Social Inequalities in Comparative Perspective

Social Inequalities in Comparative Perspective

Edited by

Fiona Devine *and*
Mary C. Waters

Blackwell Publishing

350 Main Street, Malden, MA 02148-5020, USA
108 Cowley Road, Oxford OX4 1JF, UK
550 Swanston Street, Carlton, Victoria 3053, Australia

First published 2004 by Blackwell Publishing Ltd

Library of Congress Cataloging-in-Publication Data has been applied for.

ISBN 0-631-22684-2 (hardback); ISBN 0-631-22685-0 (paperback)

A catalogue record for this title is available from the British Library.

Set in 10.5/12.5pt New Baskerville
by SNP Best-set Typesetter Ltd., Hong Kong
Printed and bound in the United Kingdom
by TJ International Ltd, Padstow, Cornwall

For further information on
Blackwell Publishing, visit our website:
http://www.blackwellpublishing.com

Contents

Notes on Contributors

HARRIET BRADLEY is Professor of Sociology and Dean of Social Sciences at the University of Bristol, UK. Her publications include *Myths at Work* (with M. Erickson, C. Stephenson and S. Williams, 2000), *Gender and Power in the Workplace* (1999) and *Fractured Identities* (1996). Current research projects include the study of minority ethnic women in trade unions, young adults' employment trajectories and an evaluation of the Connexions personal adviser system.

KIRSTEN DELLINGER is Assistant Professor of Sociology at the University of Mississippi. Her research and teaching focuses on gender and sexuality in the workplace. She has published on organizational culture and sexual harassment (*Social Problems*, 2002), dress norms and makeup at work (*Gender Issues* 2002; *Gender & Society* 1997), and organizational sexuality (*Annual Review of Sociology* 1999). She is currently working on a comparative case study of the catfish and casino industries in Mississippi.

FIONA DEVINE is Professor of Sociology at the University of Manchester. She is the author of *Affluent Workers Revisited: Privatism and the Working Class* (1992), *Social Class in America and Britain* (1997), and *Class Practices: How Parents Help their Children Get Good Jobs* (2004). She is the co-author, with Sue Heath, of *Sociological Research Methods in Context* (1999).

ELÍSIO ESTANQUE is Assistant Professor in the Faculty of Economics, University of Coimbra, Portugal, where he is attached to the Center for Social Studies. His areas of research include the sociology of inequalities and social classes; labor relations and trade unionism; youth cultures and associative movements. His is the author of *Entre a Fábrica e a Comunidade* (2000) and the co-author of *Classes e Desigualdades Sociais em Portugal* (1998).

PATTI A. GIUFFRE is Associate Professor of Sociology at Southwest Texas State University. She conducts research about sexuality in the workplace and sexual harassment in different workplace contexts. Her most recent work, a study about sexuality in a teaching hospital, appeared in *Gender & Society* (2000).

RIVA KASTORYANO is a senior research fellow at the National Center for Scientific Research and teaches at the Institute for Political Studies in Paris. Her work focuses on relationships between identity and states, on minority and community formation in western democratic societies. A recent book by her is *La France, l'Allemagne et leurs Immigré: Négocier l'identité* (1997), of which the English translation is *Negotiating Identities: States and Immigrants in France and Germany* (2002). She has also edited *Quelle identité pour l'Europe? Le multiculturalisme à l'épreuve* (1998) and *Nationalismes en mutation en Méditerranée Orientale* (with A. Dieckhoff) (2002).

PÄIVI KORVAJÄRVI is Professor of Women's Studies at the University of Tampere, Finland. Her research interests include gendering practices in work organizations, especially in the service sector. She has published articles in English in *Gender, Work and Organization*, in *Culture and Organization*, and in several anthologies.

MICHELINE LABELLE is Professor of Sociology at the Université du Québec à Montréal (UQAM). She is head of the Centre de recherche sur l'immigration, l'ethnicité et la citoyenneté (CRIEC) and the Oberservatoire international sur le racisme et les discriminations, which is part of the Institut d'études internationales de Montréal. She is the author of *Idéologie de couleur et classes sociales en Haïti* (1987); co-author of *Histoires d'immigrées. Itinéraires d'ouvrières colombiennes, haïtiennes, grecques, protugaises de Montréal* (1987), and *Ethnicité et enjeux sociaux. Le Québec vu par les leaders de groupes ethnoculturels* (1995). *Diversité et contestation transnationale: Vers une reconfiguration démocratique des espaces de citoyenneté* will be published in 2004.

CHAUNCY H. LENNON is a Program Associate in the Economic Development Unit of the Ford Foundation's Asset Building and Community Development Program. He has been a member of the research team led by Katherine S. Newman examining the employment trajectories and family dynamics of low-wage workers in New York City. He has also conducted research on racial integration and education politics.

MAIRTIN MAC AN GHAILL works in the Faculty of Social Sciences and Humanities at the University of Newcastle. He is author of *Contemporary*

Racisms and Ethnicities (1999) and *Men and Masculinities* (with Chris Haywood) (2003).

BILL MARTIN is Associate Professor of Sociology at Flinders University in Adelaide, Australia. His current research focuses on the changing experience of work, particularly among managerial, professional, and "knowledge" workers. His research with Judy Wajcman on the changing careers of managers in large firms after organizational restructuring has been published in *The British Journal of Sociology*, the *Journal of Sociology*, and *Sociology*.

KATHERINE S. NEWMAN is the Malcolm Wiener Professor of Urban Studies at Harvard University's John F. Kennedy School of Government and the Dean of Social Science at the Radcliffe Institute for Advanced Studies. She is the author of several books on middle-class economic insecurity, including *Falling From Grace* (1988) and *Declining Fortunes* (1993). Her 1999 book, *No Shame in My Game: The Working Poor in the Inner City*, received the Sidney Hillman Book Prize and the Robert F. Kennedy Book Award. Her recent volume, *A Different Shade of Grey* (2003) focuses on the lives of inner-city residents who are aging in impoverished neighborhoods.

YUKO OGASAWARA is Associate Professor of Sociology at Nihon University in Tokyo, Japan. Her recent publications in English include "Women's solidarity: company policies and Japanese office ladies," in Mary C. Brinton (ed.) *Working Lives in East Asia* (2001). She is currently researching issues on gender-based differentiation in commitment to making a living and the work-family balance among Japanese dual-earner couples.

LIVIU POPOVICIU works in the Department of Education, Communication and Language Sciences at the University of Newcastle. He is currently completing his PhD: *Conceptualizing National Identity: A Comparative Case Study of Romania and England.*

JUDY WAJCMAN is Professor of Sociology in the Research School of Social Sciences at the Australian National University and a Visiting Centennial Professor in the Gender Institute at the London School of Economics. Her books include *Managing Like a Man: Women and Men in Corporate Management* (1998), *Feminism Confronts Technology* (1991), and *The Social Shaping of Technology*, edited with D. MacKenzie (1999). Her forthcoming book, *TechnoFeminism* (2004), explores the gender relations of technology.

MARY C. WATERS is Harvard College Professor and Chair of the Sociology Department at Harvard University. Her many publications in the areas of race and ethnicity, immigration, and demography include *Ethnic Options: Choosing Identities in America* (*1990*) and *Black Identities: West Indian Immigrant Dreams and American Realities* (1999), a winner of numerous awards. She is co-director of the New York Second Generation Project, a study of the incorporation into American society of young adults whose parents were immigrants. She recently completed an edited volume, *The New Race Question* (*2002*) (with Joel Perlmann), which examines that issue in the 2000 US Census. She is currently editing, with historian Reed Ueda, *The New Americans: A Handbook to Immigration since 1965*, which will update the landmark *Harvard Encyclopedia of American Ethnic Groups*.

CHRISTINE L. WILLIAMS is Professor of Sociology at the University of Texas, Austin. Most of her research has examined gender inequality and sexual harassment in the workplace. She is the author of *Gender Differences at Work* (1989) and *Still a Man's World* (1995), and co-editor of *Sexuality and Gender* (2002). She also edits the journal, *Gender & Society*. She is currently working on an ethnography of toy stores.

Introduction

FIONA DEVINE AND MARY C. WATERS

This book brings together a collection of essays on social inequalities by contributors from around the globe, including North America, Europe, Australia, and Asia. More specifically, the chapters consider race and ethnicity, income and class, and gender and sexuality in the US, Canada, Britain, France, Finland, Portugal, Australia, and Japan. Above all else, therefore, the book is comparative in its focus. There are numerous excellent anthologies and textbooks that introduce students to the study of social inequalities in the societies in which they live. Few expose them, however, to theoretical ideas and empirical findings on race, class, and gender in other nations. This is surprising since it is now a cliché to say we live in a global world where everything is connected to everything else! It is important, to be sure, that students come to know aspects of their own society first of all. This is an obvious starting point for all students embarking on sociology degree programs. There is no good reason, however, why students should stop there and plenty of good reasons why they should learn about other places too.

A comparative focus, like international travel, broadens the mind. We are familiar with our own social worlds through our everyday lives although systematic study, of course, provides us with new insights and understanding about that world. When we study other countries, however, we are aware of how things are different. Differences strike us immediately because they are unfamiliar. Learning about the ways in which other societies vary from our own, especially why they might do so, is challenging as we come to understand things that are novel to us. Moreover, examining these differences allows us to reflect back on our own social world and appreciate how the way it is structured is neither obvious nor inevitable. A comparative perspective is not just about admiring difference, however. There are many similarities between societies that are worthy of study so they too can be understood and explained. Thinking about similarities across nations also stimulates us to think harder about the nature of our own societies. A comparative perspective, in other words, is an important quality of mind which forces us to expand our horizons – to think unaccustomed ideas, raise new questions, arouse novel curiosities, and so forth – that are so crucial to the sociological enterprise.

It is very easy to extol the virtues of adopting a comparative perspective. It is quite another matter, however, to help students begin to study topics like social inequalities in other countries. Of course, there are always students who are curious about other places because they have family ties to the country, they have visited somewhere on holiday or, quite simply, a social or political issue has aroused their interest in a particular nation. It is probably true to say, however, that these students are in a minority. Most students do not have the opportunity to explore issues comparatively. The aim of this textbook on comparative inequalities is to help students take that first step towards learning about race, class, and gender in other places. We asked the contributors to this book to aid students in this endeavor by addressing a number of issues that might be considered obvious starting points. What are the major issues of significance that have captured attention in the study of social inequalities over the years? What theoretical ideas have informed ways of thinking about race and ethnicity, income and class, and gender and sexuality and where have they come from? How have these concepts shaped empirical research on those issues and what kinds of substantial findings have been produced?

We also asked our contributors to introduce students to empirical research in their respective countries. After all, sociology is an empirical discipline and it is through systematic enquiry that sociologists uncover new findings. In doing so, we hope that students can see the ways in which important social issues have been subject to empirical investigation. All the contributors are known for their high caliber qualitative research and they have drawn on their ethnographic work, embracing intensive formal interviews and informal conversations with informants, observation and participant observation, in their individual chapters. As editors, we decided to bring together a collection of chapters that focuses on qualitative work on race and ethnicity, income and class, and gender and sexuality in particular. Again, as a first step, we thought it would be helpful for students to get a feel for the day-to-day subjective experience and meaning of social inequalities in different countries. We also wanted students to understand the processes by which the interconnected inequalities of race, class, and gender are reproduced in everyday practices and to appreciate the contexts in which social inequalities recur. Empirical facts and figures are all important to be sure and there are plenty of them in the pages of this book. However, qualitative research on social inequalities brings a special perspective to the study of social inequality, laying bare the lived experience and enormous complexity of inequality cross-nationally.

The focus on qualitative research should not be interpreted as hostility to quantitative research. Nothing could be further from the truth. All the contributors to this edited collection have been or are currently engaged in empirical research that has drawn on both quantitative and qualitative research methods and techniques. The advantages and disadvantages of both methodologies are fully appreciated. Nevertheless, we asked our contributors to think about the pros and cons of qualitative research on social inequalities specifically. We did so because sociologists are well aware that the production of sociological knowledge is not an uncomplicated affair. The choice of methods influences the nature of substantive findings in whatever country empirical research is undertaken. It is increasingly customary, therefore, for sociologists to reflect on issues of method and we thought it equally important that our contributors consider these issues here too. They do so before describing some of their own research that is either recently completed work or research in which they are still engaged. In effect, the chapters are a showcase for what we consider to be high quality empirical work that is at the cutting edge of the discipline. Again, we thought it important to introduce students to the best research being undertaken elsewhere. It is for this reason that we also asked the contributors to identify new areas of research on social inequalities. What better group of sociologists to ask?

INEQUALITIES OF RACE AND ETHNICITY

This collection starts with a discussion of inequalities of race and ethnicity. The chapters cover the United States, England, France, and Canada, all countries that have experienced large flows of immigration in recent decades. Yet while group inequality is important in all of these countries, different lines of fissure characterize the countries. In the United States new immigrants face the overwhelming importance of racial stratification. In Canada race is also quite important, but its interpretation and treatment are shaped by the divisions over language use, citizenship, and national sovereignty claims of the province of Quebec. In France, Kastorayano describes how the split between Islam and

Christianity is crucial to an understanding of the reality of the immigration experience there, and how an ideology about nationhood and social differences prevents the French from even categorizing the population by generation, religion, nationality, or race. In Britain new immigration has tended to focus attention on non-white groups and their social inequality but Popoviciu and Mac an Ghaill discuss how attention to the lived experience of those of Irish origin or ancestry in England shows continued patterns of exclusion and inequality.

Without doubt, race is the social inequality that generates significant interest in America. As Mary Waters suggests, racial and ethnic divisions have a long history reaching back to the forced migration of Africans, the expansion of the US to include the Southwest and its Spanish-speaking population and, more recently, voluntary immigration from around the world. Interestingly, while most immigrants to the US were white, the majority of immigrants are now non-white (Farley 1996). The changing nature of immigration has raised thorny problems with the concept of assimilation and the idea that immigrants gradually adopt the cultural values and lifestyles of (white) Americans. The field of ethnic studies and race relations in America was once preoccupied with understanding the immigrant experience and much qualitative research charted the declining significance of cultural distinctions among different ethnic groups living in major cities like Chicago. Such integration was seen as the source of economic and social success. Now, however, sociologists researching non-white immigrants and their children, invariably born in the US, and their experiences of living in America are interested in the continuing importance of cultural differences and especially racial and ethnic identities while also thinking about how they are changing.

In Chapter 1, Waters (1999) draws on her study of second-generation West Indians in New York City to outline three paths to identity development: identifying as American, identifying as ethnic American with some distancing from black Americans and identifying as immigrant in ways which do not engage with American racial and ethnic categories. Contrary to previous research, she shows that those teenagers who held a strong ethnic identity, valuing their Jamaican or Trinidadian background and disassociating with African Americans, were more likely to be successful in school and work. She turns the relationship between subjective identification and socio-economic trajectories, in other words, on its head. The adoption of a particular identity is closely related to social class in that the ethnically identified youngsters were more likely to be middle class while the working-class and poor American were immigrant identified. Waters has recently extended her research to think about the ways in which young people interact with many different ethnic groups in big cities like New York. New avenues of research include an exploration of multiculturalism, hybridity across minority cultures, and the fluid exchanges across group boundaries that are creating new mixes of values, lifestyles, and cultures. This hybridity will force sociologists to think about the way the boundaries between ethnic groups are situational, fluid and, above all, dynamic.

In Chapter 2, Micheline Labelle, like Waters, examines racial and ethnic identities and the sense of belonging that they generate in Quebec, Canada. The Canadian state, she argues, has promoted civic integration expecting ethnic groups to subscribe to a Canadian civic identity in return. At the same time, the Quebec state, one of the ten provisional sub-units of the Canadian state, has also fostered a Quebec citizenship identity in its pursuit of autonomy from Canada. In effect, there are two citizenships competing with each other for the hearts and minds of various ethnic groups. Labelle focuses her interests on how immigrants and racialized communities have responded to the citizenship appeals and she notes the way in which ethnic groups distrust such appeals since the rhetoric of civic inclusion does not match their experiences of racist exclusion. Rather, their experience of racism has had clear consequences for identity formation. Negative stereotypes of minority groups, labeling diverse ethnic groups as black and of inferior social status, had led to racialized groups, in turn, re-appropriating this attributed identity, subverting it and using it as an opportunity to define an identity of resistance. In this respect, identities are fluid constructs (see also Lamont 2001) that need to be understood within the context of competing claims of civic inclusion and state conceptions of citizenship.

Labelle has been doing ethnographic work in Quebec for many years, facilitating a deep understanding of ethnic group experiences. Her chapter focuses on recent in-depth interviews with young second-generation Haitians and Jamaicans living in Montreal, all of whom are middle class. She asked her informants about their national identities and found four types. First, the major identity is a hyphenated identity. Young people identified themselves with Canada or Quebec although they held a strong attachment to their country of origin and culture. The experience of exclusion has led them to hold on to their national identities associated with their country or origin rather than wholly embrace a Canadian or Quebecer's civic identity. Second, some young people identified with a unique national identity either as Haitians or Jamaicans and, again, they were proud of their background and culture.

Third, she found a Canadian civic identity although it was a minority identity. Identifying with Quebec was very weak indeed. Quebecers are viewed as intolerant especially in relation to the promotion of the French language as the official language of Quebec. Fourth, Labelle identifies a racialized identity. Again, it is a weak identity as young people have sought to distance themselves from racial categories. Overall, Labelle calls for more research on identity formation within the context of national citizenship claims by states that considers the impact of experiences of racism on identities. More research is needed on the building of diversity and multiculturalism too.

In Chapter 3, Riva Kastoryano considers the issues of race and ethnicity in France. She notes how the French state was preoccupied with the assimilation of immigrants, primarily from Algeria in North Africa, in the colonial era although immigrants were assimilated on racial rather than ethnic lines. In the post-colonial era, the official discourse changed to one of integration although she notes official census categories have been the source of great debate as critics have argued that, in failing to recognize "origins," the state has exacerbated discrimination against immigrant groups. That is to say, the state has been very reluctant to recognize and give legitimacy to cultural or religious diversity within French society. Similarly, social policies that are supposed to be color-blind affect particular immigrant groups. In turn, immigrant associations have emerged which have adopted a discourse around claims for recognition acknowledging cultural and, especially, religious particularities. This struggle between the state and immigrant groups has raised problems for French national identity that is so integrally tied up with the history of the Republic as a unitary entity. In other words, Kastoryano very much stresses that identities are constructed through interactions and negotiations between the state and immigrants groups. Most importantly, new identities emerge out of, and are forged as part of, the process of collective mobilization and organization.

Since the 1980s, Kastoryano (2002) has been doing ethnographic work with French and German immigrant voluntary associations, interviewing the leaders and members of such collective organizations, observing meetings and discussions and the processes by which collective identities are mobilized through these interactions. She has also interviewed politicians dealing with immigration issues, ministerial officials, union representatives, and those in charge of social services in the municipalities. Kastoryano describes the way in which religion is at the core of negotiations between the French state and immigrants. It has become the key issue because French national identity is tied up with the establishment of a secular Republic with a clear separation between the state and religion that is not available for negotiation. In contrast, immigrants groups have drawn on religion as the basis for public recognition of their ethnic origins, culture, and identity. They have emphasized the pride they have in Islamic moral values and social involvement. Religion, therefore, has become the way of appropriating a new identity of difference. The "headscarf" affair captured the heart of this conflict for it challenged the secular nature of the French Republic so highly valued in France. That said, the debate led to a revision of French identity so that religions are now acknowledged in the public sphere. Overall, Kastoryano argues that further research is required on the impact of politicized negotiations on both immigrant and national identities.

In Chapter 4, Liviu Popoviciu and Mairtin Mac an Ghaill consider racisms, ethnicities and British nation-making. Their interests are also framed within the context of immigration, especially post-war immigration to Britain (Mason 1995) and its implications for new identities, especially issues of becoming, for they write from a postmodern perspective. As noted in the other chapters so far, early research relations focused on the assimilation of ethnic minorities into British society with an emphasis on cultural differences and the extent to which they were declining. Later, interest shifted to the subordinate class position and experiences of ethnic minority groups from a Weberian or Marxist perspective. Post-colonial theory has seen a renewed focus on issues of cultural difference, ethnic formation, and national belonging. Questions of identity/subjectivity have become central. While retaining an interest in class inequalities, Popoviciu and Mac an Ghaill are interested in this new theoretical language around hybridity, diaspora and syncrenism. They also note that qualitative research has played a pivotal role in research on race and ethnicity in providing a space for self-representation, detailing people's everyday experiences of discrimination and how these experiences have shaped the emergence of subordinated racial identities. From their postmodern perspective, they are also increasingly conscious of how empirical research produces a "version of reality" rather than "accessing reality" in some way.

Within this remit, Mac an Ghaill and Popoviciu have also sought to challenge the black/white dualism (Roedrigger 1991) with reference to the subjectivity of seemingly invisible white immigrants like the Irish Diaspora in Britain. They describe the way in which the Irish have been de-racialized over time. In the past, popular stereotypes of the Irish portrayed them as an inferior race with reference to cultural differences such as their liking for unfettered sociability, talking, and drinking. Interestingly, these racialized differences are no longer discussed and

the Irish Diaspora have become invisible. That is to say, despite evidence
that shows they still experience disadvantage and exclusion, their cultural uniqueness has disappeared and they are seen as the same and part
of an Anglo-ethnic majority. In contrast, in-depth research on young
Irish men and women show that the Irish have only been partially
included in Britain with implications for identity formation. They found
a strong sense of belonging to Ireland and a clear dis-identification with
Britishness. Thus, they argue that more research needs to be done on
whiteness and white ethnic groups. At the same time, ethnographic work
is required on the cultural dynamics taking place between ethnic groups
in multicultural cities within nations and across nations. This research
also needs to be placed in the context of new migrants arriving to Britain
and elsewhere, the rise of European racism, and the intensification of
Islamaphobia in Europe and other parts of the globe. It should also
acknowledge how immigrant groups mobilize, and how they resist new
forms of native categorizations, stereotypes and moral evaluations.

INEQUALITIES OF INCOME AND CLASS

The second section of the book directs attention to income and class
inequalities across four countries: the US, Britain, Portugal, and
Australia. Each author shows how the use of qualitative methods allows
for an exploration of the subjective understanding of class position,
something which also reflects the particular social history of each individual country. Unlike ethnicity and race, class is not a salient identity
in America for most Americans either do not talk about class or align
themselves to a vast amorphous middle class (Walkowitz 1999). Nevertheless, it is clear that America has a sizeable population of people at
the bottom of the labor market. They occupy low-level service sector
jobs with poor market and work situations. These are, in other words,
working-class jobs. Previous research on class inequalities in the 1960s
and 1970s focused on the workplace although in the 1980s and 1990s
there was a shift in focus towards the poor and, specifically, those
outside the labor market and dependent on welfare. There is now
increasing interest in the working poor and the opportunities for and
constraints on upward mobility to which Newman, of course, has made
a major contribution. The working poor now have a higher political
profile in the context of welfare reform with the abolition of Aid for
Families with Dependent Children (AFDC) and its replacement with
Temporary Assistance to Needy Families (TANF). In Chapter 5,
Newman and Lennon make a strong case for ethnographic research on

the working poor to understand their day-to-day experiences and how they might be supported.

Newman and Lennon's chapter builds on the earlier research by Katherine Newman (1999) for her highly influential book, *No Shame in My Game*. The research involved intensive interviews with young people in the fast food industry in 1993–4 in Harlem, New York. Newman found that most of her informants were stuck in low-paid jobs and only a minority had enjoyed upward mobility to something better. This chapter reports on a follow-up study that involved Newman and Lennon talking to their informants again in 1997–8. Most of their interviewees had enjoyed improvements in their working life although a minority had secured high-paying jobs. They focus on the perceptions and expectations of both groups. Their limited experiences of advancement meant they were fully cognizant of the economic conditions they faced, the importance of education for mobility and, to an increasing extent, the structural barriers of class, race, and gender inequalities they had to confront. Yet, they had a strong sense of personal responsibility for their fate and held mainstream individualistic values about the importance of perseverance, working hard, and enjoying success. These young people held high expectations for the future, they were optimistic about what they could achieve and they were planning how they would attain greater security at work and at home. Their economic advancement, albeit of a limited nature, sustained this optimism. Newman and Lennon conclude by making a case for more research on the working poor to see how their lives unfold, including examining the experience of recent immigrants to the US and their children who are often found in the low wage economy.

In Chapter 6, Elísio Estanque also addresses the subjective experience of low-level work in his chapter reviewing the study of class and social inequalities in Portugal. As his starting point, Estanque provides us with an account of the unique development of sociology under the authoritarian regime of Salazar which was not overthrown until 1974. The regime seriously hindered the discipline and, by implication, the study of class inequalities in a predominately rural country. The eventual triumph of democracy in the 1970s facilitated research on inequality often influenced by Marxist theories of class. As in other countries, small-scale studies gave way to larger research projects seeking to map the class structure in Portugal. Portugal, for example, participated in the International Class Project initiated by Erik Olin Wright (1997) in the US. These were important exercises for providing a macro-sociological picture identifying different classes, their size, composition, and so forth. More recently, however, Portuguese sociologists have sought to escape from the "structuralist straitjacket" to look at the formation of classes, think about class trajectories, cognitive systems of classification, issues of subjectivity, and culture. This trend typifies a greater interest in questions of agency although Estanque rightly stresses that the links between socio-economic position and subjectivities should still be teased out in research.

Estanque documents his ethnographic research involving participant observation on the shop floor of a footwear factory in a rural area of Portugal. He chose this method of research to move away from analyzing classes "on paper" to seeing classes "in action" and, more specifically, forms of resistance to domination. He discusses, very frankly, the difficulties of doing participant observation, overcoming the initial distrust of workers and slowly securing their confidence. Interestingly, like Buroway (1979, 1985) he did not find overt resistance among workers to management for there was a deliberate evasion of tensions and conflicts. Rather, he uncovered covert power games, latent resistance, significant silences, and so on that highlighted the antagonistic relationship between the workforce and company hierarchy. Estanque also stresses that 60 percent of workers in the footwear industry are young women with low levels of education and he movingly describes how they were humiliated by macho supervisors and treated more harshly than their male counterparts. The workers, be they women or men, had to fight hard to retain their dignity (see Hodson 2001). It was in this context that their identities were formed. The footwear factory, he concluded, was run on the basis of despotic paternalism. In terms of new areas of research, Estanque notes that the expansion of education in Portugal is changing women's position in society and will require further exploration. Echoing other chapters, he calls for more ethnographic work on the growing number of immigrants from Eastern Europe, North Africa and South America who are increasingly working in lowly paid jobs in manufacturing and services in Portugal.

A number of contributors noted that the study of inequalities of race and ethnicity should not be confined to studying blacks, Hispanics, Asians and other so-called minority groups. Rather, issues of whiteness and dominant white identities need to be subjected to empirical scrutiny too. Similarly, it is increasingly recognized that the study of class inequalities is not just about the working class. On the contrary, the remit should include research on the middle classes, especially as they have grown so substantially and recruited from the working class (Erikson and Goldthorpe 1993). Against this background, Bill Martin and Judy Wajcman, in Chapter 7, discuss class inequalities in Australia. They succinctly outline the tradition of research on class inequalities, drawing on quantitative and qualitative methods. Early community studies of rural localities that stressed status and conformity gave way to in-depth case studies of class tensions and conflicts in industrial towns such as Williams' (1981) classic study of open-cut coalmines owned by a US multinational company. She found high levels of class consciousness that undermined Australian egalitarianism. There is still a strong body of research on working-class culture, especially resistance and deviance among working-class men. The importance of masculinity and masculine identities and lifestyles has been usefully explored within this remit. More recently, research mapping the changing class structure in Australia has led sociologists of class to study other occupational groups including white-collar workers, professionals and managers, their experiences of mobility, work, and their identities and lifestyles.

Martin and Wajcman note that early qualitative studies achieved great depth of understanding in a holistic fashion and they are enthusiastic about computer software packages that facilitate more detailed analysis of textual data. The problem of giving voice to the underprivileged is still tricky, however. They describe their research on the careers of managers and professionals in large Australian companies. They were interested in mobility trajectories and experiences as a way of understanding how social origins feed into destinations. Conversations about families revealed three ways in which education was understood as part of the mobility process. First, among parents with high levels of education, they found high expectations and assumptions that children would match, if not surpass, their parents' educational qualifications. Second, among those without formal education but with high-level skills, the development of technical knowledge was highly esteemed. Third, among working-class (and immigrant) parents, education was consciously mobilized as a resource to secure children's upwards mobility. Thus, the meaning parents attached to education powerfully influenced children's aspirations. These meanings vary among families and explain different mobility patterns. What children learn about work and careers from their parents, therefore, is crucially important for understanding class reproduction and mobility. Further research is needed on how gender, race and ethnic inequalities shape these processes.

In Chapter 8, Fiona Devine explores middle-class and working-class identities in her chapter on class subjectivities in Britain. The study of class consciousness was central to the early community studies that found highly antagonistic relations between bosses and workers. Economic affluence, however, was widely predicted to weaken class consciousness and lead to the incorporation (or, even, assimilation!) of the working class into middle-class society. Sociologists quickly refuted such ideas, emphasizing the cultural distinctiveness of the working class in terms of their experiences at work. That said, growing similarities between the working class and middle class in terms of lifestyles and socio-political proclivities were acknowledged, although the source of much debate. Be that as it may, changing economic circumstances reoriented debate about the demise of class consciousness and survey research showed that class identities remained strong. Qualitative research confirmed that class was a salient social identity although Devine's (1992) earlier work noted that people did not like talking about class for it had very negative associations with status. Her respondents preferred to stress similarities with others in terms of their ordinariness. Indeed, how people distance themselves from class labels has become a dominant theme in the study of class subjectivities. Controversy has centered on the extent to which people distance themselves from the working class or take pride in it. In turn, there is now a growing interest in middle-class subjectivities and how members of the middle class are ambivalent about this class label.

Devine argues that the study of class subjectivities has been beset with methodological difficulties. Most notably, researchers have been overly keen to get respondents to assign themselves to (usually) pre-given class categories and then claim that class is a salient social identity. A more cautious approach has been to consider the circumstances in which informants talk about class spontaneously. Devine (2003) has recently completed a qualitative study of class mobility among doctors and teachers in the US and the UK. Strangely, she found her American interviewees were often happy to describe their family backgrounds as middle class whether they were mobile or not. Her British interviewees, in contrast, rarely spoke of their background as being middle class while her upwardly mobile respondents spoke of their working-class origins. Where the middle-class label was employed, it was usually as a innocuous descriptive category although there were some expressions of class superiority in terms of academic aspirations. A working-class identity was more frequently evoked with pride in recognition of economic hardships that had been experienced and subsequently overcome. Arguably, it was a defensive pride rejecting working-class inferiority. Parents' high educational aspirations were emphasized instead. Now middle-class parents, however, they were keen to distance themselves from being labeled as middle class, which they associated with being snobbish, elitist, and pushy. Devine concludes that ethnographic work which captures feelings and emotions rather than perceptions of class could tell us more about the experiences of class and its salience in people's lives.

INEQUALITIES OF GENDER AND SEXUALITY

Gender inequalities have become central to scholars around the globe in the past 10 years as a result of the impact of feminism on the academy. The study of sexuality is growing in significance too as the studies we present here on the US, Japan, Britain, and Finland make clear. In Chapter 9, Christine Williams, Patti Giuffre and Kirsten Dellinger chart the growth and development of research on gender stratification in the US over this period. Parsons' structural-functionalist approach to the study of gender roles was famously dominant in the 1950s although a Marxist–feminist perspective superseded it in the 1960s and 1970s, emphasizing the subordination of women in society instead. Recognition of the socially structured nature of gender inequalities was subsequently combined with an interest in how gender is internalized and shapes women's (and men's) needs and dispositions as discussed by thinkers influenced by psycho-analytic theory. More recently, social constructionism has stressed that gender inequalities are reproduced in everyday interactions of "doing gender" or, to put it another way, "performing gender" (Butler 1990). This strand of thought has emphasized the malleability and contextual nature of gender and challenged the idea of static categories of gender and sexuality. Interest in everyday interactions and how they reproduce power has also ignited interest in resistance and change. Moreover, there are different masculinities and femininities and men and women of different races, ethnicities, and sexualities have varied experiences. The processes by which inequalities are reproduced via everyday inter-actions, therefore, are now central to feminist scholars.

Williams and her colleagues provide an excellent overview of the contribution of qualitative work to this research tradition. Rightly, they argue that not all aspects of gender can be categorized and quantified. Such categories are often essentialist anyway. Recognizing that gender is an emergent property of everyday interaction implies that intensive ethnographic research is highly significant. It is also the most appro-priate means of tapping people's experiences and feelings. In-depth research can also capture the way in which gender is institutionalized in various practices such as in the workplace. Williams et al. then go on to discuss various studies of sexual harassment in a variety of industries and occupations in which they have been involved (see, for example,

Williams 1995). They set out to explain the way in which sexual encounters are rarely labeled as sexual harassment. Often, for example, certain behaviors are institutionalized aspects of the jobs. There are different boundaries as to what is considered sexual harassment, what is tolerable and what is pleasurable. Thus, they found sexual banter was considered normal and acceptable in the restaurant industry although interestingly, innocuous flirting is not tolerated across races or sexualities. In conclusion, they call for more research on these fluid and ambiguous boundaries and different aspects of sexualized interaction in varied workplaces. Additional thought needs to be given to how such interactions empower some women while imperiling others, thereby acknowledging the diversity of women's experiences, to provide a fuller picture of the reproduction of inequality and sexism.

Yuko Ogasawara, in Chapter 10, provides a fascinating account of the position of women in Japanese society. More specifically, she addresses the curious fact that Japanese women occupy lowly and seemingly powerless positions in the workplace and yet they express high levels of self-fulfillment and happiness with their lives. Ogasawara notes that sociology in Japan used to speak of men and women as if they were disembodied people with no gender or sexuality. However, theory and research on gender and sexuality have developed. There is, for example, a huge body of quantitative research that has documented women's limited command over economic resources including good pay, stable employment, and high positions. Women's presence in the labor market, therefore, is extremely limited. One outcome of this research is that Japan is characterized as a society with substantial gender inequalities and it has confirmed Western stereotypes that Japanese women are powerless and are to be pitied (although, for an opposite view, see Brinton 2001). A string of qualitative studies, in contrast, has shown that women are not to be pitied for they enjoy much self-fulfillment in being autonomous from the workplace and, arguably, it is men who are in woeful positions as they continue to work long, grueling hours for corporations. Thus, a different picture of Japanese women emerges. Within constraints of course, they exercise choices in their lives, although Ogasawara rightly points out that such freedom is enjoyed more by middle-class than working-class women.

Qualitative research, Ogasawara correctly notes, has contradicted Western ideas of Japanese women as compliant because it has taken women's experiences and their hopes and dreams into account. The meaning of women's everyday lives has been central. Her own research on women office workers, or Office Ladies (OLs) (Ogasawara 1998), also confirms that women are not powerless in the workplace. To be sure, her ethnographic research highlighted much discrimination: namely, how women are referred to as "girls," how they have to perform menial chores for men and they are rarely considered for promotion even if the pretence of a grading system is maintained. Being unfettered by careers, however, gave her women informants the space to be critical of men and the system they worked for. They were not simply compliant to men for they were very critical in their evaluation of male behavior. Office talk on men's authority was important for if it was known that they could not supervise female subordinates, they were not promoted. Similarly, the women disagreed with the basic values of salaried men in their seemingly slavish devotion to their careers. All in all, they did not envy men's position within the workforce. Ogasawara forcefully argues that ethnographic research that captures the microprocesses of power is required to challenge Western feminist assumptions about non-Western culture. Moreover, the way in which masculinity shapes men's lives in pitiful ways requires more investigation. Research that considers relationships and interaction between women and men would also provide a better handle on issues of gender power and inequality.

One of the major topics in the field of gender and sexuality is the extent to which women's position at work and in the family is changing for the better. In Chapter 11, Harriet Bradley considers whether women are catching up with men in Britain. While writers such as Walby (1997) are optimistic, Bradley, rightly in our view, is more cautious. To be sure, there have been major socio-economic changes but whether attitudes and behavior have kept apace is another matter. Reviewing the study of gender inequalities, Bradley describes the dominance of Parsons' work on the family and how this was superseded by feminist academic work that highlighted gender inequalities. American feminism was very influential in Britain although there was a more Marxist slant to British theory and research that was attuned to issues of gender and class. It was during this time that a huge body of empirical research was amassed which documented women's unequal position to men in a number of spheres of life. This work, however, was sharply criticized by post-structuralist and postmodernist feminists who rejected unilinear theories of male dominance and stressed that the world should be seen as disorderly and incoherent. More attention, it was argued, should be paid to the diversity of women's experiences, ethnicity, and culture, and women should not be seen as victims but as agents capable of resistance and change. Bradley is critical of this "cultural turn" for it neglects the all-important material basis of gender inequalities. Still, she is happy to admit that it is good to see that the diversity of women's experiences and the fluidity of everyday life are now higher up on the feminist research agenda.

Early work by gender researchers took a qualitative form, Bradley argues, because they wanted to give voice to women's experiences that had been ignored by men. That said, there is a body of exemplary quantitative work on women's inequalities including, for example, Angela Dale and her colleagues' work on Pakistani and Bangladeshi women (Dale et al. 2002). Bradley had conducted mostly small-scale intensive work for she values the way in which it explores the processes by which gender relations are reproduced. She discusses various empirical projects in which she has been involved although for the purposes of this summary, her work on young adults in Bristol in the South West of England is worthy of note. While she expected to find progressive attitudes to gender roles among young women, this was not necessarily the case. Many of the young women were ambitious for what they hoped to achieve in the world of work like their male counterparts. However, they also attached far more importance to bringing up children and spending time with their family than young men. These traditional attitudes, Bradley argues, show that the domestic sphere will continue to shape and constrain these young women's lives, especially in relation to paid employment, as it has done in previous generations. Overall, Bradley stresses that future research should explore the diversity of women's experiences and how they respond to constraints and exploit opportunities. These issues are firmly tied to context. Issues of class, race and ethnicity, she concludes, are central to the study of gender inequalities.

Finally, in Chapter 12, Päivi Korvajärvi considers gender and work-related inequalities in Finland. Finland is a very interesting country because women have long participated in the labor market in that state-provided childcare has facilitated women working full-time. Moreover, cultural norms assume that women will work in paid employment and contribute to family income as much as men. Yet, Finland's occupational structure is characterized by gender segregation and women get paid about 80 percent of men's earnings. This puzzling situation has long perplexed European academics studying gender inequalities (Rubery et al. 1999) although Korvajärvi focuses on the most recent theoretical ideas seeking to explain persisting inequities in the workplace. Interestingly, she describes the enormous influence of Joan Acker's (1990) work, an American feminist scholar, on Finnish academic thinking. Acker, of course, has long argued that attention should focus on gendered practices for it is the ordinary things that women and men do as they go about their daily lives that explain the constant remaking of gender differences. It is by studying daily practices and routines that we get a sense of how gender is done. Echoing the other contributors to this volume, Korvajärvi notes the way in which this perspective has allowed Finnish researchers to challenge universal categories, understand the diversity of women's experiences, and give due consideration to their agency. Like Williams and her colleagues, she stresses the importance of the organizational context in which gender practices are performed in research on gender and sexuality.

Korvajärvi argues that ethnographic research gives us a sense of people and the lives they lead behind the numbers we collect. She stresses, however, that while it is important to collect rich qualitative data, it is imperative that methods of analysis and interpretation match the depth of the material. It is important that researchers closely examine the narratives that people tell and acknowledge that these stories have their own logic but they can be incoherent and fragmentary as well. Korvajärvi's research interests lie in women in technical occupations and she has conducted some fascinating work on call centers in Finland. In one call center, for example, she found that a shift from serving customers to selling services led to a change in the gender composition as women were replaced by men. The changing nature of the work was more associated with men's work than women's work. In another center, she found that women became the users of technology while men were the experts which meant that men rather then women were the major decision-makers in the workplace. Her case studies powerfully show the processes by which gender segregation is remade in new industries and occupations. Korvajärvi calls for more empirical research on these micro-processes and she makes a plea for research that is sensitive to the body and sexuality in the workplace. Although Finland is an ethnically and racially homogenous society, she argues the "whiteness" of workplaces outside the capital, Helsinki, should not go unnoticed. Silence around such issues does not mean they should not be subject to sociological investigation.

Conclusion

The overall aim of this collection is to encourage students to take an interest in social inequalities in other societies. We have argued that it is important to do so because a comparative focus challenges us not to take things for granted. It forces us to reject common-sense ideas about the obvious and inevitable way the distribution of resources is organized in our own and other countries. It makes us appreciate the diversity of forms that inequalities of race, class, and gender can take around the world while also pushing us to make sense of the variety by identifying similarities and patterns too. Reading sociological research on race and ethnicity, income and class, gender and sexuality makes us think hard about why things take the form that they do in particular places as well as across spaces and, in doing so, we discover new things about our own social world and other societies. The benefits of a comparative perspective, therefore, are obvious. The Introduction to this book may make the case but it is the individual chapters that comprise this collection that demonstrate it. In our view, it is the contributors to this book that make a compelling case for expanding our sociological horizons beyond national borders. In doing so, they show how challenging and exciting such an endeavor can be.

REFERENCES

Acker, J. (1990) "Hierarchies, jobs, bodies: a theory of gendered organization," *Gender and Society* 4: 139–58.

Brinton, M. C. (ed.) (2001) *Women's Working Lives in East Asia.* Stanford, CA: Stanford University Press.

Buroway, M. (1979) *Manufacturing Consent.* Chicago: University of Chicago Press.

—— (1985) *The Politics of Production.* London: Verso.

Butler, J. (1990) *Gender Trouble.* New York: Routledge.

Dale, A., Fieldhouse, E., Shaheen, N. and Kalra, V. (2002) "The labour market prospects for Pakistani and Bangladeshi women," *Work, Employment and Society* 16: 5–26.

Devine, F. (1992) *Affluent Workers Revisited.* Edinburgh: Edinburgh University Press.

—— (2004) *Class Practices: How Parents Help their Children Get Good Jobs.* Cambridge: Cambridge University Press.

Erikson, R. and Goldthorpe, J. H. (1993) *The Constant Flux.* Oxford: Clarendon Paperbacks.

Farley, R. (1996) *The New American Reality.* New York: Russell Sage Foundation.

Hodson, R. (2001) *Dignity at Work.* Cambridge: Cambridge University Press.

Kastoryano, R. (2002) *Negotiating Identities.* Princeton, NJ: Princeton University Press.

Lamont, M. (2001) *The Dignity of Working Men.* Cambridge, MA: Harvard University Press.

Mason, D. (1995) *Race and Ethnicity in Modern Britain.* Oxford: Oxford University Press.

Newman, K. S. (1999) *No Shame in My Game.* New York: Knopf/Russell Sage Foundation.

Ogasawara, Y. (1998) *Office Ladies and Salaried Men*. Berkeley, CA: University of California Press.

Roedrigger, D. R. (1991) *The Wages of Whiteness*. London: Verso.

Rubery, J., Smith, M. and Fagan, C. (1999) *Women's Employment in Europe*. London: Routledge.

Walby, S. (1997) *Gender Transformations*. London: Routledge.

Walkowitz, D. J. (1999) *Working with Class*. Chapel Hill, NC: University of California Press.

Waters, M. C. (1999) *Black Identities*. Cambridge, MA: Harvard University Press.

Williams, C. (1981) *Open Cut*. Sydney: George Allen and Unwin.

Williams, C. L. (1995) *Still a Man's World*. Berkeley, CA: University of California Press.

Wright, E. O. (1997) *Class Counts*. Cambridge: Cambridge University Press.

CHAPTER ONE

Race, Ethnicity, and Immigration in the United States

Mary C. Waters

Racial and ethnic divisions in the United States originated in three distinct historical processes: (1) slavery and the forced migration of Africans in the sixteenth through the nineteenth centuries; (2) the expansion of the US through conquest of the indigenous American Indians and the annexation of Spanish-speaking people in the Southwest; and (3) centuries of voluntary immigration from around the globe. When Americans discuss *race relations*, they have historically been concerned with non-immigrants. The small population of American Indians, Eskimos, and Native Hawaiians who survived the arrival and colonization of their land by European settlers, the large number of descendants of African slaves who comprise the African-American population of the US, and the descendants of Spanish-speaking residents of the territory conquered by the Americans in the outward expansion of the nation in the nineteenth century as well as from the territory of Puerto Rico in the Caribbean have all been studied under the rubric of American race relations. A great deal of empirical and theoretical research has documented the inequality by race in the US and has debated the reasons for such inequality and possible remedies for it.

The study of *ethnicity*, on the other hand, has primarily been concerned with immigrants and their children. American sociology owes its birth to the desire to understand the great changes that our society underwent at the beginning of the twentieth century: urbanization, industrialization, and perhaps most importantly, immigration. The last great wave of immigration at the turn of the past century filled American cities with immigrants and their children. Between 1880 and 1920 the US absorbed 24.5 million immigrants, the great majority of them from Southern and Eastern Europe. The social problems that were linked with these immigrants, along with the problems arising out of urbanization and industrialization, gave rise to the sociological studies that came to be known as the Chicago School of sociology. Associated most often with one of its founders, Robert Park, the Chicago School gave rise to numerous studies of immigrants and their children (the first and the second generation) (Park 1928, 1950; Wirth 1956; Thomas and Znaniecki 1984). Combining ethnographic methods and holistic inquiries with demographic data, these studies not only provided a wealth of data on particular groups, urban areas, and urban dynamics, but also gave rise to many of the sociological concepts and theories we use today to try to understand the experiences of immigrants – assimilation, residential segregation, occupational specialization, marginality, and race relations cycles.

Thus, we have two strands of research in the area of group inequality: ethnicity/immigration and race relations. American race relations research has primarily focused on the experience of blacks and on the legacies of slavery in American life. While slavery was ended in America after the Civil War with the Emancipation Proclamation in 1865, legal equality for blacks was not a reality until a century later when the Civil Rights Revolution of the 1950s and 1960s ended legal segregation and discrimination. Since then the differences between blacks and whites on education and income have narrowed. In 1940, 92 percent of blacks were poor, by the early 1970s, the black poverty rate had declined to 31 percent (Farley 1993). These changes, together with rising general levels of prosperity in the second half of the twentieth century, have led to the creation of a sizeable black middle class, and increasing contact and even intermarriage between the races. Yet while inequality between blacks and whites has narrowed considerably, it has not disappeared. In 2001 a substantial gap between whites and blacks remained: 22.7 percent of the black population was poor, compared to 7.8 percent of the non-Hispanic white population.

Scholars of race relations have tried to explain why prejudice and discrimination persist in American society (Bobo 2000; Wilson 1978, 1996). They have also debated the role that current discrimination in employment and education plays in explaining these disparities, compared to the role of past discrimination in creating cultures of poverty, concentrated disadvantage, and difficult family and personal experiences for African Americans (Wilson 1987; Anderson and Massey 2001). A great deal of attention has been paid to the extreme residential segregation of African Americans in the nation's large cities, and to the role of concentrated poverty, crime, substandard schools, and declining manufacturing employment in the major cities in causing and maintaining the poor economic situation of urban blacks and Hispanics.

The latter half of the twentieth century saw great improvements in the situation of black Americans, but at the same time it was marked by an era of massive immigration. Sociologists are once again trying to make sense of the impact of immigration on our society and on the immigrants themselves. The transformation of American immigration law in 1965 led to a re-opening of the US as a destination for immigrants. Since 1965 25 million immigrants have come to the US, primarily from Asia, Latin America, and the Caribbean in response to changes in immigration law and the international pattern of immigration flows (Massey *et al.* 1994). As a result the gap between those who study immigrants and those who study race relations is breaking down as immigrants since 1965 have largely been non-white (Waters 2000). In 2000 51.0 percent of the foreign-born population was from Latin America, 25.5 percent were from Asia, 15.3 percent were from Europe. Nine of the top ten countries of birth of the US foreign born in 2000 are in Latin America and Asia. The leading source country is Mexico, the source of 7.8 million people, or 27.6 percent of the foreign-born population in 2000. China was second with 1.4 million people followed by the Philippines, India, Cuba, Vietnam, El Salvador, Korea, the Dominican Republic, and Canada.

The concept of assimilation, which played such a great role in understanding the experiences of European immigrants, is now hotly debated as to its usefulness in understanding current immigration. American sociologists are busy studying the core variables and components of assimilation in order to understand the immigrant experience: How different or similar to other Americans are immigrants in terms of socioeconomic standing (measured in terms of education and income), residential segregation, language use, intermarriage, and citizenship and civic participation?

Many provocative questions about new immigrants and old minorities remain unanswered. How will new immigrants react to American race relations and categories, and how will America categorize them? Where will the color line be drawn in the twenty-first century? Are some new groups becoming white, as older groups did? What does that mean for black Americans and for immigration and poverty policy in the United States?

In this chapter I summarize recent theorizing and research about the experiences of non-white immigrants, and most especially their children: the second generation. I describe my own qualitative research on the ways in which second-generation black immigrants balance their racial identities as blacks with their ethnic identities as West Indians. I conclude with some observations on how racial and ethnic stratification in the United States might change in the future, and on promising avenues for future research in this area.

THEORETICAL AND METHODOLOGICAL APPROACHES TO THE IMMIGRANt EXPERIENCE

Qualitative sociology played a central role in the development of the field of American ethnic and race relations. The Chicago School of sociology took as one of its main subjects understanding the immigrant experience in that city. With the publication of *The Polish Peasant in Europe and America* by W. I. Thomas and Florian Znaniecki in 1918, a new agenda for sociology was set; one which, in Martin Bulmer's words, shifted sociology "from abstract theory and library research toward a more intimate acquaintance with the empirical world, studied nevertheless in terms of a theoretical frame" (1984: 45). Robert Park, Ernest Burgess and W. I. Thomas trained a cadre of graduate students to study the experience of immigrants in Chicago, and provided methodological and theoretical tools for making sense of the patterns they found.

American sociologists used both ethnographic methods and increasingly quantitative methods as data became available to study racial, ethnic, and immigrant inequality. The US government collects a great deal of information on race, ethnicity, and generation. In fact, the situation could not be more different than the French situation described in this volume by Kastaryano. A primary source of quantitative data has been the US Census, which has asked a question about race or color of the population since it was first established in 1790. Data on immigrants and their children were also available until 1970 because the Census asked a question on birthplace of respondents and of their parents. Currently, the Census asks a question on race, ethnic ancestry, birthplace, and language use. These data have been used by scholars to document differences between native-born whites and other groups. For instance, in 1999, 11 percent of the native-born population was below the poverty line, but 17 percent of the foreign born were. Some 22 percent of Latin American foreign born were poor, but only 13 percent of the foreign born from Asia and 9 percent of the foreign born from Europe were poor. As noted earlier, sharp racial differences remain. In 2001 23 percent of the black population (regardless of nativity) was poor, compared to 7.8 percent of the non-Hispanic white population. In addition, ethnographic and interview studies have examined the cultural, social, and attitudinal differences between whites and American racial and ethnic groups. The concept of assimilation – or how much groups are becoming similar to one another has guided this research.

Sociologists Richard Alba and Victor Nee (2003) define assimilation as the decline of an ethnic distinction and its corollary cultural and social differences. They stress that this decline can come about because of changes both among the immigrant groups, and among the mainstream. They also formulate a definition of assimilation for individuals:

> Individuals' ethnic origins become less and less relevant in relation to the members of another ethnic group (typically, but not necessarily, the ethnic majority group), and individuals on both sides of the boundary see themselves more and more as alike, assuming they are similar in terms of some other critical factors such as social class; in other words, they mutually perceive themselves with less and less frequency in terms of ethnic categories and increasingly only under specific circumstances. (Alba and Nee 2003: 11)

New Studies on the Second Generation

The accepted wisdom among immigration scholars is that over the course of a few generations in the United States most differences between national origin groups whose origins were in Europe have narrowed considerably or disappeared (Lieberson and Waters 1988; Alba 1990). While noting differences in the pace of change across ethnic groups, researchers have determined that the progress of once-stigmatized groups like Greeks, Slavs, Irish, and Italians merits Greeley's description as an "ethnic miracle" (Greeley 1976). In numerous studies of European immigrants and their children, time spent in the US explains success because immigrants acquire the language skills, educational credentials, and general cultural knowledge needed to compete with native white Americans. Second-generation ethnic Americans may *surpass* native Americans because of the selectivity of the immigrant generation and the drive and achievement orientation they instill in their children (Hirschman 1983; Perlmann 1988; Lieberson and Waters 1988).

In the 1990s as the children of immigrants who arrived in the 1970s and 1980s from Latin America, the Caribbean and Asia came of age, a number of scholars began to examine the patterns of academic achievement and cultural assimilation of this new second generation. This new literature grappled with the question of whether previous optimistic theories of immigrant assimilation were useful for this new population, and with problems of data availability and quality.

These studies generally included children of immigrants who were born in the United States (the classic second generation), and people who came to the US, usually with their parents, as children but who grew up and attended school in the US (the 1.5 generation). In 2000 10.4 percent of the population or 28.4 million people were foreign born, another 27.5 million people or 10 percent of the US population had one or two immigrant parents: the second generation. Using Current Population Survey data, Zhou (2000: 229) calculates that 35 percent of the second generation are Latin American in origin, and 7 percent are Asian.

The second generation, like their immigrant parents, are concentrated in gateway cities – large centers of immigrant concentration such as Los Angeles, New York, Miami, and San Francisco. Just six states, California, New York, Florida, Texas, New Jersey, and Illinois contained 70 percent of the foreign-born population. The two biggest gateway cities – New York and Los Angeles contain in their metropolitan areas one-third of the US foreign-born population – 9.4 million people. Other metro areas where the foreign-born population was 1 million people or more include San Francisco, Miami, and Chicago. These immigrant children have a strong impact on the local school systems; in these cities more than one-third of schoolchildren speak a language other than English at home (Zhou 2000: 229).

As many scholars have pointed out, it is quite difficult to study the second generation at a national level because in 1980 the Census Bureau dropped the birthplace of parents question and replaced it with an ancestry question (Zhou 1997; Waters 1999; Portes and Rumbaut 2001). So adult members of the second generation who no longer live with their immigrant parents are not identifiable through census data. An emerging body of work has sought to extrapolate future adult patterns of incorporation from the experiences of second-generation children and teenagers (Gibson 1989; Portes and Zhou 1993; Rumbaut 1995, 1997; Fernandez-Kelly and Schauffler 1994; Zhou and Bankston 1998; Portes and Rumbaut 2001). Qualitative and ethnographic studies have also been made of second-generation young adults that highlight generational transitions within immigrant communities (see Grasmuck and Pessar 1991; Smith 1994; Suarez-Orozco 1995; Bacon 1996; Waters 1999).

This literature has compared the experiences of the new immigrants to native minorities, asked how well they are doing in the labor market, examined patterns of naturalization and citizenship, measured language loss and retention, and examined strategies for economic mobility, including entrepreneurship and employment in ethnic enclaves.

Immigration scholars have generally stressed the great variation in the social origins of the immigrants. Bipolar immigrant streams have brought large numbers of skilled professionals and entrepreneurs along with uneducated and unskilled laborers. Thus immigrants are among both the most educated and the least educated Americans. While the foreign born overall have about the same percentage of college graduates as the native born (20 percent), they are over-represented at the lowest educational levels. While only 14.4 percent of native men had less than a high school diploma, 37.1 percent of immigrant men had less than a high school diploma (Smith and Edmonston 1997: 183). Immigrant educational attainment varies a great deal by national origin. Zhou (2000: 206) reports that 60 percent of foreign-born Indians have college degrees, but less than 5 percent each of immigrants from El Salvador or Mexico had a college degree. Scholars have also underscored the importance of legal conditions upon arrival, comparing legal immigrants, undocumented immigrants, and refugees. Attention has also been given to the regional distribution of the immigrants and their interaction with local labor markets and geographic mobility patterns among the native born. Finally, given the long history of caste-like exclusion of America's non-white minorities, scholars have addressed the central question of how non-European immigrants are doing, relative to native minority groups, not only to examine potential displacement effects, but also to understand the long-run prospects for nonwhite immigrants. This burgeoning literature has produced many intriguing findings and some speculation about the experiences of the new second generation. Taken as a whole, it suggests that their experience will be quite different from expectations based on inter-generational change among late nineteenth- and early twentieth-century European immigrants and their children and grandchildren.

Gans (1992), for instance, outlines several scenarios in which the children of the new immigrants could do worse than their parents or society as a whole. Gans speculates that second-generation immigrants who are restricted to poor inner city schools, bad jobs, and shrinking economic niches will experience downward mobility. Using ethnographic case studies and a survey of second-generation school children in Miami and San Diego, Portes and Zhou (1993) make a similar argument. The mode of incorporation of the first generation endows the second generation with differing amounts of cultural and social capital in the form of access to jobs, ethnic networks, and ethnic values, and exposes them to differing opportunities, which exerts differential pulls on their allegiances. Those who face discrimination and are close to American minorities, adopt a "reactive" ethnicity. Some of those groups who come with strong ethnic networks, access to capital, and fewer ties to US minorities, on the other hand, develop a "linear ethnicity" by assimilating into existing ethnic communities, while others develop a "segmented assimilation" in which they hold on to an immigrant identity in order to avoid being classified with American blacks or Puerto Ricans. Like Gans, they conclude that members of the second generation who cast their lot with America's minority groups, where peer culture takes an adversarial view of upward mobility and school success, are likely to experience downward social mobility.

In the most comprehensive study of second-generation youth published to date, Portes and Rumbaut (2001) show very divergent paths for second-generation youth from different national origin and class backgrounds. They found three different trajectories of incorporation among the youth they studied in San Diego and Miami: dissonant, consonant and selective acculturation. Dissonant acculturation occurs when young people quickly adopt American ways and the English language and their parents do not move as quickly. This is the trajectory that leads to role reversal, when children must translate for their parents and when children become more worldly and sophisticated about American ways, leaving their immigrant parents relatively powerless and often dependent on their children. Consonant acculturation occurs when parents and children learn the new culture and abandon the old at an even pace across the generations. This is most common among middle-class immigrants and their children. Finally, there is selective acculturation – when the second generation is embedded in a co-ethnic community that supports parents, slows the loss of parents' home language and norms, and cushions the move of both generations into American ways. This is characterized by a lack of intergenerational conflict, the presence of co-ethnics as friends, and perhaps the most emphasized in the text – full bilingualism in the second generation. In their last chapter Portes and Rumbaut extol the benefits of selective acculturation and call for policy initiatives to promote it.

The new scholarship on the second generation also stresses the changes in the American economy and the ways in which those changes shape the options available for the children of immigrants today. The decline in manufacturing and the growth of the service economy, along with the Civil Rights movement and the opening of universities and the economy to all groups by matter of law, mean that there are enormous opportunities available for well-educated immigrants and their children. The growth of racial and ethnic tolerance and the acceptance of multiculturalism also mean that this socio-economic success does not come at the cost of cultural assimilation. At the same time the lack of well-paid jobs for those with less than a college education and the growth of low-level service jobs mean that opportunities and outlooks for those who do not do well in school are rather limited.

What does this mean for the second generation? Concepts such as second-generation decline, segmented assimilation, and selective acculturation all stress that becoming American for the second generation could lead to downward mobility, while maintaining ties to their parents' culture and homeland could facilitate upward mobility. Portes and Rumbaut also show that first-generation immigrants with high levels of education and income are better able to provide a grounding in their own culture and language for their children.

In my own work I have addressed the question of the relation between the subjective identification of second-generation youth and their socio-economic trajectories. I have found a very different pattern from what prevailed with the earlier wave of immigration and I argue that racial discrimination and changes in the American economy have acted together to decouple the relationship that may have held before between socio-economic mobility and ethnic assimilation. Among second-generation West Indian youth I studied in New York City, those who identified as American were likely to be least successful in school and the job market, those who had a strong ethnic identity as Jamaican or Trinidadian had the best prospects.

SECOND-GENERATION WEST INDIANS IN NEW YORK CITY

In the early 1990s I began a study of West Indian immigrants and their teenage children in New York City. I was interested in exploring how they developed a racial and ethnic identity, given the overwhelming attention to race in American society. I was also interested in whether the first and second generation would follow the same patterns of assimilation, as they became American, as European origin immigrants had followed at the beginning of the twentieth century. I conducted in-depth interviews and participant observation in order to examine the ways in which first- and second-generation West Indian immigrants balance their identities as West Indian and as American. I found that for both the first and the second generation, part of coming to terms with being an American, is coming to terms with American race relations.

The overall study was designed to explore the processes of immigrant adaptation and accommodation to the United States, to trace generational changes in adaptation and ethnic and racial identification, and to explore the reactions of immigrants and their children to American race relations. The second-generation sample included 83 adolescents drawn from four sources designed to tap a range of class backgrounds and class trajectories. They include:

1   The public school sample: teenagers attending two public inner-city high schools in Brooklyn, New York, where I did extensive interviewing and participant observation (45 interviews).
2   The church and church school sample: teenagers attending Catholic parochial schools or a Catholic after-school program in the same inner-city neighborhood as the public schools (although most of these students were not themselves Catholic) (14 interviews).
3   The street-based snowball sample: teenagers living in the same inner-city neighborhood in Brooklyn who could not be reached through the school – either because they had dropped out or because they would not have responded to interviews conducted in a formal setting (15 interviews).
4   The middle-class snowball sample: teenagers who had ties to this neighborhood, who were now living there and attending magnet schools or colleges outside of the district, or whose families had since moved to other areas of the city or to suburbs (9 interviews).

The in-depth life history interviews lasted between one and two hours and were conducted by myself, a white female, and a team of three research assistants, two of whom are second-generation Caribbean Americans and one a black American.

I found some clear divisions in the ways in which the second generation balanced their race and ethnic identity. This variation in racial and ethnic identity was related to attitudes towards school and work and to the socio-economic backgrounds and trajectories of these youngsters. Some of the adolescents we interviewed agree with their parents that the United States holds many opportunities for them. Others disagree with their parents because they believe that racial discrimination and hostility from whites will limit their abilities to meet their goals. By contrasting the ideas these youngsters have about their own identities and the role of race in American society, I find a great deal of variation within the West Indian group. Some Jamaican Americans, for example, are experiencing downward social mobility while others are maintaining strong ethnic ties and achieving socio-economic success.

THREE PATHS OF IDENTITY DEVELOPMENT

The interviews with the teenagers suggest that while the individuals in this study vary a great deal in their identities, perceptions and opinions, they can be classed into three general types: (1) identifying as Americans; (2) identifying as ethnic Americans with some distancing from black Americans; or (3) identifying as an immigrant in a way that does not reckon with American racial and ethnic categories.

A black American identity characterized the responses of approximately 35 (42 percent) of the 83 second-generation respondents we interviewed. These youngsters identified with other black Americans. They did not see their "ethnic" identities as important to their self-image. When their parents or friends criticized American blacks or described what they perceived as fundamental differences between Caribbean origin people and American blacks, these youngsters disagreed. They tended to downplay an identity as Jamaican or Trinidadian, and described themselves as American.

Another 26 (31 percent) of the respondents adopted a very strong ethnic identity which involved a considerable amount of distancing from American blacks. It was important for these respondents to stress their ethnic identities and for other people to recognize that they were not American blacks. These respondents tended to agree with parental judgements that there were strong differences between Americans and West Indians. This often involved a stance that West Indians were superior to American blacks in their behaviors and attitudes.

A final 22 (27 percent) of respondents had more of an immigrant attitude towards their identities than either the American identified youth or the ethnic identified youth. Most, but not all, of these respondents were more recent immigrants themselves. A crucial factor for these youngsters is that their accents and styles of clothing and behavior clearly signaled to others that they were foreign born. In a sense, their identity as an immigrant precluded having to make a "choice" about what kind of American they were. These respondents had a strong identity as Jamaican or Trinidadian, but did not evidence much distancing from American blacks. Rather, their identities were strongly linked to their experiences on the islands, and they did not worry much about how they were seen by other Americans, white or black.

These categories capture the general tendencies of each of the individuals we interviewed and it was possible to sort each individual into one of the three categories. Yet it is best to understand these categories as ideal types that simplify a much more complicated reality. Identity is situational and fluid for all of the teens we studied and just because any one individual generally identifies as African American, for instance, does not mean that there are not times or situations where he or she might identify as Jamaican.

While the identity choices made by the young people did not differ by gender, there tended to be a strong relationship between the type of identity and outlook on American race and ethnic relations that the youngsters developed and their social class background and/or their social class trajectory. The ethnically identified youngsters were most likely to come from a middle-class background. Of the total of 83 second-generation teens and young adults interviewed, 57 percent of the middle-class teens identified ethnically, whereas only 17 percent of the working class and poor teens identified ethnically. The poorest students were most likely to be immigrant or American identified. Only 1 out of the 13 teens whose parents were on public assistance identified ethnically. The American identified, perhaps not surprisingly, were also more likely to be born in the US. Some 66 percent of the American identified were born in US, as opposed to only 14 percent of the immigrant identified or 38 percent of the ethnically identified. One question I asked about how things had changed since the Civil Rights Movement shows the different perceptions of the teens about race in United States society. The ethnically identified gave answers I suspect most white Americans would give. They said that things are much better for blacks now. They state that they now can ride at the front of the bus and that they can go to school with whites.

> Things are much better now. Cause I mean during the sixties, you couldn't get into white high schools. And you couldn't drink from the same water fountain as whites, you had to go to the back of the bus. Now it's a lot of things have changed. (18-year-old, Guyanese female, born US, American identified)

The irony of course is that we were sitting in an all-black school when this young woman made this statement. The American identified teens saw things differently. The vast majority told us that things were not better since the Civil Rights Movement. They think that the change is that the discrimination now is "on the down low," covered up, more crafty:

> It's the same discrimination, but they are more careful of the way they let it out. It's always there. You have to be very keen on how to pick it up. But it's always there. But it's just on a lower level now. (17-year-old Grenada male, three years in US, American identified)

Some of the American identified teens pointed out that we were in an all-black school, and they concluded that the fight against segregation had been lost. The result of these different world views is that the parents' view of an opportunity structure that is open to hard work is systematically undermined by their children's peer culture, but more importantly, by the actual experiences of these teens.

> It's worse now because back then at least you know who didn't like you and who like you. But now you don't know who's after you. I mean, we don't have anyone to blame for anything. I mean, we know what we feeling. We know when we got there to get a job, we can't get a job. We know it is our color . . . If you know who your enemy is, you can fight him. But if you don't know who your enemy is, you can't fight him. And they're tearing you down more and more and you don't know what is going on. And there's a lot of undercover racist people out there, institutions and firms and corporations, that's directly keeping people out. (22-year-old Jamaican male, six years in US, immigrant identified)

This 15-year-old, American-born, Trinidadian girl points to the difference between *de facto* and *de jure* rights for blacks. She is taught in school about the accomplishments of the Civil Rights Movement and her mother tells her all the time not to be "racial," yet her peer group and her own "mental map" of her surroundings give her a very different picture:

> *Q*: Do you things are better for black people now than they were before the Civil Rights Movement?
>
> *A*: In some ways I would say yes and in some ways no. Because, it's like they don't say that you can't go in this neighborhood anymore. But you know you really can't, because there will be trouble if you do. I mean you could go there, but you know you will get those looks and stares and everything like that.
>
> *Q*: What neighborhoods can't you go to?
> *A*: My friends say Sheepshead Bay is bad. They say Coney Island too, but I have to deal with that. They say by South Shore, around there. And near Kings Plaza. They say over there. And by Canarsie. They say that's really bad. (15-year-old, Trinidadian female, born US, American identified)

On the other hand, the ethnic identified teens, whose parents are more likely to be middle class and doing well, or who attends parochial or magnet schools, and not the substandard neighborhood high schools, see clearer opportunities and rewards ahead, despite the existence of racism and discrimination. Their parents' message that hard work and perseverance can circumvent racial barriers does not fall on unreceptive ears. The ethnically identified youngsters embrace an ethnic identity in direct line from their parents' immigrants identity. Such an identity is basically in part in opposition to their peers' identities and in solidarity with their parents' identities. These youngsters stress that they are Jamaican Americans, and that while, they may be proud of their racial identity as black, they see strong differences between themselves and black Americans. They specifically see their ethnic identities as keys to upward social mobility, stressing, for instance, that their parents' immigrant values of hard work and strictness will give them the opportunity to succeed in the United States, when black Americans fail. This ethnic identity is very much an American-based identity – it is in the context of American social life that these youngsters base their assumptions of what it means to be Jamaican or Trinidadian. In fact, often the pan-ethnic identity as Caribbean or West Indian is the most salient label for these youngsters as they see little differences among the groups, and the most important thing for them is differentiating themselves as second-generation non-black Americans.

The ethnic and racial identifications of these kids were also correlated with what they thought of being American. While both groups contained individuals who spoke in somewhat patriotic terms of the privileges of being American, there was a difference in the overall interpretation of American identity described by the teenagers. Ironically, the American black identified teens had more negative things to say about being American in the abstract:

Q: What does it mean to you to be an American?

A: American? Well, I live in America, so I call myself American. But America is just, like – we were brought here to do work for Americans. So, like, we work for Americans really. (17-year-old Jamaican male, born US, American identified)

The ethnic identified respondents, who were also more likely to be middle class, often gave more positive appraisals:

Q: What does it mean to you to be an American?

A: To be an American, is to, one, be free. I think that's the main thing we have in our Constitution and the Declaration of Independence. Free to vote. Free to express our ideas. Free to go out and do what we want to do. That may be to go out and start our own business. I think that being an American, gives the individual the opportunity to make the

choice to succeed, to be better . . . I felt proud to be an American when
I went overseas . . . Or when America as a whole has done something
great. Most of the time though I think of myself as a West Indian.
(22-year-old Montserrat male, born US, ethnic identified)

CREATING HYBRID MINORITY CULTURES

My more recent work has extended this study of identity and socio-
economic outcomes to a larger cross-section of second-generation
young adults in New York City. A study of young adults from a number
of different backgrounds including Chinese, Dominicans, West Indians,
Colombians, Ecuadorians and Peruvians, and Puerto Ricans, has complicated the picture of identity development presented above. While
becoming an American minority is a clear-cut avenue for West Indian
youth who are identified in American society with black Americans,
other people of color face a variety of possible outcomes. One important factor is that in major receiving cities with high concentrations of
immigrants such as New York, Los Angeles, Miami and the like,
members of the second generation interact a lot more with each
another and native minorities than with native whites, with important
consequences for the patterns of prejudice and intergroup conflict
experienced by different groups. But this intergroup contact also has
positive dimensions. They are creating a new kind of multiculturalism,
not of balkanized groups huddled within their own enclaves, but of
hybrids and fluid exchanges across group boundaries. New York City
abounds in clubs where African-American hip hop has been fused with
East Indian and West Indian influences into new musical forms, for
example. The real action is not in the interplay of immigrant cultures
with a homogenous dominant American culture, but in the interactions
between first- and second-generation immigrant groups and native
minorities. African-American young people dance to Jamaican dance
hall and imitate Jamaican patois, even as West Indian youngsters learn
African-American slang. Puerto Ricans can meringue and Dominicans
can play Salsa and rap in two languages. Second-generation youth do
see themselves as Americans and New Yorkers, but they are not assimilating into some mythical American mainstream but into an evolving
society that is very much a product of globalization, international
migration, and the consequent mixing of cultures and identities to
produce new outcomes.

This is reflected in how our respondents in our most recent study
identified themselves (Kasinitz et al. 2002). They used the term Ameri-

can in two different ways. One was to describe themselves as American compared to the culture, values, and behaviors of their parents. They definitely thought that the US had influenced them to approach the world differently from their parents. But they also used "American" to refer to the native whites they encountered at school, the office, or in public places, but whom they new far better from TV and the movies. They saw those "Americans" as a different group that would never include them because of their race/ethnicity.

Many respondents sidestepped this ambivalent understanding of the term "American" by describing themselves as "New Yorkers." This was open to them even as Blacks or Hispanics or Asians, and it embraced them as second-generation immigrants. A "New York" identity embraced the dynamic cultural activities familiar to them, but not necessarily the larger white society. "New Yorkers," for our respondents, could come from immigrant groups, native minority groups, or be Italians, Irish, Jews, or the like.

New Directions for Research

Ordinary Americans and the federal statistical system have generally divided the population into five racial ethnic categories: white, black, Native American, Asian, and Hispanic. While there has always been overlap and ambiguity in drawing the boundaries among these groups, they have remained rather stable as categories and there has been general acceptance of them as describing the major racial divisions within our society. Two processes are undermining this system of racial classification and leading to a fluid and indeterminate outcome. One is increasing intermarriage across these categories and increasing recognition of multiple identities. For the first time in 2000, the Census allowed respondents to check all races that apply to them.

Some 2.4 percent of Americans (6.8 million people) reported a multiracial response, but most analysts believe this will rise sharply in the future. The Census Bureau now reports data on 164 combinations of race categories, and some have speculated that the entire process of identifying and reporting by race will be undermined or exposed as completely arbitrary by this plethora of categories (Harrison 2002; Skerry 2002).

The other force which will change American conceptions of race and ethnicity is immigration. Immigrants from around the world who do not share the American categories of racial classification are challenging the status quo. The second-generation West Indians I studied who insist on an immigrant or transnational identity are resisting the racial status quo in the United States. The young second-generation Dominicans we studied in New York who define Americans as whites they see on TV but see little difference between themselves and Chinese and Puerto Rican young New Yorkers are also transforming and shaping new categories of belonging and exclusion.

Excellent qualitative research, including interviews and ethnographies will need to be done to chronicle and understand these changes. This research should address both how immigrants and the succeeding generations understand and identify as group members in the United States, but also how established native-born whites and blacks identify the newcomers, and how native-born concepts of race and ethnicity are transformed. One out of five Americans is currently an immigrant or a child of immigrants, but all Americans are changing as a result of these global migration flows. Whether we become a less race- and color-obsessed society and a more equal one, or whether we develop new patterns of exclusion and inequality remains to be determined.

REFERENCES

Alba, R. (1990) *Ethnic Identity: The Transformation of White America.* New Haven, CT: Yale University Press.

Alba, R. and Nee, V. (2003) *Remaking the American Mainstream: Assimilation and the New Immigration.* Cambridge, MA: Harvard University Press.

Anderson, E. and Massey, D. S. (eds.) (2001) *Problem of the Century: Racial Stratification in the United States.* New York: Russell Sage Foundation.

Bacon, J. (1996) *Life Lines: Community, Family and Assimilation among Asian Indian Immigrants.* New York: Oxford University Press.

Bobo, L. (ed.) (2000) *Prismatic Metropolis: Inequality in Los Angeles.* New York: Russell Sage Foundation.

Bulmer, M. (1984) *The Chicago School of Sociology: Institutionalization, Diversity and the Rise of Sociological Research.* Chicago: University of Chicago Press.

Farley, R. (1993) "The common destiny of blacks and whites," in Hill, H. and Jones, J. E. (eds.), *Race in America: The Struggle for Equality.* Madison, WI: University of Wisconsin Press.

Fernandez-Kelly, M. P. and Schauffler, R. (1994) "Divided fates: immigrant children in a restructured US economy," *International Migration Review* 28 (4): 662–89.

Gans, H. (1992) "Second generation decline: scenarios for the economic and ethnic futures of the post 1965 American immigrants," *Ethnic and Racial Studies* 15 (April): 173–92.

Gibson, M. (1989) *Accommodation without Assimilation: Sikh Immigrants in an American High School.* Ithaca, NY: Cornell University Press.

Grasmuck, S. and Pessar, P. (1991) *Between Two Islands: Dominican International Migration.* Berkeley, CA: University of California Press.

Greeley, A. (1976) "The ethnic miracle," *The Public Interest* 45 (4) 20–36.

Harrison, R. J. (2002) "Inadequacies of multiple-response race data in the federal statistical system," in Perlmann, J. and Waters, M. C. (eds.), *The New Race Question: How the Census Counts Multiracial Individuals.* New York: Russell Sage Foundation.

Hirschman, C. (1983) "The melting pot reconsidered," *Annual Review of Sociology* 9: 397–423.

Kasinitz, P., Mollenkopf, J. and Waters, M. C. (2002) "Becoming American/becoming New Yorkers: immigrant incorporation in a majority minority city," *International Migration Review* 36 (4): 1020–36.

Lieberson, S. and Waters, M. C. (1988) *From Many Strands: Ethnic and Racial Groups in Contemporary America.* New York: Russell Sage Foundation Press.

Massey, D., Goldring, L. and Durand, J. (1994) "Continuities in transnational migration: an analysis of nineteen Mexican communities," *American Journal of Sociology* 99: 1492–533.

Park, R. (1928) "Human migration and the marginal man," *American Journal of Sociology* 33 (6): 881–93.

—— (1950) *Race and Culture.* Glencoe, IL: Free Press.

Park, R. and Miller, H. (1921) *Old World Traits Transplanted.* New York: Harper.

Perlmann, J. (1988) *Ethnic Differences: Schooling and Social Structure among the Irish, Jews and Blacks in an American City, 1999–1935.* New York: Cambridge University Press.

Portes, A. and Rumbaut, R. G. (2001) *Legacies: The Story of the Immigrant Second Generation.* Berkeley and Los Angeles: University of California Press.

Portes, A. and Zhou, M. (1993) "The new second generation: segmented assimilation and its variants. (interminority affairs in the US: pluralism at the crossroads)," *Annals of the American Academy of Political and Social Science* 530 (Nov): 74–97.

Rumbaut, R. (1997) "Ties that bind: immigration and immigrant families in the United States," in Booth, A., Crouter, A. C. and Landale, N. (eds.), *Immigration and the Family: Research and Policy on US Immigrants.* Mahwah, NJ: Lawrence Erlbaum Publishers.

Rumbaut, R. G. and Cornelius, W. A. (1995) *California's Immigrant Children: Theory, Research and Implications for Educational Policy.* La Jolla, CA: Center for US Mexican Studies, University of California, San Diego.

Skerry, P. (2002) "Multiracialism and the administrative state," in Perlmann, J. and Waters, M. C. (eds.), *The New Race Question: How the Census Counts Multiracial Individuals.* New York: Russell Sage Foundation.

Smith, J. P. and Edmonston, B. (eds.) (1997) *The New Americans: Economic, Demographic and Fiscal Effects of Immigration.* Washington, DC: National Academy Press.

Smith, R. C. (1994) "Doubly bonded solidarity: Race and social location in the incorporation of Mexicans in New York City." Paper presented at the Social

Science Research Council, Conference of Fellows: Program of Research on the Underclass.

Suarez-Orozco, C. and Suarez-Orozco, M. M. (1995) *Transformations: Immigration, Family Life, and Achievement Motivation among Latino Adolescents.* Stanford, CA: Stanford University Press.

Thomas, W. I. and Znaniecki, F. (1984) *The Polish Peasant in Europe and America: A Classic Work in Immigration History.* Edited by E. Zaretsky. 2 vols. Urbana, IL: University of Illinois Press.

Waters, M. C. (1999) *Black Identities: West Indian Immigrant Dreams and American Realities.* Cambridge, MA: Harvard University Press.

—— (2000) "The sociological roots and multidisciplinary future of immigration research," in Foner, N., Rumbaut, R. and Gold, S. J. (eds.), *Immigration Research for a New Century: Multidisciplinary Perspectives.* New York: Russell Sage Foundation.

Wilson, W. J. (1978) *The Declining Significance of Race: Blacks and Changing American Institutions.* Chicago: University of Chicago Press.

—— (1987) *The Truly Disadvantaged: The Inner City, the Underclass and Public Policy.* Chicago: University of Chicago Press.

—— (1996) *When Work Disappears: The World of the New Urban Poor.* New York: Knopf.

Wirth, L. (1956) *The Ghetto.* Chicago: University of Chicago Press.

Zhou, M. (1997) "Growing up American: the challenge confronting immigrant children and the children of immigrants," *Annual Review of Sociology* 23: 63–96.

—— (2000) "Contemporary immigration and the dynamics of race and ethnicity," in Smelser, N., Wilson, W. J. and Mitchell, F. (eds.), *America Becoming: Racial Trends and their Consequences.* Washington, DC: National Academy Press.

Zhou, M. and Bankston, C. (1998) *Growing Up American: How Vietnamese Children Adapt to Life in the United States.* New York: Russell Sage Foundation.

FURTHER READING

Alba, R. and Nee, V. (2003) *Remaking the American Mainstream: Assimilation and Contemporary Immigration.* Cambridge, MA: Harvard University Press.

Bean, F. and Stevens, G. (2003) *America's Newcomers and the Dynamics of Diversity.* New York: Russell Sage Foundation.

Portes, A. and Rumbaut, R. (2001) *Legacies: The Story of the Immigrant Second Generation.* Berkeley and Los Angeles, CA: University of California Press.

CHAPTER TWO

The "Language of Race," Identity Options, and "Belonging" in the Quebec Context

MICHELINE LABELLE

The racial discrimination experienced by certain minorities in the Americas constitutes a structural obstacle to the full exercise of citizenship in its broadest sociopolitical sense (rights and obligations, membership, participation, and belonging). Racism contradicts the most basic human rights. It represents a blatant disregard for the principles of justice, dignity, and equality upon which rest a number of these rights. Racism weakens the sense of belonging individuals are expected to feel toward a given political community, denies diversity, demeans the conditions of social and political membership, and leads the way to the expression of antagonistic and socially divisive identity claims. Racism is largely responsible for the resentment felt by many racialized social groups in North America (Aboriginal Peoples, historical minorities created by the slave trade, new minorities emerging in the wake of post-colonial migrations). Any normative discourse on citizenship must take this resentment into account and address it.

Canada, like most western, liberal-democratic societies, has been taken to task on issues of exclusion and discrimination (Li 1999; Satzewich 1994, 1998; Frideres and Pizanias 1995; Driedger and Halli 2000; Abu Laban and Gabriel 2002). The Canadian state has responded with a Charter of Rights and Freedoms which celebrates and protects difference and diversity, as well as with laws and policies that actually extend the benefits and privileges of membership in the Canadian political community to all, without distinction of origin, culture, race or creed. In the past decade, the Canadian state has been particularly active in promoting the seamless integration of immigrants and members of racialized minorities through a number of policy initiatives, clearly expecting in return, indeed demanding, that they develop a strong Canadian civic identity.

Yet, in a controversial and polemical book, Neil Bissoondath (1994), argues that Canadian multiculturalism policies are based on the cult of ethnicity and do not encourage immigrants to consider themselves as wholly Canadian. More recently, philosopher Will Kymlicka has adopted the counter-position (1998). He argues that one of the key explanations for the Canadian success story lies in its policy of multi-culturalism, and in the fact that immigrants are encouraged to keep their own cultural identities. Among the "visible minorities," the con-ditions for "blacks" are better than in the United States because Canada does not have the same historical relationship with slavery as its neigh-bor to the South, and the problems with which they are confronted today are comparable to the experiences of certain other immigrant groups in the past. However, Kymlicka admits that "Blacks" risk devel-oping "an oppositional stance toward the mainstream society," if certain measures are not taken (1998: 80–9).

For its part, the Quebec state (which, despite its legal status as one of the ten provincial sub-units of the Canadian state, is laying claim to a self-contained, autonomous and Quebec-based citizenship) has stood increasingly firm to ensure that all who reside on the territory upon which it is allowed to legislate embrace Quebec as their primary home of civic attachment, and not Canada.

To understand contemporary Quebec, we have to look at the period preceding the creation of Canada in 1867. In 1663, the first permanent French European settlement was established in Quebec City. Mohawks, Cree, Algonquin, Huron/Wendats, Innus, Abénaquis, Naskapis, Micmacs and Malecites nations were living at the site of present day Quebec. In 1663, King Louis XIV of France proclaimed the French colony "*la Nouvelle France*." In 1763, *la Nouvelle France* became a British possession by conquest, forming the "Province of Quebec." At this time, the native French (more than 55,000) already identified themselves as *Canadiens*, expressing a "collective identity firmly established during the French regime" (McRoberts 1997: 2). They had a sense of distinct nationality constructed from "the merging of various French regional identities that colonists brought to New France" (ibid.: 3). By contrast, the English-speakers saw themselves very differently. Most adopted a British colonial identity until the Confederation of 1867. This identity was gradually displaced by a Canadian identity. Consequently, the *anciens Canadiens* have been forced to define themselves as *Canadiens français*. Today the term *Québécois* that has expanded after the 1960s refers to Quebecers of various origins.

In 1774, the colony's French subjects "who had lived entirely under the system of English laws since the conquest, obtained from London the right to live under the rule of their French laws and customs with respect to property and civil law" (Chevrier 1996: 3). This was established through the Quebec Act of 1774 that recognized religion, education, language and culture as legitimately belonging to the French themselves, not to the British government. The colony was later divided into Lower Canada (French) and Upper Canada (English). Each had a local parliament overseen by a governor appointed by London.

In the 1830s, the elected officials of Upper and Lower Canada (*Canadiens*, Irish and English democrats) called for a responsible government. This movement led to a violent rebellion in 1837–8 suppressed by the British colonial army as a political response. The Act of Union of 1841 merged Upper and Lower Canada into one Province of Canada, aiming to force assimilation of the French-speaking population (650,000) to the English-speaking one (450,000). In 1848, France recovered some of its rights in institutions.

During the following decades, constitutional demands emerged in both language groups because the Act of Union created tensions between the two communities. In 1867, Westminster approved the British North American Act establishing the Dominion of Canada. It comprised one central government and four provinces: Nova Scotia, New Brunswick and the Provinces of Canada that became Ontario and Quebec. The 847,000 French Canadians represented barely one-third of the population of the new federation. Today, the population of Quebec of various origins represents around 23 percent of the Canadian population.

The federation itself remained a colony, a constitutional monarchy. As Chevrier puts it:

> The federal parliament had broad general powers such as the power to legislate on peace, order and good government and to make laws on trade and commerce. Few jurisdictions were shared, except immigration and agriculture, subject to the preponderance of federal laws. The federal government that emerged from the Constitution of 1867 resembled a unitary government, in no way hindered by the action of provinces and their participation in its choices. In short, it was a narrow and frail autonomy that the Constitution of 1867 recognized for the unsettled community that was once again called Québec. (1996: 4)

The federation gave the province of Quebec control over issues like education, language, and culture. Nevertheless, the Confederation was seen among certain politicians as "a pact between two nations, a bilateral agreement between two founding peoples who, recognized by right as equal, chose federalism so they might live better together" (ibid.).

But this was a false perspective and since the Confederation, Quebec's demands have focused mainly on defending provincial autonomy facing a unitarian and centralized concept of federalism (McRoberts 1997: 11; Chevrier 1997: 6; Rocher 2002).

During the 1960s, what was called a "Quiet Revolution" took place in Quebec with the creation of sovereignist parties and a challenge to the dominance of the English economic class of Quebec. French Canadian discontent with their socio-economic subordination and their lack of power within federal institutions brought them to see the Quebec state as the only political institution that they could fully control. The "Quiet Revolution" brought huge transformations: the democratization of society, a greater equality in the access to education and to health, the control of major economic structures, the modernization of the Quebec public service, the emergence of a sovereignist political movement and the adoption of a *Charte québécoise de la langue française*, which made French the official language of Quebec (Rocher 2002).

The process of nation-building in the past 40 years have made Quebec a "world leader" in the knowledge-based economy (Gagnon 2001: 38). The construction of a true national space has been accompanied by the erasure of disparities between Anglophones and Francophones in terms of social mobility. Dieckhoff notes a strong convergence of values and behavioral patterns with the rest of Canada (consumerism, birth rates, divorce rates, civil liberties, ethics) (2001: 31). Yet, within this national space, two citizenship systems face off and compete with one another.

The Quebec state proposes a vision of citizenship based on the values of justice, equality, democracy and pluralism, using international norms as guidelines on these issues (Québec 2000: 17). The Quebec discourse on citizenship focuses on countering the ethnicization of Quebec's social dynamics, on breaking down community isolationism, and on promoting new relationships "between citizens" rather than between linguistic or cultural communities (Labelle and Rocher 2001).

Beyond the inevitable political tug-of-war between the federal and the provincial governments – a tug-of-war in which the loyalty of immigrants and racialized minorities to either the Canadian or the Quebec state appears as the ultimate prize – beyond their institutional and administrative divergence over issues of membership and belonging, the Canadian and the Quebec states address the problem of racial discrimination and minority exclusion in very similar fashion. Both genuinely encourage immigrants and racialized minorities to become full and free participants in a civic and institutional framework that, theoretically, includes them unconditionally. Both are driven by a strong will to inclusiveness, which has become a major plank in their citizenship-focused nation-building project. Although the Canadian state emphasizes multiculturalism, and the Quebec state insists on the convergence of the various ethnocultural groups that make up the social fabric of contemporary Quebec society around a common public culture, both are intent on achieving the social unity and the political primacy of their respective jurisdictions.

Some among immigrant and racialized communities fully endorse either Quebec's or Canada's aspiration – or even both – to stand as a civic nation. Others, however, are rather wary. They distrust the pluralist and civic discourses of the (Quebec and Canadian) state, they denounce the unfulfilled promises of inclusion of both Canadian and Quebec citizenship, and they resentfully point to the significant distance that separates the state rhetoric from the actual economic and political marginalization that important segments of immigrant and racialized populations continue to experience on a regular basis.

The main aim of this chapter is to explore the basis of this distrust and, in the process, examine how the complex intersection of race, identity claims, and belonging bring out the inherent limits of the state's conception of citizenship in Quebec. The analysis proceeds first by contextualizing the issues of diversity and racism in Canada and Quebec. A critical reflection on the racialization process that affects certain socials groups follows. This reflection will shed light on empirical data presented in the third section about the identity choices of second-generation Caribbean immigrants in Montreal. Finally, the factors that influence civic incorporation will be discussed in the fourth and last section.

DIVERSITY AND RACISM IN THE CANADIAN AND QUEBEC CONTEXTS

Canada has a national francophone minority concentrated in Quebec. The mother tongue of more than 81 percent of Quebecers is French and more than 85 percent of all Canadians whose mother tongue is French are residents of Quebec. The Aboriginal peoples, who are more dispersed across the Canadian territory, represented approximately 4 percent in the 1990s (1.3 million of the total population, estimated at 31,110.6 in 2002). Ethnocultural diversity in Canada results in large part from the decline of European immigration in the 1960s and 1970s, a period during which Canada was, among all the developed countries, the one that welcomed the highest proportion of Third World immigrants (Frideres 1992: 50). Social and political tensions, the end of the colonial era, the ensuing restructuring of the global migratory system, the increasing role played by Canada within the Third World, and international pressures aimed at ending racial discrimination through legislation and immigration rules are generally mentioned as the main causes of this situation. In 2001, the number of Canadians born abroad represented 18.4 percent of the total population. In 1881, groups other than those of British or French origin only represented 10 percent of the population. Over a century later, by 1991, the same groups represented 42 percent of the Canadian population. The so-called "visible minorities" represented 13.4 percent in 2001. It is estimated that this proportion will exceed 19 percent in 2016 (Samuel 2001: 23; Kalbach 2001).

"Visible minority" is a term first proposed by the federal government in order to designate groups that are victims of discrimination. The Employment Equity Act defines "visible minorities" as persons, "other than aboriginal peoples, who are non-Caucasian in race or non-white in colour." Under this definition, the following groups are identified as visible minorities: Chinese, South Asians, Blacks, Arabs and West Asians, Filipinos, Southeast Asians, Latin Americans, Japanese, Koreans and Pacific Islanders (Statistics Canada 1998). The term has been widely criticized because of its racializing connotations and its globalizing and imprecise nature. It echoes the notions of "race" and "racial group" found in classical sociology, which are still widely used in the scientific community and among Canadian public policy-makers (Kobayashi 1992). I prefer to use the expression "racialized minorities" as a replacement. In this chapter, I refer to the terms "race," "blacks" and "whites" in quotation marks in order to clearly delineate my position, which is opposed to the racializing ideology that still imbues current academic discourses.

All the elementary forms of colonial or classical racism (prejudices, discrimination, segregation, violence) have been a part of the nation-building process in Canada and they have reached the level of state racism (supremacist movements, discrimination entrenched in laws and policies, specifically immigration policies up until the 1960s). This racism based itself openly on theories rooted in a presumed genetic inferiority of certain minority groups. This type of racism operated concurrently in North American societies along the lines of an inegalitarian logic of domination and exploitation, and a difference-driven logic of distancing and exclusion.

Racism has undergone transformations. Neo-racism (also referred to as symbolic, modern or differentialistic racism) brings in a new dimension. It postulates that certain national or migrant groups are incompatible with mainstream society. We find evidence of this in opinion polls and in public policies (Satzewitch 1998).

In the 1960s, Canada, like many other countries, began to apply in earnest the principles of "equality" and "respect for diversity" to its policies. The Canadian Declaration of Rights marked the first time that a federal law prohibited discrimination on the basis of "race," country of origin, religion or sex and spurred the first wave of immigration policy reform and employment equity, culminating in the policy of multiculturalism. Despite these measures, Aboriginal peoples and racialized minorities still face significant disadvantageous socioeconomic conditions (Harvey et al. 1999). This is true, for example, of many members of the "black community." Although their level of educational attainment is comparable to that of the general population, they are still likely to be more often unemployed and for longer periods than most Canadians, their average income is lower, they are poorer, and they suffer from income disparities attributable to discrimination in hiring policies and promotion within the workplace (Torczyner 1997; Fleras 1999; Driedger and Halli 2000). In addition, this group is underrepresented in the public service, in the media and in the political sphere. Along with Aboriginal Peoples and Arabs, the minorities categorized as "blacks" remain preferred targets of discrimination based on racism in the Canadian social space.

As far as Quebec is concerned, at the time of the 2001 census, the immigrant population accounted for 10 percent of the total population (7,417.7 million). Racialized minorities represent 7 percent of the Quebec population. 90 percent live in the Montreal Metropolitan region and comprise 13.6 percent of the area's residents. Persons defined as "Black" represent 2.1 percent of the total population in Quebec, Arabs and West Asians 1.2 percent, Latin Americans 0.8 percent, Southeast Asians 0.8 percent and Chinese 0.8 percent.

Like its federal counterpart, Quebec has initiated over the past 30 years a number of laws against discrimination, and several job-creation and ethnic community funding programs geared towards eradicating racism. But despite this string of policy measures, studies continue to reveal the persistence of disproportionate poverty levels and economic disadvantages among racialized minorities, much like those found in the rest of Canadian society (Québec 1996, 1999, 2001; Torczyner 2001). The *Commission des droits de la personne et des droits de la jeunesse* has published several reports on discrimination and racial harassment in the workplace, in housing, in the judicial system, etc. The studies concluded that racialized minorities were under-represented, subject to inequalities in remuneration, and professionally segregated (Québec 1999).

MINORITY IDENTITIES

The process of racialization

Racism and, in general, obstacles to the egalitarian incorporation of racialized minorities into North American societies, have had discernible consequences on identity. Researchers have not given as much attention to these consequences as might be hoped. Yet categories of ethnicity and "social race" are central to contemporary identity politics and narratives of belonging. Like other major forms of social division, they are social and political constructs and they take on different meanings depending on their historical or national contexts.

Minority status has two dimensions: "the *self-definition* of a group is based on its members' perception of shared language, traditions, religion, history and experiences; the *other-definition* results from the dominant group's use of its power to impose social definitions on subordinate groups" (Castles and Davidson 1999: 62). Negative other-definition of a minority leads to the racialization or the ethnicization of social relations. Differences are interpreted and attributed to "race," culture or religion, rather than to a process of social differentiation resulting from socioeconomic positions, or historical, unequal relations of power (ibid.: 63). The overpowering action of dominant regimes of representation, and the "epistemic violence" of their underlying narratives on the "other" – the colonized, orientalism, the exotic, the primitive, the anthropological, the folkloric (Hall, in Donald and Rattansi 1992: 255) – are largely responsible for this outcome.

However, as Anthony Appiah points out, there are differences among differences. It is harder to resist racial identification than ethnic identification for two reasons: (1) racial ascription is more socially salient; and (2) "race" is taken to be the basis for treating people differentially (Appiah and Gutman 1996: 81). Conversely, racialized and subaltern groups can re-appropriate attributed identity, subvert it, and use it as an oppositional stance. Diverse forms of identity consciousness (diasporic, separatist, transcultural, etc.) can result. This new "identity of resistance" explains the emergence of "identity politics" (Castells 1997). But as Stuart Hall and Anthony Appiah have noted, it also often signals the "end of innocence" as minorities who attempt to unite around a unique and illusory category are faced with the inevitable acknowledgement of their differences and specificities.

Racialization stems from a historical and ideological process. It imparts racial meaning to social relations, social practices or groups which had originally no particular, *a priori* racial grounding (Omi and Winant 1986: 69). Thus, at the end of the seventeenth century, Africa's Ibos, Yorubas, Fulanis, etc., were reduced, within the Americas, to the category of "Negroes," a term which at first designated a social condition rather than a skin color (Labelle 1987). In the case of the United States, the American term "Negro" would be replaced by the following categories: "colored race," "Black," "Afro-American," "African-American" (Appiah and Gutman 1996: 76). In the Canadian context, the census attests to the innate racialism of public policies geared toward the management of diversity in the last two centuries. The terms "Negro," "mulatto," "coloured people," "Indian," appear as early as 1851. The expression "visible minorities," which today defines people who are not of the "Caucasian race or of the White race" or who do not have "white skin" perpetuates the "language of race" and rests on the following assumptions:[1] "1) races of people exist; 2) theses races have social relations; 3) these relations are, or have the potential to become, conflictive" (Kobayashi 1992; Satzewich 1994: 39).

Contemporary immigrants who come from the segmented societies of the Caribbean, of Brazil and Latin America live through a particular type of experience. In these societies, the infinitely varied and nuanced lexicon of identity is expressed in complex forms within social strata. The prevailing ethno-racial lexicon, itself a product of colonialism and of slavery, differentiates individuals and social groups along a scale based on color categories, following a set hierarchy of skin tones ranging between the archetypal "black" and "white." Dozens of terms are used in the Caribbean and in Brazil in order to designate this variation and this phenotypical hierarchy. This situation should not be interpreted as an example of racial democracy or of referential ambiguity on account of *métissage*, as some theories have sometimes suggested. On the contrary, this lexicon was and remains the main yardstick of segmentation in societies born out of triangular commerce. In the case of the contemporary French Caribbean, for example, it resulted in a near total inability to develop a fully-fledged civic identity (Labelle 1987; Dahomay 2001). Those who emigrated from these countries to the United States or Canada, might have been seen as "*Griffes*," "*Mulâtres*," "*Quarterons*," "*Bruns*" or "*Marabouts*" (including many subcategories for each basic term) in their homeland, but their former identity is reduced to the global category of "black" once in their new host society. They are thus readily associated with the group with an inferior social status as dominant, othering narratives purposely avoid having to deal with the ambiguity of intermediate identities.

Flux and identity constructs

The straight line assimilation theory which prevailed in North America until the end of the 1960s maintained that new immigrants would first experience acculturation by adopting the values, language, and manners of the *core group* of the host society, and would then develop a sense of belonging, which would in turn modify their identity. In the final phase, civic assimilation was considered successful when there were no conflicts between majorities and minorities over political issues, when immigrants participated in and became committed to the public affairs of the host society, the acquisition of citizenship representing, at this point, the best indicator of the success of the assimilation process.

Numerous sociological studies have disproved this theory. It is possible to observe that identities have variously been reshaped among European minorities in the United States. These variations can be explained by sociological factors such as: the status of the reference groups, social class, and the life cycle (Waters 1990; Rumbaut 1997). Within racialized minorities, choices are more restricted, but they exist depending on the specific cases and contexts (Waters 1998, 1999).

These distinctions demonstrate that it is necessary to take into account the historical, social, and political context in which identities are developed, transformed, and combined. Contemporary factors are still active in the perpetuation of the racialization process. Systemic discrimination, categorization linked to public policies geared toward the management of diversity, the segmentation of the labor market, the socio-demographic characteristics of the migrants, the legal status and the duration of residence, the representation or presence within the public sphere, the ideological and political stakes inherent to the host societies, all these factors have an influence on the ways identities are shaped.

The case analysis which follows will attempt to shed light on the impact of certain of these structural factors on the discourse associated with identity building and with the rationale on which it is based, in a specific societal context, that of Quebec.

THE IDENTITIES OF THE "SECOND GENERATION": A QUEBEC FIELD STUDY

For over 15 years, I have been studying the representations which are commonplace within minority environments on the issues of integration, citizenship and inter-community relations within Quebec society as a whole (Labelle and Lévy 1995; Labelle and Salée 2001). I have carried out this research through participant observation and field studies. This qualitative method requires that the researcher become immersed in the context, and that he or she takes charge personally of the majority of the in-depth interviews, in order to be able to determine when the saturation point has been reached. This method has many advantages when compared to opinion polls or quantitative methods. The qualitative interview, as long as it is reinforced by a rigorous theoretical framework and well-documented research on the social environment being studied, allows for the acquisition of a deeper knowledge of the perspective of the social actors, and a better understanding of the stakes as well as of the difficulties experienced by the actors.

In 1998, in the context of the social climate that followed the 1995 referendum on Quebec sovereignty,[2] with two other colleagues, I tried to circumscribe the discourse specific to the "second generation" of Haitian and Jamaican immigrants in terms of their integration into Canadian and/or Quebec society, and of their experience with racism (Labelle et al. 2001).

In looking at Haitian immigration to Canada, we distinguish between two distinctive waves. The first, from the late 1950s to early 1970s, was made up largely of professionals in the fields of health and education, as well as students, forced out by political persecution – this group had relatively little difficulty integrating. During the rapid expansion of the welfare capacities of the Quebec state in the 1960s and 1970s, their skills were in great demand. The second, post-1970s' wave consisted of unskilled or semi-skilled laborers fleeing economic hardship and political repression in Haiti. They headed mainly for Quebec's manufacturing and service sectors. Their lack of professional qualifications and a slumping Quebec economy through the better part of the 1980s and 1990s made for more difficult conditions of integration than what their predecessors had experienced. The Haitian community is the fourth-ranking ethno-cultural group established in Quebec. It numbered 75,705 individuals in 1996, 45,465 of whom were born in Haiti. The second generation represents two-fifths of the community (Statistics Canada 1996). Over 94 percent of this population is concentrated in the francophone neighborhoods of the Montreal metropolitan area, and has an educational profile relatively comparable to the general population. Two-thirds of immigrants of Haitian origin speak only French; 30 percent know both French and English; 3 percent speak neither. A little more than half of the individuals born in Haiti have declared Creole to be their mother tongue.

The Jamaican community has deeper historical roots in Quebec society. The first important waves of immigration from the West Indies began early in the twentieth century. In Jamaica, as in the rest of the Caribbean, limited economic prospects and demographic pressures were the principal motivating factors behind emigration. In 1928, West Indian immigrants represented 40 percent of Montreal's "black" population (Williams 1997). According to Williams, they were better educated and more "British" than the Afro-Americans who had arrived in Montreal before them, which created a certain social distance between the two groups, reminiscent of the situation in New York (Kasinitz 1992). Beginning in 1955 and into the mid 1960s the immigration of women was more prevalent due to the West Indian Domestic Schema. Many of these women lived in Montreal temporarily, only to emigrate to Toronto and Vancouver later (Williams 1989). As of 1968, following the opening in Jamaica of the first immigration office able to handle immigration requests on site, the number of immigrants rose quickly. This immigration was youthful, urbanized and bipolar, much like Haitian immigration. But the majority of individuals headed for English Canada.

In the 1996 Census, 10,075 people in Quebec declared that they were of Jamaican origin. The second generation is estimated to be made up of 4,230 individuals. Data show that the Jamaican community in Quebec remains almost entirely concentrated in the Anglophone communities of Montreal. Some 79 percent are unilingual and speak only English, while 20 percent declared that they were bilingual. The knowledge of French is more widespread among the educated youth in Quebec. This population has an educational profile comparable to the general population of Quebec.

It is often assumed that second-generation immigrants have an easier time than their parents and as a result should feel more readily Canadian and/or Quebecers. The ultimate aim of our exploratory study (from which we are quoting partial results for the purpose of this chapter) was to verify this assumption. The study is based on 24 in-depth interviews with Montreal-area young adults (ranging in age from 18 to 34) (chosen according to the snowball sampling method), who were either born of Haitian or Jamaican parents in Quebec or immigrated to Quebec with their parents as pre-schoolers. In other words, they have been primarily socialized and raised within Quebec institutions and normative environments (for the methodology employed, see Labelle et al. 2001). The two principal researchers conducted the interviews personally.

Given the limited scope of the research, we deliberately chose to focus on young people from the middle classes, who did not display any particular commitments to social, political or community issues. The fathers were well educated (75 percent of them held a university degree) and were employed at the time or previously in socially enviable positions (engineers, professionals, teachers, administrators). Many of the mothers, although less educated, were active in the workplace (nurses, businesswomen, employees of the service sector, laborers).

All the young people of Haitian origin interviewed were educated in French at the elementary and secondary levels. Half of the young Jamaicans were educated in English at the elementary level and 90 percent went to English-language high schools. All of the respondents had received either post-secondary technical training or university-level education. The majority were actively part of the labor force at the time of the interviews (however, in many fields not necessarily related to their initial training).

We focused on their experience of racism in the school environment throughout their socio-professional development path. We investigated their social networks, their views on intercultural relations in Quebec, the personal significance of trans-border links with family members and relatives, and their views on national and civic identities.

We wanted to find out whether, inasmuch as these young adults had been imprinted in a sustained and even exclusive way by the Canadian and Quebec social environments, they felt a sense of belonging to the Quebec and/or Canadian political communities. We also asked whether they embraced Quebec's civic identity in any way, and, despite the experience of racism which was part of our hypothesis, what meaning should be ascribed to their identity options.

During the interview, we asked for their reaction to the following statement: "People can describe themselves in several ways, for example as Haitian or Jamaican, Haitian-Canadian, Canadian, Quebecer of Haitian origin, Quebecer, Black or by some other name. How do you identify yourself?" Four or five types of identity options stood out: a unique national identity based on Haitian or Jamaican origin (29 percent of cases); a hyphenated identity, for example, Canadian-Haitian or Jamaican-Canadian, or Quebecer of Haitian origin (42 percent of cases); a unique Canadian civic identity (17 percent); a racialized identity: "Black" (8 percent). In one last case, an interviewee identified herself as a "citizen of the world" and explained her choice as coming from a feeling of double rejection.

Haitian and Jamaican identities

The young people interviewed justified their choice of a single identity, Haitian or Jamaican, by differences in culture, education, values, lifestyles and the characteristics of their informal networks. The interviewees made a clear distinction between their own identity and the Canadian or Quebec identity. One can debate this identity's status: Is it based on immigrant values, on ethno-racial considerations, or is it linked to citizenship? It all depends on one's point of view: that of the country of origin or that of the host society. Whatever the case may be, the respondents (some among them were born in Canada) who chose a single identity, that of their parents, stated that they see Quebec and/or Canada as a place of residence, but they attach no symbolic value to this condition and feel no sense of belonging to either Canada or Quebec:

> Haitian first, because of my surroundings, my friends. I have my home and my own way of being myself. If I said that I was a Quebecer, I would be assimilated . . . I have integrated into the Quebec milieu, but I am Haitian . . . And proud of it . . . It is a way of setting myself apart. (Woman born in Canada, translated from the French)

> I feel Haitian . . . For me, a Quebecer is a White Francophone. I do not fit this image. (Born in Canada, translated from the French)

> I'm Jamaican. Not Jamaican-Canadian. I wouldn't say I'm Black I would just assume, you look at my skin and you know I am Black. I am very proud of it. I don't feel like I am a Canadian or a Quebecer. I feel like they want me out of here . . . (Born in Jamaica)

> Jamaican. Most people would probably categorize me as Jamaican-Canadian because I speak a certain way and I know certain things . . . but I have never felt that I am Canadian or a Quebecer. I just don't do a lot of the Canadian things . . . (Born in Jamaica)

Hyphenated identity

This choice of identity is made by respondents who came to Canada at a very early age, but also by some individuals who were born in Canada. Their attachment to the culture and to the country of origin is reaffirmed, more often than not, as a reaction to a feeling of exclusion. Thus, a young woman, born in Canada, declares that she is "Jamaican-

Canadian": "I wouldn't say just Quebecer or Canadian because I was born in Jamaica. I still have the cultural influence."

A young man speaks of the fluidity of identities that are transformed depending on the generation. He clearly refers to himself as a "Haitian-Canadian born in Montreal," who cannot be considered automatically as a "Quebecer or a Canadian," because he is the son of immigrants who possess another culture and another "race," but whose children may one day call themselves or be designated as "neo-Quebecers."

Identity building is manifest among the interviewees as a part of a dynamic relationship between themselves and their vision of a Quebec identity. Their vision of the "Quebecer" is ethnically charged (it connotes White Francophones), and non-civic. These interviewees therefore declared, inevitably, that they harbor feelings of non-belonging towards Quebec. Whatever the case may be, they declare, people have always insisted on knowing where they are from, and have ceaselessly made them feel like the "other" (or have underscored their "otherness").

> Jamaican-Canadian . . . I wouldn't really say I am a Quebecer because to be a Quebecer is to be White and French . . . I guess since elementary school [people ask]: Where are you from? And you realize from young (*sic*) that you're not a Quebecer, you are whatever your parents are. (Woman born in Canada)

The interviewees demonstrated a strong sensitivity, much like first-generation immigrants, to the political connotations associated with the competing national/civic identities in the Canadian social space (Labelle and Saléc 2001). They have learned to take the context and the interlocutor into account in order to select a situational identity:

> If I find myself in a *Québécois* milieu, I will say Quebecer of Haitian origin, perhaps because that pleases people. If I am among Allophones,[3] I am Canadian. I do not simply say Canadian or Quebecer, because that is not what people want to hear. (Translated from the French)

Only one respondent claimed to be Quebecer-Haitian: "I would not simply say Quebecer, because people could tell from my skin color that I am not truly Quebecer. Because in our heads, when we see a Quebecer, we see a White person" (translated from the French).

The Canadian identity

Those who identify themselves exclusively as Canadians underscore the distance that they have taken in terms of their parents' country of origin, their integration into Quebec society, or the political connotation of their choice:

> Canadian. Because when I go to Jamaica they all look at me like a foreigner. I am a second-generation . . . I have more in common with the *Québécois* child. I have done the *cabane à sucre.* I have done all that. I come from here.

Or from another respondent: "I would probably call myself Canadian. I would probably call myself Quebecer. I think it's all I really know. I was raised here. I was raised in a fairly French-speaking community here . . .". And finally: "I describe myself as Canadian. It's political . . ." (translated from the French).

The racialized identity

Two young people of Jamaican origin opted for the "Black" designation: "Black is a powerful word and it's right to the point," one of them remarked.

RESULTS OF THE SURVEY

Three observations stand out concerning this empirical data: (1) the dominant tendency to adopt a hyphenated identity that, in most cases, demonstrates a resistance in accepting a unique Canadian or Québécois civic identity; (2) the weakness of the Quebec identity and its polarization; and (3) the weakness of the racialized identity. Let us examine the possible reasons behind this state of things.

The weakness of the racialized identity

When questioned on the topic of the ethno-racial lexicon used in governmental circles and public institutions, one-third of respondents felt it was normal to recognize "race" via the terms "whites" and "blacks," seen as accurately reflecting biological, social and cultural differences.

In reaction to a historical legacy of "white" dominance, the bedrock of racist ideology, many recalled a parental caution against trusting "whites," as well as emphasis on solidarity between "brothers and sisters" of color, the idea of "looking out for one's own."

A majority, however, found the "black/white" dichotomy to be reductionist, oversimplified, even hurtful, pointing to the dangerous precedent set by those wishing to biologize difference, as well as to homogenize an otherwise vastly diversified group of persons. It is also seen as a very "American" delineation, unreflective of particular Canadian realities, and reinforcing the racist stereotypes of generations past in the current popular imagination.

They point to the great national diversity of populations aggregated as "black" and their internal differences. One interviewee remarked that, in general, "white" people are referred to in terms of their national origin, whereas this is not the case for people of color. Being Haitian or Jamaican is linked to specific national histories that are highly valued by their parents. These opinions confirm the results of many studies that demonstrated the resistance shown by Caribbean immigrants (and their descendants) to being reduced to a "black" identity against which they are then forced to define themselves either positively or negatively (Kasinitz 1992; Waters 1996; Williams 1997; Labelle and Midy 1999). The young people, for their part, have a rather mitigated view of "black" solidarity in North America. In this sense, the Jamaican or Haitian communities of Montreal, Toronto, New York or Miami all have, in their eyes, their own specificities. Some also referred to a climate of competition and mistrust, and even prejudice, between groups categorized as "blacks." Many indicated that Quebec's preoccupation with linguistic concerns, and the ensuing geographical divide of francophone and anglophone groups in Montreal, are often transposed onto "black communities," influencing the integration process: "It is more a question of language. We are French and they are English (referring to Jamaicans) . . . So there is a barrier" (Haitian-born woman).

The respondents therefore distanced themselves from the essentialist theory of "race," a product of the racist ideology of the colonial period in the Americas. It must be said that two-thirds of the young people interviewed remembered being called a variety of disparaging names during their school years: "chocolate," "nigger," "*bougalou*," "*négresse*" (feminine form of "nigger"), "*patinoire*" (a play on words whose literal meaning is "ice rink," but which, in its derogatory, deconstructed meaning is a deformation of "*petit noir*" (*pa-ti-noir*, or "little blackie"). In order to face up to racism, quite real in its diverse manifestations (prejudices, discrimination, violence), they were raised to abide by a strong ethic of performance which held that they must work twice as hard as others to counterbalance the prejudices.

Michèle Lamont demonstrated how white Americans promote a *disciplined self*, whereas black Americans portray themselves, in terms of a distinct race, as the defenders of humanism and of the ethics of community solidarity – the *caring self* (Lamont 2001). The same dialectic operates in the discourses of some of our interviewees, but in reverse. Racial discrimination, the lack of available resources and economic opportunity, prejudiced methods of selection and fierce labor force competition, all result in parental pressure to succeed and overcome, to "be better than whites" in compensation for the social handicap of color: "You've got to work twice as hard . . . As a black person you have to prove yourself more than double time to get the job. As a parent this is a notion that you would pass on to your kids . . ." (Jamaican-born woman).

The predominance of hyphenated identity

We have already analyzed the reasons for the persistence of multiple identities in first-generation immigrants. National pride and transnational linkages, the perverse effects of state-generated categorization, the role played by discrimination based on racism, ethnicity, religion, etc. and a certain feeling of exclusion in the cultural and symbolic order, all explain the reticence to relinquish national identities linked to the country of origin (Labelle and Midy 1999; Labelle and Salée 2001).

In the present case study, transnational linkages are unevenly maintained. Half our respondents keep some ties with the country of origin of their parents, but not to the same extent that their parents did or still do with the friends, relatives or associates left behind. The other half hardly knows anyone from the old country, or never even set foot there. Transnational practices in this regard remain relatively limited, contrary to what we note in the first generation of migrants.

Social categorization, prejudices, and discrimination are more important factors. Both the Jamaican and Haitian communities in Quebec report unemployment levels of twice the provincial average. Studies reveal clear evidence of discrimination in both hiring practices and job security due to feelings among employers that hiring minorities constitutes a "risk," and adherence to racial stereotyping that characterizes blacks as "lazy," despite candidates displaying the required necessary knowledge and skills.

Again, the racist incidents reported left unpleasant memories which have tended to reinforce symbolic boundaries in the minds of our interviewees. And despite their relative success at securing satisfying jobs, they feel that job hunting has been for them a more difficult and lengthier process than for other Quebecers. Less than one-third of respondents reported no difficulties in the professional realm, the rest describing a variety of obstacles including an implied lack of experience, lack of connections and "contacts," insufficient knowledge of French, as well as overt prejudice and racial discrimination. Anglophone Jamaicans in particular feel that French language requirements represent an additional obstacle for them in the labor market. In consequence, for some, continental mobility is an important element of their social mobility project, even though, paradoxically, they perceive racism to be worse in the United States than it is in Quebec and Canada.

Personal networks and professional connections are essentially woven within the Haitian and Jamaican communities themselves. The choice of friends and spouses follows a certain logic based on community closure to the outside. And even if relations between "blacks" and "whites" are widely perceived as problematic, 90 percent of interviewees declared that the racialized minorities clearly wish to integrate into Quebec society.

The politicization of the Quebec identity

Historical tensions surrounding the debate over nationhood, and the discourses leading toward the ethnicization of the people of Quebec, which are still prevalent in the Canadian public space (in the Canadian press outside Quebec and within a certain minority-based leadership), contribute in certain cases to slowing down the process of civic incorporation for Quebec's minorities. Conversely, in other cases, the same factors produce a strong adhesion to the Quebec civic identity, perceived as the key to a shared citizenship.[4] These divergent social positions are underpinned by several theoretical arguments (Labelle and Lévy 1995; Labelle and Salée 2001) and are the source of heated debates.

In this case study, many respondents shared an ethnicized view of the Quebec identity (which is reflected by the recurrent and pejorative image, markedly present in their discourse, of *Québécois pure laine* – old-stock Quebecers or Quebec-born residents of French descent). The majority were unaware of the debates and of the notions of common public culture and of common civic framework put forward and defended by the Government of Quebec (Québec 2000). They were unaware of the principles and values that underlie Quebec's public policy of interculturalism.[5] They were also uninformed about the societal debates surrounding the issue of the Quebec civic nation that might have led them to qualify their points of view.

As a result, only a minority declared that the integration of racialized minorities has nothing to do with the political situation, but is rather linked to the perpetuation of racist ideologies and to limited opportunities within the labor market. However, the majority readily positioned the debate on the political level. They foresee that the treatment of minorities will be worse in a sovereign Quebec. Minorities experience, according to them, feelings of insecurity, fear, and reticence towards Quebec nationalism.

The sovereignist movement causes them to feel frustrated and uncertain. In a first case profile, individuals felt excluded from the Quebec social and political community. They do not feel like *Quebecers* because they are not themselves considered as fully-recognized Quebecers: "There are many immigrants who are in favor of Quebec independence. [For my part], the movement for the independence of Quebec is too 'white' and too Quebecer to allow any room for immigrants" (translated from the French). Or, from another respondent:

> Certain Quebecers are proud of Quebec and want separation, no matter what ethnic groups it may contain. Many others do not want to have anything to do with the English, or with Blacks. They want to live amongst born and bred white *Québécois*. (Translated from the French)

In a second case profile, individuals delineate themselves by attributing to a "cultural other" (the French majority or the French sovereignists), a propensity toward intolerance. Under a "separatist regime," said one respondent, immigrants would no longer be accepted, minorities would be ghettoized and would not be allowed the same liberties as "French Canadians": "It would be worse. Minorities would be ghettoized."

Linguistic policy serves as an important vector in the analysis of this situation. Perceived as an ethnic language rather than as a common public language, the French language is seen as a strategic element for domination and exclusion: "The *Québécois pure laine*, the real Quebecers, those that have been here forever, that's what they really want, Quebec for themselves."

Certain sovereignist leaders have come to embody the presumed rejection of minorities and immigrants who were accused of being responsible for the failure of the 1995 Referendum on the sovereignty of Quebec. This discourse consolidates and perpetuates the stereotypes linked to non-liberal values that are ascribed to the attributed nature of "ethnically" defined *Québécois* or sovereignists (Potvin 1997). It is therefore understandable that, armed with such prejudices, the young people interviewed developed an oppositional stance and did not identify themselves as Quebecers. The positions observed are indeed marked by ambivalence. They oscillate between a feeling of exclusion and a sense of reversed rejection, in a dynamic relationship that underpins the desire to belong.

This study is not fully representative of all racialized minorities youth, nor of minorities in general. But the analysis of the perceptions and the discourses that we have conducted do in fact lift the veil on a reality that is infinitely more complex than the one delivered by opinion polls on identities or prejudices, the common indicators of social distance. We may conclude that professional uncertainty, empirically experienced racism, non-inclusive societal categorization, stereotypes developed in reverse, and community closure to the outside reinforce the feelings of otherness experienced by these young people in the country where they were born and/or grew to adulthood.

CONCLUSION

In Western countries, structural transformations in the labor market have contributed to the exploitation and to the precariousness of large segments of the population. The coexistence of classic racism (which takes root in the hypothesis of biological and hierarchized races), and of neo-racism (based on the incompatibility and irreducibility of cultures and the necessity of their distance), perpetuates in turn the material and symbolic marginalization of individuals and groups. The societal enunciation of racism and social segmentation explains the quite diversified modes of incorporation of historical minorities subjected to conquest, annexation and slavery, and of contemporary migrants.

The ideological and political stakes proper to each society also factor into this enunciation. In Quebec, despite the orientations that guide the construction of a Quebec civic and diversified nation and despite the contributions of artists and intellectuals from minority groups to these same orientations, we are forced to note that the Quebec identity is more often than not a pretext for the expression of resentment.

How do we conceptualize the incorporation of racialized minorities in particular into the greater citizenry, in keeping with the perspective of a broadening of democracy? Civic incorporation must necessarily be attained through the concrete application of social and economic rights (the right to work, the right to fair remuneration, the right to dignity in the workplace, the right to unionize, the right to social security, etc.) and by the fight against systemic discrimination within the public and private sectors. In this perspective, the public policies that set in place equal opportunity access programs to employment (and the qualitative measures to which they are associated in the workplace: job training, vigilance against racial harassment, etc.) play an exemplary role. The same applies to policies and measures designed to favor equitable access to public services (education, health, etc.).

Citizenship is also linked to the concrete exercise of civil and political rights. Canada and Quebec, much like other countries in the Americas, have made commitments to international and regional human rights instruments in order to fight racism and xenophobia (legislative, administrative and judicial measures targeting propaganda and racist organizations). Many community organizations in the civil society work towards the inclusion of these measures into social practices. A lot remains to be done, however, in terms of the broadening of democratic spaces (measures to improve access to public affairs through presence if not active participation in institutions, social movements and political parties; measures aimed at recognizing and supporting community action dedicated to the fight against racism, etc.).

Finally, in the Quebec context, asking these questions solely in terms of multicultural or intercultural relations, or of the co-integration of "communities," defined as homogenous blocks or entities, is just not enough. We believe that a new discourse focused on cultural rights is a necessity, along with its corollary, the subversion of the current ethno-racial discourse. What is at stake is the building of neither a "*communauté des citoyens*" as individualized monads, nor a "*communauté des communautés*," and requires institutional creation to take into account the deep diversity of our societies (Balibar 2000).

The world Conference of the United Nations against racism, racial discrimination, xenophobia and the intolerance with which it is associated, held in Durban in 2001, highlighted various claims. Among them, the measures of symbolic reparation represented by the recognition of the cultural and identity rights of Aboriginal Peoples and of the minorities of African descent, which includes the possibility of "calling themselves by of their own names." The right to identity can be interpreted as the right not to be reduced or subsumed into a presumed racialized group. It thus appears necessary to subvert this reductionist and dominant discourse. Quebec, like other Western societies, has its own narrative that can recounted otherwise than by means of the "white/native" or "white/black" dichotomies, and this, without falling into the trap of an abstract and leveling citizenship. On the contrary, a differentiated or multicultural citizenship presupposes the public recognition of diversity as a principle, but does not tie down the groups carrying various identity markers to an exclusive specificity, whether it be ethnic or racialized. Moreover, how could they be defined or delimited?

ACKNOWLEDGMENTS

This article is adapted and draws in part from the author's essay published in French and entitled "Options et bricolages identitaires dans le contexte québécois," in A. G. Gagnon and J. Mclure (eds.) *Repères en mutation: Identité et Citoyenneté dans le Québec Contemporain,* (Montréal: Québec Amérique, 2001), pp. 295–325. I thank the editors for allowing it to be used here. I also thank my colleague Daniel Salée for his useful feedback, comments and contribution.

NOTES

1   For many decades, the term Caucasian has been rejected by anthropologists as non-scientific and ideologically perverted.

2   In September 1994, the *Parti Québécois* won the provincial election. The government announced an extensive consultation process on the independence of Québec. It created 15 regional consultative commissions to debate a proposed Bill and to participate in the writing of a declaration of sovereignty. Following the consultation, the document would become a Bill, be passed by the National Assembly, and then be submitted for approval by Quebecers in a referendum. This referendum took place on October 30, 1995. The question was: "Do you agree that Quebec should become sovereign, after having made a formal offer to Canada for a new Economic and Political Partnership, within the scope of the Bill respecting the Future of Quebec and of the agreement signed on June 12, 1995?" The turn-out level was 93.5 percent, with 50.6 percent voting No side, and 49.4 percent voting Yes side (Rocher 2002: 15; McRoberts 1997: 230).

3   In the Quebec context, the term "Allophones" means speaking neither French or English.

4   The civic and territorial notion of Quebecer the *Parti québécois* government has been bandying about is the following: "anyone who is a Canadian citizen residing on the Quebec territory at the time of independence will

automatically be considered a Quebec citizen" (Québec, Assemblée Nationale 1995: 13–15).

5 The Trudeau government's policy of multiculturalism implemented in 1971 has been considered by all the Quebec governments "as a denial of their understanding of Canada" and they have vigorously rejected it. The fact is that it denies the national character of Québec within the federation and perpetuates the ethnicization of the "French Canadian" (considered an ethnic group among others) (McRoberts 1997: Chapter 5 and Labelle and Salée 2001). As McRoberts puts it: "This did not prevent the Quebec government from establishing programs that paralleled measures adopted by Ottawa under the rubric of multiculturalism" (1997: 130). The term multiculturalism was systematically eschewed in favor of *interculturalisme*. This notion insists on the dynamics of exchanges (versus the "Canadian mosaic") and on a common public and civic culture. It refers to a demo-cratic and pluralist *société québécoise*: "open to multiple influences within the limits imposed by the respect for fundamental democratic values and the need for intergroup exchanges" (Québec 1990; see also Kymlicka 1998 on this subject).

REFERENCES

Abu Laban, Y. and Gabriel, C. (2002) *Selling Diversity: Immigration, Multicultur-alism, Employment Equity, and Globalization.* Peterborough, Ontario: Broadview Press.

Appiah, A. and Gutman, A. (1996) *Color Conscious: The Political Morality of Race.* Princeton, NJ: Princeton University Press.

Balibar, E. (2000) *Droit de Cité: Culture et politique en démocratie* [City Law: Culture and Politics in Democracy]. Paris: PUF.

Bissondath, N. (1994) *Selling Illusions: The Cult of Multiculturalism.* Toronto: Penguin Books.

Castells, M. (1997) *The Power of Identity.* Malden, MA: Blackwell Publishers.

Castles, S. and Davidson, A. (1999) *Citizenship and Migration: Globalization and the Politics of Belonging.* New York: Routledge.

Chevrier, M. (1996) *Canadian Federalism and the Autonomy of Quebec: A Histori-cal Viewpoint.* Quebec: Direction des Communications, Ministère des Relations Internationales. http://www.mri.gouv.qc.ca/la_bibliotheque/federalisme/fede_canadien_an.html

—— (1997) *Laws and Language in Québec: The Principles and Means of Québec's Language Policy.* Quebec: Direction des Communications, Ministère des Relations Internationales. http://www.mri.gouv.qc.ca/la_bibliotheque/langue/loi-langue_an.html

Dahomay, J. (2000) "Identité culturelle et identité politique" [Cultural identity and political identity], in Kymlicka, W. and Mesure, S. (eds.), *Comprendre les Identités Culturelles*, No. 1. Paris: Presses Universitaires de France.

Dieckhoff, A. (2001) "Le nationalisme dans le monde global" [Nationalism in the global world], *Bulletin d'Histoire Politique* 10 (1): 30–40.

Driedger, L. and Halli, S. S. (2000) *Race and Racism: Canada's Challenge.* Montreal: McGill-Queens University Press.

Fleras, A. and Elliott, J. L. (1999) *Unequal Relations: An Introduction to Race, Ethnicity and Aboriginal Dynamics in Canada.* Scarborough, ON: Prentice-Hall and Allyn and Bacon Canada.

Frideres, J. (1992) "Changing dimensions of ethnicity in Canada," in Satzewich, V. (ed.) *Deconstructing a Nation: Immigration, Multiculturalism and Racism in '90s Canada.* Halifax: Fernwood Publishing.

Frideres, J. and Pizanias, C. (1995) *Freedom Within the Margins: The Politics of Exclusion.* Calgary: Detselig Enterprises.

Gagnon, A. G. (2001) "Le Québec, une nation inscrite au sein d'une démocratie étriquée" [Quebec, a nation inscribed on the bosom of a cramped democracy], in Maclure, J. and Gagnon, A. G. (eds.), *Repères en mutations.* Montréal: Québec Amérique.

Hall, S. (1992) "New ethnicities," in Donald, J. and Rattansi, A. (eds.), *Race, Culture and Difference.* London: Sage Publications.

Harvey, E. B., Siu, B. and Reil, K. D. V. (1999) "Ethnocultural groups, period of immigration and socio-economic situation," *Canadian Ethnic Studies* 31 (3): 95–113.

Kasinitz, K. (1992) *Caribbean New York: Black Immigrants and the Politics of Race.* Ithaca, NY: Cornell University Press.

Kobayashi, A. (1992) "Représentation de l'ethnicité: statistextes politiques," in Statistique Canada (eds.), *Les Défis que Pose la Mesure de l'Origine Ethnique: Science, Politique et Réalité.* Ottawa: Statistique Canada.

Kymlicka, W. (1998) *Finding Our Way: Rethinking Ethnocultural Relations in Canada.* Toronto: Oxford University Press.

Labelle, M. (1987) *Idéologie de couleur et classes sociales en Haïti* [Ideologie of Color and Social Class in Haiti], 2nd edition. Montréal: Les Presses de l'Université de Montréal et le CIDHICA.

—— (2000) "La politique de la citoyenneté et de l'interculturalisme au Québec: défis et enjeux" [The politics of citizenship and of interculturalism in Quebec: challenges and risks], in Greven, H. and Tournon, J. (eds.), *Les Identités en Débat: Intégration ou Multiculturalisme.* Paris: L'Harmattan.

—— (2001) "Options et bricolages identitaires dans le contexte Québécois", in Gagnon, A. G. and McLure, J. (eds.), *Repères en mutation: Identité et Citoyenneté dans le Québec Contemporain.* Montréal: Québec Amérique.

Labelle, M. and Lévy, J. J. (1995) *Ethnicité et enjeux sociax: Le Québec vu par les leaders de groupes ethnoculturels.* Montréal: Liber.

Labelle, M. and Marhraoui, A. (2001) "Intégration et multiculturalisme: discours et paradoxes" [Integration and multiculturalism: discourse and paradoxes], in Resh, Y. (ed.), *Définir l'intégration.* Montréal: XYZ.

Labelle, M. and Midy, F. (1999) "Re-reading citizenship and the transnational practices of immigrants," *Journal of Ethnic and Migration Studies* 25 (2): 213–32.

Labelle, M. and Rocher, F. (2001) "People who live in a glass house. . . . citizenship and national identity in Canada and Québec," in MacInnes, J. and McCrone, D. (eds.), *Stateless Nations in the 21st Century* (*Scottish Affairs*, special issue). Edinburgh: University of Edinburgh, Institute of Governance.

Labelle, M. and Salée, D. (1999) "La citoyenneté en question: L'État Canadien face à l'immigration et à la diversité" [Citizenship in question: The Canadian plight regarding immigration and diversity], *Sociologie et Sociétés* 31 (2): 125–44.

—— (2001) "Immigrant and minority representations of citizenship in Quebec," in Aleinikoff, T. A. and Klusmeyer, D. (eds.), *Citizenship Today: Global Perspectives and Practices.* Washington, DC: Carnegie Endowment for International Peace.

Labelle, M., Salée, D. and Frenette, Y. (2001) *Incorporation citoyenne et/ou exclusion? La deuxième génération issue de l'Immigration Haïtienne et Jamaïcaine* [Citizenship Incorporation and/or Exclusion? The Second Generation Outcome of Haitian and Jamaican Immigration] (*Rapport de Recherche*). Toronto: Fondation Canadienne des Relations Raciales.
http://www.crr.ca/FR/Publications/fPubHome.htm

Lamont, M. (2001) *The Dignity of Working Men: Morality and the Boundaries of Race, Class and Immigration.* Cambridge, MA: Harvard University Press and New York: Russell Sage Foundation.

Li, P. (1999) *Race and Ethnic Relations in Canada.* 2nd edition. Toronto: Oxford University Press.

McRoberts, K. (1997) *Misconceiving Canada: The Struggle for National Unity.* Toronto: Oxford University Press.

Omi, M. and Winant, H. (1986) *Racial Formation in the United States, from the 1960s to the 1980s.* New York: Routledge and Kegan Paul.

Québec (1990) *Let's Build Québec Together: A Policy Statement on Immigration and Integration.* Québec: Ministère des Communautés Culturelles et de l'Immigration.

—— (1995) *National Assembly: Bill 1, An Act Respecting the Future of Québec including the Declaration of Sovereignty.* Québec: Éditeur Officiel.
http://www.sfu.ca/~aheard/bill1.html

—— (1996) *Le racisme au Québec: Un Élément de Diagnostic* [Racism in Quebec: An Element of Diagnosis] (*Collection Études et Recherches*, No. 13). Québec: Ministère des Communautés Culturelles et de l'Immigration.

—— (1999) *L'Équité en emploi: De l'Égalité de droit à l'Égalité de fait* [Using Fairness: From Equality under the Law to Equality in Practice]. Québec: Conseil des Relations Interculturelles.

—— (2000) *Forum national sur la citoyenneté et l'intégration: Document de consultation* [National Forum on Citizenship and Integration, Document of Consultation]. Québec: Ministère des Relations avec les Citoyens et de l'Immigration.

Rocher, F. (2002) "The evolving parameters of Quebec nationalism," *MOST Journal on Multicultural Societies, UNESCO* 4 (1): 1–21.
http://www.unesco.org/most/vl4n1rocher.pdf

Rumbaut, R. G. (1997) "Paradoxes (and orthodoxies) of assimilation," *Sociological Perspective* 40 (3): 483–511.

Samuel, J. T. (2001) "Perspectives on Canadian diversity," in Nancoo, S. (ed.), *21st Century Canadian Diversity*. Mississauga: Canadian Educators' Press.

Satzewich, V. (1994) " 'Race relations' or racism: Unravelling the new 'race' discourse in Canada," in Samuelson, L. (ed.), *Power and Resistance: Critical Thinking about Canadian Social Issues*. Halifax: Fernwood Publishing.

—— (1998) "Race, racism and racialization: Contested concepts," in Satzewich, V. (ed.), *Racism and Social Inequality in Canada*. Toronto: Thompson Educational Publishers.

Statistique Canada (1998) "Recensement de 1996: Origine ethnique et minorités visibles," *Le Quotidien*, February 17.
http:\\www.statcan.ca\Daily\Français\980217\q980217.htm

Torczyner, J. M. (1997) *Diversity, Mobility and Change: The Dynamics of Black Communities in Canada*. Montréal: McGill Consortium for Ethnicity and Strategic Social Planning.

—— (2001) *L'Évolution de la Communauté noire à Montréal: Mutations et Défis*. Montréal: Consortium de McGill pour l'Ethnicité ct la Planification Sociale Stratégique.

Waters, M. C. (1990) *Ethnic Options: Choosing Identities in America*. Berkeley, CA: University of California Press.

—— (1996) "Ethnic and racial identities of second generation black immigrants in New York City," in Portes, A. (ed.), *The New Second Generation*. New York: Russell Sage Foundation.

—— (1998) "Multiple identity choices," in Katkin, W. F., Landsman, N. and Tyree, A. (eds.), *Beyond Pluralism: The Conception of Group and Group Identities in America*. Urbana and Chicago, IL: University of Illinois Press.

—— (1999) *Black Identities: West Indian Immigrant Dreams and American Realities*. Cambridge, MA: Harvard University Press.

Williams, D. (1989) *Blacks in Montreal 1628–1986: An Urban Demography*. Qúbec: Les Éditions Yvon Blais, Inc.

—— (1997) *The Road to Now: A History of Blacks in Montreal*. Montreal: Vehicule Press.

FURTHER READING

Abu Laban, Y. and Gabriel, C. (2002) *Selling Diversity: Immigration, Multiculturalism, Employment Equity, and Globalization*. Peterborough, Ontario: Broadview Press.

Labelle, M. and Saléc, D. (2001) "Immigrant and minority representations of citizenship in Quebec," in Aleinikoff, T. A. and Klusmeyer, D. (eds.) *Citizenship Today: Global Perspectives and Practices*. Washington, DC: Carnegie Endowment for International Peace.

Li, P. (1999) *Race and Ethnic Relations in Canada*. 2nd edition. Toronto: Oxford University Press.

CHAPTER THREE

Race and Ethnicity in France

RIVA KASTORYANO

French political and sociological traditions have long resisted the concepts of race and ethnicity. This resistance was justified by the Republican ideal of public life. This ideal is embodied in the preamble to the French Constitution of October 27, 1946 which specifies that: "France forms with its overseas peoples a Union based on equality of rights and duties, without distinction of race and religion."[1] The 1946 preamble became Article 2 of the Constitution of the Fifth Republic of 1958. According to it, "France is an indivisible, secular (*laïc*), democratic and social Republic. It assures all its citizens equality before the law without distinction of origin, race and religion. It respects all beliefs." Consequently, both concepts are somewhat obscure in intellectual, social, and political discourses.

The concept of race has been used historically in France in varied ways. But it still remains ambiguous. Theorists have argued many questions ranging from the "objectivity" of racial inequality to the existence of cultural hierarchies.[2] The lack of clarity is due partly to the fact that "race" was often used interchangeably with "nation" in the nineteenth century. Todorov's study of "human diversity" in French thought shows that some interpretations made blood and color the key to race – the most famous example is Gobineau's *Inequality of Races* – while other authors like Renan made membership in a linguistic group the main criterion. Taine spoke of a historical race. Colonialism preoccupied all of these early writers. Colonialism provided the basis for a juridical categorization of "race." mainly in terms of skin colors: "black and white." This translated into social science terminology as categories of belonging. "Race" or "ethnicity" were also superimposed on linguistic communities as political, sociological and demographic classifications in colonial Algeria. Ethnicity designated "local" populations and their "ethnic" communities were also classified by regional characteristics, language and customs.

In the colonial era, race as a juridical category distinguished the "Metropolitan" from the "Autochtone." The former was a citizen, and the latter a subject (an African or an Algerian, for example). "Autochtones" were later reclassified as "indigenous," and defined by civil and personal status.[3] Within the "Metropole" a "confessional category" was established for the "Jewish race" in the Vichy years (1939–42). The Vichy experience generated a strong reaction against the use of the term "race" in political and social terminology as well as in social science. Post-war Republican France, returning in part to the eighteenth- and nineteenth-century tradition focused instead on the ideal of citizenship.[4] The preamble to the Constitution of 1946 was in the aftermath of Vichy, and at a time when colonialism was being contested. The Constitution was conceived therefore in opposition to any type of inequality imposed on people because of "race." or "origin" or "religion." The term "Union" defines France inclusive of its colonies. The goal, at least in part, was to correct determinist approaches which classified races according to physical, moral, and cultural criteria and used those distinctions to establish relationships of superiority and inferiority among populations.

The Republican principle excluded racial and ethnic definition of citizens: words like difference, community and/or people came to be used to designate the Other.[5] Republicanism influenced the French sociological tradition as well; the state and its institutions became the locus of the analysis of social relations. Whether inter-ethnic or inter-racial, or inter-religious, social relations were analyzed through the prism of state institutions.

The last wave of immigration brought this tradition and their values into question. Since the 1980s passionate debates have introduced the concepts of ethnicity, minority, and community (with reference to culture, religion and nationality) into the political vocabulary; French society has been redefined as multicultural, multiracial, and multi-confessional. The use of these terms represents an initial acceptance that France is *de facto* a pluralistic society. But *de facto* acknowledgement changed into a political argument when the Socialist Party, after its 1981 election, legitimized a politics of "difference." Government measures promoting (social) integration were joined to discourses about "recognition." The word "integration" replaced "assimilation"; identity became the focus of collective interests which often blurred private and public spaces. Claims were made for institutional representation by the state based on cultural/religious particularities.

The change in vocabulary reflected a complex new reality. Official rhetoric still stressed the "indivisibility" of the Republic. It reminded public opinion that the national community was the only political community, and that culture and identity belonged to the private sphere.[6] However, a redefinition of the public sphere led to arguments between "Republicans" and "Democrats."[7] The former objected to the recognition of any community other than the "unified" political community; the latter defended a more liberal vision which granted identity rights to communities and recognized their places in political life. For the "Republicans," a "community of citizens" rests on individual membership.[8] This normative claim reflected the representation of France as universalistic because it was assimilationist.[9] "Democrats" want to see identity claimants in France as surrogates for a fading labor movement which was once the source of social change and unrest.[10] Group demands become for Democrats a normal dimension of pluralistic political life. In sum, French debates concern the compatibility of a Republic as "one and indivisible" with linguistic, religious or national communities who assert a collective identity as political expressions of belonging. The debates reflect a mix of ideology, normative claims, and social realities and the politics reveal contradictions between myth and reality, discourse and action, rhetoric and practice leading to paradoxes: ethnicization of politics without data;[11] recognition of differences without naming them.

What, then, is the relation between the concepts and the reality of "race" and "ethnicity" in France? To what extent do they intersect and interact? How does an analyst deal with an issue when in some ways it is not named? This chapter will confront these questions by looking at the following:

1   ethnicity as "origin" that appears in census categories;
2   ethnicity as organization and a process; that is the emergence of ethnicity as a collective expression of belonging and claim for recognition of particularities;
3   the state and the substance of ethnicity;
4   the question of recognition and the formation of a minority, defined in religious terms, in France.

This last assumption is the empirical result of my research on the immigrant population in France since the early 1980s, focused on the expression of their collective identities and their interactions with the state. I concentrated on voluntary associations of immigrants, whether they define themselves as social, cultural, religious or national. I carried out in-depth interviews with their leader and members, observed their meetings, discussions and mobilization over a long period. Based on the assumption that collective identities are constructed through inter-actions mainly with the state in order to gain legitimacy, I also inter-viewed politicians in charge of issues of immigration, ministerial departments, union representatives and those in charge of social ser-vices in some municipalities.

Intense interactions between political actors on both sides – repre-sentatives of the states and individuals chosen to represent the relevant population according to their nationality or religion – led to a process of *negotiations of identities*.[12] This negotiation resulted in the reciprocal influences that produce institutional, discursive, and normative changes. Based on these interactions I show how the state creates eth-nicity. Moreover, the substance of ethnicity is itself defined through negotiations of reciprocal identities, since negotiations mainly concern the contradictions between principles and realities. I attempt to show empirically how interactions between states and immigrants have situated religion at the core negotiations in France, in reconsidering *laïcité* – French understanding of secularism – as a non-negotiable value while leading immigrants to claim religious recognition as a basis for ethnicity.

ETHNICITY AS "ORIGINS": THE CENSUS CATEGORIES IN FRANCE

In France, the official census classifies the whole population under three categories: French by birth, "French by acquisition" (naturaliza-tion), and foreign. Thus, once the foreigner is naturalized, he moves into the column of "French by acquisition" (that is naturalization); his children born on French soil are declared "French by birth." Unlike the American census since 1980, which has tried to highlight ethnic ancestry, in France, the national and ethnic origin of citizens does not appear in official documents, and consequently, has no legal or statis-tical validity. The Code of Nationality sets up statistical categories that exclude the "origin" once French nationality is obtained.[13] This leads to a statistical invisibility of any "ethnic ancestry." In the official census of 1990 however, a new category of "previous nationality" of naturalized French citizens was introduced into the presentation of statistics on for-eigners. The Preface of the resulting census of the foreign population referred directly to changes in the laws of nationality.[14] The last census of 1999 made a distinction between "immigrant population" and "foreign population." The "immigrant population" is classified by

"country of birth."[15] Whether "immigrant population" refers to the previous nationality of a new citizen, or to membership of a nation of those
who have been established for several generations, to mention it suggests the persistence of an ethnic identity separate from that of the
majority. It relegates the individual to an "immigrant identity." to the
country of birth and to the previous nationality as a permanent marker
and creates thereby an ambiguous "category" that is ethnicized and
omitted from an identification with the "acquired" French nationality.
The "previous nationality" or that of the parents for younger generations, or even a "country of birth." was then expressed by demographers
in terms of "origin" as a clarification about the past and an awareness
of the conditions of belonging throughout generations.[16]

The meaning of "origin" became more explicit in the recent survey
done by Michèle Tribalat entitled "Geographical mobility and social
integration."[17] In this study as a response to the inadequacy of classical
censuses to analyze immigration and integration, the author calls children of immigrants "persons of foreign origin" and she adds, "If we
want to follow the future of immigrants and their children, we should
stop referring to nationality."[18] She challenges the official census categories by including the criteria of "ethnic belonging" and "ethnic
origin" based on the mother tongue of immigrants and their children
in the home country of their parents. By creating these categories, she
aims at "freeing" the French social sciences from the "taboo of origins."

Another demographer, Hervé Le Bras, reacted with virulence to
Michèle Tribalat in his book entitled *The Evil of Origins*.[19] He argued
that use of the term "origin" in demographic classification is a source
of racial discrimination. He sees in this vocabulary and assessment of
the population a "convergence between the new direction that French
demography has taken and the ideology of the extreme right with
regard to immigrant population." Such a categorization of generations
of immigrants creates another category called "*Français de souche*" (of
French stock), which according to Hervé Le Bras becomes a way to "eth-
nicize French nationalism by transforming the French population to an
ethnic group."[20]

Is the classification of the population by generation, language use,
ethnic ancestry or foreign birth an acknowledgment of "origins" or a
stigmatization of the immigrant as "other" because of their "origins"?
To acknowledge, argues Patrick Simon, another demographer, has
become a scientific requirement. Simon argues that the statistical invisibility of ethnic categories aids discrimination; whereas a reference to
"origins" helps to define a social phenomenon, such as the reality of a
multicultural society. Despite methodological problems concerning the

sociological analysis of the immigrants (social mobility, level of education, marriage), the ignorance of the reality of how immigrants and their children and grandchildren are doing raises the problem of a political action.[21] In other words, Simon argues that "to acknowledge" makes "action" possible.

This statement criticizes the French approach that is defined as universal. In *The New Social Question* Pierre Rosanvallon pointed out that universality is based on opacity, and that "information promotes differentiation."[22] To maintain the principle of universality, French governments, both Right or Left, deal with the issue of immigration or immigrants' integration (housing, education, job market) under a "social" coverage. The state, the "schoolmaster of society" in Pierre Rosanvallon's words, uses its administrative and ideological influence to secure social cohesion. What is at stake is the "social bond" (*lien social*), a term inspired by a sociological or political tradition that refers to the idea of national solidarity, cohesion, and integration. The motto is therefore "social integration." in opposition to "exclusion." as a source of unrest in French society. Exclusion is not simply geographically peripheral; it also refers especially to social institutions and to the labor market, to educational failure, to unemployment. In discourse, the evil is primarily social and must be corrected by society. This logic reflects the political rhetoric of denying any "special treatment" of the foreign population or immigrant. No government measure is specifically oriented toward immigrants or their descendants or foreigners, at least officially.

The reality contradicts discourses and ideals. In reality, the social element is closely linked to the cultural – not named although recognized as such through policies. The rule of a political intervention is "color blind" but its application targets specific areas and groups. For example since 1982, suburbs with high concentrations of immigrants, particularly Muslims, have been called "priority urban zones" (ZUP).[23] They are recognized by the government as a source of unrest. Their schools are codified as "priority education zones" (ZEP),[24] which "from their preparation and development to their implementation emphasize concerns about foreign children and children of foreign origin in order to settle suitable educational and pedagogical answers."[25] The "zones" are thus the focus of specific measures justified by the principle that "more must be done where there is less." In discourse, "less" is determined economically, like social handicaps. To calm fears and antagonisms, the less must be integrated into the more.

This logic leads to the French rejection of the very idea of "ghettoes." According to public authorities "zones" are not supposed to be seen as "ghettoes." Based on the criterion of nationality, French specialists in urban policy point to the national heterogeneity of the immigrant population to report that there is no "ghetto" in France, especially in comparison with the United States where race is the decisive factor. Reflections on the French suburbs are initially social but actually ethnic. The new term is "*cité-ghetto*"[26] characterized by conflicts between civil society and the forces of order, between generations and cultures and between national, local, and community institutions, by tensions between the school and the students who flaunt their "differences" as members of an "ethnic community." As François Dubet notes, "Residents of HLM [low rent housing] seem to get away from traditional representations of the working class on the one hand and of poverty on the other."[27]

To avoid the use of race or ethnicity in political and sociological vocabulary reflects a reluctance to legitimize division on a cultural or religious basis within the society and in politics. But this does not imply a rejection of all forms of collective representation of the Other. Ironically racism is denounced and the word "racism" is used in laws against discrimination. Even when "race" is not mentioned, it is expected that laws against racism, intolerance and discrimination affect *mentalités* as well as the social and political relations. Thus committees are created and policies defined to prevent exclusion, inequality, and discrimination. In 1998 an Observatory to fight against discrimination was established to denounce racial discrimination. Reports on racism and xenophobia in France clearly mention the targets: Maghrebis and more generally the Arab population in France.[28]

ETHNICITY AS A PROCESS

In the United States, the term ethnicity has now entered the scientific vocabulary and even the spoken language, and no longer needs to be defined. But in a 1975 collection of essays with that title, Nathan Glazer and Daniel Moynihan, the editors, stated that "Ethnicity seems to be a new term" and they added, "a change of relative status is going on here."[29] The term in France has, according to Nancy L. Green, a comparative assumption; it is used to differentiate France from the United States.[30] Although if ethnicity is defined as the expression of cultural, religious, and racial identities in the political realm, as they rally to demand recognition in the public space, in France too, since the 1980s, immigrants have been organized and mobilized, seeking public recognition. Ethnicity emerged in France, in large part from political measures that add an identity element to traditional practices, restructuring the society in such a way that social demands are transformed into cultural or identity demands. It is based on the claim for recognition of an "origin."

The ensuing policies are *a priori* far from affirmative action or any positive measurement to compensate for past inequality as applied in the United States, where classifying ethnic groups by "chosen" ancestors elucidates a targeted policy. In France, racism, public debates, ambiguities in naming the immigrant or the foreigner, on the one hand, targeted policies; access to the economy and to national communities, on the other, have generated an "awareness of belonging" among individuals of immigrant descent. This awareness found an institutional basis with the "right to difference" promoted by the Socialist Government in 1981. This right was followed by the liberalization of the law allowing foreigners to create their own voluntary associations and therefore "institutionalize" their difference.[31] The law concerning associations goes back to 1901. But the right allowing foreigners to create their own associations was forbidden in 1939 and then liberalized in 1981. Spontaneous gathering based on interpersonal relations in concentrated areas therefore found an institutional and formal structure through associations perceived as identity organizations. The associations appeared then as a refuge, sometimes even a sanctuary, where culture, religion, ethnicity, and nation (of origin) were interpreted, materialized, and took root. It is as if all the anthropological diversity that had been eclipsed by a concern for the cultural homogeneity in the native nation-state has reappeared in some form, as if it were "liberated" in the country of immigration where each specific feature constitutes an element of distinction. In addition, ideological divisions affecting some of the Islamic religious associations also come into play, along with positions for or against the government in power in the homeland and positions on policies in the country of immigration. There, too, the battle against racism unites young people, but at the same time, the "sexism of the leaders and activists" puts off the women who would like "to have their say as women."[32] Each of these concepts and identity elements has intervened to transform an informal local community, constituted *de facto* by spatial proximity, into an ethnic or cultural one, imagined in terms of common identifications and as a basis for new solidarities to be constructed.[33]

During the vote on the law of October 9, 1981, to liberalize associations of foreigners, parliamentary debate justified that phenomenon:

> The association is the expression of national, cultural, and social soli-
> darities and the instrument of their improvement. In that capacity, they
> constitute a means of breaking the isolation transplanted persons may
> suffer, of renewing the bonds with the homeland, and of reappropriat-
> ing a cultural identity.

The leader of an association of North African women speaks in the
same tone: "If I use the term re-appropriation, it is because I am convinced that it is full of completely different things from the French. We
must not deny those aspects, we must bring them to light but empty
them at the same time." She went on: "Reappropriation means that I
try to improve the little bit my parents transmitted to me and that makes
me aware that the talk about 'we are all the same' is really not true."
Ever since the liberalization of the law of associations in 1981, foreigners acting in labor unions or parties (particularly the French Commu-
nist Party) or other political organizations have adjusted their policies
around special cultural features, invented and reaffirmed in their relation to politics. While in the 1960s or 1970s immigrants expressed their
interests in terms of class, today the younger generation expresses their
concern in terms of culture or religion, in an "identity of origin," rein-
terpreted within the framework of new collective actions. "There is no
continuity with the original activities, there is a change," stated the representative of the Association of Moroccan Workers in France: "Our
goal was to provide them with moral support at the beginning, but also
to show in time a will to take care of problems of housing, childhood,
culture, health, education, and so on." A cultural identity corresponding to the process of permanent settlement must now be defined, and
that requires getting away from the influence of teachers and imams
sent by the homeland, and taking charge of instruction in the language
and the culture imagined as that of origin, regardless of bilateral agreements the homeland has made with the host country. In sum, it is necessary to mark autonomy and perhaps even to break with colonial
history, aiming primarily at "changing the image of immigration in
France," even at constructing a new identity by rewriting history. The
first step in this process is to change the image of the homeland by integrating the history of immigration into it. In short, to develop a pride
that is both national and immigrant.

Religion becomes another way of "reappropriating" identity. Its introduction, according to Youssour Roty, founder of the association "Living
Islam in the West," is "a supreme urgency to give the children at least
an awareness of Islamic values, and elementary ritual principles that
they haven't developed here. And it is terms of these points of anchor

. . . that moral values, social involvement, and so on can be developed."
The idea is that a positive image of Islam in French society can make
young people identify more closely with their religion and "their
origin." He continues, "Young people now have to be awakened to this
culture, helped to discover it and tell it." An imam in Marseilles asserts
that "Islam is a religion that manages all society, even brings remedies
to it, is not there to destroy but to build and improve human relations,
and you can find that in all the verses of the Koran."

Identification with a religions group does not exclude social affiliation, it reinforces it. The discourse accompanying their action is gen-
erously supported by the Fund of Social Action (FAS), the largest source
of funds for institutions concerned with cultural and social identity.
This organization, created in 1958, aimed originally "at promoting a
general social initiative on behalf of wage-earners working in metropolitan France in professions targeted by the Algerian regime for family
grants and whose children reside in Algeria."[34] But after its activities
were decentralized and dispatched in different regions with appropriate structures in 1982, the FAS reoriented its initiative toward "the specific representation of immigrant communities." Its declared objective
is to "create intermediaries" in order to facilitate the integration of
immigrants. In the integration of immigrants, "the FAS is the state,"
affirmed its director, Michel Yahiel when I interviewed him in 1988.

The state, governmental policies and national institutions thus have
intruded more and more into identities, reserved until now for the
private domain. Moreover, the reciprocal engagements between states
and immigrants in France have created a space of transaction, an
"ethnic market" where groups compete for public resources in order
to publicly express their cultural and identity differences. The competition created by the state to enable identities to be organized and
expressed results in a situation similar to the one in America, that
is, the emergence on to the political stage of ethnic or religious
communities seeking public recognition.

Such a demand generates the politicization of identities which proceeded from the interaction between groups and state, from the struggle for recognition and a representation within national institutions.[35]
In the United States immigrants or foreigners demand equal treatment
and equal rights as a fundamental principle of democracy in the Toc-
quevillian sense. In France, however, the state has encouraged the creation of associations whose purpose is to be intermediaries between a
group formed around common interests and the public authorities.
This is the corporatist logic of the *Ancien Régime*, which in the Republic recognizes labor unions, professional organizations, or other

interest groups based on collective interest, while the original logic does not refer in principle, to identities, local, regional, religious or ethnic. Associations of foreigners fit into this scheme *a priori*, at least in its objectives. Yet the ethnic content of these organizations contradicts French corporatism that rejects issues related to cultural, religious or ethnic identities considered as private. The implicit strategy of the French state was to see an "elite" emerging among the immigrants or their descendants, which then assumed the role of spokesman representing a collectivity to the public authorities. This followed the classical pattern of elite formation among the working class in the nineteenth and early twentieth centuries. The state recognizes elites who mobilize and negotiate their interests with public authorities. "Immigrant elites" are expected to serve as examples of "successful integration" into the society and politics.[36]

The politicization of identity is therefore closely linked with the emergence of this new "class" of intermediaries. It is actually a cause and effect relation. Manufactured to serve as spokesmen with the public authorities, these intermediaries trigger a realization of "basic" ethnic affiliation. The intensity of a collective consciousness and the sense of belonging to a cultural or ethnic group obviously depend on the ability of those intermediaries to harmonize the codes of the host society and the cultural symbols they use to restructure the group. They are judged by their skill in mobilizing financial resources, on the one hand, and human resources on the other, for both are indispensable to the survival of their associations. The image of success they reflect is based, therefore, on their new function among the immigrants and on their talent for creating identification with the individuals they appeal to and who accept them *a priori* as spokesmen. Their role becomes to represent and negotiate identities with the state apparatus and to maintain identification with the populations they appeal to.

The declared objective of public authorities is to make public opinion accept "differences," and to counter racism. By institutionalizing collective identities through the associations, the state thus intended to give "instructions" for differences in a republican state where it is important to integrate them into the ideological framework and its structures, even though there is an instrumental use of them. This is how rhetoric meets policy. From the point of view of the association activists, identities are now the element structuring a community in order to compete for state resources.

Hence, the creation of associations is based on an obvious duality of objectives: developing a collective awareness of belonging and, at the same time, integration into the structures of the state. Official reports, particularly those of the High Council on Integration, drew the attention of the association leaders and of public opinion to the "French model of integration." Association activists also altered their tone, rejecting any idea of ethnic or cultural community and its representation in the public domain; instead, they insisted on the role of representation assigned to the individual, the only intermediary between a structured collectivity and the state. Parallel to an official discourse on the "French exception," immigrant activists "invented" new solidarities that would allow the construction of a community that would distinguish itself from the national community and situate themselves in relation to the state. Both parties use the same rhetoric for their intentions. Discourse becomes universalist in the struggle against racism. Faced with the National Front – the Far Right Party – that has campaigned against foreigners, assigning responsibility for "French ills" to immigration and immigrants and presenting them as a threat to society and French identity, their movement by and large is defined as anti-racist. "Something has to be done," said the young activists in the associations, thus justifying the existence of their organizations, which they defined as "political weapons." Racism becomes the most important element of mobilization in the associations.

THE STATE AND THE SUBSTANCE OF ETHNICITY

Race and ethnicity are thus constructed through a collective fight against racism and social exclusion combining national and social "origins," both perceived as a permanent status. Public resources have legitimized the organization of immigrants into associations. I show in my research on France and in Germany that the "substance" of ethnicity emerges through the negotiations between the state and the immigrants.[37] Confronting communities trying to win legitimacy, states either redefine or reinforce the fundamental principles that had prevailed at their inception, as a way to set limits on that recognition in order to place identity demands within an institutional framework, while leading immigrants to define their own identity in reaction to the national identity.

The emergence of these communities in France reveals contradictions between social reality and the ideology behind the creation of the nation-state. It raises the question of an individual's loyalty to the national community. The political class and public authorities evoke the founding values of the nation they want to protect and they ask the groups that express other identifications and other allegiances to adapt.

In return, those groups elaborate an identity that they can use to search for recognition, whose limits are included in the legitimacy of the host states. Thus, immigrants' community formation is the result of social policies (intended or unintended), but also is the result of the terms of negotiation that are established by the state. It is through negotiations with the state that immigrants have defined a core identity around which a community can be constructed, giving substance to ethnicity. The substance of ethnicity reveals in reality the contradiction or at least the unresolved questions at the core of the foundation of the nation-state.

In France, the negotiations between the state and immigrants were crystallized around the so-called "headscarf affair" situating Islam, the religion of the vast majority of post-colonial immigrants, at the core of negotiations challenging the relation between state and religion. The issue shook French society for the first time in November 1989, when three teenage girls attended public school wearing Islamic headscarves. The event unleashed a flood of commentary on identity: the identity of the latest wave of immigration, but also that of national identity. The emphasis lay on Islam and, its compatibility with the secular principles of French society. More than that, the issue struck at the heart of *laïcité*, French secularism, which differentiates itself from the secularism in other Western states in that it is defined as a total separation of church and state, and asserts itself as a French exception. Public opinion and public authorities were torn between a defensive Republicanism and a pluralistic liberalism. The political class and certain intellectuals took it upon themselves to remind society of the basic principles of the Republic, principles that constitute the "core of national identity" and appear to the migrants as a "way of life" in a *laïc* country. At its creation, the French Republic, then called "the oldest daughter of the Church," *laïcité* had taken on a holy character. It had become a new doctrine, any public display of religion was rejected.[38] From a legal standpoint, the Constitution of 1795 had already introduced a partial secularization in marriage, health, and education, but the legal separation of church and state dates from 1905, after the Dreyfus Affair. But it was not until the Constitution of October 27, 1946, that secularism became law, and was reiterated in the Constitution of 1958.

Nevertheless, secularism, rather than *laïcité*, is ambiguous about the boundary between culture and religion. Culture refers to religious identity and religion to belief or practice. Research on French religious expression shows a constant decline of practice, which is easily measured, unlike the cultural reference which remains abstract and hard to measure, but which appears whenever it confronts another religion, like Islam today. In reaction to issues raised by the headscarf affair, French society redefined *laïcité*. It has become the very definition of French secularism. This principle of the Republic has undergone several interpretations since November 1989, without reaching a final version, except that it appears as the "official religion" of France. Today, Islam is at the core of the redefinition of *laïcité* and serves as its mirror.

Yet, the idea of *laïcité* is inseparable from the "indoctrination" implemented by the public schools under the Third Republic. Jules Ferry, Minister of National Education in the Third Republic, introduced a radical change in 1882 by making the public, secular, free primary school compulsory for everyone, including girls. The school then became the instrument for propagating secularism. The secular school played the role of foil to Catholicism in the definition of *laïcité* in the early twentieth century, and to its function and its ideology.[39] It is not surprising then that the contemporary challenge to *laïcité* was triggered when some young Muslim girls wore their "headscarf" in school. The scope of the polemic was similar to that of the church against the secular school. The centralization of instruction, the creation of secular teachers' training schools conferred upon the school the right "to unify the nation and establish social order",[40] an argument that has been transposed into recent parliamentary debates of October 1994, that "French national identity is inseparable from its school."

That is certainly why the issue was perceived as an assault on the public school, an institution that, more so than others, is represented as the very embodiment of national ideology as being egalitarian, *laïc*, inclusive. The headscarf was perceived as if it defied the long historical process of forming the nation-state, and the transformation not only of "the peasant," but also of the foreigner, or the immigrant "into the Frenchman."[41] Compulsory education and instruction in French (the abandonment of regional languages) for everyone (immigrants from a region or foreigners) based on equal opportunity, naturally spread a national ideology, but also created the sense of belonging to Republican France. Moreover, shaping the nation-state entailed the creation of collective memory and consciousness aiming at the ideal of cultural homogeneity.[42] That is where the "assimilation" of the individual was assured. This effort of standardization is reformulated now as the *intégration à la française*.

The case of the headscarf revealed the issue in a power balance between French national identity on the one hand, and that of the last waves of immigrants on the other, the former remolded around *laïcité* (secularism) and the latter around Islam, as if the law of the Republic were being challenged by the law of the Koran spread by the local

Muslim institutions in the suburbs. Even though the politicians rallied around the case of the headscarf in the name of secularism or *laïcité*, that mobilization elevated Islam to the core of the collective identification of the descendants of the North African immigrants. At the same time, the state's refusal to acknowledge associations of a religious nature reinforced Islam as the locus of identity components, since it is perceived as a source of pride for independent action from public or social agencies which subsidize supposedly secular, cultural associations. Forming a community hence became the way to define an identity perceived as a basis for action and public self-assertion.

Thus, the headscarf issue has led to a re-evaluation of the principles of the Republic and of secularism, which until then had been considered to be the pillar of social cohesion that had to be maintained as a constitutive value of the nation-state. In reaction, the North Africans defined the solidarities around Islam when confronting *laïcité* in France. Negotiations have strengthened both the frontiers of the identity manifested by the national political communities while "ethnicizing" religion has challenged the religious/secular dichotomy, with its high emotional charge in France. For Muslim migrants, the reference to religion, radicalized mobilization by giving it an emotional substance that reinforced identification.[43] From the standpoint of the French authorities, who see themselves as guarantors of national identity (or at least of an image or representation of it), the perceived threat to secularism is emotional, because it attacks the basic principles of the national state.

The negotiations over the headscarf really concerned recognizing new ways and means of including immigrant groups into the political community, based on a different balance between national institutions and immigrant associations. Indeed, the "case" made politicians realize that one more religion had entered society and its institutions. Islamic association activists experienced it as the moment when assertion of an identity on the part of the immigrant population occurred. These immigrant association leaders negotiated with the public authorities the permanent and structural presence of Islam and its cultural and public expression.

THE QUESTION OF RECOGNITION AND THE FORMATION
OF A MINORITY

The assertion of Islam opposes the doctrine of a nation characterized by its cultural unity and the common identity of its citizens. This republican principle of unity claims to obscure all cultural, regional, linguistic, or any other difference in the public domain. This was confirmed by the Constitutional Committee's rejection of the term "people" applied to the Corsicans, emphasizing that the expression, "the people," applied to the French people, must be considered a unifying category and not open to any division by virtue of the law."[44] The idea of assimilating a "foreign body" defined by its nationality obeys that logic of integral inclusion of naturalized foreigners or their children who are French either at birth or at the age of 16.

Yet, according to Danièle Lochak, "the state's ignoring of differences is confined to religion."[45] The author states, in fact, that while France rejects the notion of "minority," the term does appear in legal texts only in reference to a "religious minority." This is proved by the fact that there is no problem of recognition and representation for the almost 400,000 Portuguese who form all kinds of associations and whose bonds of village solidarity are undeniably characteristic of a community organization. Is it because Portuguese adhere to the same religion, even if they attend separate churches that they are invisible to public opinion? Similarly, referring to the community of Italians, Poles, and Armenians in the recent past was meant to denounce prejudice, racism, and rejection that all newcomers face.[46] The monographs about these groups focused on local structure facilitating the transition between past and future, and did not refer to the question of citizenship, loyalty or to a permanent institutionalization.

But this view of community seems to disappear when religions are felt to be different, especially in the case of Islam. The separation of Church and State confers institutional legal status on the Catholic clergy, the Protestants of the National Federation of the Protestant Churches of France, and to the Jews governed by the Consistory created under Napoleon. That "recognition" is seen as an expression of respect for freedom of religion and the neutrality of the secular state.

Demands for recognition clash with the founding principles of the French state. The place of Islam in France revived the old duality between religion and state in the public discussion. Asking for recognition as a minority allows the Muslim population in France to declare a specific identity and to emerge from their political marginality, and to express a struggle for liberation. But unlike the liberation of the Enlightenment which separated religion from public life and the individual from his community to guarantee his essential identification with the national community, the demand for recognition in this case is spawned by a wish for participation with equal rights recognized for religious or community identities within the structures of the state. In fact, the recognition of Islam is as serious as for other religions. It has arisen almost a century later.

The demand for recognition of Islam has led association activists to reorganize. At the local level, they have attempted to go beyond the national, ethnic, and ideological divisions and define common elements uniting all Muslims in each community, such as building a mosque. Shaping a "community" became "an option"[47] in order to define an identity of action or reaction and to assert it publicly through representative institutions recognized by the state.

Many heated discussions about the place of religion in French society followed the case of the headscarf. Successive Ministers of Interior (who are at the same time Minister of Cult) tried to create an institution to represent Islam. In 1990, the Socialist Minister, Pierre Joxe, initiated a Council of Thought on Islam in France, the CORIF. The idea was to try to assemble the Muslims of France "symbolically,"[48] so that the Council might become the embryo of a representative structure of Islam for the public authorities on the model of the Episcopal Conference or the Protestant Federation of France."[49]

In 1994, shortly after the publication of a circular letter by François Bayrou, Minister of National Education (UDF), banning all ostentatious religious symbols in educational establishments, Charles Pasqua (RPR) officially recognized the Representative Council of Muslims of France, created the previous year, and he declared: "I have always wanted Islam to go from the status of a tolerated religion in France to that of a religion accepted by everyone and part of the French spiritual landscape." Recently Jean-Pierre Chevènement created a group "Consultation" and declared that he wished "to see Islam like Judaism and Protestantism at the time of Napoléon, to be a minority religion in France,"[50] and in December 2002, Minister Nicolas Sarkozy created the French Council of the Muslim Cult as a representative institution. Thus, Islam has been integrated into a scheme defined by Danièle Lochak as "a pragmatic handling of differences," consisting of "gradually introducing the minimal dose of institutionalization needed for a concrete resolution of the practical problems created by the existence of 'minority groups' who want to end up with 'official recognition,' which would then produce the institutionalization of differences."[51]

This process clearly aims at orchestrating a shift from Islam in France to Islam of France, from a simple presence of Muslims and their practices visible in France to an Islam that is expressed and developed within national institutions, assuming its freedom from "foreign" influences, especially those of the homeland. The discussion is far from over. "Nationalizing" Islam, making it a "French Islam," might thus introduce a liberating process. This was how the shift of the Jews of France to "French Judaism" took place, if only in terminology. In both cases, representation obviously brings a legal protection more broadly guaranteed by all the representative organizations initiated by the state, which, in this case, intervenes both as arbiter and as dispenser of official recognition. This experience makes existing representative organizations, particularly Jewish institutions, which are older, and were produced and developed with respect to secularity, the reference point for associations of non-Islamic immigrants. France-Plus, for example, proposes the creation of a Muslim Consistory, one of its activists arguing that "secular Islam is completely compatible with life in France." The chairman of the Federation of the Muslims of France, on the other hand, rejects this plan precisely because of the argument advanced by France-Plus: "They want us to copy the model of the Consistory made up of people who are Jews but not religious." Note that the same quarrel divided observant or believing Jews from secular Jews when the Consistory was centralized and its leaders insisted on secularizing it by removing all religious content.[52]

While Muslims now refer to the legal status of Jewish institutions, some Jews increasingly draw on the claims for Muslim recognition to express the sense of belonging to a "Jewish community," signaling the rejection of the concept of French Judaism for that of "Jews of France." Inspired by Muslim aspirations and the permanent redefinitions of secularity they suggest, even the Church of France has revived the discussion of its relations with the state. Recognition of Islam has thus spawned a general revision of the place of religions in the public sphere, challenging the concept of republican secularity, its universalism, and its practices, as well as the connection between church and state in France. More then is given to the substance of the concept of "ethnicity" even if its use remains "taboo." As if to assert the historic continuity, the state takes refuge behind an "inclusionist" strategy and discourse that lead it to encourage representative institutions to make their chairmen its main spokesmen and consider their members full partners in the political community. The big change is, however, the explicit reference to religion and its representation leading to the recognition of an implicit "ethnicity" in France.

The stakes riding on such recognition are high, depending among other things on the size of the "Muslim electorate," no matter how sociologically varied and politically differentiated it is, but it will appear in the public arena as an implicit "ethnic vote." Researchers pointed out that during the presidential elections of 1988, "a new type of correlation between the Le Pen vote, inclusion in the slates, and the Beur vote was taking shape."[53] This fast-growing collective strategy does not contradict individual strategies. It complements it, challenging the representation of the "French model of integration" and not the politically defined status of citizen. Cultural and political acculturation has made inroads so much so that the representation of a group of French citizens of the Muslim denomination has made itself felt, even if it is not expressed in those terms.

The discussion of immigration, race, and ethnicity relates to the discussion of national identity. The evolution in France since the 1980s shows that the "individual foreign immigrant" is now perceived as the "the immigrant of foreign origin" belonging to an "ethnic community," struggling for state legitimacy. In this perspective the concepts of race and ethnicity developed in the American social sciences in relation to immigration were useful to "name" the collective identification and mobilization of immigrants in France. The linguistic contagion acknowledges the similarities in all democratic plural societies and the justification of a political convergence among them, even though each country gives a different meaning to the same word, since words are related to national history and its representations and they appear in national rhetoric. In France the dynamic of the interactions between the state and immigrants leads to the role of the state in creating an ethnic community with a sense of belonging to a specific collective identity inscribed in the historical tradition. But there remains an unresolved question: the place of religion in the public space, which gives its content to the definition of ethnicity.

The nation, "imagined" or invented, defines its modes of inclusion and exclusion according to its representation, its cultural component that makes each nation-state historically unique, each of them following their own path to political unification and national integration. From this point of view, the past serves to legitimate the present and provides ways to elaborate "models" to make each national experience specific by fixing the past. The settlement of post-colonial immigrants in France questions the validity of the "French model" and the capacity of the state to set up new arrangements. France must come to terms with how to establish new relations between the state and society, the state and immigrants, the state and identities that are woven in the connections between representations of political traditions and the assertions of new identity constructs, shifting the boundaries between what was defined as private and public, and what was based on the bond between church and state in France.

The discussion ultimately leads to the relationship between culture and politics developing new codes of co-existence by redefining some values or reinforcing others in order to calibrate the "idea" of a united nation-state with the "fact" of the pluralism of modern societies and its institutional representation, to guarantee an historical continuity and to recognize the unique features that crop up in the public space. What is a stake is the balance between civil society and the state, the relationship between cultural diversity and citizenship which does not threaten either civic principles or the final identity of the collective as a whole.

The European Union reinforces the ambiguous relations between culture and politics, between identity and rights, between nation and states, between membership and citizenship that characterize a political community. The projects of a political Europe have stimulated migrants to extend their networks to other countries and elaborate a transnational solidarity. Such a structure helps the immigrants to skew national, even nationalist, policies of each state towards them and to negotiate their rights and the public recognition of collective identities (religious, linguistic or regional) in European supranational institutions, which in return are imposed on member states. Even though it is with the state that ultimately identities are negotiated, the normative supranationality leads the "French exception" to a more realistic approach towards differences and fulfills the requirements of democratic societies with regard to immigration and differences.

NOTES

1 "La France forme avec les peuples d'outre mer une Union fondée sur l'égalité des droits et des devoirs sans distinction de race ni de religion," quoted by Claude Liauzu, in *La société française face au racisme*. Paris: Editions Complexe, 1999: 129.

2 Tzevan Todorov; *Nous et les autres: La pensée politique française sur la diversité humaine*. Paris: Editions du Seuil, 1988.

3 Danièle Lochak, "La race: Une catégorie juridique?", in "Sans distinction de . . . race," Special issue of *Mots/Langage du politique* 33, December 1992: 291–303.

4 In 1992 a conference discussed in depth whether or not the term should be used in the Constitution, even if it aims at equality and protection: see the special issue of *Mots/Langage du politique*. "Sans distinction de . . . race." December 1992. See mainly the articles of Simone Bonnafous and Pierre Fiala, "Est-ce que dire la '*race*', présuppose l'existence," ibid.: 11–12; Etienne Balibar, "Le mot '*race*' n'est pas de trop dans la Constitution française," ibid.: 215–41; Chantal Millon-Delsol, "Pertinence et dénonciation du mot '*race*' dans la Constitution, " ibid.: 257–61.

5 Jacqueline Costa-Lascoux, "La relativité des mots et la prégnance des faits," in *Mots/Langage du politique*, December 1992: 317–29.

6   Jean-Loup Amselle, *Le multiculturalisme français: L'empire de la coutume.* Paris: Aubier, 1996.
7   This has become a dichotomy in French public discourse.
8   See D. Schnapper, *La communauté des citoyens.* Paris: Gallimard, 1994.
9   Emmanuel Todd developed this argument contrasting France to Germany categorized as "segregationist" and the United States as "differentialist" in *Le destin des immigrés: Assimilation et ségrégation dans les démocraties occidentales.* Paris: Editions du Seuil, 1994.
10 M. Wievorka (ed.) *La société fragmentée: Le multiculturalisme en débat.* Paris: La Découverte, 1996; Alain Touraine, *Comment vivre ensemble?* Paris: Fayard, 1999; *Qu'est-ce que la démocratie?* Paris: Fayard, 1993.
11 See. Ariane Chebel d'Appollonia, "The ethnicization of immigration in France and class/urban conflict," paper presented at the 13th International Conference of Europeanists, Chicago, March 14–16, 2002.
12 Riva Kastoryano, *Negotiating Identities: States and Immigrants in France and Germany.* Princeton, NJ: Princeton University Press, 2002.
13 R. Silberman, "French immigration statistics," in D. L. Horowitz and G. Noiriel (eds.), *Immigrants in Two Democracies: French and American Experience.* New York: New York University Press, 1992: 112–23.
14 INSEE (Institute for National Statistics) *Étrangers,* 1992.
15 INSEE, *Recensement de la population,* March 1999.
16 For the history of census classification, see Patrick Simon, "Nationalité et origine dans la statistiques française. Les catégories ambiguës," *Population* 3, 1998: 541–68.
17 Report published by INED, INSEE, supported by the DPM (Direction Populations Migrations) and the FAS (Fonds d'Action Sociale).
18 M. Tribalat, *Faire France: Une grande enquête sur les immigrés et leurs enfants.* Paris: Editions La Découverte, 1995.
19 H. Le Bras, *Le démon des origines: Démographie et extrême droite.* Paris: Editions de l'Aube, 1998.
20 Ibid.: 194.
21 P. Simon, "Sciences sociales et racismes, où sont les docteurs Folamour?" in *Mouvements,* 3, March–April 1999: 11–115.
22 P. Rosanvallon, *La nouvelle question sociale.* Paris: Editions du Seuil, 1994 (*The New Social Question.* Princeton, NJ: Princeton University Press).
23 Where low-income families, both French and foreign, were "relocated" in the 1970 and settled in HLM, translated as low rent apartments. Today, foreigners or the foreign-born constitute sometimes up to 55 percent, of the total population, unemployment reaches a high of 20 percent and obviously affects mainly young people. In some suburbs, that rate even goes beyond 50 percent and affects youth of Algerian "origin" in particular.
24 The "zones," are areas where 28.9 percent of the students are children of foreigners, as opposed to 10.8 percent at the national level; see S. Boulot and D. Boyzon-Fradet, *Les immigrés et l'Ecole, une course d'obstacles: Lectures et chiffres 1973–1987.* Paris: L'Harmattan, 1988.

25 Hubert Prévot, Secretary of State for Integration in a document on social policies of integration presented to the OECD (Organization for Economic Cooperation and Development) in March 1991.

26 Chebel d'Appollonia, "The ethnicization of immigration."

27 F. Dubet, "Les figures de la ville et la banlieue," *Sociologie du Travail* 2, 1995: 127–51.

28 Commission nationale consultative des droits de l'homme, 2001, *La lutte contre le racisme et la xénophobie: Rapport d'activité*. Paris: La documentation Française, 2002.

29 N. Glazer and D. Moynihan, (eds.), *Ethnicity: Theory and Experience*. Cambridge, MA: Harvard University Press, 1975: 1.

30 Nancy L. Green, "Religion et ethnicité: De la comparaison temporelle et spatiale," in *Annales, Histoire, Sciences Sociales* 57, 1, January–February 2002: 127–44; see also N. L. Green, *Repenser les Migrations*. Paris: PUF, 2002.

31 Riva Kastoryano, *Negotiating Identities*, ch. 6.

32 Interview with the chair of "Nana Beur" in France. A similar thought was formulated by the activists of the Association of Women in Berlin.

33 R. Kastoryano, "Relations interethniques et formes d'intégration," in Pierre-André Tagueiff, *Face au Racisme* (vol. 2: *Analyses, hypothèses, perspectives*). Paris: La Découverte, 1991: 167–77.

34 Statute of December 21, 1958, signed by General de Gaulle, cited by M. Yahiel, "Le FAS: questions de principe," *Revue Européenne des Migrations Internationales* 4, 1988: 107–13.

35 R. Kastoryano, *Negotiating Identities*, Chapter 6.

36 See Vincent Geisser, *Ethnicité républicaine: Les élites d'origine maghrébine dans le système politique français*. Paris: Presses de Sciences-Po, 1997.

37 Kastoryano, *Negotiating Identities*.

38 See C. Nicolet, *L'idée républicaine en France (1789–1924)*. Paris: Gallimard, 1995.

39 Yves Déloye; *Ecole et citoyenneté: L'individualisme républicain de Jules Ferry à Vichy, controverses*, Paris: Presses de Sciences-Po, 1994.

40 Ibid.

41 Reference to Eugen Weber's classical book *From Peasant into Frenchmen: Modernization of the Rural France, 1870–1914*. Stanford, CA: Stanford University Press, 1979.

42 S. Rokkan, "The formation of the nation-state in Western Europe," in S. N. Eisenstadt and S. Rokkan, *Building States and Nations*. London, Sage Publications, 1973.

43 For a useful comparison with the United States concerning the substance of ethnicity, see A. Zolberg and Long Litt Woon, "Why Islam is like Spanish: cultural incorporation in Europe and the United States," *Politics and Society*; 27 (1), 1999: 5–38.

44 Decision 91/290 DC, status of Corsica (May 9, 1991). According to that decision, the "Corsican people," a component of the French people, is contrary to the Constitution, which recognizes only the French people composed of "every French citizen without distinction of origin, race, religion" (Art. 2).

45   D. Lochak, "Les minorités dans le droit public français: du refus des dif-
     férences à la gestion des différences," *Conditions des minorités depuis 1789*.
     CRISPA-GDM, Paris: L'Harmattan, 1989: 111–84.

46   See Ralph Scor, *L'opinion française et les étrangers, 1919–1939*. Paris: Publi-
     cations de la Sorbonne, 1985.

47   Harry Goulbourne develops the concept of "communal option," which he
     analyzes as a reaction of ethnic minorities confronting the majority and
     the universal values it defends. H. Goulbourne, *Ethnicity and Nationalism
     in Post Imperial Britain*. Cambridge: Cambridge University Press, 1991: 41.

48   "Unable to represent Islam, I have withheld a suggestion of Jacque Berque
     who told me that it was possible, on the other hand, to symbolize Islam,"
     explained Pierre Joxe in "La France vue de l'intérieur: Entretien avec
     Pierre Joxe," *Débat* 61, September–October 1990: 15.

49   Interview with A. Boyer, Minister of Religion, at the Ministry of the Inte-
     rior, *Actes*, April 1992.

50   *Consultation*, no. 1, 1999.

51   D. Lochak, "Les minorités dans le droit public français."

52   See P. Cohen Albert, *The Modernization of French Jewry: Consistory and Com-
     munity in the Nineteenth Century*. Hanover, NH: Brandeis University Press,
     1977.

53   F. Dazi and R. Leveau, "L'intégration par le politique, le vote des 'Beurs',"
     Études, September 1988: 1–15.

FURTHER READING

Hargreaves, A. (1995) *Immigration, "Race" and Ethnicity in Contemporary France*.
   New York: Routledge.
Horowitz, D. and Noiriel, G. (eds.) (1992) *Immigrants in Two Democracies: French
   and American Experience*. New York: New York University Press.
Kastoryano, R. (2002) *Negotiating Identities: States and Immigrants in France and
   Germany*. Princeton, NJ: Princeton University Press.

CHAPTER FOUR

Racisms, Ethnicities, and British Nation-Making

Liviu Popoviciu and Mairtin Mac an Ghaill

Introduction

This chapter is written against a British background of the theoretical, conceptual and methodological underdevelopment that surrounds the interplay of racialized social relations, ethnic identity formations and nation-making within contemporary transformations. The main themes of the chapter are: (1) the need for theoretical/conceptual space to rethink this field of inquiry; (2) holding onto the productive tension between earlier (class-based) and more recent (cultural) theories of racism and ethnic relations; (3) exploring the productiveness of qualitative research; (4) examining a move beyond the dominant black–white regime of representation; and (5) an examination of emerging questions in the sub-discipline.[1] Importantly, bringing together early and more recent theoretical and empirical work produces a critical reflection on the relative adequacy of different sociological frameworks. An advantage of this kind of structure is that it allows us to consider not only the relative adequacy of different theoretical accounts through a series of contrasts, but also encourages a view of these theories as alternative explanations, which make different assumptions about ethnic minority and majority communities and associated processes of racialization, national exclusion and inequality.[2] In turn, this suggests different political and policy interventions in addressing cultural difference and racial inequality at both local and global levels.

Currently, we are caught between the decline of old political identifications and new identities that are in the process of becoming, marked by the implosion of the British color paradigm with its vocabulary of post-war immigrants, the black–white dualism and fixed cultural affili-

ations, and ethnicities. Based upon our own qualitative work, we suggest
that imagery traces of the past and the future are present in the lives
of diverse diasporic groups in Britain and the Anglo-ethnic majority, as
exemplified in emerging academic representations (Rutherford 1990;
Brah et al. 1999a and b). These are located within the contexts of the
break-up of a (Dis)United Kingdom; Euro-racism, the intensification of
Islamaphobia and the arrival of new migrants, "illegal" immigrants,
refugees, and asylum seekers (Kinealy 1999). In this chapter we explore
a range of contemporary forms of ethnic, national, and religious exclusions, that have been subsumed within the black and white model of
racism. The latter involved representations of racism that privileged
post-war New Commonwealth immigration and settlement as the dominant (color) paradigm. This involved the construction of a specific
hierarchy of fixed racialized identities that displayed predictable signs,
most notably color, as the central marker of difference. From our own
work, in deconstructing the collective subject position of whites, there
is a specific examination of the cultural invisibility of the Irish in Britain,
who are of central significance as major representational resources in
making sense of the formation of the British nation and the political
specificities of British nationalism. At the same time, in terms of the
racial dichotomy of domination/dominated, the Irish are not either/or
but both/and, representing an ideal type (understood as a heuristic
device rather than a normative ascription) of contemporary European
racialization. Furthermore, the "white" Irish within an English context
suggest that ethnicity, rather than being a marker of essential cultural
differences, is now marked by contingency, indeterminacy, and fluidity.
In other words, (Irish) ethnicity may now be performed, mobilized, and
contested transnationally within shifting contexts.

SOCIO-HISTORICAL MAPPING OF THE FIELD

We begin with a critical engagement with British sociology of race, ethnicity, and racism that provides an overview of the central issues that
have defined this area of inquiry during the past 50 years. As is made
clear in the other chapters in this book, comparative material from
Europe and the United States makes explicit the specificities of the
British position (Guillaumin 1988; Balibar and Wallerstein 1991; Goldberg 1993; Wieviorka 1995).

Race relations studies

The primary focus of race relations studies used to be inter-ethnic relations between minority and majority communities in such institutions as employment, housing, and education (Patterson 1963; Banton 1977). They examined minority communities' distinctive cultural attributes, suggesting that social behavior was primarily to be understood in terms of culture. This culturalist perspective was preoccupied with questions of assimilation or integration of ethnic minorities into British society and the problems facing the "second" generation, who were seen as being "caught between two cultures." Although the culturalist perspective received much theoretical criticism from other sociological approaches, it nevertheless informed a significant "common-sense" understanding of minority communities' experience of British society. It was particularly important in helping to develop multicultural policies. The legacy of this perspective is still to be found in different parts of the country, illustrating the uneven translation of theories into practice.

Class-based analyses

The race relations problematic was challenged by Weberian and Marxist analyses on the grounds of its assumed limited theoretical explanation. They argued that a major weakness of the culturalist approach was that by focusing on the "ethnic attributes" of the black community, they failed to recognize the significance of their social class location in advanced capitalist societies. The Weberian approach examined the incorporation of different immigrant groups into Britain and the forms of social stratification emanating from status distinctions based primarily on race (Rex and Moore 1967; Rex 1970). For Marxists, the emphasis was on the economic exploitation of immigrant groups with a focus upon the inter-relationship between class, racism, and colonialism (Castles and Kosack 1973; Miles 1982). Weberian and Marxist accounts were of particular political importance in the development of anti-racist theories. They established commonalties of experience of racism, investigating the different institutional positioning, particularly of Asians and African Caribbeans, living in a multi-racist Britain, and provided these social groups with a vocabulary to talk about their experience of society in terms of racism (see CCCS 1982; Solomos 1993).

Recent cultural theorizing needs to recover the history of earlier class-based accounts and in the process re-read these texts as providing innovative understandings of racial conflict, inequality, and social change (see Mac an Ghaill 1999). This enables us, from a late modernity perspective, to engage with the structural continuities of racist and nationalist exclusions, for example, in areas of employment, training, housing, and social services – alongside the discontinuities – of late capitalist consumer society. It also enables us to address key absences in the rather narrow ahistorical accounts generated by current theoretical frameworks, as well as illustrating the complexity of developing conceptually and politically adequate understandings of processes of racialization. Most importantly, analyses of the relationship between racism and class are currently of strategic political importance in challenging a growing pessimism that there is little that can be done, for example, in relation to global forces that are seen to be determining immigration controls and welfare policies at the level of nation-states (Renan 1990; Brah et al. 1999a). This is not to suggest a "simple" return to class-based explanations. Rather, with their revisionist tendency to forget, new theoretical frameworks and empirical studies of racialized minorities and a de-racialized Anglo-ethnic majority need to re-engage critically with earlier theoretical issues of class analysis, concerning the state, migration and forces of social regulation. However, they must address the contemporary concerns of a restratified working class in relation to the cumulative effects of structural unemployment in regional spaces, the crisis of the welfare state, and the restructuring of scarce public resources to an emerging "underclass," who are experiencing multiple social exclusions (Bradley 1996; Savage 2000). This is part of a broader picture, explored below, in which global economic restructuring, advanced technological communications, and increasing cultural exchange are highlighting a wide range of emerging processes of social exclusion and marginalization that have challenged older models of racial inequality.

The new politics of cultural difference position

By the early 2000s we have been provided with theoretical frameworks in which the changing nature of ethnic minority communities' lives have been much debated (Rattansi and Westwood 1994; see Barker 1981). These texts, in reclaiming culture as of central importance to ethnic minority communities, provide a critique of class-based explanations. They have begun to suggest the need for a more complex understanding of racial difference, ethnic formation, and national belonging that is not reducible to a single source. In the 1980s earlier academic and political analyses were criticized for class reductionism and economic determinism. It was claimed that such representations were conceptually inadequate in explaining the complex social and psychological processes involved in the development of changing forms of racialized and ethnic identity formations. Placing the capital–labor relationship at the center of theory was seen as closing off more open approaches. New social movements, including feminism, black struggles, national liberation movements, gay and lesbian rights, and antinuclear and ecology movements, challenged the privileging of class relations, through which other social categories were mediated. The question of identity has emerged as one of the key dynamic concepts in the context of rethinking change in late modernity. As Bradley (1996) argued in *Fractured Identities: Changing Patterns of Inequality*, sociocultural change is marked by the disintegration of older social collectivities, such as social class, and increased fluidity of social relationships, with an accompanying interest in identity and subjectivity. More specifically, there has been a focus on the pluralization of identities involving processes of fragmentation and dislocation (Hall 1992). Alongside this, theorists of late modernity have suggested that western societies are experiencing a surge of individuation, in which globalized change is bringing an end to the constraining influence of social class and other forms of industrial society (Giddens 1991; Beck 1992). It is argued that late modernity is characterized by an increased capacity for cultural reflexivity, as individuals are impelled into decision-making, negotiation, and individual strategies about every detail of how we live together in multi-cultural societies.

This mapping of a more complex picture has been greatly developed by ethnic minority feminist theorists (Mama 1995; *Feminist Review* 1995; Hickman and Walter 1995; Brah 1996; Gray 2000). Reading through these texts on cultural forms of racism and new ethnicities, one becomes aware of the current influence of particular ideas on poststructuralism and postmodernism that are discussed in terms of: difference, diversity and cultural pluralism (Hall 1992; Brah et al. 1999b). Some post-structuralist theorists have adopted psychoanalytic accounts, highlighting the complex psychic investments that individuals have in dominant racist and nationalist discourses that cannot simply be explained in rationalist terms (Parker et al. 1992; Cohen 1992; see Fanon 1970).

Of particular influence here has been post-colonial cultural theorists, who have developed a new language around such notions as diaspora (movement of people-cultural dispersal), hybridity (mixing of cultures) and syncrenism (pluralistic forms of cultural belonging) (Spivak 1988; Gilroy 1993; Said 1993; Bhabha 1994). They have suggested that in constructing human identity, we cannot appeal to any fixed or essential characteristics that exist for all time, and that racialized social relations are better understood within the specific contexts in which they are played out. More specifically, they have argued for a shift beyond the black–white model of racism – the color paradigm – towards one in which cultural and religious identities are foregrounded. In questioning the fixed boundaries around color racism that were established by political and academic discourses in the 1970s and 1980s, there is the suggestion that the conditions of late modernity are helping to produce multiple forms of racisms and new political subjects.

Summary

The above presents a potted history over the past 40 years of British academic and political representations of race, racism, and ethnicity. An earlier race relations position focusing upon inter-ethnic relations in a multi-cultural society was challenged by a class-based position that highlighted the structural power relations operating against black people, as indicated in the notion of institutional racism. In turn, this position was challenged by the new politics of cultural difference, with its focus upon culture, diversity and difference.

RESEARCHING THE FIELD: QUALITATIVE MOMENTS: A YOUNGER GENERATION

In attempting to hold on to the tension between materialist (class-based) and post-structuralist/post-colonial accounts of racism, ethnicity, and national belonging, we have found that theory-led qualitative research grounded in individuals' own narratives is highly productive. Empirical work with young people highlights that their lived experience and explanations of racial and national difference are ahead of theory (Cohen 1993). For example, we have found fascinating insights into the changing cultural dynamics taking place between inter-ethnic groups within the multicultural cities of Cluj and Newcastle upon Tyne (Popoviciu 2002). At the same time, our work suggests that in order to develop sociological perspectives that engage comprehensively with the range of theoretical representations of emerging ethnic identity for-

mations, there is a need for a continual referral to social relations themselves within institutional contexts. The hard work of theory-led qualitative investigation makes clear the productivity of engaging with a
younger generation's meanings, not only by testing out theory, but also
providing alternative avenues of enquiry. In this way, the challenge
centers not so much upon underlying different representations of identity formations but a need to address more fundamental issues of the
processes involved in nation-making, identity formation, and racial
inequality.

Since the 1970s, unlike the sociological perspectives that held onto
traditional social science conceptions of objectivity and neutrality,
critical qualitative social researchers, from certain strands of Marxism,
feminism and anti-racism, have argued for a mutually informing
interdependency between theory and methodology. This theory-
informing research has been productive in rethinking the dynamics of
methodology. For instance, it has promoted the discussion about
knowledge production, notions of objectivity, and the question of
reflexivity around power relations within the research process
(Ramazanoglu 1992). At the same time, qualitative research methodology was of central importance to earlier work on racial inequality. A
major appeal of qualitative methods, for example, such as in-depth
interviewing, was that it provided a space for self-representation by
ethnic and other social minorities. This work was embedded in broader
debates about the epistemological status of social minorities. Feminist
scholarship was of particular significance here, in celebrating standpoint epistemology, arguing that truth can be found in the accounts of
people in specific social and cultural situations. Such anti-oppressive
research frameworks invited the operation of particular scripts for the
researcher and research participants, with the latter positioned as
having special insight into what is "really going on" in the social world
(Smith 1987).

An earlier development of qualitative studies was successful in getting
young black people's "different experience" of institutional life and
explanations of institutional racial inequality onto the social map (Mac
an Ghaill 1988; Gillborn 1990; Mirza 1992). This ethnographic work
was important in moving beyond state, psychology-based positions that
were grounded in a dominant British empiricist epistemology.[3] These
official social regulatory perspectives, in their explanation of differential institutional outcomes in schooling/training and social destinies in
the market place focused upon individual "problem black young
people," thus excluding institutionalized social and discursive practices.
Furthermore, politically and theoretically, earlier qualitative studies

were important in emphasizing black young people's active construction of subordinated racialized identities within the inter-related nexus of: schools and training places that did "nothing but boss them about," their survivalist peer-group cultures; adolescent psychosexual development and the anticipation of their future location on low status training schemes, in low-skilled labor markets. At the same time, the studies documented young black people's creative responses to the racially regulated processes that circumscribed their lives.

Other qualitative researchers have explored a younger generation's experiences, illustrating a wide range of new pluralistic forms of collective belonging that broaden the public sphere of multicultural society (Hewitt 1986; Jones 1988; Mac an Ghaill 1994a; Back 1996). They describe how Anglo-ethnic majority and ethnic minority young people are involved in constructing new syncretic versions of transculturally based identities. For example, young men living in England have developed emotional investments and cultural attachments to US black popular cultural forms, such as music and sport, that act as significant resources in their creative explorations of the shifting contours of cultural and political identities among and between ethnic majority and minority young people. For example, Haywood and Mac an Ghaill (2002), in exploring the formation of young masculinities through the dynamics of ethnicity, suggest that this is not simply about exploring the inter-subjective dimensions of "blackness" and "whiteness" but is also contained within lived and imagined ethnic (national) histories. In their ethnographic study of a sixth form college (post-compulsory), race created a number of complexities for white English males in their articulation of particular masculine heterosexualities. These male students conflated notions of Englishness and whiteness that became key components in circuits of desire. Those males who were part of a heterosexual culture that was premised on sexual athleticism experienced a range of psychic and micro-cultural contradictions because of their racist and homophobic dis-identifications with black men and women. Englishness, from their perspective, was about being "not black and not gay." Through the performance of their masculinities, that is, repetitive stylized ritualistic practices, these young men were simultaneously articulating a radicalized politics. At the same time, such dis-identifications limited, restricted and thus contested their claims to a sexual desire that was "uncontrollable": a mainstay of their heterosexual masculinities. The relations between them also involved a psychic structure, including such elements as: desire, attraction, repression, transference and projection in relation to a racialized "sexual other" (Pajackowska and Young 1992). There is much work to be done in this area in order to understand the ambivalent structure of feeling and desire embedded within social institutions.

Such qualitative work is particularly important in showing subjectivity/identity not as a product, not as something possessed but rather a complex and multifaceted process – the focus shifts from a anti-racist emphasis on *being* ethnic to a post-structuralist emphasis on *becoming* ethnic. This move from an anti-racist to a post-structuralist position can be seen as signaling a shift from a concern with *laboring with* the racialized body, for example, in work on black slavery, labor migrants and the over-representation of minority ethnic communities in low skilled employment, to that of *laboring on* the body, for example, in the work on the complex investments of a younger generation of white working-class men inhabiting black youth styles. One way of moving forward here is to link questions of the body to an exploration of the function of binaries within the formation of ethnic, racialized, and national identities. For example, this process might involve deconstructing how Anglo-ethnicity gains an ascendant position in relation to ethnic minority groups through these binaries. In doing this, ethnic identity formation can be read as performative.

Although there has been a growing exploration of the implications of post-structuralism and post-modernism, within a British context, there has been little application of those theoretical and conceptual insights to the research process. Sociologists' general lack of transparency of their research methodology exacerbates this invisibility. In short, it may be argued that the current explosion of *new* knowledges are accompanied by *old* methodological techniques. In order to explore this, briefly, we focus upon three key components of contemporary theorizing: (1) the crisis of representation; (2) multiple subjectivities; and (3) methods of research as technologies of truth production.

First, earlier approaches to research have undergone what Marcus and Fischer (1986: 8) term a "crisis of representation," where authorial status is deemed problematic. This resonates with Derrida's (1978) focus on the indeterminacy of the author in the articulation of ideas. He questions the notion of the text as simply conveying the author's ideas. Derrida contends that meanings within texts are subject to multiple interpretations. Therefore the author's representations are active attempts to stabilize (justify and legitimate) interpretations of fieldwork incidents. Research accounts become the *forcible* presentation of a semantic unity between researcher and the researched. Hence, an approach to researching racism, ethnicity and nation-making questions the author's authority and the meanings that he or she attempts to stabilize. Importantly, reflexive awareness of how qualitative research may simply *produce versions of reality* rather than being a mirror or device to *access reality* is a key departure from an anti-racist position. Post-structuralist methodology deploys a reflexivity that allows the researcher to examine the researcher/researched relationship as a localized, dialogical production; understanding *research as praxis* is of key concern (Lather 1991).

Second, an immediate concern for post-structuralists is that social relations often operate through a series of historically-situated discourses. These contain categorically organized narratives that use techniques such as binarism, othering, repositioning, and inverting. As a result, Davies and Harre (1994: 46) suggest that: "An individual emerges through the process of social interaction, not as a relatively fixed end product but as one who is constituted and reconstituted through the various discursive practices in which they participate." As an individual in different discourses, he or she is located in a number of subject positions that results in the constitution of multiple *subjectivities*. The task of the post-structuralist researcher in carrying out qualitative work is to develop sensitivity to an individual's differentiated subject positions.

Third, although sociological methodologies have undergone considerable revision over the past century, little attention has been paid to the techniques of data collection. For example, sociological researchers on racism continue to use research techniques as methods of truth production. In an article that exemplifies one style of post-modern writing, Tyler (1991: 85) argues: "Method, the technology of truth, the rational means that make truth, relativizes truth not to time, place or purpose, but to its instrumentality. Method is the ritual that brings forth the truth." With post-structuralism making visible the semantic technologies that systematically produce truth claims, research methods also need examination. A post-structural qualitative approach to methods emphasizes that interviews are constituted through local contexts, multiple identities, and cultural scripts. These affect the emergence of truth about categories of racism, ethnicity, and nation-making.

Summary

Anti-oppressive qualitative methodologies have helped push the limits of sociological analysis, by inviting alternative readings of the research process. The increased recognition of the research process as generated by gendered epistemological and theoretical positions has produced increased visibility of reflexivity on research designs, data collection, coding, and analysis. In turn, post-structuralism is subjecting anti-oppressive approaches to intellectual interrogation. This raises the question: how can traditional qualitative methodological formats, such as in-depth interviewing, continue to make sense against post-structuralist claims about the multiplicity of selves, notions of decentered forms of power and the intersections of highly relational social categories? In our response, we have found that theoretical and conceptual developments tend to remain under-connected to methodological reflexivity. For example, while there is much talk of post-structuralist accounts of ethnic and national identity formations, these have not yet produced a consistent methodology. In fact, sustained methodological discussions in this field have yet to take place.

THE SOCIOLOGICAL INVISIBILITY OF THE IRISH DIASPORA IN BRITAIN

In current work, in which one of us has been involved, there was an exploration of the dominant British racial regime of representation and the accompanying conceptual absences, as illustrated in earlier anti-racist and more recent new cultural theory texts (Mac an Ghaill 1999). This involved rethinking the histories and geographies of social closure and cultural exclusion as defining elements of the politics of race and nation. More specifically, as argued above, this suggested the need to move beyond the Americanization of British race-relations – the color paradigm – to a critical engagement with European explanations, focusing on questions of nation, nationalism, and migration (Wieviorka 1991; Silverman 1992; Kiberd 1996). This shift beyond the modernist black-white dualistic model serves to critique the long academic tradition of "over-racializing" selected groups of "non-whites," while deracializing the Anglo-ethnic majority and white minorities. A main issue that has tended to be underplayed in the literature on racialization and racial inequality is the collective subject position of whites, which operates within a hegemonic logic in which "whiteness" is absent to the "racial majority," who assume that racialization is "something to do with blacks." Whiteness as the signifier of dominance has become the unexamined norm. We illustrate this with reference to theory-led qualitative research with the Irish diaspora in Britain (see Williams and Mac an Ghaill 1998; Bielenberg 2000; Gray 2000; Walter 2001).[4]

There is a long historical narrative of the relations between Britain and Ireland in which images of the Irish have been mobilized as major changing representational resources for the making of the British nation, identity, and culture. Irish labor migrants and immigrants represented strategic *economic* and *cultural* elements of this imperial project. Economically, Ireland as the emigrant nursery to the world economy provided, at different historical periods, a reserve army of cheap and flexible labor for British capitalism (Mac Laughlin 1994; see also Kearney 1990; O'Sullivan 1992). Culturally, specific subject positions were produced for the Irish as "colonial others," within the context of a "shared life" between migrants and the "host" society at the imperial center (Jackson 1963; Miles 1982; Holmes 1988; Dummett and Nicol 1990). This was an important moment for the British, in the re-production of their collective self-identity as a "superior race," who actively dis-identified with the Irish as an "inferior race." Curtis (1968: 84) describes the pervasiveness of popular images of the Irish that circulated in Victorian England. There was a wide range of cultural markers of difference that juxtaposed the dirtiness, drunkenness, laziness, and violence of the rootless, alien Irish with the purity, industriousness and civilization of the settled English. At this time, dichotomies of race and nationality were frequently conflated in popular journals and newspaper editorials (Hickman 1995).

The acknowledgement of the racialization of the Irish during this earlier period contrasts with its systematic absence from contemporary representations of racism and ethnicity.[5] In response to British theorists' production of the conceptual invisibility of the Irish diaspora and its attendant denial of cultural difference, Irish community activists have produced a broad range of empirical evidence of structural discrimination and inequality that the Irish have experienced across Britain's institutional sites in the post-war period until the present. This has included studies on: migration, work, health, education, policing, the legal system, and welfare rights (Conner 1985; Lennon et al. 1988; Hazelkorn 1990, Greenslade 1992; Gribben 1994; Kowarzik 1997; Hickman and Walter 1997; Williams et al. 1997; Williams and Mac an Ghaill 1998).

Alongside the above important work on the structural location and social exclusion of the Irish in Britain, qualitative research is especially productive in helping us to address the equally important question of the changing cultural formation, shifting subjectivities, and emerging representations among the Irish diaspora (Mac an Ghaill 2000; see Kiberd 1996). As argued above, the question of identity has been of major political significance for post-war social movements in Britain. In focusing on the taking up of identities, there has been a particular concern with how social and symbolic systems classify people and mark social collectivities. More recently, questions of difference and otherness have become organizing concepts across a number of disciplines. In contrast to the conceptual and policy visibility of "difference" in the dominant racial regime of representation, the idea of "sameness" remains under-explored, subsumed under the concept of identity. Questions of sameness, identification, and cultural belonging are currently of particular salience and demand urgent critical engagement. This requires the development of conceptual frameworks that enable us to achieve a more comprehensive understanding of the cultural zone within and through which dominant and minority social groups live out and negotiate their differences *and* similarities with others and between themselves. For example, empirical work carried out with the Irish diaspora in Britain has illustrated the limitations of conceptions of racial difference, based exclusively on color racism, which serve to position the Irish in Britain as racially the same as the white Anglo-ethnic majority (Williams and Mac an Ghaill 1998). British sociologists are unaware that as Lebow (1976) in his book *White Britain and Black Ireland*, clearly illustrates, for much of British colonial history, the Irish were seen as black (Curtis 1984). Such work converges with American texts on how the Irish became white in America (Roedrigger 1991; Ignatiev 1995). However, there is a tendency in these narratives to conceptualize whites and blacks as reified social collectivities, in a way that does not resonate with the complexity of contemporary conditions in a European context. In other words, such work operates within a modernist framework with its accompanying binary of a racialized either/or.

What is under-stated here is that historically, the structural contradictory location of the Irish diaspora within racialized discourses emerges out of their ambivalent involvement in both American and European colonialism and imperialism (O'Toole 1997). In terms of the racial dichotomy of domination/dominated, the Irish are not either/or but both/and, representing an ideal type of contemporary European racialization. Within a British context, historically the Irish were not simply excluded but partially included (albeit a forced inclusion) within the British extended family, while experiencing widespread discrimination and social exclusion (Walter 1998). This is not a simple narrative of *what was done to* the Irish diaspora in Britain, they were and continue to be *active agents* in their own cultural formation. In their study of twentieth-century Irish women, Hickman and Walter (1995: 5) suggest: "It is all too easy for 'whiteness' to be equated with a homogenous way of life. What is necessary is research on the deconstruction of 'whiteness.'" For many people from the Republic of Ireland, the cumulative experience of colonialism and contemporary forms of anti-Irish racism, the British involvement in Northern Ireland and their own national and ethnic sense of belonging to Ireland mean that they actively dis-identify with Britishness (Popoviciu and Mac an Ghaill forthcoming). At the same time, there is a need conceptually to focus upon the self-insertion of the Irish into whiteness, as a central mechanism of producing cultural invisibility (Mac an Ghaill 1996, 2000). Furthermore, developing broader frameworks of racial difference and sameness that are inclusive of diverse diasporic groups in Britain, such as the Irish, may help us to reconnect the issue of color (whiteness), to wider questions of class, migrant labor, nation, and cultural belonging (Williams et al. 1997).

EMERGING QUESTIONS: CONTEMPORARY FORMS OF ETHNIC, NATIONAL, AND RELIGIOUS EXCLUSIONS

As suggested above, recent social and cultural changes, involving global economic restructuring, advanced technological communications, and increasing cultural exchange, have highlighted a wide range of processes of social exclusion and marginalization that have challenged older models of racial inequality. Within a British context, four main issues have been of particular significance; that of: Euro-racism, the intensification of Islamaphobia, the arrival of new migrants, "illegal" immigrants, refugees and asylum seekers and the diverse range of contemporary ethnic minority community mobilizations and struggles. The re-emergence of the Far Right and neo-fascist parties in Eastern and Western Europe with the accompanying increased physical and symbolic violence against migrant and Jewish communities, and the wider dimensions of a rapidly changing world of ethnic nationalisms and religious fundamentalisms in Europe and beyond have served to illustrate the parochialism of much British anti-racist theorizing (Alund and Schierup 1991; Balibar and Wallerstein 1991; Webber 1991; Silverman 1992). By the end of the 1990s important work had been carried out that traced developments of racism within individual European nation-states (Wieviorka 1991; Ford 1992; Willems 1995). However, such work offers only a partial insight into the rise of Euro-racism. As Bonnett (1993: 30) makes clear: "moves toward militant rejectionism have taken place in the context of the integration of the European community (EC) and the emergence of pan-EC immigration, refugee and social surveillance controls." He illustrates this with reference to former British Prime Minister, John Major's desire to construct a "perimeter fence" around Europe to protect the continent from immigrants (see CARF 1991).

There have been different explanations for the phenomenon of Euro-racism. For Miles (1993) the new comparative interest in contemporary European racisms was an important analytical development in the late 1980s that followed the weakening of the race relations paradigm. He maintains that the notion of Euro-racism signals an intensification of nationalisms associated with the crisis in the nation-state in the latest stage of globalization. While sensitive to the particularity of the political and ideological form of each nation-state, he identifies a common set of problems facing EU societies resulting from the restructuring of capitalist economies in a period of continuing reorganization of the capitalist world economy. The politics of immigration is one such problem, with the need for EU member states "to continue to regulate the political and ideological consequences of large-scale labor migrations that occurred during the 1950s, 1960s and early 1970s and the resulting rise of nationalisms" (ibid.: 16).

Whereas for Miles racism is conceptualized as integral to the development of capitalist societies, Wieviorka (1991, 1995) places his work within analytical frameworks that place modernity and postindustrialism at the center of his explanation of the rise of contemporary European racisms. He distinguishes four forms of racism located within modern social and political conditions: (1) a universalist type, evident in conditions of colonial expansion which inferiorizes "pre-modern others"; (2) a racism associated with downward social mobility – a "poor white" response common at times of economic recession and unemployment in modern industrial societies; (3) an anti-modernist stance, that appeals to traditions of nation, religion and community, often directed against the Jews and economically successful Asians; and (4) inter-group tensions that have complex relations with the conditions of modernity. Wieviorka maintains that all contemporary European societies are experiencing huge transformations that define what he calls, in the case of France, *une grande mutation*, manifested in "the era of destructuration," that is constituted by crises in industrialism, the welfare state, and national identity. For Wieviorka, these changing conditions in Europe have allowed each form of racism to develop as a space of racism, with racists taking up a complex mixture of various positions.

A major feature of Euro-racism has been increased levels of state surveillance and exclusion alongside an upsurge in popular violence against Muslims. For example, within France, the headscarf affair of 1989 helped to generate a major moral panic against Islamic people. It involved the suspension from a state school of three Muslim girls, who insisted on wearing headscarves that their principal judged to contra-

vene French laws on *laïcité* (secularism), a term denoting the separation of state and religious institutions. The principal's decision was
eventually overturned by the Minister for Education, Lionel Jospin
(Silverman, 1992; Hargreaves 1995). A range of reasons have been identified for the intensification of the racialization of Islam, including: that
in many European societies Muslims form the largest non-European
minority; that following the collapse of communism, Europe is returning to an earlier historical conflict between Christians and Muslims; that
the early 1970s' world recession was associated with "greedy oil sheikhs"
(Mason 1995). More recently, the Islamic revolution in Iran and the
Gulf War have been represented as a direct challenge to Western, and
more specifically, North American hegemony. Most significantly the
September 11 attack on the United States is currently projected as illustrative of the major threat of religious fundamentalists against liberal
social democratic Western societies – a "clash of civilizations." As
Hoogvelt (1997:182) has argued "In the last twenty years or so a number
of apparently political and social events all over the world have led
Western commentators to speak of a militant Islamic revival." Hence,
as Castles and Miller (1993: 27) point out: "Muslim minorities appear
threatening partly because they are linked to strong external forces,
which appear to question the hegemony of the North, and partly
because they have a visible and self-confident cultural presence."

Within a British context, Muslims have emerged as a major target of
official racial discourses and increased levels of popular violence. Historically, one can trace the shift in central government political rhetoric
with Sikhs represented as the "others" in Enoch Powell's speeches
during the 1960s and 1970s. At this time there was much debate in the
media concerning the problem of Sikhs refusing to assimilate to British
culture and enforcing it on their children. Equally interesting is the way
in which different cultural objects, here, Sikh turbans, come to signify
a cultural threat to the nation. By the 1980s, Muslims had become
demonized as the main "enemy within," threatening the "British way of
life." Most recently, this was articulated by the Conservative MP, Winston
Churchill: "He [Major] promises us that fifty years from now, spinsters
will be cycling to communion on Sunday mornings – more like the
muezzin will be calling Allah's faithful to the high street mosque" (see
Runnymede Trust 1993). As Anthias and Yuval-Davis (1993: 55) have
pointed out:

> Since the "Rushdie Affair," the exclusion of minority religions from the
> national collectivity has started a process of racialization that especially
> relates to Muslims. People who used to be known for the place of origin,

or even as "people of color" have become identified by their assumed religion. The racist stereotype of the "Paki" has become the racist stereotype of the "Muslim fundamentalist."

This racial discourse is being mediated within state institutions. For example, schools are in the process of constructing a new hierarchy of ethnic masculinities (Mac an Ghaill 1994a). For over two decades, African-Caribbean boys have been positioned as the main disciplinary problem. They are currently being joined by Muslim boys as the new folk devils, with corresponding negative categorization, stereotyping, and moral evaluation.

A third example of emerging contemporary forms of social exclusions within the context of global transformations that have challenged older models of color racism is illustrated by the growing significance of new migrants, "illegal" immigrants, refugees and asylum seekers. Hooper (1997: 16) describing Italy as a death trap for recent immigrants, highlights the varied migrant population of modern European societies with: "its Filipino, Ethiopian and Dominican daily helpers, its Albanian squeegee merchants, North African farm workers and Sri Lankan street vendors." Equally significant is the social positioning of Gypsies and Travellers in Britain, who are currently receiving much negative media attention (Popoviciu 2002). There is a long history of neglect, both by the state and anti-racist movements, of the material and cultural experiences and needs of Gypsies and Travellers. Hawes and Perez (1995) have explored the cumulative effects of this long history of neglect alongside recent changes, including Court of Appeal decisions on the definition of a Gypsy, the provisions of the 1994 Criminal Justice and Public Order Act and the impact of European legislation. Acknowledging the complexity of the social location of Gypsies within a new politics of cultural difference situation, they argue the case for the use of the concept ethnic cleansing to describe "the actions and attitudes of British society to the most maligned of its minorities, the Gypsies."

In response to the development of contemporary forms of social exclusions, a diverse range of community mobilizations and struggles have emerged. An historical account of the sociology of racism serves to link these current political mobilizations to their histories of protest in colonial and post-colonial conditions. More recently, there has been a move beyond images of a unitary history, for example, of Asian and African-Caribbean communities, to recording the fragmentation of racialized identities and the under-reported forms of resistance to racialization that are not reducible to academic accounts of anti-racist movements (Knowles and Mercer 1992; Gilroy 1993). This helps us to go beyond the exclusive focus of materialist accounts of blacks and whites, to explore the continuing political significance of anti-racism with reference to other "non-white" minority groups and white minority ethnic groups. These forgotten histories of protest highlight the different cultural forms of state incorporation of minority communities into the British state, particularly with regard to labor and housing locations, and experiences of the state and civil society, including immigration, the courts and the police.

At the same time, ethnic minority communities have developed their own forms of accommodation, contestation, and resistance. These strategies are currently evident, for example, in Irish and Muslim mobilizations. The former has included the long political campaigns, such as those against the imprisonment of the Birmingham Six and the Guildford Four, which form part of the wider contestation of the state criminalization of the Irish diaspora, lobbying the Office for National Statistics for inclusion of the Irish as an ethnic minority in the Census and the development of counter-discourses to anti-Irish racism. For Muslims, the term Islamaphobia is gaining increasing acceptance as signifying that existing anti-racist discourses do not adequately address questions of cultural and religious discrimination. This has been a central argument among sections of the community, highlighted in two main issues: their campaign for government financial support for Muslim schools and their mobilizing against the publication of Salman Rushdie's book *The Satanic Verses* (Modood 1989; Asad 1993; Al-Azmeh 1993). Irish and Muslim political activism serves as evidence of the unsettling of liberal multiculturalists and radical anti-racists, who developed their respective positions in opposition to each other around the highly contested concept of culture. These campaigns enable us to begin to ask critical questions about the relationship between minority communities and anti-racist movements. They also open up questions concerning the disconnection of anti-racism from other social movements, including trade unionism, Northern Ireland struggles, ecology, feminism, and "queer politics," as well as links with Europe and Euro-racism. In turn, these campaigns may open up questions about contemporary global forms of contestation by recent migrants, "illegal" immigrants, refugees and asylum-seekers from increasingly diversified places (Sivanandan 1989). As Popoviciu (2002) argues, of particular importance here is the use of comparative research. He illustrates the nuanced local (national) responses of Romanian and English young people, who are constructing individual and collective cultural identities, marked by pervasive feelings of increased global anxiety, risk and dislocation within conditions of late modernity (Kearney 1997; Brah et al. 1999a).

CONCLUSION

Questions of migration, nation-making and ethnic belonging are currently key elements of rapid social and cultural changes. However, contemporary British debates between anti-racists and cultural theorists are providing a limited discussion, with the former emphasizing common experiences of racial inequality and the latter focusing upon the differentiated experiences of diverse diasporic communities. We need to explore how future studies of these communities in England, informed by the principle of ethnic inclusiveness, including the Anglo-ethnic majority, might help to move beyond the limits of dominant anti-racist positions in trying to understand the politics around ethnicity, racism and difference. A key question that arises here is whether we can develop a new civic nationalism for the 2000s that challenges the racist and nationalist exclusions currently experienced by diasporic groups, while addressing the fears of the Anglo-ethnic majority in a rapidly changing de-industrializing society (Wieviorka 1995).

The shifting semantics of race are historically specific in the production of racialized political subjects. We can trace the shift from a narrative of immigration from New Commonwealth Countries and Pakistan (NCWP countries) (1950s/1960s), through one of institutional discrimination against black ethnic minorities and their "finding a voice" (1970s/1980s), to narratives of the emergence of diverse diasporic communities and the search for a lost white British national identity within the context of an ambivalent Anglo-ethnic response to "Fortress Europe" (1990s/2000s). However, a re-reading of earlier race and ethnic relations texts in the early 2000s shows them to have been largely developed in reductionist and essentialist terms of "what white people have done to black people," rather than the broader category of racialized social relations between a wide range of ethnic groups. A further limitation of earlier work was the under-theorization of subjectivity, and ethnic identity formation. Contemporary cultural theory suggests that the changing meanings around racism, ethnicity and national belonging can be seen to be multi-dimensional, experienced and negotiated in different ways within specific historical and institutional arenas. There has been a strong tendency in earlier anti-racist work to adopt a monocausal explanation of racial exclusion and inclusion that disconnected it from other forms of social divisions and cultural processes. Contemporary racialized processes are temporally and spatially specific, and connect in complex ways with other categories of social difference. More specifically, much was written out of the overly simplistic black–white oppositional couplet, including issues of migration, nation-making, religious and cultural identities and generation. Furthermore, in assuming that blacks and whites were homogeneous collectivities, there was a tendency to concentrate on inter-racial differences to the exclusion of intra-ethnic differences, both within and between black and white social groups. Hence, racial/ethnic/national categories can be read as being shaped by and shaping the processes of colonization, of racism, of class hegemony, of male domination, of heterosexism and other forms of oppression. In short, we need to make the case for seeing changing forms of racialized social relations and ethnic identities as crucial points of intersection of different forms of social differentiation, subjectivity, and identity formation (Mac an Ghaill 1994b).

Qualitative studies provide evidence of a younger generation living in multicultural urban settings, who have moved beyond the era of post-war colonial migration to that of English-born ethnic minorities such as Birmingham Irish, Leicester Indians, Liverpool Chinese, London African Caribbeans and Newcastle Bangladeshis. This marks a shift from the old certainties of color as the primary signifier of social inequality to more complex processes of regionally and institutionally based inclusions and exclusions. However, at conceptual, political and policy levels, the ongoing narrative of the post-war immigration of Asians and African Caribbeans is still being told in an older language of race and empire that is not able to grasp the generational specificities of emerging inter-ethnic social relationships and their engagement with a different racial semantics. Within the context of global transformations, contemporary comparative research illustrates the complex emerging reconfigurations of national and ethnic identities (Popoviciu 2002). This chapter has argued that theory-led qualitative research is highly productive in helping us to develop a conceptual language to engage with issues of ethnic, national and religious difference and how we might contribute to the transformative nature of racism within the wider frameworks of social justice, civil rights, and citizenship. In turn, this needs to inform and be informed by political and policy interventions in specific institutional arenas that resonate with a wide range of constituencies and the way that we live with difference (Mercer and Julien 1988; Young 1993).

ACKNOWLEDGMENT

Thanks to the editors of the book for their comments on this chapter.

NOTES

1 The term "black" emerged in Britain in the 1970s as a political concept emphasizing the collective experience of white racism. In the literature the major focus of color racism has been African Caribbeans and Asians (from the Indian subcontinent: India, Pakistan and Bangladesh). Currently, in a school context the concept of black is often used to denote British-born children of African, African-Caribbean and Asian-born parents. For a critique of the terms black and Asian, see Mac an Ghaill (1999).

2 For example, in the literature the concept of racialization has been deployed in a number of ways. Banton (1977) used the concept to refer to the use of the idea of race to structure people's perceptions of different populations. Others, including Reeves (1983) and Troyna (1993) have used the notion as a key signifier of meanings in a range of discourses. Changing processes of racialization are operationalized through the impact of changing race imagery in diverse institutional settings as well as processes of deracialization (Husband 1982; Gillborn 1995).

3 Empiricists view the social world as an arrangement of social facts. The collection of these social facts, via objective methods, is seen to generate valid, reliable and "testable" theories. Empiricist approaches tend to operate in a positivistic manner so that a set of independent objective laws and formulae can be identified. Research in this tradition generally takes a quantitative form, associated with the collection of numerical data, as opposed to qualitative approaches, focusing upon the exploration of meanings.

4 For further information, see Williams et al. (1997) and Williams and Mac an Ghaill (1998), exploring respectively the economic needs of the Irish diaspora in England and older Irish men's health and social care needs. This included qualitative and quantitative methods with Irish men and women in the city of Birmingham in the mid-1990s.

5 See Crowley (2002) for a discussion of journalist Julie Burchill in *The Guardian*, who described the Irish flag as "the Hitler-licking, altar boy-molesting, abortion-banning tricolour." Her article was referred to the Crown Prosecution Service by John Twomey of the London Irish Centre, who claimed that her article contravenes Section 70 of the 1976 Race Relations Act. The complaint has been rejected by the CPS.

REFERENCES

Al-Azmeh, A. (1993) *Islams and Modernities.* London: Verso.

Alund, A. and Schierup, C. U. (1991) *Paradoxes of Multiculturalism: Essays on Swedish Society.* Aldershot: Avebury.

Anthias, F. and Yuval-Davis, N. (1993) *Racialised Boundaries: Race, Nation, Gender, Colour and Class and Anti-Racist Struggle.* London: Routledge.

Asad, T. (1993) *Genealogies of Religion: Discipline and Reasons of Power and Islam.* Baltimore, MD: Johns Hopkins University Press.

Back, L. (1996) *New Ethnicities and Urban Culture: Racisms and Multiculture in Young Lives.* London: UCL Press.

Balibar, E. and Wallerstein, I. (1991) *Race, Nation and Class: Ambiguous Identities.* London: Verso.

Banton, M. (1977) *The Idea of Race.* London: Tavistock.

Barker, M. (1981) *The New Racism.* London: Junction Books.

Beck, U. (1992) *Risk Society: Towards a New Modernity.* London: Sage.

Bhabha, H. (1994) *Nation and Narration.* London: Routledge.

Bielenberg, A. (ed.) (2000) *The Irish Diaspora.* London: Longman.

Bonnett, A. (1993) *Radicalism, Anti-Racism and Representation.* London: Routledge.

Bradley, H. (1996) *Fractured Identities: Changing Patterns of Inequality.* Cambridge: Polity Press.

Brah, A. (1996) *Cartographies of Diaspora: Contesting Identities.* London: Routledge.

Brah, A., Hickman, M. J. and Mac an Ghaill, M. (1999a) *Global Futures: Migration, Environment and Globalization.* London: Macmillan.

—— (1999b) *Thinking Identities: Ethnicity, Racism and Culture.* London: Macmillan.

Campaign Against Racism and Fascism (1991) "Comment," *CARF* 4: 2.

Castles, S. and Kosack, G. (1973) *Immigrant Workers and the Class Structure.* London: Oxford University Press/Institute of Race Relations.

Castles, S. and Miller, M. J. (1993) *The Age of Migration: International Population Movements in the Modern World.* London: Macmillan.

CCCS (1982) *The Empire Strikes Back: Race and Racism in 70s Britain.* London: Hutchinson.

Cohen, P. (1992) "'It's racism what dunnit': Hidden narratives in theories of racism," in Donald, J. and Rattansi, A. (eds.), *"Race", Culture and Difference.* London: Sage/Open University.

—— (1993) *Home Rules: Some Reflections on Racism and Nationalism in Everyday Life.* London: University of East London.

Conner, T. (1985) *Irish Youth in London Research Report.* London: Action Group for Irish Youth.

Crowley, J. (2002) "Burchill case is referred to CPS," *Irish Post* August 3, p. 4.

Curtis, L. P. (1968) *Anglo-Saxons and Celts.* Bridgeport, CT: University of Bridgeport.

Curtis, L. (1984) *Nothing but the Same Old Story*. London: Information on Ireland Press.

Davies, B. and Harre, R. (1990) "Positioning: the discursive production of selves," *Journal for the Theory of Social Behaviour* 20 (1): 43–64.

Derrida, J. (1978) *Writing and Difference*. Chicago: University of Chicago Press.

Dummett, A. and Nicol, A. (1990) *Subjects, Citizens, Aliens and Others*. London: Weidenfeld and Nicolson.

Fanon, F. (1970) *Black Skins, White Masks*. London: Paladin.

Feminist Review (1995) "Editorial: The Irish issue, the British question," 50: 1–4.

Ford, G. (1992) *Fascist Europe: The Rise of Racism and Xenophobia*. London: Pluto Press.

Giddens, A. (1991) *Modernity and Self-identity: Self and Society in Late Modern Age*. Cambridge: Polity Press.

Gillborn, D. (1990) *"Race", Ethnicity and Education: Teaching and Learning in Multiethnic Schools*. London: Unwin Hyman.

—— (1995) *Racism and Antiracism in Real Schools: Theory, Policy and Practice*. Buckingham: Open University Press.

Gilroy, P. (1993) *The Black Atlantic: Modernity and Double Consciousness*. London: Verso.

Goldberg, D. T. (1993) *Racist Culture*. Oxford: Blackwell.

Gray, B. (2000) "From 'ethnicity' to 'diaspora': 1980s emigration and 'multicultural' London," in Bielenberg, A. (ed.), *The Irish Diaspora*. London: Longman.

Greenslade, L. (1992) "White skin, white masks: psychological distress among the Irish in Britain," in O'Sullivan, P. (ed.), *The Irish in the New Communities*, vol. 2. Leicester: Leicester University Press.

Gribben, P. (1994) "A community haemorrhage: Number of Irish people working in Britain dropped by nearly 100,000," *Irish Post* June 16, p. 1.

Guillaumin, C. (1988) "Race and nature: The system of marks," *Feminist Studies* 8 (2): 25–44.

Hall, S. (1992) "The question of cultural identity," in Hall, S., Held, D. and McGrew, T. (eds.), *Modernity and its Futures*. London: Polity/Open University.

Hargreaves, A. G. (1995) *Immigration, 'Race' and Ethnicity in Contemporary France*. London: Routledge.

Hawes, D. and Parez, B. (1995) *The Gypsy and the State: The Ethnic Cleansing of British Society*. Bristol: Bristol University, School for Advanced Urban Studies.

Haywood, C. and Mac an Ghaill, M. (2002) *Men and Masculinities: Theory, Research and Social Practice*. Buckingham: Open University Press.

Hazelkorn, E. (1990) *Irish Immigrants Today: A Socio-Economic Profile of Contemporary Irish Immigrants in the UK* (Irish Studies Centre Occasional Paper Series, No. 1). London: Polytechnic of North London Press.

Hewitt, R. (1986) *White Talk, Black Talk: Inter-Racial Friendship and Communication amongst Adolescents*. Cambridge: Cambridge University Press.

Hickman, M. J. (1995) *Religion, Class and Identity: The State, the Catholic Church and the Education of the Irish in Britain*. Dartmouth: Avebury.

Hickman, M. J. and Walter, B. (1995) "Deconstructing whiteness: Irish women in Britain," *Feminist Review* 50: 5–19.

—— (1997) *Discrimination and the Irish Community in Britain.* London: Commission for Racial Equality.

Holmes, C. (1988) *John Bull's Island: Immigration and British Policy, 1871–1971.* London: Macmillan.

Hoogvelt, A. (1997) *Globalisation and the Postcolonial World: The New Political Economy of Development.* London: Macmillan.

Hooper, J. (1997) "Italy 'death trap' for immigrants," *The Guardian* June 13, p. 16.

Husband, C. (ed.) (1982) *'Race' in Britain: Community and Change.* London: Hutchinson.

Ignatiev, N. (1995) *How the Irish Became White.* New York: Routledge.

Jackson, J. A. (1963) *The Irish in Britain.* London: Routledge and Kegan Paul.

Jones, S. (1988) *Black Youth, White Culture: The Reggae Tradition from JA to UK.* London: Macmillan.

Kearney, R. (ed.) (1990) *Migrations: The Irish at Home and Abroad.* Dublin: Wolfhound.

Kearney, R. (1997) *Postnationalist Ireland: Politics, Culture and Philosophy.* London: Routledge.

Kiberd, D. (1996) *Inventing Ireland: The Literature of the Modern Nation.* London: Vintage.

Kinealy, C. (1999) *A Disunited Kingdom? England, Ireland, Scotland and Wales.* Cambridge: Cambridge University Press.

Knowles, C. and Mercer, S. (1992) "Feminism and anti-racism: an exploration of the political possibilities," in Donald, J. and Rattensi, A. (eds.), *Race, Culture and Difference.* London: Sage/Open University.

Kowarzik, U. (1997) *Irish Community Services: Meeting Diverse Needs.* London: Action Group for Irish Youth/Federation of Irish Societies.

Lather, P. (1991) *Getting Smart: Feminist Research and Pedagogy with/in the Postmodern.* New York: Routledge.

Lebow, N. (1976) *White Britain and Black Ireland: The Influence of Stereotypes on Colonial Policy.* Philadelphia, PA: Institute for the Study of Human Issues.

Lennon, M., McAdam, M. and O'Brien, J. (1988) *Across the Water.* London: Virago.

Mac an Ghaill, M. (1988) *Young, Gifted and Black: Student-Teacher Relations in the Schooling of Black Youth.* Milton Keynes: Open University Press.

—— (1994a) *The Making of Men: Masculinities, Sexualities and Schooling.* Buckingham: Open University Press.

—— (1994b) "(In)visiblity: sexuality, masculinity and 'race' in the school context," in Epstein, D. (ed.), *Challenging Lesbian and Gay Inequalities in Education.* Buckingham: Open University Press.

—— (1996) "Irish masculinities and sexualities in England," in Adkins, L. and Merchant, L. (eds.), *Sexualizing the Social: Power and the Organization of Sexuality.* London: Macmillan.

—— (1999) *Contemporary Racisms and Ethnicities: Social and Cultural Transformations.* Buckingham: Open University Press.

—— (2000) "What about the lads? Emigrants, immigrants, ethnics and transnationals in late 1990s diaspora," in Lentin, R. (ed.), *Emerging Irish Identities.* Dublin: National Consultative Committee on Racism and Interculturalism.

Mac Laughlin, J. (1994) *Ireland: The Immigrant Nursery and the World Economy.* Cork: Cork University Press.

Mama, A. (1995) *Beyond the Masks: Race, Gender and Subjectivity.* London: Routledge.

Marcus, G. and Fischer, M. (1986) *Anthropology as Cultural Critique: An Experimental Moment in the Human Sciences.* Chicago: University of Chicago Press.

Mason, D. (1995) *Race and Ethnicity in Modern Britain.* Oxford: Oxford University Press.

Mercer, K. and Julien, I. (1988) "Race, sexual politics and black masculinity: a dossier," in Chapman, R. and Rutherford, J. (eds.), *Male Order: Unwrapping Masculinities.* London: Lawrence and Wishart.

Miles, R. (1982) *Racism and Labour Migration.* London: Routledge and Kegan Paul.

—— (1993) *Racism after Race Relations.* London: Routledge.

Mirza, H. S. (1992) *Young, Female and Black.* London: Routledge.

Modood, T. (1989) "Religious anger and minority rights," *Political Quarterly* July: 280–4.

O'Sullivan, P. (ed.) (1992) *The Irish in New Communities.* Leicester: Leicester University Press.

O'Toole, F. (1997) *The Ex-Isle of Erin: Images of Global Ireland.* Dublin: New Island Books.

Pajackowska, C. and Young, L. (1992) "Racism, representation and psychoanalysis," in Donald, J. and Rattansi, A. (eds.), *"Race", Culture and Difference.* London: Sage/Open University.

Parker, A., Russo, M., Sommer, D. and Yaeger, P. (1992) *Nationalisms and Sexualities.* London: Routledge.

Patterson, S. (1963) *Dark Strangers.* London: Tavistock.

Popoviciu, L. (2002) "National identity formation: Secondary education systems in Romania and England," unpublished PhD thesis, University of Newcastle upon Tyne.

Popoviciu, L. and Mac an Ghaill, M. (forthcoming) "Local knowledges of nation-making: Education, citizenship and nation making," in Popoviciu, L. and Mac an Ghaill, M. (eds.), *Race, Ethnicity and Education.*

Ramazanoglu, C. (1992) "On feminist methodology: Male reason versus female empowerment," *Sociology* 26: 207–12.

Rattansi, A. and Westwood, S. (1994) "Modern racisms, racialised identities," in Rattansi, A. and Westwood, S. (eds.), *Racism, Modernity and Identity: On the Western Front.* London: Polity Press.

Reeves, F. (1983) *British Racial Discourse: A Study of British Political Discourse about Race and Race-related Matters.* Cambridge: Cambridge University Press.

Renan, E. (1990) "What is nation?" in Bhabha, H. (ed.), *Nation and Narration*. London: Routledge.

Rex, J. (1970) *Race Relations in Sociological Theory*. London: Routledge and Kegan Paul.

Rex, J. and Moore, R. (1967) *Colonial Immigrants in a British City*. London: Routledge and Kegan Paul.

Roedrigger, D. R. (1991) *The Wages of Whiteness*. London: Verso.

Runnymede Trust (1993) *The Runnymede Bulletin* 257 (July/August). London: Runnymede Trust.

Rutherford, J. (1990) "A place called home: Identity and the cultural politics of difference," in Rutherford, J. (ed.), *Identity: Community, Culture and Difference*. London: Lawrence and Wishart.

Said, E. W. (1993) *Culture and Imperialism*. London: Vintage.

Savage, M. (2000) *Class Analysis and Social Transformation*. Buckingham: Open University Press.

Silverman, M. (1992) *Deconstructing the Nation: Immigration, Racism and Citizenship in Modern France*. London: Routledge.

Sivanandan, A. (1989) "New circuits of imperialism," *Race and Class* 30 (4): 1–19.

Smith, D. (1987) *The Everyday World as Problematic: A Feminist Sociology*. Milton Keynes: Open University Press.

Solomos, J. (1993) *Race and Racism in Britain*. Basingstoke: Macmillan.

Spivak, G. (1988) *In Other Worlds: Essays in Cultural Politics*. New York: Routledge.

Troyna, B. (1993) *Racism and Education: Research Perspectives*. Buckingham: Open University Press.

Tyler, A. (1991) "A post-modern in-stance," in Nencel, L. and Pels, P. (eds.), *Constructing Knowledge: Authority and Critique in Social Science*. London: Sage.

Walter, B. (1998) "Challenging the black/white binary: The need for an Irish category in the 2001 census," *Patterns of Prejudice* 32 (2): 73–86.

—— (2001) *Outsiders Inside: Whiteness, Place and Irish Women*. London: Routledge.

Webber, F. (1991) "From ethnocentricism to Euro-racism," *Race and Class* 32 (3): 11–17.

Wievioka, M. (1991) *L'Espace du racisme*. Paris: Seuil.

—— (1995) *The Arena of Racism*. London: Sage.

Willems, H. (1995) "Right-wing extremism, racism or youth violence? Explaining violence against foreigners in Germany," *New Community* 21 (4): 501–23.

Williams, I., Dunne, M. and Mac an Ghaill, M. (1997) *Economic Needs of the Irish Community in Birmingham*. Birmingham: Birmingham City Council.

Williams, I. and Mac an Ghaill, M. (1998) *Older Irish Men: An Investigation of Health and Social Care Needs*. Birmingham: DION.

Young, I. M. (1990) *Justice and the Politics of Difference*. Princeton, NJ: Princeton University Press.

—— (1993) "Together in difference: Transforming the logic of group political difference," in Squires, J. (ed.), *Principled Positions: Postmodernism and the Rediscovery of Value*. London: Lawrence and Wishart.

FURTHER READING

Bielenberg, A. (ed.) (2000) *The Irish Diaspora*. London: Longman.

Grant, C. A. (ed.) (1999) *Multicultural Research: A Reflective Engagement with Race, Class, Gender and Sexual Orientation*. London: Falmer Press.

Mac an Ghaill, M. (1999) *Contemporary Racisms and Ethnicities: Social and Cultural Transformations*. Buckingham: Open University Press.

CHAPTER FIVE

Working Poor, Working Hard: Trajectories at the Bottom of the American Labor Market

KATHERINE NEWMAN AND CHAUNCY LENNON

INTRODUCTION

The first thing a student typically learns in a course on stratification in the United States is that Americans generally do not talk about class at all. A fundamental concept almost everywhere else in the developed world, it is an idea whose time has never come in the US.[1] Why is class absent from the American lexicon? One explanation points to the tendency of Americans to see the United States as a society so mobile (especially in an upward direction) that neither birthright nor current occupation constitute a barrier. This wisdom holds that if one works hard, anything is possible. Another explanation has to do with the way in which many Americans, rich, poor, and in between, see themselves as part of the vast cultural "middle class." From this perspective, only those on the extreme ends of the income and wealth distribution reject the values that are the ticket to membership of the American middle class.

While most Americans do not see themselves in class terms, there has nonetheless been a considerable scholarly attention paid to class stratification in the United States. Much of this work has been quantitative, focusing on the issues of industrial organization and occupational structure; of social and economic status, mobility, and segregation; and of wealth, poverty, and income inequality. Ethnographers and other qualitative researchers have weighed in as well. The ethnographic studies of class in the United States can be characterized in terms of location – communities, workplaces, or schools – and vantage point – looking at the class tensions within these settings or at the way these settings are shaped by the larger framework of class relations. Perhaps the best known ethnography of community life in

America, the Lynds' classic *Middletown*, examined the dynamics of the business and working classes within a typical 1920s American city, Muncie, Indiana. Taking a similar approach to a very different locale, Ulf Hannerz's *Soulside* detailed class tensions within the segregated African-American community of late 1960s' Harlem. In contrast, Gans's classic study of suburbia, the *Levittowners*, looked at the creation of a new community by a group of middle-class families.

The classic ethnographies of work in the United States, such as Chinoy's 1955 *Automobile Workers and the American Dream*, Burawoy's 1979 *Manufacturing Consent* and Halle's 1984 *America's Working Man*, tend to focus on the ways that class shapes the experience of the workplace. Likewise, the ethnography of education typically approaches the issue of class by looking at the way class relations structure the experience of schooling. McLeod's 1987 *Ain't No Makin' It* provides an interesting elaboration on this approach by contrasting the experiences of working-class white and African-American high school students.

Collectively, the quantitative and qualitative literature on class in the United States elaborates the ways in which class dynamics both structure access to opportunity in American society and inform the experience of daily life. However, these insights rarely travel very far outside academic settings. Other than the occasional claim of some conservatives that progressive taxation is a form of "class warfare," the language of class is rarely heard in debates about governmental priorities. On the campaign trail or in the halls of Congress, the only real conversation about class that takes place has to do with the poor. For most of the past two decades, the focus of this discussion has been on the ways in which the work-related values of the poor are believed to deviate from the mainstream and, in turn, the ways in which welfare policies exacerbate this putative divergence.

WORKING AT THE BOTTOM

Nearly 12 percent of Americans were living in poverty at the tail end of the twentieth century (Beers 2001). Most of these 32 million people are children or adults who were not in the formal labor force, defined by the Census as neither working nor looking for work in the past year. However, some 6.8 million people – 1 in 5 Americans in poverty – meet the Census definition of the "working poor" – adults who spent at least half the year working or looking for work but did not earn enough to make it out of poverty. Though many of these workers have part-time jobs, the majority, 64 percent, are full-time employees and more than half worked for at least 50 weeks. Low-wage jobs that do not pull these workers over the poverty line are the root of the problem.

The experience of the working poor has received comparatively little attention (Levitan and Shapiro 1987; Swartz and Weigart 1995). The bulk of social science research on poverty, quantitative and qualitative, has focused on the public assistance system and its recipients (Heclo 1994; O'Connor 2000). Until recently, a major component of the welfare system in the United States was a national program, Aid to Families with Dependent Children (AFDC), providing means-tested income support to poor families. In 1996 AFDC was abolished and replaced by a state-operated program, Temporary Assistance to Needy Families (TANF), which both required most recipients to work for benefits and placed life-time limits of five years on support. Only in the wake of these reforms, which have pushed many off the dole and into the low-wage labor market, has the problem of working poverty taken its place on the research and policy agenda.

We refer to the working poor to emphasize the central role that low-wage jobs and structural barriers to mobility in the labor market play in the lives of the poor, not to divide the poor into the false dichotomy of workers and welfare recipients. Despite popular, political, and academic obsession with the putative problem of "welfare dependence" feeding on and off an "anti-work culture," welfare recipients have always been part of the working poor and low-wage workers have long relied on family members who receive public aid (O'Connor 2000). Most welfare recipients use public support as a temporary response to unexpected events such as losing a job (Bane and Ellwood 1994). Even when they are on the dole, few welfare recipients can get by on their benefits alone. Many make up the shortfall by working off the books or in the informal economy (Edin and Lein 1997). Another group of recipients, particularly welfare mothers and grandmothers, serve as child care providers so other members of the household, sons and daughters, siblings and cousins, can go to work to support the family budget (Newman 1999). In the new era of TANF, most welfare recipients must work for benefits, performing a variety of municipal services such as cleaning parks or providing clerical assistance in government offices.

Of course, welfare reform did more than require that recipients must work for benefits; it also cut hundreds of thousands from the rolls. Nearly all of these former welfare recipients find themselves in the low-wage labor force. While they may be a little better off in terms of income than they were on the dole, most are still struggling to get by with jobs that do not pay enough to make ends meet, that do not offer benefits, and that don't hold much promise for the future (Danziger et al. 2001).

Indeed, their standard of living may be lower because of additional costs of child care, transportation, and other work-related expenses.

Social scientists and others interested in social inequality in the United States have little to gain from asking the question "How are the working poor different from the welfare poor?" But if we want to understand the experience of the poor in the wake of welfare reform, attention will need to be paid to the increasing importance of labor markets and the decreasing role of government support in the lives of low-wage workers. In this chapter we discuss the role that qualitative research can play in the study of low-wage work. We then present some of the findings of our current research, and we conclude with a discussion of new directions in research on the lives of the working poor.

THEORY, RESEARCH, AND THE WORKING POOR

In the post-welfare reform era, one of the most important questions to be studied is the transition from a system of state support for the poor (however inadequate) to a system in which the labor market is the primary source of financial support for the poor. Most studies that take on this question will rely on large data sets, capable of tracking low-wage workers and TANF recipients over the long term. Although the best of these will undoubtedly link outcomes experienced in the labor market to the family circumstances with which the working poor must simultaneously contend, the focus of most large-scale research will be limited to employment. Employment is where the interests of most state governments lie because if the working poor lose their jobs in the current economic downtown, local authorities will be faced with a crisis.

Large-scale surveys will provide the best purchase on these questions if we are satisfied with extensive, but relatively superficial, answers. Indeed, results from surveys can reach across the particularities of millions of poor individuals and their families while showing us the patterns. Resource questions facing the states – where best to spend funds to meet the needs of the working poor – must necessarily flow from these survey studies.

There are two reasons not to stop there, however. First, at the most pragmatic level, numbers alone will not do the trick in the public debate on how much support is due to the working poor. Neither politicians nor the general public can interpret logistic regressions. They are not moved or influenced by chi squares. All too often, the findings of survey research are inconclusive or contradictory; like many a nutritional study (eat butter, don't eat butter), they end up exhausting the patience of their intended audience. This is not to suggest that they be abandoned, for that would be foolish. It is to suggest that if the social science community wants to weigh in with its assessment of how to help the working poor, it should couple survey research, especially panel studies, with qualitative research that is meaningful to a broader audience (Newman 2002).

It is the rare survey that can tell us *why* the documented patterns exist. For example, quantitative research will show us the negative outcomes from growing up in a poor family. But this pattern begs many qualitative questions: What are the social processes that push children out of school, and how are they connected to the stresses their parents face as a consequence of work below the poverty line? (Chin and Newman 2002). What is it about work that makes children in families better or worse off than those from more advantaged families? (A more honored identity? Hopeful future? Income? Or time poverty?) How do families think about child care? What governs their choices? What choices do they really have? How stable are their alternatives? If child care arrangements fall through, how effectively can they scramble to patch together an alternative? What is the relationship, if any, between the moral messages the government conveys through policy changes such as welfare reform and the messages that are received, internalized, and acted on? Such questions demand more context, texture, and nuance to answer. They go to the heart of *why* we see the patterns that surveys reveal.

This is what qualitative research does best. It attempts to dig deeply into the daily lives of those whom government policy seeks to help to examine the structural and cultural issues that define the life chances of the working poor, including: the set of resources families draw on in adapting to economic shocks; the internal dynamics of a family as they deal with the demands and protections afforded by their wider kinship and friendship networks; the internal consistency in normative expectations that govern the roles of parents, partners, and fictive kin; and the patterned variations between race, ethnic, and class cultures in the subjective experience of poverty, exclusion, and economic self-sufficiency. This barely scrapes the surface of the contextual and cultural domains that inform the study of working poverty.

Such an intensive inquiry almost always precludes the kind of extensive coverage and attention to representativeness that are the hallmark of survey research. Hence, questions are routinely, and appropriately, raised about how qualitative findings based on studies with a small number of informants can be generalized to a larger population. We may learn a great deal from Elliot Liebow's classic qualitative study,

Tally's Corner, about the culture of poor black men, but how many corners are there like Tally's? Do street corner denizens in cities in the 2000s have the same beliefs and behaviors as those Liebow observed in Washington, DC, in the 1960s? If not, what produces the differences? Qualitative research rarely addresses these questions. For policy-makers, however, these are issues that cannot be sidestepped.

How can one best use the rich insights that qualitative research provides while taking the need for generalization seriously? In recent years, we have seen the emergence of a blended methodology that embeds qualitative "samples" in survey research designs. Intensive interviews, participant observation, discursive diaries, household studies, and ethnographies of neighborhoods are all built within a sampling framework generated by a larger survey project. *The Project on Human Development in Chicago Neighborhoods* is probably the richest study of this kind. The unique design of this interdisciplinary project provides new focus on the question of how communities influence individual development, particularly as this question relates to the causes and processes of juvenile delinquency, crime, substance abuse, and violence. The project combines intensive qualitative and quantitative research on the social, economic, political, and cultural dynamics of Chicago's neighborhoods with longitudinal studies of 7,000 randomly selected children, adolescents, and young adults.

This is not the only large-scale project blending qualitative and quantitative research. The evaluation of the New Hope Project, an anti-poverty program directed at the working poor in Milwaukee, Wisconsin, carried out by the Manpower Demonstration Research Corporation (MDRC) is another example. In this random assignment study, extensive administrative data on benefits and services and survey data on the lifestyles and well-being of program and control group members is complemented by qualitative research. To develop a more in-depth understanding of the impact of the program on the children of participants, there was also an ethnographic study of a group of families who participated in the study. A third example of the "blended-methodology" approach is *Welfare, Children, and Families: A Three City Study*. Conducted in Boston, Chicago, and San Antonio, this project evaluates the effects of welfare reform on the well-being of children and families. The design of this study includes not just comparative longitudinal surveys but also comparative ethnographic studies that capture the various ways in which changes in welfare policy influence neighborhood resources and impact the day-to-day experiences of working poor families. This multi-method research design is clearly what will be needed for qualitative work to count in the arenas where we most want it to be heard.

In endorsing this approach, however, we think it is important not to lose sight of the special contribution qualitative research can make. Qualitative work is not simply about generating hypotheses. It does not exist only to illustrate quantitative findings. It can be useful for both of these purposes, but it has the potential to make more influential contributions than that.

Qualitative research illuminates underlying questions that are often hard to access through other means: How households work in consort; how the interests of individuals within them may be subordinated (and possibly damaged) by the needs of collectivity; how the shifting prospects of one person (e.g. a welfare recipient) are shaped by those of others in his or her network. These questions must be understood through "extensive" field studies, projects big enough to consider: differences by race and ethnicity; differences between states that are generous and those that are less generous; differences between families living in tight labor market areas and those in places with high unemployment; differences between families with transnational ties and obligations and those that have severed them; and differences between families with multigenerational ties (especially those that are nearby) and those that have become more "nuclear" (and geographically separated).

CAREER TRAJECTORIES OF THE WORKING POOR

Among the "front burner" questions for poverty research in the post-welfare age, few are more important than the career trajectories of workers who start out in low-wage jobs (Pavetti and Acs 1997). Whether we are talking about the working poor who were firmly lodged in the labor market when welfare reform descended; those who move off the rolls of their own accord and into poorly paid jobs; or those who reach their time limits and are pushed into the marketplace, the question of who among them "gets stuck" and who "moves up" from the bottom of the occupational structure is critical. If welfare reform merely succeeds in exchanging one kind of poverty for another, a better life may elude millions of poor families. If, on the other hand, movement into the labor market is the first step on the way to a future of significantly higher earnings, we may witness significant, durable improvement in the poverty picture.

For many former welfare recipients and low-wage workers, the less appetizing of these outcomes is the most likely (Burtless 1995, 1997). They will spend years in working poverty, even if they are employed year-round and full-time (which is less likely at this end of the labor market, where part-time and part-year work are more plentiful) (Blank, 1998). For others, however, job experience, even at the low end, will permit the accumulation of experience, skills, references, enhanced social networks, and education that position workers to move up into something better (Gladden and Taber 1999).

What makes the difference? Which factors help to push a low-wage worker above the poverty line over the long haul? According to the sparse literature, the prospects for occupational mobility and earnings growth over time for low-skilled workers seem rather dim. Arguments persist over the causes of this pattern. Some of them include: low human capital and declining demand for low-skilled workers; high worker turnover and inconsistent work experience; the part-time, no-benefit nature of low-wage jobs; and low returns for work experience. But there is a reasonable consensus that whatever the causes, workers at the bottom of the occupational structure who lack education are, for the most part, destined to remain there. It should be noted that most of these studies draw upon data collected during periods of higher unemployment than we see at the moment. The most comprehensive studies we have now tend to cut off the longitudinal portrait around 1993, when labor market conditions were noticeably weaker than they were in the 1998–2000 period.

To examine the question of the career trajectories of low-wage workers and job-seekers, Newman (1999) took a random sample from among the workers and the unsuccessful applicants of four Harlem fast food restaurants in 1993–4. These jobs certainly qualify as "bad" jobs; they are typically low-wage, part-time positions, which offer no health benefits, retirement contributions, or sick leave (or sick pay). The research discussed here began with this question in the context of a larger study of the working poor in one industry (fast food) in one big city ghetto: Harlem, New York (Newman 1999). As originally conceived, the project was not longitudinal and did not focus on the question of the long-term careers of these workers. Instead, it focused on one period of time (1993–5), examining the work and family lives of 200 workers – the entire universe of workers in four Harlem "Burger Barn" restaurants – and 93 job seekers who had been turned away from the same establishments. Having observed these workers, at varying levels of intensity, over 18 months, many questions about their long-term futures remained. Most had made efforts to find better jobs but few had succeeded. Among those who had experienced upward mobility, two patterns became evident from this rather thin database. One small group of people had been elevated off the entry level of the shop floor and had been promoted into management. They were long-time workers who attracted the positive attention of management which, in turn, was in an expansionist mode. As the owners opened new restaurants, they created vacancies for entry-level management and chose to recruit from the shop floor to fill them.

Another, equally small, group had found their way to jobs that made use of skills they used their low-wage earnings to acquire. For example, a young Haitian immigrant had used his salary to pay for a certification course in air conditioning and refrigeration. After three years of working at Burger Barn to pay for this training, he finished and within three months had found a job in his new field for $12/hour, nearly three times his Burger Barn wage. His entry into the higher-skill end of the service sector was made possible by the willingness of his aunt and uncle to let him live with them without charge, which freed his earnings to pay for trade school.

These two patterns were the only forms of occupational mobility visible in 18 months and they were exemplified by only a handful of people. However, 18 months is far too short a time to reach any meaningful conclusions. For a sizeable proportion of these inner-city workers and job seekers, the future was a long way off (and potentially more promising than their original circumstances might have suggested) because they were still in high school or community college. Hence, four years after the first intake survey, we set out to find out what happened to a random sample of both employed and rejected applicants from this cluster of central Harlem fast food restaurants (Newman 2000). Here we present a preliminary answer to this question along the following lines: brief statistical comparisons for the whole sample at Time 1 (1993–4) and Time 2 (1997–8) in terms of their employment experience and occupational mobility, and a discussion of the changes over time in perceptions of employment opportunities and expectations for the future.

BEFORE AND AFTER

The "bad jobs" our respondents had in 1993 were located in the middle of one of New York's poorest ghettos, where unemployment was over 18 percent, public assistance was a mainstay in nearly 30 percent of the households, and the poverty rate exceeded 40 percent. By 1997, when the first follow-up study was conducted, unemployment in Manhattan was running at 7.8 percent (still well above the national average) while Central Harlem unemployment was approximately 17.5 percent. If ever

Table 5.1   *Hires vs. rejects at T1 and T2*

	Hires at T1	*Rejects at T1*
Employed at T2	82%	53%
Mean numbers of workers in household at T2	1.79	1.28
Mean number of AFDC recipients in household at T2	0.32	0.72
Living independent of natal family at T2	68% (46% at T1)	45% (23% at T1)
Educational attainment at T2	82% completed GED (46% at T1) 27% have some college (7% at T1) 23% job training/voc-ed (0% at T1)	67% completed GED (33% at T1) 32% have some college (13% at T1) 4% job training/ voc-ed (0% at T1)

there was a challenging place from whence to launch a career for a low-wage worker, this is arguably it.

Yet the dire predictions drawn from the literature turned out to be, for many people, completely out of line with experience. In a broad sense, both the "hires" and the "rejects" were doing substantially better in 1997 (T2) than they were at the first point of contact in 1993 (T1). As Table 5.1 indicates, both had acquired more education; a majority of the rejected applicants were working; and in both groups there has been a substantial movement toward independent living. However, the rates of change differ, indicating that the hires and rejects were not simply the same people caught at different moments in their employment history; instead, they were qualitatively different to begin with. There is also clearly a difference between the hires and the rejects in terms of who was working in 1997. Regardless of gender or race, those who were employed at the beginning of the study were far more likely to be working at the follow-up point.

The original aim of the follow-up study was to understand the prospects of "graduation" from the low-wage labor market. Most of the respondents who were hires at T1 were low-wage earners in "bad" jobs. Some had been in the job for a long period of time, while others were relative newcomers, but the jobs that formed the catchment for the study were all fairly close to the minimum wage (in 1993 the minimum

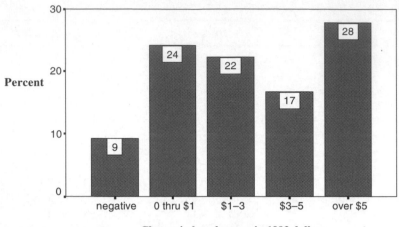

Figure 5.1   *Wage change among the employed*

wage was $4.25). Hence in 1993–4 the median wage of all those who were working was $4.37 per hour (1993 dollars). Four years later, the median wage of those people who were working had increased substantially to $7.24 per hour (1993 dollars). This trajectory reflects improvement in the labor market in the 1990s, the increase in 1996 of the minimum wage to $4.75, the benefits of steady work experience, and human capital improvements among our subjects. Despite these gains in workers' median wages, the trajectory of the low-wage labor force in this inner city labor market is still high on unemployment compared to the national average.

Figure 5.1 shows that many of the people in this study have done well over the four years between the first and second interviews, though there are pockets of stagnation and wage loss. Overall, 9 percent of these workers are worse off and 46 percent have remained close to their prior real wages. Yet 45 percent have clearly moved up, earning higher wages.

What kinds of jobs do the high earners have now? The modal job category among those earning more than $10 per hour was a store manager at Burger Barn, reflecting the importance of internal promotion for low-wage workers in this industry. Twenty percent of the high earners are now managers in the firm where we originally found them (though not necessarily in the same establishment). The fast food business is known for its practice of recruiting management from the shop floor (Newman 1999). Moreover, inner-city communities are still considered growth areas for this industry, which has largely saturated more affluent communities and now turns both to poor neighborhoods and overseas locations for its growth. This finding suggests that bad jobs are not all created equal. Low-wage jobs in growth industries may offer a more positive trajectory for entry-level workers. Growth industries that sport internal job ladders leading from the bottom to middle management are even more desirable. It is not clear that these success stories would have enjoyed this good fortune if these conditions had not existed.

Promotions within the fast food industry were not the only avenue to success. Most of the high earners are now working in jobs that are medium- to low-skilled positions. Those that are not in the managerial ranks of the industry are now found in unionized positions elsewhere. Hospital attendants, mail carriers, janitors, payroll clerks for the city, and unionized porters in an apartment building are all represented among the success stories. Collective bargaining appears to be a critical part of the picture. A porter who handles garbage collection in an apartment building and keeps the boiler running may well be deemed more skilled than someone who runs a french fry station, but this skill differential is probably not enough to account for a wage difference of nearly $8 per hour.

While it is true that only a minority of the participants in this study have truly broken free of low-wage jobs, they are a sizeable minority. Another sizeable group has moved into middle-earning positions which, though not spectacularly better than where we first found them, are no longer at the minimum wage. Many of the sample have acquired more education, but take longer to reach the zenith of their human capital on this score than is typically the case among more middle-class populations.

The group that is unemployed or still locked into low-wage jobs is in the most trouble. They are not trivial in size, but the proportion is smaller than one might have expected given that the study was situated in the middle of a very poor ghetto community. Now well over 25 years old, most of this group is unlikely to acquire much more education. While no one in this study had been out of the labor force for their entire adult lives, this particular group has had a more sporadic job history, with more unemployment spells for a longer duration, than any of the others. They are more likely to be living with people on welfare or to be on TANF themselves, and have fewer network contacts with steady jobs. This is the group that looks most like the problem cases Pavetti (1997) and others foresee developing among long-term welfare recipients who are facing time limits.

However, for the working poor who have been in the labor market fairly consistently (even at a low wage level), the prospects for mobility are better than we would have expected. This is testimony to the benefits of tighter labor markets. And for most of these workers, the high flyers and low riders alike, expectations remain positive and a sense of personal responsibility for their fate strong, even in the face of recognized inequalities along the lines of race and gender.

CULTURAL PERSPECTIVES

It is not enough to chart the different trajectories of the working poor through the post-welfare reform labor market. If we want to understand the positive and negative ways in which labor markets structure the lives of the working poor, we also need to look at the cultural context of labor market dynamics. Some observers look at the mobility of the working poor and, in particular, at the labor market experiences of former welfare recipients and proclaim a transformation in the "culture of welfare" into a "culture of employment." Our research tells a very different story.

The respondents in this study were either low-wage workers or job seekers looking for entry-level, minimum wage jobs when they were first interviewed in 1993. Since then some have seen a fair amount of good fortune, others have tread water, and still others have bumped along the bottom of the occupational structure with a fair amount of unemployment. What difference, if any, have these divergent experiences made in the way they look at the world? Labor markets have tightened, not as much in Harlem as elsewhere, but even in Harlem the lines of job seekers are somewhat shorter than they were in 1993. Welfare reform has become the law of the land, a change that has had an impact on members of their families, neighbors and friends. Have the changes in the economic/policy landscape, coupled with the changes that have occurred in these individual lives, made a difference in their understanding of the opportunity structure and of future prospects?

Open-ended interviews conducted during the first wave and the four-year follow up suggest considerable stability in respondents' understandings of the economic universe within which they live and the role of personal responsibility in determining the outcomes they have experienced thus far. In 1997 the respondents in our sample were older and had been in the labor market for quite a few years. They have come to realize that it is much harder to find a high-paying job than they thought it would be when we first interviewed them in 1993, particularly the younger respondents. For example, respondents who were in high school when we last interviewed them believed that after graduating from high school or acquiring their high school graduate equivalency degree (GED), they would automatically find a well-paid job that would enable them to support themselves and live on their own. Many have come to the unexpected revelation that these diplomas are not enough to secure a high-paying, office job. Nonetheless, most believe that continued effort is required and that whatever the future may hold, it is largely theirs to either make or break.

Who makes it?

Some people say that anyone who wants to make it in this city or in America can do it. All they have to do is try or work hard. Other people take the opposite point of view and say that they have many obstacles against them from the beginning. This is a very general question, but what do you think? Can anyone make it? Why or why not?

This question, asked in the first round of interviews as well as four years later, was intended to give respondents a chance to think out loud about two polar opposite perspectives on opportunity. The responses were particularly instructive for the way they echo mainstream values of individuality, perseverance, and the belief (which many social scientists would dispute) that "making it" is a function of personal effort rather than luck, connections, or advantageous identities (race, class background, or education).

The majority of our respondents continue to believe that anyone can make it if that person tries hard, stays focused, and perseveres. Everyone has obstacles that may impede their success, but the key is to overcome them and to keep trying. Even people in our sample who are not doing well, who are unemployed, or who have been in prison, feel that anyone can make it. The respondents still subscribe to the dominant ideology that there is an open opportunity structure, regardless of limits they experience personally. Some of the respondents acknowledge that their race or gender may be disadvantageous in the labor market initially, but argue it is up to the individual to prove other people wrong. Their view of who succeeds and who fails is extremely individualistic.

Toni is a West Indian immigrant who currently works full-time as a cashier for a major toy store, where she earns $5.75 per hour (placing her at the bottom of our "middle earner" category). Toni never finished high school, but she is currently enrolled in a program designed to lead her through the GED exam and onto an Associates Degree. She has had three other jobs in the past four years, all cashiering. She has also had a brief internship in a law firm, an experience that sparked a desire to pursue a career in the law some day. When asked in 1993 whether anyone could make it in New York, she argued that race and gender would pose problems for her, but that she had what it takes to overcome these barriers:

> My Momma will tell you, "If you want something real hard try for it." And she knows I want to be a lawyer. She says I have things are against me right now: I'm black and I'm female. It's gonna be hard for me. But if I try I can make it. I could be a lawyer. But I have those two things against me. They are gonna try their damnedest to stop me. So from my point of view, I see where people coming from when they say [anyone can make it]. My mother tell me that all the time, and I understand why she's telling me.

Four years later, when asked the same question, Toni acknowledges that there may be some obstacles against blacks who are trying to make it, but she also feels that blacks have a tendency to blame and criticize everyone else for their failures instead of trying to improve their own situation. She believes that blacks should work harder for themselves if they want to get ahead and even refers to blacks as "lazy." Though there are strikes against her, they present obstacles she must surmount. But Toni does not believe this attitude is universally embraced in her own community. She generalizes from the question (intended to focus on labor market prospects) to a broader critique of the behavior of some people in the black community, whom she feels are losing out through apathy, self-pity, and lack of personal responsibility. Toni in 1997:

> A lot of people say blacks got a lot of obstacles ahead . . . I have a lot of obstacles ahead of me because I'm black and I'm a female. But that doesn't make it right that I could say that, and then not try to work harder to get to where I want to get. I feel that a lot of black people are lazy, because if they hear people say this, they should want to work harder to get where they want to go . . . They want to stay home and they want to criticize people, and you can't criticize people if you're not doing anything about it. Like, a lot of people got mad. They said, "Oh, Dinkins lost." But a lot of people were sitting home on their stoops. They weren't voting. So how can you expect the man to win if you're not out there? So now they get what's coming to them. Whatever Pataki and Giuliani do to us, we deserve it. Because if we would have all pulled together, and all got out there, something would have changed for us.

Toni's views on this point have changed very little in the course of the four years. If anything, they have hardened or expanded beyond what she tells herself about obstacles and opportunity in her own life to what she thinks is problematic about her own community. Though her own trajectory has, thus far, not borne enormous fruit, she does not think of the jobs she has held as indicative of her real future. For that, she is going to school, with a view toward better things over the horizon.

Although the majority of the respondents feel that anyone can "make it" if they try, there were a few who did not subscribe to this ideology. These respondents believe that race and gender bias make it very difficult for everyone to have an equal shot. This is particularly evident to people like Lauren, a 21-year-old African-American student who also receives TANF and food stamps for her 2-year-old daughter. Lauren was rejected by Burger Barn four years earlier, but in the interim has both graduated from high school and held down a number of jobs, mainly in summer youth programs (as a payroll clerk). At the time of the 1997 follow-up, she was among the low-wage workers, earning $4.75 as a bookkeeper, but she was also attending a community college, which she funded through government loans.

Lauren thinks that she will probably do all right when she has finally finished school, but she does not believe men her age are managing. Indeed, she believes that black men face a stacked deck. It is hard for them to get hired, she says, because there are so many negative stereotypes they have to combat, even if they have a great deal of work experience. Employers will always favor white males over blacks, regardless of how much knowledge and experience black male candidates may have.

> Black males, it's really hard for them to make it in society. . . . I see a lot of negativity towards black men when they go look for jobs. You know, I could give you a good example. Let's say a guy comes in. He has dreadlocks. He's dressed up. Let a Caucasian guy come in. He's nicely cut, but the black guy has a lot of experience. They're not going to really look at the black guy, because they're going to look at his outside, they're not going to be looking to his experience, because they're like, "Well, we can't have him representing our company, looking like that." I think it's really hard on black men.

Personal success, whether in education or the labor market., does not necessarily lead to support for the mainstream proposition that effort is all that is needed to succeed. Adam is one of the most successful respondents in our sample. Indeed, he comes from a family of success stories. His father worked for the sanitation department. Growing up in Brooklyn, he was surrounded by people with "city jobs": bus drivers, school teachers, and park service workers. Adam was a 29-year-old African-American and single parent, a high school dropout and a rejected applicant from Burger Barn in 1993. Although he didn't get that job, he was working two jobs by the time we caught up with him in 1994 and was raising a daughter in Harlem. By 1997 he had become a truck driver for an overnight package delivery firm, earning $38,000 per year (the equivalent of $19 per hour), a job he had held for more than three years. He certainly thinks of himself as a success story, but as he has become more experienced in the work world, he has become less sure that the windows of opportunity are open for everyone. In 1994, he had a mixed opinion on this issue:

> Some areas and jobs . . . may discriminate against you because of your color, but there's some places, some big businesses that I see that I go into and it looks like they don't care. You're an individual, they treat you like an individual.

By 1997, Adam had become a bit more skeptical, even though he was doing quite well. He thinks minorities are at a marked disadvantage when they have to compete with whites:

> No [I don't believe anyone can make it] . . . That's a universe there. You can't say that. Color, first of all, is an obstacle. Income, another obstacle, because it be black, not just black, minority. If you're a minority, or if you're black, Puerto Rican, whatever, it's very hard to get a job. A lot of employees going to, even if you have the benefits, if the white person wants it too, even if they're less qualified, they're going to hire them. Standard procedures. Even though they got these procedures going out there saying, "affirmative action" and all this. "We don't do [biased hiring] like that." They do.

Prospects for the future

The first round of interviews with both the successful "hires" and the unsuccessful "rejects" revealed a high degree of optimism, coupled with an orientation toward planning. This was more than talk. Even then, both the workers and the job seekers were active in looking for entry-level work and opportunities for advancement. Even those who had little to show for their efforts beyond a low-wage job valued that status, particularly in comparison to the non-workers in their households and among their friends. The follow-up study was developed in part to determine whether that same positive orientation would hold four years later, even in cases where there was still only modest (or no) success.

In the 1997 interviews, we asked respondents what they expected to be doing five years down the line. Most imagine a future in which they will have a "good paying job" and perhaps own their own house or apartment. Those who are in college or who aspire to go to college see themselves finished with higher education and therefore in line for a good job that will make use of their degrees. They hope to move to better neighborhoods and, in some instances, to get out of the city altogether. In general, they continue to believe this future is within their grasp. For the 30 percent who are now in the high earning category and for the students who are moving ahead with higher education, this is perhaps not very surprising. However, these goals are equally alive among those who are middle- and even low-wage earners. They also see themselves moving ahead, though perhaps not at the pace they had hoped.

Tyandra, a high school graduate, but college drop-out who is currently earning $5 per hour and living at home, expects that she will land a full-time job, finish the last two years of college, and get her own apartment. At the age of 20, with none of these pieces in place, she was chafing at her dependent status and hoped it would not last too long. A good job was key to her plans, but so was "getting married [and] having a house." Children, she thought, could wait.

Cassandra, who at 33 lived with her boyfriend and her 12-year-old son from a prior relationship, earned $8 per hour working as an operator for a long-distance company. She knew this was a good job and hence was determined to hold onto it. For Cassandra, marriage was a key to a stable future, because with two incomes she would be able to afford a house. She imagined the house would be in North Carolina where her mother and siblings live and where her boyfriend might work for a freight company. She had also begun to think about college for her son and possibly a return to school herself since her "raising days of [her] son will be pretty much over" and she would have more freedom. At $8 per hour, many of these ambitions had to be regarded as distant hopes. But she still had them and thought of them as attainable.

In this, Cassandra was very much like Tamara, who expected she would "be working with a good-paying job, a very good-paying job; living in a house, hopefully, with a job in a church, and a car." Or Toni, a 20-year-old West Indian living with her mom and four siblings, working for $5.75 per hour, who saw herself in five years having graduated from college with "a nice management job." Or Antonia who, at 26, was still living with her mother and earning $7 per hour after five years at Burger Barn. Antonia wanted "to have my own children . . . I want a husband . . . and a house, a business in [the Dominican Republic]." These low-wage workers had *not* become astounding success stories in the years between the first interview and the follow up. Yet, they still saw themselves as moving toward a set of goals, not as stagnating in the face of impossible obstacles.

The women in our sample who do not have children realize that having children would slow down their chances for upward mobility. They know that if they were to have children, it would be more diffi-cult for them to finish school or to find a good-paying job. Even those who have children admit that finding a good-paying job would have been easier were they not burdened with child-care responsibilities. Hence, when asked what would stand in the way of realizing their ambi-tions, most of the female respondents noted that getting pregnant would be a huge blow. As Toni put the matter:

> The only problem I [would] have is getting pregnant, and I pray, I hope I don't. That's the problem for a lot of youth. I ain't gonna get pregnant. No. I'm very smart when it comes to that. All my cousins, all my nieces, they all pregnant. They all have kids. I'm the only one without kids. And they always say, I say they jinx me, because they always say, "Oh, we can't wait for you to have yours." So I can be a part of you all? I don't want to be in that clique.

Toni has to work at separating herself in a normative sense from these friends and relatives. Staying away from childbearing is key to this plan. In this she resembles most of the other women in the follow-up study, especially those who have already had a child and now know what an impediment this can be in the pursuit of upward mobility.

One should not conclude that all of these women have decided never to have children. It would be more accurate to say that they want to avoid having children outside of marriage. Like many middle-class women, these respondents are also thinking about how they can combine a good family life with employment. Key to their vision is the prospect of getting married, followed by raising children in a decent home. Those who have steady boyfriends, who are often the fathers of their children, hope to marry and, by combining incomes, afford a more comfortable home. As Cassandra, the long-distance company operator, puts it: "In five years time I would be married in my house, still working for [the same firm]. My job will help me get where I want to go financially. You know, along with my boyfriend's income."

Among those who have already become parents, what the future holds for their children is at least as important as what they foresee for themselves. Cassandra expects to see her son graduate from high school and on his way to college:

> My son is in seventh grade now. I see he'll be out of high school. I'm not going to put him in the service because I don't think black men should be in the service. So he'll either go to college or he'll get out. So that's pretty much his choice. Either you go to college or you pack your bags and you decide what you want to do after that, because I don't tolerate laziness. I don't even allow that word in my house. I just believe in striving, because I came from the street. Literally. And if I can do it, you can do it.

Adam, a divorced father who has now remarried, wants to spend more time with his daughter from his first marriage, who is now 8. He has plans for his son, now 15 months old:

> We already started looking for private schools to put him in. Public schools is good. Don't give me nothing wrong with that, but they just overcrowded right now, and I really want my son to have an education. . . . Hopefully in five years, he'll be a computer whiz kid.

Having made something of themselves, these workers can now imagine a better future for their children. For recent immigrants like Antonia, the plan involves taking the family she imagines having back to the Dominican Republic where she could stretch the dollars she earns into a more comfortable retirement.

How close reality will come to the futures so many of our respondents envision is hard to forecast. About one-fifth of them are no longer among the working poor. Those who are on track with higher education will probably follow in the footsteps of these success stories. For the rest, the future is harder to predict. If the labor market remains tight, they will be more likely to remain employed and over time their earnings will probably increase. But they have a long way to go to achieve the level of economic security they imagine. For the 16 percent of the sample that is in the low-wage group, combined with the 33 percent who were unemployed at in 1997 and only episodically employed in the previous four years, one imagines the future will be bleak.

Given the divergence of experience, the stability of our respondents' views of opportunity and personal responsibility is notable. One might expect that those who have done well would see the world through positive lenses and argue that everyone is the master of his or her own destiny. It is testimony to the power of mainstream values that even those who have had less positive trajectories generally subscribe to the views they held when first interviewed four years earlier. Virtually all of them agree that whatever obstacles they face, ranging from those they have had a hand in creating, like poor educational track records, to those bequeathed to them by a society that still erects racial barriers, are theirs to surmount. They are insistent about holding others to a standard of personal conduct and condemn not only those who fail, but those who seek to offload accountability for failure onto anyone else: the white world, other racial minorities, management, welfare agencies, or powerful people in the city. The durability of these views is impressive for the way in which it displays the power of mainstream, middle-class morals. Conservative thought infuses the lives of the working poor and their fellow job seekers in the inner city.

New areas of research

The "end of welfare as we know it" has redirected the focus of poverty research away of welfare and welfare dependency and onto the working poor. This does not mean, however, that poverty research will need to be rebuilt from the ground up. The quantitative work being done on the macro and micro structure of the labor market will tell us about the characteristics of jobs available to the working poor (Kalleberg et al. 2000), the spatial and social distribution of these jobs (Kasarda 1995; Wilson 1996, 1987; Waldinger 1996), employer behavior and preferences (Holzer 1996), and discrimination (Reskin 2000).

The next stages of qualitative research on the working poor will build on of the literature on economic restructuring. The research we have presented in this chapter looks at the movement of low-wage workers through an urban labor market in which service-sector jobs predominate. A crucial question to ask has to do with the effects of labor market conditions on the employment trajectories of the working poor. To that end, we are currently conducting a third wave of research with the Burger Barn hires and rejects we first met almost 10 years ago. At the time of the second wave of this study in 1997 the unemployment rate in New York City was at a historic low. A rapidly deteriorating economy and the events of September 11, 2001 have now pushed the unemployment rate back up. Welfare rolls in New York City have also started to rise for the first time since 1995 at the same time that a number of recipients are due to reach their life-time limits. The working poor now

find themselves grasping at a declining economy without a governmental safety net to cushion any fall. Some of them will prosper because
their own initiative, coupled with favorable conditions in the job
market, will have made them valuable to their employers. We need to
know how true that is and for what kinds of workers. Ethnographic and
life history research will be critical to understanding this "up side." It
will also need to pay close attention to the other side of the coin: low-
wage workers forced out of their jobs by a looming recession, who lose
the ground they gained during an era of tight labor markets.

We are interested not only in the career trajectories of the workers in
our study. We are also examining the consequences these precarious
economic conditions have on issues such as family formation and educational attainment for the children of the working poor. For many
working poor families an older relative supported by welfare was the only
affordable child-care option. Work requirements and time-limits have
eliminated this option, undermining both a source of cohesion and
tension with families. These new economic realities have also upped the
ante as far as education is concerned. Yet, in a city with a severe short-
ages in affordable housing and a crippled school system, the options
available to working poor parents are problematic, to say the least.

Scholars will need to look at the economic and household strategies
of the working poor who make it out of the ranks of the low-wage labor
market and those who manage to get by. There will also need to be
attention paid to those who cannot make it at all. During the debate
over welfare reform, most acknowledged that there would always be a
certain number of the poor who would need government support over
the long run. With time limits in the near future, we need to understand who cannot make it the labor market. Many of those who are
unable to eke out a subsistence income will turn to their network of
family and friends for support. For working poor families earning
barely enough to get by, these demands for help will create numerous
conflicts.

A related issue in the next wave of research on the working poor will
be the role of men in families. Declining economic conditions both
heighten the need for the income contributions that non-custodial
fathers can make at the same time they undermine their earnings. The
welfare dependency focus of the previous generations of poverty
research offers very little insight into the ways in which family relationships respond to economic shifts. This is an important area of
research that demands attention. New qualitative research by Kathryn
Edin, Laura Lein, and Timothy Nelson (2001) on non-custodial fathers
will add greatly to our understanding.

New research on the working poor will also build on the work that has been done on recent immigration to the US. Already the subject of much scholarly attention (Smith and Edmonston 1997; Hirschman et al. 1999; Borjas 2001; Waters 2001), the experience and effects of immigrants in low-wage labor markets will continue to be an crucial area of study. Attention will also need to be paid to the experiences of the children of this recent wave of immigrants (Portes and Rumbaut 2001). Many will grow up in homes where the disadvantages of being in a working poor family will be compounded by the barriers faced by immigrants. Even for those members of the second generation whose parents arrive with the credentials, skills, and human capital to avoid the low-wage labor market, the threat of downward mobility into the working poor is all too real.

The goal in these new areas of qualitative research is not simply to shift the focus of poverty research from the "welfare poor" to the "working poor." Rather, it is to examine the ways in which changes in the structure of work and labor markets and the dismantling of the government safety net have remade the structure of opportunity in the United States. We will need the contributions of qualitative researchers to understand how poor Americans make their way through this new terrain.

NOTE

1   Strictly speaking, this is not an entirely accurate characterization, for there were times in American history, for example, the 1930s, when the lexicon did include the concept of class. Yet even then, loud voices emerged declaiming the idea that the US was a class-riddled society and extolling the virtues of upward mobility.

REFERENCES

Bane, M. J. and Ellwood, D. T. (1994) *Welfare Realities: From Rhetoric to Reform.* Cambridge, MA: Harvard University Press.

Beers, T. M. (2001) "A Profile of the Working Poor, 1999" (Report 947). Washington, DC: US Department of Labor, Bureau of Labor Statistics.

Blank, R. (1998–9) "Labor market dynamics and women's part-time work in the United States," *Focus* 20: 37–40.

Borjas, G. J. (2001) *Heaven's Door: Immigration Policy and the American Economy.* Princeton, NJ: Princeton University Press.

Burowoy, M. (1982) [1979] *Manufacturing Consent: Changes to the Labor Process under Monopoly Capitalism.* Chicago: University of Chicago Press.

Burtless, G. (1995) "Employment prospects of welfare recipients," in Nightingale, D. S. and Haveman, R. H. (eds.), *The Work Alternative: Welfare Reform and the Realities of the Job Market.* Washington, DC: Urban Institute.

—— (1997) "Welfare recipients' job skills and employment prospects," *The Future of Children* 7(1): 39–51.

Chin, M. and Newman, K. S. (2002) "High stakes: Time poverty, testing, and the children of the working poor" (Working Papers Series). The Foundation for Child Development, New York.

Chinoy, E. (1955) *Automobile Workers and the American Dream.* Garden City, NY: Doubleday.

Danziger, S. H., Heflin, C. M., Corcoran, M. E. and Oltmans, E. (2001) *Does it Pay to Move from Welfare to Work?* (Research Report 00–449). Michigan: Population Studies Center, University of Michigan.

Edin, K. and Lein, L. (1997) *Making Ends Meet: How Single Mothers Survive Welfare and Low-Wage Work.* New York: Russell Sage.

Edin, K., Lein, L. and Nelson, T. J. (2001) "Taking care of business: The economic survival strategies of low-income non-custodial fathers," in Munger, F. (ed.), *The Low Wage Labor Market.* New York: Russell Sage.

Gans, H. J. (1982) [1967] *The Levittowners: Ways of Life and Politics in a New Suburban Community.* New York: Columbia University Press.

Gladden, T. and Taber, C. (1999) "Wage progression among less skilled workers." Unpublished paper written for the conference *Labor Markets and Less Skilled Workers,* sponsored by the Joint Center for Policy Research.

Halle, D. (1984) *America's Working Man: Work, Home, and Politics among Blue-Collar Property Owners.* Chicago: University of Chicago Press.

Hannerz, U. (1969) *Soulside: Inquiries into Ghetto Culture and Community.* New York: Columbia University Press.

Heclo, H. (1994) "Poverty politics," in Danziger, S. H., Sandefur, G. D. and Weinberg, D. H. (eds.), *Confronting Poverty: Prescriptions for Change.* New York: Russell Sage and Cambridge, MA: Harvard University Press.

Hirschman, C., Kasinitz, P. and DeWind, J. (1999) *The Handbook of International Migration: The American Experience.* New York: Russell Sage.

Holzer, H. J. (1996) *What Employers Want: Job Prospects for Less-Educated Workers.* New York: Russell Sage.

Kallenberg, A. L., Reskin, B. F. and Hudson, K. (2000) "Bad jobs in America: Standard and nonstandard employment and job quality in the United States," *American Sociological Review* 65 (2): 256–78.

Kasarda, J. D. (1995) "Industrial restructuring and the changing location of jobs," in Farley, R. (ed.), *State of the Union: America in the 1990s.* New York: Russell Sage.

Levitan, S. A. and Shapiro, I. (1987) *Working But Poor: America's Contradiction.* Baltimore, MD: Johns Hopkins University Press.

Liebow, L. (1967) *Tally's Corner: A Study of Negro Streetcorner Men.* Boston: Little, Brown.

Lynd, R. S. and Lynd, H. M. (1982) [1929] *Middletown: A Study in American Culture.* San Diego, CA: Harcourt Brace Jovanovich.

McLeod, J. (1987) *Ain't No Making It: Leveled Aspirations in Low-Income Neighborhoods.* Boulder, CO: Westview Press.

Newman, K. S. (1999) *No Shame in My Game: The Working Poor in the Inner City.* New York: Knopf/Russell Sage.

—— (2000) "In the long run: Careers patterns and cultural expectations in the low wage labor force," *Journal of African American Public Policy* VI (1, Summer): 17–62.

—— (2002) "The right (soft) stuff: Qualitative research and the study of welfare reform," in Moffit, R. (ed.), *Studies of Welfare Populations: Data Collection and Research Issues.* Washington, DC: National Academic Press.

O'Connor, A. (2000) "Poverty research and policy for the post-welfare era," *Annual Review of Sociology* 26: 547–62.

Pavetti, L. (1997) *Against the Odds: Steady Improvement among Low Skill Women.* Washington, DC: Urban Institute.

Pavetti, L. and Acs, G. (1997) *Moving Up, Moving Out or Going Nowhere? A Study of the Employment Patterns of Young Women.* Washington, DC: Urban Institute.

Portes, A. and Rumbaut, R. G. (2001) *Legacies: The Story of the Immigrant Second Generation.* Berkeley, CA: University of California Press.

Reskin, B. F. (2000) "Getting it right: Sex and race inequality in work organizations," *Annual Review of Sociology* 26: 707–9.

Smith, J. P. and Edmonston, B. (eds.) (1997) *The New Americans: Economic, Demographic, and Fiscal Effects of Immigration.* Washington, DC: National Academy Press.

Swartz, T. R. and Weigart, K. M. (eds.) (1995) *America's Working Poor.* Notre Dame, IN: University of Notre Dame Press.

Waldinger, R. (1996) *Still the Promised City? African-Americans and New Immigrants in Postindustrial New York.* Cambridge, MA: Harvard University Press.

Waters, M. C. (2001) *Black Identities: West Indian Immigrant Dream and American Realities.* Cambridge, MA: Harvard University Press.

Wilson, W. J. (1987) *The Truly Disadvantaged: The Inner City, the Underclass, and Public Policy.* Chicago: University of Chicago Press.

—— (1996) *When Work Disappears: The World of the New Urban Poor.* New York: Random House.

FURTHER READING

Ehrenreich, B. (1999) *Nickeled and Dimed: On (Not) Getting By in America.* New York: Henry Holt.

Newman, K. (1999) *No Shame in My Game: The Working Poor in the Inner City.* New York: Knopf /Russell Sage.

Wilson, W. J. (1997) *When Work Disappears: The World of the New Urban Poor.* New York: Knopf.

CHAPTER SIX

Class and Social Inequalities in Portugal

From Class Structure to Working-Class Practices on the Shop Floor

Elísio Estanque

This chapter addresses the emergence and development of class analysis in Portugal. Starting with a reference to the process of institutionalizing sociology, I will discuss the influence of different schools of thought in the light of the political context, i.e. the 1970s, in which social class theories and Portuguese sociology itself were born. I will refer to different theoretical and methodological perspectives, and, in particular, discuss the interconnections between quantitative and qualitative approaches, while emphasizing the advantages of the latter. These will be illustrated with examples of my own research based on the participant observation method, showing some aspects of daily life on the shop floor where I worked. Finally, I will propose some new lines and prospects for future developments in research into social inequality.

CLASS ANALYSIS IN PORTUGUESE SOCIOLOGY

Sociology has only been able to develop fully in Portugal, since the triumph of democracy with the Revolution of the Carnations (April 25, 1974), but it would be wrong to say that only after that did we have Portuguese sociologists. As we all know, during the 1960s, in European universities sociological thinking was strongly influenced by the new social movements. During this time, the authoritarian regime of Salazar in our country not only gave rise to huge class inequalities, but also made it impossible for them to be studied sociologically. Sociology was then considered a synonym for socialism. However, many young students, who left their country during this period to escape both the decaying and repressive regime and conscription into the colonial war, studied in Europe (mostly in France) and thus came into contact with the debates in the social sciences. This would later be of great importance to the academic institutionalization of Portuguese sociology.

The foundations of Portuguese social sciences, together with class analysis, were laid by a small group of researchers led by Adérito Sedas Nunes.[1] His first sociological text (Nunes 1964), covered the theme of the dual society, and drew attention not only to the general poverty of the country but also the stark contrast that characterized the increasing gulf between the urban centers (Lisbon and, partly, also Porto), which absorbed almost all the professionals, while the country as a whole was still predominantly rural and under-resourced.

Studies which followed, on higher education and the recomposition of the labor force (Nunes 1968; Guerra and Nunes 1969; Miranda 1969) provided an important critical diagnosis of the "backwardness" of Portuguese society during the period and denounced the elitist nature of the universities. The class origin of students was presented as a clear inversion of the stratification pyramid. The texts published in *Análise Social* (*Social Analysis*)[2] interpreted this underdevelopment as the result of an autocratic and coercive regime, designed to guarantee the security and reproduction of the dominant classes (Nunes and Miranda 1969).

While the so-called "Sedas Nunes group" started pivotal work in the country, in the late 1960s in Britain H. Martins[3] had also begun an interesting set of essays on Portuguese society. The central aspects of these studies focused on issues such as European fascism and the nature of the *Estado Novo* (the New State), in which he discussed some of the classic Weberian concepts and tried to use them to understand our society during the late phase of Salazar's regime. It was a society considered "culturally homogeneous" and subjected to a class dictatorship, as distinct from the so-called apparatus dictatorship and characterized by its coastal basis, the fragility of the middle-class strata and the "dualism" between rural and "modern" trends (Martins 1998).

Both these contributions played an important role in shaping future studies on class inequality in Portugal within the first generation of our sociologists. Therefore, it can be said that the first approaches to social inequality in Portugal combined stratification theories and structural class analysis. In the early 1970s a few texts were published on mobility, paying particular attention to the importance of social and personal trajectories – including, for example, notions of "expectations of mobility," "anticipated socialization" and "reference groups," and to the symbolic significance of "upward" or "downward" agent mobility (Almeida 1970).

It is worth remembering at this point that the context in which sociology developed in Portugal not only favored attention to class issues and social inequalities, but, since it coincided with the late institutionalization of democracy, was clearly framed by the revolutionary social climate (1974–5), within which class language played a leading role (Estanque 1999). This explains the strong presence of Marxism within sociology and was woven into abstract debates that revolved around the concept of social class.

From the mid-1980s onwards, class analysis witnessed greater development and conceptual elaboration through the work of the ISCTE[4] sociology group. Stressing the multidimensional nature of the concept of class, the authors developed their own typology of classes, combining the models of Poulantzas (1974), Wright (1978, 1985) and Bourdieu (1979) in strict articulation with multiple theoretical influences, to produce a rigorous model of class typologies which contributed significantly towards shaping class analysis in Portugal (Marques and Bairrada 1982; Ferrão 1985; Almeida 1986; Costa et al. 1990). The starting point was the study by João Ferreira de Almeida (1986), in which the author used a wide range of theoretical and methodological tools in order to overcome the "structuralist straitjacket," on the one hand, and "individualist idealism" on the other (Almeida 1986: 86). This critical revision of functionalist sociology led him to a sociological explanation of the way in which the recomposition of classes was processed in a rural context (north of Porto city), characterized by flows of daily migration, with part-time rural workers and local family networks acting as a "reserve labour force" within a peripheral community exposed to the structuring effects of the industrial nucleus of the city of Porto.

In analyzing recomposition and social mobility in Portugal the same authors portrayed the evolution of the class structure from the 1960s onwards, discussing the results of "social mobility" in the light of the deep structural change that was occurring in the country. This includes the huge expansion in the education system (together with its markedly female presence), mirrored in the tertiary sector workforce. In addition, intergenerational social mobility not only showed downward and upward trends (with the latter more significant than the former) but, at the same time, a marked tendency towards social reproduction or "immobility," which is particularly evident in the most extreme categories of the class structure (Almeida et al. 1994; Machado and Costa 1998).

The presence of the structuralist approach brought together concepts such as "class trajectories," "family networks," and "lifestyles," which helped to direct analysis towards the role of social actors in the cultural field. The influence of Bourdieu was significant among the new generation of Portuguese sociologists, particularly his conception of a class structure intertwined and reproduced through the individual and class *habitus*, that is, through the incorporation of cognitive systems of classification and practices. The attention given to cultural lifestyles, as well as to aspects such as symbolic consumption, the social construction of taste, the building of social schemes of distinction and imitation etc., have been important and innovative dimensions for studies in class inequality.

The most recent approaches to social class and mobility have progressively abandoned the structural approach, since the old abstract analyses have given way to more subjective or culturalist studies. Doubtless it is not by chance that these new trends seem to be moving from Marxism towards the Weberian vision, as a prerequisite for focusing more closely on political and subjective elements (Erikson et al. 1993). Recent studies have set the tone for Portuguese perspectives on inequality and self-identification of class, seeking explanations for the lack of citizenship and equity in Portuguese society (Cabral 1997, forthcoming). This research has confirmed the restricted dimensions of the middle classes and little empirical evidence of upward mobility. In terms of subjective attitudes, a widespread feeling of injustice in the distribution of wealth, together with a sense of being impotent to change the direction of events are prevalent traits in Portuguese society today. The Portuguese seem to share greater subjective feelings towards wide levels of power distance (Hofstede 1980) between the strata immediately above or below them, but – paradoxically or not – they tend to identify themselves with the "middle class" (sometimes, even when they are in fact manual workers). In this respect the field of consumption might be considered a central element, since it gives the lower and middle classes the impression of gaining access to life styles viewed as similar to those of the strata immediately above them.

In a recent study on the working-class district of Alfama in Lisbon, A. Firmino da Costa (1999) provides a good example of how class analysis can be enriched by multidimensional perspectives and plural theoretical concepts. The structure–agency dilemma, for example, is embedded in the effort to forge new links between different levels of analysis (macro-meso-micro) and this is directed towards an understanding of the practices, networks, and patterns of identities and cultures in which the actors move. This is, in fact, a demonstration of how an approach to class inequality can create a more consistent understanding of interaction contexts, that is, the spaces within which identities are structured, given that these contexts obey and interact with socio-economic structural conditionings. These conditionings, far from being imposed or "determined" on a macro-level, are first incorporated by the agents into their representations, subjectivities, and practices, and it is in this way that they participate in the restructuring of inequalities, both cultural and social, and in the production of the Alfama society.[5] The crucial importance of understanding the cultural traditions and associative practices in this urban community of Lisbon has been sustained as a condition for preserving local identity and its popular roots. Through case studies like this, the full potential of action-research programs becomes clear. Proximity and involvement with the social actors have been decisive factors in defining forms of action and of negotiation to minimize the risk of gentrification and to revitalize this traditional environment through urban redevelopment policies.

We have seen how Portuguese sociology was born under the direct influence of class analysis and how the structuralist approach was strong, especially during the second half of the 1970s, notwithstanding the plurality of theoretical influences, including social stratification. But, in spite of the growing importance of the culturalist approach, I believe there is a risk of a split between the ethnographic perspective and socio-economic class analysis. So, as previously mentioned, qualitative case studies may deal with the structural dimension by trying to connect the social interaction under observation with the macro frameworks within which collective action takes place.

QUALITATIVE METHODS AND PARTICIPANT OBSERVATION

The problem of qualitative versus quantitative methods in social sciences is linked to the wider issue of epistemology and the history of science. When we look back to the late nineteenth century it can be said that theoretical controversies within universities and amongst sociologists were always influenced by the impact of workers' struggles (AAVV 1996). This kind of permeability between theoretical conceptions and social struggles and between social sciences and the "real world" is the main reason why theoretical divergence persists. Just as we cannot ignore the large amount of theory accumulated over more than 150 years, equally we cannot ignore the fact that the social world has changed profoundly and some of the old perspectives are no longer capable of explaining new trends.

In fact, the difficulties involved in reconciling a critical sense of analysis with the rigor and complexity of the quantitative methodology employed did not abate (Wright 1985, 1989). The efforts of analytical Marxism to confer greater scientific legitimacy on class analysis continued at the expense of concessions to the positivist principles of methodological individualism (Burawoy 1989; Pakulsky and Waters 1996). In addition, the most stimulating dimensions of Wright's work moved significantly closer to Weberianism, thus lending credibility to those who claimed that "class consciousness" could not be understood through abstract determinisms. We may agree that *Class Counts* (Wright 1997), but this becomes a mere nostalgic cliché if the question of class does not incorporate or connect with other forms of inequality emerging in society which are difficult to capture with the old class schemes or quantitative instruments. In my opinion, it is therefore fundamental that an analysis of these questions makes use of various methodologies, in particular qualitative methodologies and case studies (Reay 1998; Grusky and Sorenson 1998).

In a study I conducted into the footwear industry in Portugal, I used the participant observation method to address questions such as class practices, group subjectivities, and identity structuring (Estanque 2000). The company where I worked employed about 60 workers and was located in S. João da Madeira (SJM), on the southern coast of Portugal, north of the Aveiro district. During this period I worked an 8-hour day on the assembly line and shared many of the workers' experiences, not only inside the company but also during leisure and free-time activities.

I believe the option for this methodological approach requires a very strong attempt to break with positivist science. The classic epistemological presumption based on the idea that ordinary people live in a world of "illusio" – the Durkheimian belief that common sense is guided by "illusions" and distorted impressions while the scientist represents reason – must be challenged, since no understanding can be completely neutral. The search for objectivity is not synonymous with absolute neutrality (Santos 1995). For participant observation to be used successfully, it is essential not to neglect the self-reflexive critique which the problem of interaction between the observer and the observed demands (Bourdieu 1996; Fowler 1996).

The methodological strategy I followed corresponded to the so-called extended case method[6] and was dedicated to avoiding determinism and relativism, by establishing a multiple interactive causality which aimed to intersect the micro-foundations of macrosociology with the macro-foundations of microsociology (Collins 1981; Fine 1991).

Observing the phenomena from below, but still paying attention to the external forces which model them, and through a form of experimental fieldwork in social involvement with individuals with whom I shared work routines, physical labor, jokes and many complicities over three months, is the method of checking pre-existing theories, hypotheses and sociological knowledge directed towards a wider social context (Burawoy 1991).

Participant observation implies, of course, an infinite number of risks and problems. Although there are advantages to experimentation in terms of the overall depth of the study, it also raises innumerable perplexing issues since, in spite of previous knowledge of the field and because this knowledge is fundamentally either theoretical or superficial, the researcher is soon led to feel let down by his expectations. This situation forces us to question the power of the social scientist and to pay more attention to alternative points of view, namely those of the actors being observed. Obviously it is a complex task and one that can never fully be achieved, given that, even knowing that social practices are always practical knowledge, "they can only be recognized as such to the extent that they are the mirror image of scientific knowledge" (Santos 2001: 266).

Let me describe briefly my experience in the factory. The cultural bias of my own class condition made me feel inadequacy, discomfort, and misunderstanding, especially at the outset when the workers viewed me with distrust, if not as an outright "enemy." In my personal case, if I had had any doubts at all, this fact alone would have constituted direct evidence of the symbolic force of a class rift. At first, there was immense speculation among the factory workers about my presence there, since the absence of a strong pair of callused hands, as much as the way in which the line supervisor (who knew of my status) addressed me, made them sense immediately that "he isn't one of us." Some insisted that I was a "psychologist" working for the boss, others were sure that I was from the police and was tracking down a gang of drug dealers and yet another group insisted that I was a member of the boss's family who was learning about factory procedures. My strategy was ruled by discretion and I aimed not to draw attention to myself, although at the same time I needed to gain their confidence. So, little by little, as I began to make friends, I told them vaguely that I was trying to "study the footwear sector."

After three weeks of hard work, standing for eight hours a day to carry out various tasks, my fingers were swollen from undoing boots manually at dizzying speeds. I considered giving up because, in addition to physical exhaustion, the workers, contrary to my expectations, showed no interest in talking about the company, the union or the working conditions (the issues which at the time seemed most important to me), even after they had begun to trust that I was on their side. I resisted, with difficulty. I reflected painstakingly and, after many theoretical dilemmas and much existential anguish, began to incorporate the significance of the workers' deliberate evasion of their problems with the company, and even with myself, into the analysis. The volume of sympathy and information I received and my "privileged" position towards the various actors (the director, supervisors and workers) conferred a special status upon me, which I attempted to benefit from as much as possible. I began to pay more attention to the little symbolic power games of daily life and I have done as much as I could to understand how these processes, made up of tacit agreements, significant silences or latent resistance, were constructed by the workforce.

Nevertheless, many questions remained unanswered, although the fact that they had been formulated was fundamental. Indeed, I believe sociological research cannot provide all the answers, and so the questions that emerge during the observation process must be shared. They should even be published whenever possible. For this reason, in the book which was subsequently published, I left fragments of my *Diário de Campo* (*Fieldwork Diary*) printed on alternate pages of the chapter in which I analyzed the relations in production (Burawoy 1985), thus creating a mirror effect (cf. Estanque 2000: 243–321).

The results of my research were the object of some public discussion, ably promoted by the local press, in which workers and unionists in the sector participated. Because of this, I also had to face a violent reaction from my "ex-boss" in which he afterwards accused me of treason, ingratitude and even of being involved in a "set-up" with the trade union leaders. I should add that, in the beginning, I made a deal with the owner of the company in which I agreed to write a "diagnostic report" before leaving the factory, which I have done. The overall information delivered in that report identified several communication and functional problems within the firm, but never identified individuals. I now believe his intentions were different. The fact that he expected to obtain detailed information about the "motivation of the workers," together with the use he made of my presence – a sociologist studying his company – to promote an image of a modern entrepreneur, help to explain his cooperation with my research but also his disappointment in the end. I think this is a good illustration of the multiple power games involving the researcher in a case study like this.

The analytic importance of participant observation only becomes relevant when its results are integrated into a wider theoretical framework.

This confirms that, in reality, methodologies cannot be considered separately from the analytical perspective as a whole. In this particular case, I had attempted to pursue the study within the historical process of local industrialization and its spatial and socio-cultural impacts. This effort not only enabled the qualitative study to be combined with an extensive survey of regional class structure[7] but also required an analysis of cultural identity, within the company and in the surrounding community, as different dimensions involved in the making of the local working class.

In this second section I have briefly discussed qualitative methods, focusing on my fieldwork in order to show the advantages and complexities of participant observation. I have given some examples of the daily life on the shop floor and referred to the efforts made to link observations of the working class from the bottom up with the structural framework and historical background.

CLASS INEQUALITIES AND CONTEXTUAL ANALYSIS: A CASE STUDY OF THE SHOP FLOOR

I will start this topic by summarizing some results of my former research on social classes, and then I will give some detailed attention to my case study on the working class in the footwear industry. The study of social classes in Portugal which I undertook a few years ago (Estanque et al. 1998) was based on a Marxist theoretical model and aimed for a systematic understanding of the class structure based on a critical view of social inequality and its dynamics. It allows us to see both the overall configuration of the Portuguese class structure and in particular the complex divisions among employees, which I believe has been an interesting contribution (Wright 1985). However, this is a mere abstract model, the Wrightian topologic model of class locations, designed to characterize the class structure. It refers to classes on paper and not classes in action. For that reason I tried to interpret the results from the Weberian perspective paying special attention to historic and contextual aspects (Wright 1997).

For example, the statistical weight of the "petty bourgeois" owners (22.6 percent) and, principally, of the "proletarian" class category (46.5 percent) together with the low rates for middle class positions (14.5 percent)[8] clearly revealed the deep contradictions present in Portuguese society (Estanque et al. 1998). Still an eminently rural society in the early 1970s, the country suffered a very intense process of social change in just two decades. The large number of "proletarians" is a result, on the one hand, of the rapid industrial restructuring and privatization processes in the early 1980s and, on the other, of increased flexibility and fragmentation in the job market.

When we compare the national results with those of the region referred to in the previous section (SJM), the contrasts between the different class fractions widen dramatically. Here, middle-class categories, already barely represented at national level, practically disappear. The most highly qualified positions in the workforce waver between 0.3 percent and 0.7 percent, while the proletarian category rises substantially to 60.2 percent. The entrepreneurial framework, composed primarily of micro-companies whose owners are almost entirely former workers, is always turbulent. Very high flows of individual mobility combine with high levels of class reproduction. The regional class structure remains virtually unchanged over two generations (Estanque 2000). Furthermore, the regional working class has shown very low levels of involvement in protests and associative participation. Many workers even declare themselves to be relatively optimistic about their future. The ideological effect of an illusion of affluence functions alongside the relative affluence of some segments of the labor force, leading to positive expectations on an individual level. How can these contradictions be explained? What is the significance of class in a context such as this?

The experience of working-class resistance to capitalist exploitation also took place in this region, but it has always been shaped by a community and family-based paternalism which is typical of the artisan tradition. The impact of industrialization instigated a regulatory logic with specific characteristics, within which class capacities were redefined between resistance and adaptation to the community context. When, in the early decades of the twentieth century, a strong movement to promote a modernist community in S. João da Madeira emerged (led by the emerging capitalist class), it aimed to be based on "local pride" and founded in the productive ideal. The word "LABOUR," which is still displayed today on the local county flag, embodies the symbolic triumph of the official discourse in its historic and cultural struggle against the class language inscribed in the experiences of the working-class movement during the same period.[9]

As we know, the community cannot be viewed in a purely territorial or substantive sense (Ferrara 1997). It is, above all, a dynamic socio-cultural process, which produces collective subjectivities and witnesses many struggles, discourses, and forms of identification. If class is essential in structuring economic inequality, it is also decisive as a discursive or identifying element. In both cases it is inscribed within the community; it becomes part of the culture and takes part in the struggle for recognition and the collective dignity of a segment of society: the industrial working-class (Fraser 1997; Honneth 1996).

When I analyzed everyday life on the shop floor more closely, several perplexities emerged. In a working-class sector like this, which earns some of the lowest wages in the EU, collective struggle scarcely exists and trade union involvement is very low (even though affiliation rates are above average, at around 35 percent). Contrary to what might be expected, there is no approval by the workers for management policies. What prevails is tacit resistance, a covert rebellion, which signifies the existence of a wide rift in culture and identity between the collective workforce and the company hierarchy. As previously mentioned, the factory workers demanded a clear statement of my position, "one of them or one of us," which reflects the antagonistic way in which they perceive interests within the factory. Yet although I seemed to be in the presence of a clearly visible class instinct, the workers did not openly contest the bosses and viewed the role of the unions with a certain mistrust. The game playing that was always breaking out during production in the form of petty sabotage and petty outbursts against the system seems to function as a form of escape from a constraining discipline and an unwanted exploitation (Collinson 1992). The subtle tactics and transgressive behavior of the workers (de Certeau 1984)[10] express a working-class identity on the shop floor as a collective response to defending dignity under assault. Yet, at the same time, these small symbolic power games ultimately serve to fuel the manufacturing of consent (Burawoy 1979).

The assembly line supervisor told me some revealing stories. He complained that the workers always tried to do things their own way and said that some of them were trying to "make my life a misery . . . and test me out to see how soft I was. And the more they felt I was soft on them, the more they took advantage . . . sometimes I pretended not to notice but I understood what was going on all right!" When I asked him why he shouted at the workers from a distance when they were, as he put it, "filing their nails" (meaning that they were chatting or slacking), he gave me the following explanation: "before, I used to go up to them and point out what they were doing and control things. But I began to realize that they just wanted to give me the runaround. When I went up to someone who was talking or fooling around, they understood and so the others behind me would call me over to sort something out as well."

Still, F.'s arrogant shouts were much more in evidence when the boss was around and were usually directed at the youngest and least qualified workers. Resistance varied according to individual cases and could involve more dramatic reactions or more subtle kinds of games. Uncle António (a 60-year-old who worked alongside me) would sometimes yell in desperation to the supervisor when the belt was running too fast, but never straight to his face and not when he was nearby: "Can't he see he can't do this? Any minute now, I'm going to walk out of here!"

On other occasions they adopted a deliberate *laissez-faire* attitude if they saw that the supervisor was not paying attention to the excessive speed of the belt. Since they knew that they couldn't win by protesting openly, and yet at the same time did not want to cooperate, they deliberately slowed down and remained calm, as if whistling to themselves, pretending not to understand what was going on. It was a silent revolt, noticeable in attitudes of non-cooperation and mockery designed to counteract the "airs" and the authoritarian attitude of the supervisor, whose technical competence was, in the eyes of the workers, dubious, to say the least. The delight with which they related situations such as the following was symptomatic: a shoe had a slight fault so the boss asked one of the workers to "fix it" and he said, "Leave it here, then." A little while later the supervisor came back to check and was shown the same shoe which was supposed to have been repaired but in fact had not been touched and he said, "That's good, put it back on the belt and send it on." They laughed a lot at him behind his back and took great delight in doing so. These were just fleeting moments of fun in a daily routine marked by the extreme pressures of discipline and physical and psychological exhaustion. Yet they served as important escape and compensation mechanisms. In this way, it may be said that consent, being both partial and composed of countless moments of camouflaged dissent, was the result of a social process in which all parties were, in one way or another, implicated.

Of course, this connection between the structuring of class inequality and the cultural dimension is also created by other means. The way in which women, for example, take part in the power games within the company is clearly illustrative of gender-based class relations. It should be remembered that more then 60 percent of the workers in the footwear industry are women. In a segment of society such as this, characterized by low levels of education, economic poverty, and close connections to the rural world, the behavior of the female workforce clearly reflects the secondary status of women and the types of discrimination they are subjected to. My observations confirmed, on an almost daily basis, the discriminatory way in which the authoritarian behavior of the supervisor was always more violent when directed towards the young female workers. Sometimes a manufacturing fault was a reason for punishment and "sending them out" for a certain time (which, obviously, was deducted from the wages, at the minimum rate of half an hour, even if the period spent outside was less), a punishment preceded by the inevitable public reprimand. The humiliation was so great that it usually resulted in tears. The sexist games in which the girls were always involved also clearly revealed their status as "sex objects," in which they often colluded. In addition to discrimination in terms of wages, there are countless cases of sexual harassment, restrictions on visits to the WC, arbitrary dismissal of pregnant women and, sometimes, physical violence. As I said before, this is a sector in which women form the majority of workers, but that does nothing to create an equivalent distribution of managerial positions: almost all the supervisors are men. The factory is a world defined by virility and this is reflected in the relations of production, even though the women themselves play an active part in reproducing this masculine logic. The fact that the female workforce is composed predominantly of youngsters with few educational assets, who are more dependent on the family and more docile, at least in this cultural context and class condition, in the face of both capitalist and male power, leads me to the conclusion that the female majority not only reflects gender segregation but also contributes towards accentuating conformism and the reproduction of class inequality.

What I aimed to show in this study, through the vision of M. Burawoy (1979, 1985, 1991), was precisely the way in which the working class, through the informal practices of everyday production, contributed actively towards legitimizing rules which had been instituted and obscuring certain elements of the production process, namely exploitation. The hegemonic despotism exercised over the working class is, in this context, directly linked to local paternalism, which results from the ambivalent relations between industry and the community. This is in part due to ties of loyalty, personal affinities, and family networks being transported from the community to inside the company, leading bosses (mainly in the small companies) to believe that their employees feel a kind of debt of gratitude towards them that can never be repaid. When workers take part in a strike or become involved with the trade union, this is seen by the employers as an act of treason.

In addition, the permeability between the company and the community is also evident in the fact that many bosses tend to use the personal connections they have in the community to control, from their positions of authority, certain aspects of the workers' family lives. As SJM is a small community, it easily offers forms of social control which, with due discretion, allow the boss access to aspects of his subordinates' private life and enables him to seek in them the reasons for any behav-

ior considered "strange" or "abnormal." For example, in the company
where I worked, a lack of dedication or punctuality in a worker could
justify the fact that, in his own interests – and those of the company too,
naturally! – the management paid special attention to these situations.

This context proves, therefore, the interdependence of a class logic
which reproduces inequalities and a cultural dynamic that, paradoxically, fuels it while resisting it. The increasing globalization of markets
has brought about in this region a contradiction between the hegemonic pressures of the global economy and local forms of action
seeking to resist it. Since this is an industrial sector which is directly
dependent on global markets (around 80 percent of production is destined for export), this situation creates new difficulties but, at the same
time, opens up new horizons for working-class organizational structures
within the footwear industry. In spite of the aforementioned difficulties
in mobilization, the union has played an extremely important part in
the search for new forms of intervention and emancipatory action.
According to the trade union leader, the strategy is now to resist capitalist power in the industry through cultural movements within the local
community, while at the same time taking part in transnational movements to resist global capitalism. In addition, the old language of
Marxist orthodoxy has given way to a pragmatic sense of action, in
which dialogue and radicalism are combined and practicalities exist
alongside utopian reinvention. This may mean that, in political terms,
class action can only be activated when it is aligned to other social movements and actors.

In this section I began by identifying some of my most recent
research relating to the theme of social class in Portugal and I
attempted to focus reflection on the case study, in which I made use of
participant observation. I then presented a series of examples and discussed some aspects of the social dynamics observed in the daily life of
the factory where I was a manual worker. Situations involving humor
and informal power games were used to illustrate the socio-cultural
complexity of this segment of the working class, in which relationships
of dependency, as well as micro-rupture, consent, and rebellion,
combine in a framework of domination characterized by despotic paternalism, and in which class inequalities are reproduced on the basis of
the close connections between the factory and the community.

NEW RESEARCH LINES ON CLASS AND OTHER INEQUALITIES

The challenges faced by class analysis are, of course, connected to the
wider changes emerging in global society. Issues of economic inequal-

ity, poverty, and ethnic, sexual and cultural differences are now taking on a new shape and, in my opinion all of them are, in one way or another, related to the class problem. In a world increasingly defined by mobility and the breakdown of national frontiers, the neo-liberal discourse of new opportunities, empowerment and competition go together with both old and new situations of oppression, exploitation and exclusion. As all international institutions recognize, inequality is increasing day by day and there are no glimpses of any credible measures on the horizon that can halt this process. What can class analysis contribute towards a consideration of these problems? From among the vast array of possible lines of investigation, I would like to focus on two areas which appear to me to be crucial for the times ahead, from the perspective of Portuguese society.

The first is related to education as a channel of mobility affecting the restructuring of classes, as well as gender inequalities (Crompton and Mann 1986). The impact of educational policies and the so-called knowledge society on class structure is full of several contradictions. The opening up of the education system to the working classes, in addition to offering new opportunities, has also created typically middle-class values and subjective expectations, reference groups, and lifestyles. Moreover, current information technology is producing new divisions, not only among the qualified and unqualified sectors, the new "info-excluded," but also in the very process of converting and reshaping professions. Those who had previously held qualified posts in the services sector and whose professions had entered into decline, nowadays face rising instability, in addition to a loss of status (Esping-Andersen 1993).

In Portugal the position of women in education and in the employment market presents interesting paths for studying social class. The greater success rate of women in education, as well as their increasing presence in qualified jobs, is already well known. Although the top jobs remain in the hands of men, Portuguese universities today contain the highest number of women in Europe and levels of academic success also remain much higher for girls than for boys. At a time in which educational qualifications are becoming the main factor in career promotion, in the face of this apparent female hegemony in the universities (of around 60 percent), can we expect that there will be a repositioning of women in the stratification structure in the next ten years? What repercussions will this have on the recomposition of social classes?

There would have to be more systematic and up-to-date research into this phenomenon in order to assess its real sociological significance. However, it is worth remembering that the family structure in Portugal remains a core variable in these types of studies. Although strong patriarchal values remain inscribed in the division of domestic tasks, if this patriarchal tendency is considered in the light of the symbolic significance of educational status within the family, we may conclude that it, in fact, favors women. That is to say that, in spite of the rising attraction of higher education qualifications to the working classes,[11] their low economic means do not permit families to put all their children through university. In such situations, the girls are chosen, since patriarchal logic demands that the boys make an early start in working life, thus reserving the opportunity to continue studying for the girls.

The second area, which I believe will be particularly important in the near future, relates to changes in the employment market and their implications for the recomposition of classes. Here, class and ethnicity must be connected. It is clear that the instability and fluidity, which nowadays characterize employment, whether in the service sector or in the productive industries, are leading to the expansion of segments which Esping-Andersen has termed the stand-by classes (1993: 234). Yet, in the current global economy, post-Fordist systems are also consolidating processes for transferring investments and moving labor forces that are profoundly altering the entire class structure. Increasing international mobility, above all at the top and base of the stratification pyramid, requires a more systematic study, especially in its European context. Nevertheless, it is possible, by starting from the Portuguese situation, to outline some hypotheses for a sociological interpretation of these types of phenomena.

Portugal's position in the past 15 years has changed from that of a country of emigrants to a country of immigrants, and it has now assumed an important position as an entry point to Europe for African and Latin American migrants (mainly from the former Portuguese colonies such as Cape Verde, Angola, Guinea-Bissau, and Brazil). Although debates on ethnicity and class are not recent, new areas of enquiry are emerging within the current framework of intensifying transnational flows, suggesting new lines of research. The emergence of overclasses and underclasses on a transnational scale is an area which merits further study within the context of an enlarged Europe. The increasing transfer of the clandestine workforce to the EU countries makes the problems of the underclass, racism, and social exclusion more visible.

In the case of Portugal, with the arrival of significant numbers of workers from Eastern European countries (particularly Ukrainians, Moldavians and Romanians) and their rapid absorption into precarious and badly paid jobs, these problems have become very evident. In the building construction sector, for example, which employs a large proportion of immigrants from Africa, it can already be seen that there is a difference in the distribution of professional tasks between these two groups. The East Europeans tend to assume positions of higher responsibility more quickly and also are better paid, in comparison with the Africans. Parallel to this, after the recent policies to authorize residence for these workers, a union-style association has already been established for East European workers. While the Cape-Verdians usually remain in more precarious employment situations and tend to live in more closed communities (often the reason for racial segregation and accusations of urban violence), the new emigrants from the Eastern countries find it easier to integrate, whether in companies or, for example, in the type of domestic work (such as daily or company cleaning staff) which is beginning to absorb many newly-arrived Ukrainian women.

It is impossible to know to what extent these phenomena are transitory or how deep a structuring effect they will have on the recomposition of classes. But, no doubt, they do show that ethnic and identity differences in this new context bring new complexities to class inequalities. Racial prejudice seem to be more decisive here than language difference, since, in spite of speaking Portuguese, the Africans are dispatched to the ghettos and resist integration while the Ukrainians and Moldavians integrate better, although they do not speak Portuguese. The wounds of post-colonialism, on the one hand, and questions of religion and color, on the other, are, without doubt, factors that must be taken into account. It is known that the construction of racism has always been connected with class (Balibar 1991), but it will be important to investigate exactly how this connects with class and collective action in present times. The fact that black workers are oppressed and socially excluded cannot, of course, be separated from the conditions of hyper-exploitation to which they are subjected at work. Furthermore, the fact that Eastern European workers have won better positions in the employment market is inseparable from the similarities of color and culture they share with the Portuguese. It should be added that they are better trained and have higher levels of education, which is, of course, a very relevant advantage.

If, in the future, the associations promoted by the Luso-Africans manage to establish alliances with the Eastern European immigrants within the context of work, it will be possible to consider a new "class struggle" of the displaced proletariat of the twenty-first century. It will certainly be difficult for the new struggles and movements to be simply "about class." This struggle, if it expands, as one can expect, must be articulated together with a whole set of NGOs, anti-hegemonic movements and associations formed to combat poverty, exclusion, racism, etc.

In conclusion, it may be said that Weberian and Marxist-inspired class analyses will continue to draw closer together in search of the reciprocal enrichment necessary for the analysis of many of the problems emerging today. The theme of inequality, far from becoming irrelevant, seems to have assumed a new central focus. The rising injustices in the contemporary world demand that critical approaches should be revitalized in order to grasp the growing complexities. If the social sciences in general cannot ignore the turbulence and social conflict which surrounds us all, class analysis in particular must not only look at inequalities and social differences, but also at the actors and the social and political movements which lead the struggles against these inequalities and differences today.

It is certain that the development of new lines of analysis relating to these themes will require the use of appropriate research skills. Qualitative methods will also continue to be essential in studying their true sociological scope. The way we observe spatial contexts within which social life is restructured, even when this process results in much broader structural effects, is undoubtedly a decisive factor in penetrating the real world and understanding the pulse of society. I am convinced that understanding the rising complexity of social change, which affects us today, requires redoubling our attention to the orientation of subjects, their representations and interactions in practical life where identities and inequalities are constantly being rewritten, propelled or inhibited by collective action.

Even in a global society in which mobility and flux of all kinds are defining new features, the impact of globalization only has meaning because it affects concrete people, groups or social sectors. The counterpart to globalization is localization. Giving priority to qualitative methodology means, in my opinion, giving priority to a critical approach to society and its problems and also to a critical vision of sociology itself. Direct observation and participant observation of micro-spaces and micro-realities require proximity to concrete groups and the sharing of their lives and problems. It means doing this there, in the place where they live. Obviously this is one methodological option among others. But it is an option that will not be content with an aseptic interpretation of reality, preferring instead to construct a citizen-science not simply limited to identifying exclusion and inequality but able to contribute towards discovering possible paths towards inclusion and social justice.

NOTES

1   A professor of Economics who had connections with democratic Church movements, via the circles of progressive Catholicism, who dedicated his work to a study of corporatism within a State institution, thereby becoming introduced to the major contemporary sociological writers. In 1963 he was authorized to establish the Gabinete de Investigações Sociais (Bureau for Social Research) and the journal *Análise Social* (*Social Analysis*), and thus became the founder of Portuguese sociology.

2   Particularly during the period 1968–72, known as the *Primavera marcelista* (the Marcellist Spring), when Salazar left office and was replaced by Marcello Caetano and there were some signs of greater political openness and relaxation of censorship.

3   Living in England at the time, he became a professor at Leeds University.

4   The Institute for Higher Education, Business and Administration, University of Lisbon. The team consisted of João Ferreira de Almeida, António Firmino da Costa, Fernando Luís Machado and José Luís Casanova.

5   Alfama is a very well known historical area in the city of Lisbon, located between the St George castle and the Tagus river.

6   Developed and employed in many field studies including Boaventura Sousa Santos (1983 and 1995) and Michael Burawoy (1979, 1985, 1991).

7   I applied the survey to two different samples, one at a national level and the other at a regional level.

8   Using Wright's terminology I should say, instead, contradictory class locations.

9   It has been noted that, following the triumph of the Salazar fascist regime in 1926, this local neighborhood movement became the target for powerful ideological manipulation by the *Estado Novo*, supported by disciplinary policies to control the workers' free time activities, which further contributed towards emphasizing the construction of an adaptable community.

10 This transgressive activity is also present at a cultural and community level, when the local history of the construction of the popular culture and leisure activities of the working class in the region are analyzed (Estanque 1995).

11 At Coimbra University, for example, about 40 percent of the students of working class origin (Estanque et al. 2002).

REFERENCES

Almeida, J. C. F. (1970) "Mobilidade e posições sociais," *Análise Social* 29: 5–21.
Almeida, J. F. (1986) *Classes Sociais nos Campos: Camponeses Parciais Numa Região do Noroeste*. Lisbon: Instituto de Ciências Sociais.

Almeida, J. F., Costa, A. F., and Machado, F. L. (1994) "Recomposição socio-profissional e novos protagonismos," in Reis, A. (ed.), *Portugal – 20 Anos de Democracia*. Lisbon: Círculo de Leitores.

AAVV (1996) *Para Abrir as Ciências Sociais*. Mem Martins/Lisbon: Europa-América.

Balibar, E. (1991) "From class struggle to classless struggle," in Balibar, E. and Wallerstein, I., *Race, Nation and Class*. London: Verso.

Bourdieu, P. (1979) *La Distinction: Critique Sociale du Jugement*. Paris: Minuit.

—— (1996) "Understanding," *Theory, Culture and Society* 13 (2): 17–37.

Burawoy, M. (1979) *Manufacturing Consent*. Chicago: University of Chicago Press.

—— (1985) *The Politics of Production*. London: Verso.

—— (1989) "The limits of Wright's analytical Marxism and an alternative," in Wright, E. O. (ed.), *The Debate on Classes*. London: Verso.

—— (1991) *Ethnography Unbounded: Power and Resistance in the Modern Metropolis*. Berkeley, CA: University of California Press.

Cabral, M. V. (1997) *Cidadania Política e Equidade Social em Portugal*. Oeiras: Celta.

—— (forthcoming) *Desigualdades Sociais e Percepções da Justiça*. Lisbon: ICS–Imprensa de Ciências Sociais.

Collins, R. (1981) "On the microfoundations of macrosociology," *American Journal of Sociology* 86: 984–1014.

Collinson, D. (1992) *Managing the Shopfloor: Subjectivity, Masculinity and Workplace Culture*. Berlin and New York: Walter de Gruyter.

Costa, A. F. (1999) *A Sociedade de Bairro: Dinâmicas Sociais da Identidade Cultural*. Oeiras: Celta.

Costa, A. F., Machado, F. L., and Almeida, J. F. (1990) "Estudantes e amigos: Trajectórias de classe e redes de sociabilidade," *Análise Social* 105–6: 193–221.

Crompton, R. and Mann, M. (eds.) (1986) *Gender and Stratification*. Cambridge: Polity Press.

de Certeau, M. (1984) *The Practice of Everyday Life*. Berkeley, CA: University of California Press.

Erikson, E. and Goldthorpe, J. (1993) *The Constant Flux: A Study of Class Mobility in Industrial Societies*. Oxford: Clarendon Press.

Esping-Andersen, G. (1993) *Changing Classes: Stratification and Mobility in Post-Industrial Societies*. London: Sage/ISA.

Estanque, E. (1995) "O lazer e a cultura popular, entre a regulação e a transgressão: um estudo de caso," *Revista Crítica de Ciências Sociais* 43: 93–122.

—— (1999) "Acção colectiva, comunidade e movimentos sociais," *Revista Crítica de Ciências Sociais* 55: 85–111.

—— (2000) *Entre a Fábrica e a Comunidade: Práticas e subjectividades no operariado do calçado*. Porto: Afrontamento.

Estanque, E. and Mendes, J. M. (1998) *Classes e Desigualdades Sociais em Portugal: Um Estudo Comparativo*. Porto: Afrontamento.

Estanque, E. and Nunes, J. A. (2002) "A Universidade perante a transformação social e as orientações dos estudantes: o caso da Universidade de Coimbra," *Oficina do CES* 169: 1–22.

Ferrão, J. (1985) "Recomposição social e estruturas regionais de classes (1970–81)," *Análise Social* 87–9: 565–604.

Ferrara, A. (1997) "The paradox of community," *International Sociology* 12 (4): 395–408.

Fine, G. A. (1991) "On the macrofoundations of microsociology," *Sociological Quarterly* 32 (2): 161–77.

Fowler, B. (1996) "An introduction to Pierre Bourdieu's 'Understanding'," *Theory, Culture and Society* 13 (2): 1–16.

Fraser, N. (1997) *Justice Interruptus: Critical Reflections on the "Postsocialist" Condition*. London: Routledge.

Grusky, D. B. and Sørensen, J. B. (1998) "Can class analysis be salvaged?", *American Journal of Sociology* 103 (5): 1187–235.

Guerra, J. and Nunes, A. S. (1969) "A crise da Universidade em Portugal: reflexões e sugestões," *Análise Social* 25–6: 5–49.

Hofstede, G. (1980) *Culture's Consequences*. London: Sage.

Honneth, A. (1996) *The Struggle for Recognition*. Cambridge, MA: MIT Press.

Machado, F. L., Costa, A. F., and Almeida, J. F. (1989) "Identidades e orientações dos estudantes: classes, convergências, especificidades," *Revista Crítica de Ciências Sociais* 27–8: 189–209.

Machado, F. L. and Costa, A. F. (1998) "Processos de uma modernidade inacabada," in Viegas, J. M. and Costa, A. F. (eds.), *Portugal, que Modernidade?* Oeiras: Celta.

Marques, A. and Bairrada, M. (1982) "As classes sociais na população activa portuguesa, 1950–1970," *Análise Social* 72–4: 1279–97.

Martins, H. (1998) [1971] *Classes, "Status" e Poder*. Lisbon: Instituto de Ciências Sociais da Universidade de Lisboa.

Miranda, J. D. (1969) "A população universitária portuguesa," *Análise Social* 25–6: 158–66.

Nunes, A. S. (1964) "Portugal, sociedade dualista em evolução," *Análise Social* 7–8: 407–62.

—— (1968) "A população universitária," *Análise Social* 22–4: 295–385.

Nunes, A. S. and Miranda, D. (1969) "A composição social da população portuguesa," *Análise Social* 27–8: 333–81.

Pakulsky, J. and Waters, M. (1996) *The Death of Class*. London: Sage.

Poulantzas, N. (1974) *Les Classes Sociales dans le Capitalisme d'Aujourd'hui*. Paris: Seuil.

Reay, D. (1998) "Rethinking social class: qualitative perspectives on class and gender," *Sociology* 32 (2): 259–75.

Santos, B. S. (1983) "Os conflitos urbanos no Recife: o caso do 'Skylab'," *Revista Crítica de Ciências Sociais* 11: 9–60.

—— (1995) *Toward a New Common Sense*. London: Routledge.

—— (2001) "Toward an epistemology of blindness," *European Journal of Social Theory* 4 (3): 251ff.

Wright, E. O. (1978) *Class, Crisis and the State*. London: New Left Books.

—— (1985) *Classes*. London: Verso.

—— (ed.) (1989) *The Debate on Classes*. London: Verso.

—— (1997) *Class Counts*. Cambridge: Cambridge University Press.

FURTHER READING

Bourdieu, P. and Wacquant, L. (1992) *An Invitation to Reflexive Sociology.* Chicago: University of Chicago Press.
Burawoy, M. et al. (2000) *Global Ethnography: Forces, Connections, and Imaginations in a Postmodern World.* Berkeley, CA: University of California Press.

CHAPTER SEVEN

Understanding Class Inequality in Australia

BILL MARTIN AND JUDY WAJCMAN

INTRODUCTION

Australia's colonial history, its emergence into full nationhood during the twentieth century, and its relationship with the "core" capitalist economies of Britain, the US, and Europe form the essential context for Australian studies of social class and inequality. While many of the theoretical concerns of this research have been derived from British, European, and US sociology, a few are distinctively Australian, and most have developed new inflections in Australian research. Qualitative styles of research were the natural choice in early Australian studies focused on class inequality, particularly community studies. They produced an impressive record of in-depth understanding of how class inequalities were structured and operated in rural towns. However, their extension to urban areas was limited, and many researchers turned to survey-based research using quantitative techniques to develop their understanding of the issues. Nevertheless, qualitative researchers periodically continued to offer unique insights into class cultures, mechanisms of class reproduction, and class relationships. More recently, new questions about the changing experience of work and its relation to class and culture have led some researchers to reincorporate qualitative elements at the center of their research. In selectively reviewing the Australian literature on class and inequality, we indicate the major theoretical issues that concerned researchers in all traditions. Although we focus on findings from qualitative work, other results are sometimes a necessary reference point. Reflecting on the contribution of Australian qualitative research to the field, it is possible to identify methodological aspects of such research that are central to its usefulness. We illustrate some of these points by examining interview data on the role of education in Australian managers' careers, arguing that our expectations about the implications of future shifts in social mobility patterns should partly depend on research of this kind. In thinking about likely future directions for the field, both contemporary social change and past research achievements (and missed opportunities) are likely sources of inspiration.

Social Class and Inequality in Australia: A Selective Review

The first wave of Australian research on social class arose as a central element in community studies, particularly those of rural towns. Researchers typically immersed themselves in the life of a town, collecting data in a variety of ways. They lived in the town for up to two years, interviewed residents both formally and informally, observed and participated in community events and meetings, and sometimes undertook systematic surveys as well. The early dominance of these approaches was largely due to the unusual history of sociology in Australia. Indeed, there was no distinct sociology department or group in Australia until 1959, and several of the key members of the first and second generations of Australian sociologists were initially trained as social anthropologists (e.g., Martin, Oxley, Wild), particularly at the University of Sydney. One of the early studies was undertaken in two "semi-industrial" rural towns in the 1960s by Oxley, who saw himself in the "tradition of social anthropology" (1978: 4).

Like other social class researchers of the period, Oxley was greatly concerned with "Australian egalitarianism," a tendency, widely perceived in popular discourse, for Australians to reject status distinctions in their social relationships (see Ward 1958). Oxley sought to understand how an egalitarian culture could co-exist with palpable wealth and income inequalities. Based on his interviews with many townspeople and his observations of local politics and voluntary organizations, he argued that the struggle for status in the towns revolved around two independent "value complexes." There was indeed an egalitarian value system that emphasized the fundamental equality of townspeople, and required them to treat each other equally outside the workplace. But, in different ways depending on their position, townspeople also recognized a "stratification" system based on the structural features of unequal class positions. These two principles jostled with each other in community life, as the example of local voluntary association leadership showed. Oxley found that, while stratification position greatly affected the likelihood that a person would be regarded as an appropriate voluntary association leader and become one, it was necessary for leaders to conform to the egalitarian norms in order to lead an organization effectively. While Oxley's study was widely read and respected, it did not produce consensus on the issues at stake.

Studying a pastorally based town that was older than the ones Oxley researched, Wild (1974) showed how status perceptions infused almost all day-to-day social relationships. He argued that the status system of the town, traceable to English class-based status culture, placed a small group of wealthy land-owning families in a distinctive upper position. Australian egalitarian culture made little headway against this status system. But Wild's most controversial claim was that the town's status system (made up of common styles of life, behavioral norms, and relations of deference and superiority) was not reducible to its class structure, defined by "varying connections to the means of production" (1974: 3). Indeed, he argued, the status system was far more important in town life than was class position. Despite the great influence of Wild's study, most later analysts came to agree with Dempsey (1990: 156) that Wild overestimated the autonomy of the status system from the "objective" class structure that underlaid it. One important reason for this view was that a number of later studies focused on rural towns with a strong industrial base where the picture of fairly cohesive communities that arose from work like Oxley's and Wild's could not be sustained (e.g., Kriegler 1980; Williams 1981). In a path-breaking study, Williams (1981) showed the strong class antagonism to be found in a town whose only significant industry was two large open-cut coalmines owned by a US multinational company. Finding substantial distrust of managers by workers, with frequent industrial disputes over apparently minor issues, she saw strong evidence of "a union-based working-class counter-hegemony" among the mine workers. Australian egalitarianism meant little in this context! But Williams added a very important further dimension to research on Australian class relations by using a Marxist-feminist approach to analyze the relation between working-class men and women in the town. She concluded that women could develop an opposition to patriarchal relations parallel to men's opposition to capitalist relations (see also Collis 1999).

Despite the dominance of urban life in Australia, studies of class relations and inequality in urban communities have provided limited insight into the lived experience of class. Some early research made a promising start by echoing British and American work and focusing on class variation in the structure and character of social networks and the class communities they constructed (Martin 1967, 1970). Other studies examined the objective inequalities in a suburb, and related these to its community life, in one case showing how middle-class "caretakers" dominated civic leadership in a working-class suburb (Bryson and Thompson 1972). A follow-up to this latter research explained the declining fortunes of the suburb's residents by a range of national and global developments which removed traditional employment opportunities from residents of *Newtown* and reduced state support for them (Bryson and Winter 1999, Winter and Bryson 1998).[1] Focusing on residents' views and understandings of life in their suburbs did allow some researchers to connect the relative homogeneity of suburban "dreams" to more objective aspects of class position (Richards 1990). However, there is no substantial body of work that might produce a comprehensive understanding of how such patterns vary by social class. Indeed, the most recent work on these issues suggests that in working-class suburbs, the ravages of economic restructuring have made any form of coherent class-based culture and identity almost impossible (McDonald 1999).

Since the 1970s, issues of Australian class structure have attracted steady attention from Australian sociologists. As in other industrial societies, the growth of intermediate occupations has received attention. Williams (1988), for example, focused on telephone company technicians, bank employees, and flight attendants, examining the complex class relations of these positions and showing how gender relations are integral to class patterns and positions. Others have focused on the broader mapping of class structure, adopting models from Britain and the US (e.g., Holton and Martin 1987; Baxter et al. 1991). This has suggested a class structure broadly comparable to European and North American countries, though Australia appears to have a somewhat smaller working class and larger managerial middle class than its obvious comparitors. Some explanations for the larger managerial middle class echo Encel's early assessment of the importance of bureaucracy and bureaucrats arising from Australia's origins as a state-sponsored penal colony (1970). However, recent evidence suggests an important shift in the Australian middle class towards a market-based, private sector-dominated managerial segment (Martin 1998a, 2001; Wajcman and Martin 2001). Another major dimension of middle-class restructuring – the increase in "knowledge workers" and the restructuring and globalization of expertise and expert labor markets – remains under-researched and a matter of controversy in Australia. Connell and Wood's (2002) argument that such workers carry out the will and tasks of a "ruling class" contrasts with other analyses suggesting a new form of middle-class autonomy (e.g., Martin 1998b). Recent research on the Australian capitalist class has indicated that it is relatively open, particularly to entrepreneurs, and somewhat less densely connected than in some other countries (Alexander et al. 1994; Alexander 1998; Carroll and Alexander 1999; Gilding 1999), though it remains a dominating force. This suggests something of a contrast to historical analyses which saw tighter organization of the class (Connell and Irving 1992).

A wave of post-World War II migration to Australia raised important questions about the ethnic structuring of the Australian class system, particularly in regard to the working class. Adopting accounts developed in Britain, Collins (1975, 1978, 1991) argued that immigrants performed the function of a "reserve army" of labor in Australia, providing a pool of available labor when it was needed and weakening the working class in conflicts over wages and working conditions. This analysis was sharply rejected by Lever-Tracy and Quinlan (1988) who showed that ethnic segmentation meant that migrants were usually core workers in the industries and occupations where they were clustered, notably the undesirable, dangerous, low-skilled jobs that fuelled the post-war economic boom in Australia (see also Lever-Tracy 1983). Moreover migrant workers' varying experiences before coming to Australia and their world-wide networks meant that they introduced a new volatility into Australian class and industrial relations. While this analysis applied well to post-war immigration to Australia from southern and eastern Europe, the end of the White Australia policy and a growing emphasis on skilled and business migration presented new challenges for class analysts. Recent research has focused on such issues as ethnic small business (Collins et al. 1995; Lever-Tracy et al. 1991) and its global reach (Lever-Tracy et al. 1996), and skilled migration in an increasingly globalized middle-class labor market (Inglis 1999).

Class imagery and class consciousness have been studied in Australian sociology using a variety of approaches. One consistent, early finding was simply that people's images of class structure varied considerably (Davies 1967; Hiller 1975a, 1975b), though the origins of this variation were matters of controversy. In an early finding that greatly influenced the field, Connell contradicted a common view, exemplified by Davies (1967), that people's images of class structure arose from their own direct experience.[2] When he interviewed children of varying ages, Connell (1971, 1972) found that beliefs about the class structure and class schemas did not vary systematically according to the class location of children's families. Instead, children's images of class structure, and their place in it, appeared to arise from historically embedded "traditions" which have only a limited connection to contemporary experience. In later theoretical work, Connell developed this idea, connecting it more systematically to his brand of Marxist class theory, to argue the crucial role of cultural hegemony in maintaining and reproducing "ruling class" dominance in Australia and similar societies (1977).

By the early 1980s, Connell's position was itself hegemonic in leftist Australian sociology. Chamberlain's important study took it as one of three competing accounts of "the sources and character of class imagery in contemporary Australia" (1983: 1). He found that a "structural" theory, in which class consciousness and imagery arose from direct experience with little influence from ruling class culture, particularly that passed on through the media, was best able to predict the patterns he found. However, while his research provided an important and powerful corrective against over-estimation of the power of the media in dictating social imagery to the mass of the working class, it was widely regarded as oversimplifying matters. Some research centered on the cultural and linguistic mechanisms that allowed working-class people to combine both support and rejection of dominant values in their images of social structure and social processes (e.g., Emmison 1985). One quantitative study found that class identification was a weak aspect of social identities for most Australians (Emmison and Western 1991), with another concluding that the lack of salience of class identity for many people accounted for the weak association between class location and class images and affiliation (Graetz 1983, 1986). Connected to this work, a long tradition of research in Australia has investigated the connection between social class and politics, particularly voting. Most recent research suggests that, although there has been some decline in class voting, it has been less in Australia than in many other advanced capitalist societies (Weakliem and Western 1999).

Despite these findings, obvious continuing class inequalities have stimulated research on class reproduction. One strand emphasized the cultural and social relational basis for class reproduction. In a path-breaking study, Connell and his collaborators (1982) used material from an intensive study of schools, students, parents and teachers to argue that non-government "ruling-class schools" were organized so as to reproduce social relationships and personal dispositions appropriate to a dominant market-based capitalist class. In contrast, government "working-class schools" embodied a bureaucratic, individualistic structure and ethos which was alien to children from working-class families, and thus functioned to disempower them and ensure their confinement to working-class destinations. Other research confirmed the key role played by some elite private schools in reproducing Australian elites (Peel and McCalman 1988). Although quantitative studies often obtained equivocal results when they tried to locate the independent effect of school type on later achievement (e.g., Graetz 1990), Connell's finding gained wide acceptance as representing the powerful mutually reinforcing effects of class background and schooling in the reproduction of class inequalities.

A related strand of research aimed to understand working-class cultures and subcultures, particularly focusing on aspects of their resistance and deviance. One study showed how riots at an annual motor cycle race meeting could be understood as expressive of a working-class subculture and its relationship to police authority (Cuneen and Lynch 1988; see also Stratton 1993). An important theme in recent work in this genre has been identifying the gendering and sexualization of working-class cultures. Connell et al. (1991) and Walker (1998a, 1998b) have examined aspects of the construction of masculinity among young working-class men, showing both how forms of masculinity affect relations between men and women, and how they are implicated in wider class relationships. Other studies have looked at deviant working-class masculinities (Connell et al. 1993). Some research has also examined the tension between neglect, sexual abuse and resistance in the school experience of working-class girls (Walker 1993). The labor market experience of working-class people, and its effect on working-class culture, have occasionally been studied (Watson 1993). Effectively, this research has studied cultures, identities, and life patterns that maintain and reinforce the social position of working-class people. In an innovative study, Zadoroznyj (1999) examined class differences in how women consume birthing services. She showed how working-class and middle-class women bring different consumption styles to their first birth, but that these styles converge in second and later births. Other research has examined the complexities of mobility via education for a small group of working-class men (Gleeson 1996).

The record of Australian research on social class and inequality reflects both important changes in Australian society, and significant shifts in sociological approaches to the problem of inequality. The early studies focusing on rural communities reflected a society in which social change was relatively slow, and it created a picture of cohesive communities despite major class and status divisions. Rapid industrial development, a shift towards the US as a source of foreign investment, quickly growing cities and mass migration from southern and eastern Europe all undermined the sense of stability from these early studies. Moreover, new intellectual influences sensitized Australian sociologists to class conflict and its relation to gender, ethnic, and racial inequalities and tensions. The result was research that illuminated the shifting contours of inequality and conflict, from Williams' study of a coal mining town to research on the class dimensions of the new migrant experience to studies of how working-class cultures structure conflict. But the theme of enduring patterns of class structure and outcomes has remained a strong one. Not only research directly on class structure, but also much of that on class consciousness and class reproduction, and some on class communities and cultures, emphasises social processes and patterns that are slow to change and have persistent effects on Australian social life. Balancing a sensitivity to changing class patterns and processes with research on enduring inequalities seems likely to be the same challenge in the future that it has been in the past.

METHODOLOGICAL ISSUES

The significant place of community studies in the Australian literature on class inequalities provides a basis for assessing the opportunities and limitations broadly "ethnographic" approaches offer the study of social class. As the work of Oxley, Wild or Williams illustrates, classic community studies' variety of methods (from observation and interviews to surveys) and long engagement in the field can produce research with unique depth and resonance. In describing this method, A. P. Elkin, instigator of many of the "first wave" of Australian community studies, implied an underlying holistic social reality:

> In this approach, a community is studied as a whole, and from all aspects – history, geography, kinship, group divisions, economics, recreation, politics, religion and external relationships; and an attempt is made to ascertain the functional relationships of these different factors in the community's life. (1945: vii)

The assumption of unproblematic community boundedness and unity worked well in small rural towns, especially in an era of limited geographic mobility. Even in Williams's *Open Cut*, with its focus on a town dominated by two mines owned by an American multinational, the lived reality of class inequality in the town could be separated from the contextual effects of its "external relationships" (the role of the parent company, of the Australian industrial relations system, of the exigencies of a capitalist economy, etc.). However, among urban residents, geographic and community boundaries could not be equated so easily. Focusing on a single working-class suburb could produce a striking picture of its relative economic disadvantage and its residents' patterns of life (e.g., Bryson and Thompson 1972), or of how residents understood their suburb (e.g., Richards 1990). However, much of the class content of peoples' daily lives in cities necessarily involved relationships which extended beyond their suburb, as, for example, with employers and managers. Early research which attempted to deconstruct the notion of community in urban settings, suggesting its sociological meaning needed to be extended to include "cultural construct" and "non-local relationships and 'belonging together'" (Martin 1970: 339), may have offered a route forward. Learning from these traditions, contemporary researchers could put together the multiple method approaches of the successful rural community studies with a focus on how networks of local and non-local relationships in urban areas constitute class relationships and, possibly, a variety of communities. Such an approach may still provide an unexploited pathway to understanding contemporary urban class inequalities.

While not strictly community studies, some research has shown the benefits of multi-method approaches focused on social relationships. When Connell et al. (1982) researched students, parents, and schools by treating students as the center of clusters of relationships, they were able to study groupings much more like Martin's non-local community relationships defined by participants "belonging together." One of the most powerful aspects of Connell et al.'s (1982) argument is the way in which the points of view of students, teachers, and parents are used to construct a complex picture of how class is lived through the relationships that constitute and reproduce it. It is striking that the networks of relationships they describe are not closed or fixed, but open and mutable; yet they clearly constitute community-like groupings. It may be that the language of sampling is a useful way to conceptualize the methodological issue here (see Becker 1998). Connell et al. used sampled students as a route to a sample of network "clusters." But these "clusters" were guaranteed to have points of intersection because students were grouped through the schools they attend, so that the study was able to empirically assess the character and density of intra-class relationships without prejudging them. A focus on understanding class structure and class experience in urban situations through networks thus appears to offer significant pay-offs.

Australian research on class inequalities also illustrates the usefulness of combining qualitative research methods aimed at exploring meanings and social relationships with quantitative ones more oriented to definitively establishing relevant social patterns or statistically based hypothesis testing. One standard way of combining such approaches is to use qualitative techniques such as observation and unstructured interviewing to develop initial ideas about a topic, and then to use these ideas as the basis for survey-based data collection which is analyzed quantitatively. Williams's (1981) study illustrates this approach, and its pay-offs. She claims that without her initial interview-based fieldwork, the survey of workplace experience she later completed would have neglected key aspects of class experience and relationships in the town. Although other community studies often combined research techniques of the kinds used by Williams, many were not so clear-cut about the logical relation between the methods. These studies illustrate a second approach to combining methodologies in which Denzin's term "multi-method triangulation" is appropriate. Here, data collected using different approaches is used as the researcher sees it to be appropriate either to buttress results by showing that they are found irrespective of the kind of data used, or in the hope that if one method does not produce data on a crucial issue, then another will. Studies like Oxley's and Wild's illustrate this orientation. Studies of this kind often appear to develop research designs as they progress, with almost opportunistic decisions about data collection techniques being made along the way. In Wild's case, for example, a series of different data sources, such as results of observation and participation, opinions of key informants and a survey, were used cumulatively to develop a clear picture of the town's status hierarchy and the place of key actors in it.

In a third approach, what are usually seen as both quantitative and qualitative approaches are melded. Chamberlain's (1983) study of class consciousness illustrates this technique. While one strand of Chamberlain's analysis focused on the results of cross-tabulations of Likert items, they were constantly interrogated and interpreted using interviewees' comments about the questions and their discussions of what the questions meant to them. This approach allowed Chamberlain to convincingly demonstrate that he understood the meaning of questions to respondents. Chamberlain's approach shows the potential advantages of collecting data in a form that allows both quantitative and qualitative analysis, particularly where a researcher is interested in attitudes, beliefs, or the meanings actors attach to actions and events. One reason that Chamberlain's model has not been widely emulated may be that his quantitative analysis was very rudimentary, being essentially bivariate, and it is not immediately obvious how his style of qualitative analysis could be used effectively alongside more sophisticated multivariate quantitative analysis.

Although much less centrally concerned with class inequality, Richards's (1990) community study shows the advantages of some quantification in an essentially qualitative study. One of the first major pieces of Australian qualitative research to use the now well-known NUD.IST software that Richards helped develop, *Nobody's Home* focuses on a new suburb in a large city. It deals with residents' images of the suburb (including its class composition, along with other issues such as the meaning of home ownership), and the ways family life is constructed and understood in the suburb. Richards's data analysis techniques were inspired primarily by Strauss (see Glaser and Strauss 1967; Strauss 1987), and involved, first, the inductive development of core themes in actors' meanings, followed by elaboration of these meanings and how they vary. The use of computer software appears to both permit and encourage systematic analysis of such "tree"-structured systems of meaning, including some quantification of results. For example, Richards's analysis of the meanings given to home ownership locates "control" as a key factor. She is then able to break this down into various senses, such as freedom from control by landlords and freedom to do as one likes. These are further elaborated, with the number of interviewees offering the various connected meanings providing a sense of how quantitatively important each was in the data. Richards's study is symptomatic of the early promise offered by the wave of methodological writing and interest in qualitative research which began in the early 1980s, along with the development of software for assisting with qualitative data analysis. These developments raised new possibilities of both combining quantitative and qualitative analyses, and analyzing textual data more systematically and in greater detail. Perhaps rather surprisingly, however, the potential of these methods has not been realized in a new wave of findings in the areas of class inequality in Australia.

While it would be going too far to say that the new systematic techniques for qualitative data analysis are a method in search of a question, it may be that they did not provide especially attractive routes to answering the questions which concerned Australian analysts of class inequality over the past 10 to 15 years. Most obviously, one set of questions was deeply bound up with quantitative techniques. These were the questions about the impacts of neo-liberalism and workplace and industrial relations change on class structures and inequalities: Are some classes growing or declining? Is there rebalancing between various class segments? How have inequalities between classes been changing? What has been the effect of workplace and industrial relations change on inequality and working conditions? Questions like these were framed in Australian debates so that quantitative analysis of survey data was the obvious route to answers (e.g., Martin 1998a, 2001; Pusey 1997, 2003; Western 2000). At the same time, another major strand of research in the 1990s really concerned class cultures, particularly the lived cultures of working-class sub-groups and how class interacted with other aspects of social location in identity formation (e.g., McDonald 1999; Watson 1993). Here, small scale studies, usually interview-based, were generally assumed in the way the research questions were asked. In this research, the new qualitative technologies did not offer major advantages over older lower-technology approaches. However, as the issues that concerned quantitative researchers increasingly come together with those of culture, identity, and action in a new "individualized" social environment (see below), it may be the new qualitative technologies will come into their own. This will be especially so in large-scale research that combines quantitative analysis of surveys with close qualitative study of particular groups of interest, possibly with a longitudinal dimension.

One growing concern among analysts of class inequalities in Australia, particularly those using qualitative techniques, has been both methodological and substantive, and has cross-cut the focus on more systematic and technically sophisticated qualitative research and data analysis. This is the political and ethical problem of the "voice" of those studied in this research. Although it has been of concern to researchers for some time, the issue has attained a new prominence with the rise of post-structuralist and post-colonial literatures. In some studies, the concern has been to make understandable and legitimate the activities of groups seen as deviant in mainstream Australian culture, such as rioters at motorcycle race meetings (Cuneen and Lynch 1988) or working-class homosexual men (Connell et al. 1993). Although voicing the self-image of such groups is rarely an explicit aim, much of this research appears predicated on the belief that the researchers' account of a group or individual's activities and self-understandings gives voice to them in ways that are beneficial to those studied. To some extent, these studies continue the long tradition in sociology, most notably in Marxist-influenced research, of speaking for groups and people taken as oppressed, exploited, or marginalized. However, they represent a new departure in two connected ways. First, they focus on the broadly cultural logic of the self-definition and actions of those they study, as opposed to the more material or structural aspects at the center of earlier Marxist studies. Second, they use data, notably verbatim material from interviews, in ways which appear to express more authentically the self-images and aspirations of the researched, especially compared to studies that assume the central explanatory role of particular social structures such as structurally defined social classes. Nevertheless, these studies still ultimately privilege the voices of researchers over those of the researched, both through their monopoly of control of the research design and of reporting the research results. In a recent example, McDonald (1999) attempted to construct a research design that would allow young working-class people with poor labor market prospects to raise grievances and concerns with people they regarded as significant and/or powerful in their local area. Perhaps, as McDonald implied, this process served the participants' interests while also allowing him, as a sociologist, to observe the struggles for identity formation as they happened. Such issues are likely to continue to concern qualitative researchers, particularly those studying inequalities.

When Australian research on class inequalities first appeared, the training in social anthropology of its authors ensured that qualitative, broadly ethnographic, methods would be dominant. With the consolidation of sociology as a discipline distinct from anthropology, and with the influence of American and some British research, more quantitative approaches became popular among many researchers. In some quarters, a fairly unproductive debate ensued about the "right" way to undertake the study of social inequality. Fortunately for the continued development of the field, a number of researchers, though noting these debates, pragmatically chose the research methods they saw as most suited to their objectives. In doing so they often found that different methods complemented each other, and even produced unexpected "synergies." It seems likely that future methodological progress will come from this more pragmatic approach to research techniques, rather than from doctrinaire insistence on one style of research rather than another. But one lesson that the most productive of Australian research demonstrates, like that elsewhere, is that careful thought and deliberate choices are necessary to fulfil the promise that a pragmatic, methodological pluralism can offer.

SOME EXAMPLES

In this section of the chapter we will discuss two components of our recent research on the careers of professionals and managers in large Australian companies.[3] This project involved interviews with 136 managers and professionals in 6 large companies, along with a survey of 525 such employees in the companies, including those interviewed (see Martin et al. 2000; Wajcman and Martin 2001). Here we will focus on research which primarily uses the interview data to examine class reproduction and class mobility. Interviews were taped and transcribed for analysis, generating a mass of data. This material was analyzed with the assistance of NUD.IST.

The study of social mobility (and immobility) has been dominated by large-scale quantitative research for the past couple of decades. It has been remarkably successful in establishing a good understanding of the relative openness of "mobility regimes" in a variety of societies, cross-national similarities and differences in the structure of patterns of mobility, and how these have changed over time (Erikson and Goldthorpe 1992). Such research has focused on the mobility due purely to the "openness" of a society's mobility regime, the so-called "circulation" mobility, by statistically controlling "structural" mobility, that due to shifts in occupational or class structure. Yet this distinction does not refer at all to the social processes that individuals experience in their own "mobility trajectories." Indeed, the widespread assumption seems to be that, so long as circulation mobility patterns remain relatively unchanged, the social processes which produce mobility and immobility remain the same. The implausibility of this assumption has recently been highlighted through Noble's (2000) speculative analysis of the likely impact of the end of the expansion in managerial and professional occupations on British gross mobility patterns during the first half of the twenty-first century. Without substantially violating the assumption of unchanging circulation mobility patterns, Noble shows that, during the next 50 years, British managerial and professional occupations are likely to shift from drawing most of their recruits from lower backgrounds to being primarily self-recruiting. Under these circumstances, the dominant social processes which determine mobility experiences are likely to shift from being ones which sort potential recruits into middle class occupations to ones which maintain the barriers for outsiders' entry into these positions (see, for example, Brown 1995). The implications of such shifts are obvious and significant, and include those for social tensions between classes.

The possibility of important changes in the social processes that generate social mobility also highlight limitations to current knowledge about them. Sophisticated statistical analyses of mobility patterns accurately describe associations between origins and destinations and, sometimes, how a few key variable such as education mediate these associations (Western 1999), but they are not satisfying accounts of precisely how mobility and immobility are generated (Devine 1998). Qualitative research has the potential to contribute significantly on both scores, by providing more complete and nuanced understandings of how social origins feed into destinations, and by illuminating changes in these processes. To illustrate this potential, we focus here on interviewees' responses to questions about the families in which they grew up, and about how they began their careers, from the above-mentioned study. While it is well established that various aspects of family background significantly affect people's occupational achievements, exactly how this occurs is less firmly known. One important issue is the mediating role of education in intergenerational transmission. Our data suggested that there may be at least three distinct ways in which education is understood in families, and thus is able to act as a transmitter of class position, or as a mechanism for upward mobility.[4]

First, we found ample evidence that confirms earlier findings and assumptions that where one or both parents have high educational achievements, children learn early to expect the same of themselves. In some cases parents virtually directly organized their children's tertiary education by finding them cadetships or accompanying them to universities. In these cases, education, particularly tertiary education, is seen by parents as part of the normal route to entry into a desirable career, and children adopt this meaning for their own educational pathways. But what of families where parents had not achieved particularly high levels of formal education? Here we found two distinct patterns, two further meanings of education. In one small group of cases, a parent, usually the father, had been a skilled technical worker and his son became a tertiary qualified professional in a similar area to his father's. For example, two interviewees had fathers with metal trades skills and both became mechanical engineers (and subsequently managers in large multinational engineering companies). Here, professional tertiary qualifications were not assumed as a general route into a desirable career path. Instead, they represented the highest possible development of knowledge in a quite particular technical area which was regarded as intrinsically interesting. Fathers' craft pride and commitment to the area seemed to have been transmitted to sons who pursued it by seeking university qualifications which would allow full development and participation of those skills.

Education is sometimes seen as an important route for upward mobility: educational qualifications allow children from working-class backgrounds entry into middle-class careers. An important sociological issue is whether it is possible to locate systematic differences between families from which this route is and is not successful. Many previous studies have shown how schools and working-class orientations to education make it difficult for them to use education as a route to social mobility. But, why do some families use this route despite such factors? Focusing on these issues led us to a third meaning education had for some interviewees. Some immigrant families had seen education as a resource that they could actively secure for their children to ensure their upward mobility. For example, one interviewee described how his

Greek immigrant parents had chosen one of Sydney's elite private schools for his education, and of the contrast with his classmates:

> That was a fairly major jump in life, to go into an all boy's school, seeing kids whose parents and themselves were rather affluent and here's my working class parents struggling away to make sure that I get an education which they thought was important, to get me out of the public system and get me to what they thought was the best education at the time . . .

Q: Do you know why your parents chose School X?

A: My father did a bit of a study, I guess, and talked to people that he knew. (Financial controller, engineering company)

He went on to do a commerce/accounting degree and was on a quite successful career path when interviewed. In cases like this, children's educational achievements were part of an immigrant family's conscious strategy, along with the decision to immigrate itself, for providing their children with the resources that would allow them to achieve upward mobility. For these children, educational opportunities had been powerfully charged with the hopes and aspirations of their parents.

In essence, these examples suggest that the meaning education is given within families is extremely important for understanding how it affects mobility, and that it varies between families. But more generally, it indicates that if we are to understand class reproduction and mobility, we may need to look closely at what children learn about work and careers in families, even when formal education is not a key element. Two patterns from our data illustrate this point. First, it is well established that the children of managers are particularly likely to become managers, and that formal education is often not a crucial aspect of this class reproduction. Indeed, most of our interviewees with managerial fathers had not completed tertiary degrees before beginning their careers. They had made their own managerial careers by entering large companies in entry level clerical or administrative positions, particularly in the financial services sector, and moving up the organization. While in a few cases, fathers appeared to have provided direct contacts into companies, in most the influence of family was in conveying knowledge about how a career of this kind might be pursued and imagining oneself in it. One middle manager in an insurance company had a father who had become a senior HR manager at a large commercial TV station after working his way up through office administration jobs in an industrial company. Throughout the interview, there were indications of the tacit understanding of such careers he had gained from his father, and the fact that he had never imagined himself doing anything else. Yet this influence had become so naturalized that he could hardly see it:

> *Q:* When you went to look for a job, was your father's experience . . . important in the kind of job that you looked for? . . . did you take explicit advice from him about where you might look for a job?
>
> *A:* No, not really . . . my brother . . . was always the trades type of person. I was totally opposite, I was more the office style . . . what kickstarted it off was work experience. Because I'd worked in a couple of offices, I thought this was my caper . . . Dad would have . . . helped us with our resumes, given us a helping hand with . . . how to handle yourself and present yourself, but it was really up to me, I suppose.

Interviewees from working-class backgrounds who had pursued organizational careers without prior tertiary education also indicated the importance of family influences, but in a quite different way. Remarkably, most of these people were the children of immigrants or had migrated to Australia themselves. For them, upward mobility was an intrinsic part of the narrative in which they or their parents understood and motivated their decision to migrate. Their family stories and their own identities were tightly tied to a story of "bettering" themselves. One portfolio manager in an insurance company, the son of Macedonian immigrants, described the significance of his entry into the company where he had made his career:

> I guess in those days when you looked at parents who came across with very limited money and resource opportunities, I suppose anything was better than what they had . . . having an office job or a clerical job of some type was defined as being . . . one step above Mum and Dad. It was more of a status thing, I guess.
>
> *Q:* Was insurance something that they encouraged you to get into?
>
> *A:* No, no. I didn't know anything about it. (Portfolio Manager)

Here, the legacy of parents was not formal education or direct knowledge and understanding of managerial careers in large companies. It was simply powerful aspirations and understandings of social hierarchy that allowed our interviewee to take advantage of the career opportunities offered by the insurance company.

To illustrate the use of qualitative research in an area that has been heavily dominated by quantitative approaches, we have focused on understanding the meanings people give to widely recognized routes to class reproduction or upward mobility. Insofar as these meanings can be taken as at least partial explanations for the actions that have led interviewees to their present positions, they offer important insights into the social processes which underlie class reproduction and social mobility. They suggest likely tensions and contradictions if, as Noble suggests, the expansion of middle-class positions ends, and absolute upward mobility is reduced. Such developments would put pressure on the various meanings that education and ambition have. The existing processes that protect managerial labor markets from working-class aspirants might be modified to harden these protections through mechanisms like rising educational requirements or increased use of informal cultural barriers (see Brown 1995). On the other hand, greater competition might weaken such protections. In the former case, working-class experiences that challenge the meanings education and ambition have for achievement might reduce the legitimacy of social class inequality among these groups. In the latter case, the middle-class sense of order and life guarantees might be threatened, leading to attempts to construct new barriers to entry. In either case, understanding the meaning of individuals' strategies and actions is likely to be central to anticipating the effects of shifts in mobility patterns on social class and inequality.

THE FUTURE

The study of class inequalities in Australia might be seen as at something of a crossroad. On the one hand, it is the central focus of relatively little current research. Theorists writing in Australia have been strong advocates of the "death of class" thesis (Pakulski and Waters 1996) and, although they have not clearly won the day, their skepticism about the continuing relevance of the concept has undoubtedly had an almost subconscious effect on many sociologists' thinking. Attempts to explicitly defend the relevance of class analyses have sometimes seemed rather arid exercises in statistically based semantics, and have failed to capture the imagination of most sociologists, let alone the wider intellectual public. Indeed, despite significant public interest in a range of issues which might be fertile ground for sociological research focused on class inequalities, such research has been largely absent, with limited presence of sociologists in the wider public debates. The relevant issues include growing income and wealth inequality, high rates of single parent family poverty, the emergence and expansion of the working

poor, a solidifying "underclass" of the virtually permanently unemployed, reduced labor market and workplace regulation, changing
family and gender dynamics with rising female labor force participation, and an expanding and globalizing private sector professional-
managerial grouping.

Ideally, investigations of the social class dimensions of these issues
should offer unique insights into the social processes underlying them,
and the individual and group strategies that constitute and reconstruct
these processes. The existing class literature does not provide so much
a set of ready answers to questions about the origins of these problems,
as beginning points for conceptualizing them, albeit ones which may
require considerable rethinking. A class focus should sensitize
researchers, first, to inequalities in the construction, possession, and
distribution of valued resources including material capital, cultural
resources such as education, skills, group cultures and reputations, and
control over significant organizational resources. But it also needs to
deal with the problem of how class experience is lived and reproduced
(or not lived or not reproduced) in patterns of everyday life and community networks. At the same time, future research on class needs to
maintain and develop existing awareness of the complex intertwining
of class relations with those of gender, ethnicity, and race.

Shifting patterns of wealth and income inequality, and changing
structures of employment and lifetime working arrangements, offer
fertile but challenging ground for social class researchers. For example,
the orthodox literature on changing income inequality has generally
used a simple market-based demand and supply model to explain
growing inequality in terms of shifts in demand for employees with different skills (e.g., Hancock 2002: 19). Recent class approaches have
increasingly suggested the importance of understanding the processes
by which some resources (or "assets") become defined as valuable and
in short supply, and how at certain junctures they may be "converted"
into other assets with greater value (see Martin 1998b; Savage et al.
1992). Extending and developing these ideas, particularly through
careful field research in and across organizations, may offer important
insights into the construction of demand for currently ascendant
middle-class groups like some private sector managers and "knowledge
workers." The growing importance of inter-disciplinary and hybrid
forms of knowledge, for example, suggests a destabilization of
credential-based institutionalization of skill or knowledge resources. At
the same time, networks of experts in particular problems appear to
be increasingly important as reference points for claims to expertise
and solutions to problems.[5] There is some evidence that reputations

based in such networks are also increasingly important in managerial appointments and careers (see Wajcman and Martin 2001). For class analysts, the central issue here is whether research on the structure and operation of these networks can show that the labor market ascendancy of some managers and knowledge workers arises through their formation into distinct class groupings with identifiable monopolies of expertise. In other words, can analysis of the construction and distribution of new kinds of knowledge assets help explain patterns of growing income inequality in which these groups are particularly successful? The complexity of the processes here, along with exploratory character of the necessary research, makes qualitative approaches particularly attractive.

An important dimension of such research will be investigation of the global reach of the relevant networks. This is likely to be one aspect of a recasting of the old Australian concern with the embeddedness of the Australian class system in Australia's place in the international system. Expanding skilled and business migration to Australia, the increasing penetration of global companies in the Australian economy, and the general globalization of managerial and knowledge worker labor markets have all contributed to the declining relevance of national boundaries in defining the contours of upper middle-class Australians' careers. The tensions between these globalizing developments and the continuing strength of reworked local commitments remain a largely unresearched area, despite an important literature on the complexities of work and family life. How class dimensions of this story play off gender ones will be a key issue in such research. For less privileged classes, analysis of the impact of globalization will raise different issues. Some refer to the impact of shifts in global organization of production and trade patterns on local employment opportunities. But others relate to how changing global relationships alter the ways unskilled migrants are used by employers and try to find and exploit opportunities for themselves and their families, especially in using family networks as the basis for moving back and forth between countries. Here again, various aspects of social networks are likely to be central, as are issues of race and ethnicity. Any research on global networks and inequalities would be greatly strengthened by cross-national comparative studies. Australia's position as a small developed society open to international markets in labor, goods, and services makes it a particularly useful case in comparative research.

At least as prominent as the impact of globalization in research on the working class is likely to be the issue of class culture and its relation to community structure. Perhaps paradoxically, many contemporary Australian sociologists seem to find the analytical bite of the concept of social class to be greatest in relation to issues of culture and "habitus." Distinctive "working-class" or "middle-class" fashions, consumption patterns, leisure habits, aspirations, and identities are readily identifiable, both by sociologists and many Australians. However, the existing literature has only made limited connections between the several disparate groupings of such life patterns, and more "structural" aspects of social life. As a result, it remains unclear whether designating patterns as "working class" or "middle class" offers analysis and explanation as opposed to mere labeling. McDonald's (1999) recent work does suggest the value of an Australian extension of Skeggs's (1997) British research, in which the focus is on understanding the variety of ways people construct their identities in relation to the signifier of "working class" or "middle class," and how their response to these signifiers relates to their class experience. However, research which assesses whether readily identifiable class cultures can be connected to class experience, irrespective of whether they are identified by those who participate in them as "class" cultures, will also be necessary. Here again, a focus on careful qualitative investigation of network patterns and structure may bear fruit. Indeed, the importance of sustained interaction between individuals as a basis for entering and adopting cultures and habitus remains a largely open field, as does investigation of variation in network types and structures. This approach may be particularly effective where employment relations can be directly analyzed in network terms, so that relationships with workmates, employers, unions, etc. can be assessed for their centrality in understanding an individual's wider network connections and adoption of class cultures or habitus.

The experience of working-class people also raises an issue that runs across all current social class analysis: the impact of neo-liberal reforms and market-based individualism on class experience and relationships. In Australia, as in most other advanced capitalist societies, reforms to labor market regulation (see Wooden 2002) and welfare state arrangements (see Castles 2001) have produced an institutional environment that has sharply increased the scope and incentives for people to focus on individualized as opposed to collective identities and life strategies. In industrial relations, for example, the unique Australian arbitration and conciliation system has been largely replaced by a system of enterprise level and individual bargaining, while unionization rates have continued to fall (Richardson 1998). The social welfare system increasingly uses market mechanisms to provide its "customers" with routes into paid employment. And superannuation and aged pension policy increasingly force individuals to see their retirement income and capital as a product of market choices they make as individuals. Similar trends are evident in health and education policy. For some theorists such trends need to be connected with a more general "individualization" of life experience (Beck and Giddens). The challenge for researchers in the social class tradition is to develop their concepts to take account of these changes, and conduct research that provides new insights into the social processes currently generating inequality. A particular challenge is likely to be integrating class effects into accounts and explanations of individuals' labor market experiences and choices, and the employment trajectories that result. This may involve more carefully mapping individuals' labor market histories to assess the common idea that they are becoming increasingly diverse. As well, it will undoubtedly require continued attention to gender, ethnic, and racial identities and orientations. But it will also demand investigation of the meaning individuals attach to these histories, the identities they adopt in acting out their careers, and how these relate to class signifiers and experience. Again, qualitative research will necessarily be a central aspect of this agenda.

If a focus on the variety of ways class life and inequality are structured through social networks is one possible way forward for Australian researchers, then attention to how they unfold over time is another. Labor market deregulation in the "new capitalism" (Sennett 1998) appears to open up a range of insecurities for individuals and new complexities for the social structuring of classes, even where these are understood in network terms. Much of this effect apparently arises as experiences of uncertainty and the possibility of rapid change in individuals' circumstances unfolds over time. However, as yet, there is virtually no research that uses longitudinal designs to investigate these issues. As a result, analysts are reduced to inferring major change in patterns of social experience from cross-sectional or, at best, retrospective studies. It seems likely that research which uses both qualitative and quantitative approaches in a longitudinal design will be necessary to fully understand social actors' experiences, self-understandings and ensuing actions, and how they build and rebuild structures of social class and inequality in the new century. Australian research along these lines will provide important self-understanding and interesting comparisons with results elsewhere. In an increasingly globalized world, Australia's place as a small developed society opening itself to the forces of the world economy may provide unique insights into the impact of such forces on class and inequality.

NOTES

1   The extensive literature on the end of the Australian post-war settlement, with its unique "wage earners' welfare state" (Castles 1985) is beyond the scope of this chapter. On these issues, see Kelly (1994), Beilharz (1994).
2   Idiosyncratically, Davies had argued that it was the experience of family structure and an individual's location in family structure that explained their class image.
3   We acknowledge funding for this research through a Large Grant (1997–9) from the Australian Research Council.
4   It is obvious that the nature of our study meant that we did not see cases of downward mobility, only of transmission of status or of upward movement.
5   Braithwaite and Drahos (2000) refer to "epistemic communities" of experts who have influence in regulating the activities of global businesses.

REFERENCES

Alexander, M. (1998) "Big business and directorship networks: The centralisation of economic power in Australia," *Journal of Sociology* 34: 107–22.

Alexander, M., Murray, G. and Houghton, J. (1994) "Business power in Australia: The concentration of company directorship holding among the top 250 corporates," *Australian Journal of Political Science* 29: 40–61.

Baxter, J., Emmison, M., Western, J. and Western, M. (eds.) (1991) *Class Analysis and Contemporary Australia*. South Melbourne: Macmillan.

Becker, H. (1998) *Tricks of the Trade: How to Think About Your Research While You're Doing It.* Chicago: University of Chicago Press.

Beilharz, P. (1994) *Transforming Labor: Labour Tradition and the Labor Decade in Australia.* Melbourne: Cambridge University Press.

Braithwaite, J. and Drahos, P. (2000) *Global Business Regulation.* Cambridge: Cambridge University Press.

Brown, P. (1995) "Cultural capital and social exclusion: Some observations on recent trends in education," *Work, Employment and Society* 9: 29–52.

Bryson, L. and Thompson, F. (1972) *An Australian Newtown: Life and Leadership in a Working-Class Suburb.* Blackburn, Victoria: Penguin.

Bryson, L. and Winter, I. (1999) *Social Change, Suburban Lives: An Australian Newtown 1960s to 1990s.* St Leonards, NSW: Allen & Unwin.

Carroll, W. K. and Alexander, M. (1999) "Finance capital and capitalist class integration in the 1990s: Networks of interlocking directorships in Canada and Australia," *Canadian Review of Sociology and Anthropology* 36: 331–54.

Castles, F. G. (1985) *The Working Class and Welfare: Reflections on the Political Development of the Welfare State in Australia and New Zealand, 1890–1980.* Wellington: Allen & Unwin.

—— (2001) "A farewell to the Australian welfare state," *Eureka Street* 11: 29–31.

Chamberlain, C. (1983) *Class Consciousness in Australia.* Sydney: Allen & Unwin.

Collins, J. (1975) "The political economy of post-war immigration," in Wheelwright, E. L. and Buckley, K. (eds.), *Essays in the Political Economy of Australian Capitalism,* vol. 1. Sydney: ANZ Books.

—— (1978) "Fragmentation in the working class," in Wheelwright, E. L. and Buckley, K. (eds.), *Essays in the Political Economy of Australian Capitalism,* vol. 3. Sydney: ANZ Books.

—— (1991) *Migrant Hands in a Distant Land: Australia's Post-war Immigration,* 2nd edition, Leichhardt, NSW: Pluto Press.

Collins, J., Gibson, K., Alcorso, C., Castles, S. and Tait, D. (1995) *A Shop Full of Dreams: Ethnic Small Business in Australia.* Sydney: Pluto Press.

Collis, M. (1999) "Marital conflict and men's leisure: How women negotiate male power in a small mining community," *Journal of Sociology* 35: 60–76.

Connell, R. W. (1970) "Class consciousness in childhood," *Australian and New Zealand Journal of Sociology* 6: 87–99.

—— (1972) *The Child's Construction of Politics.* Melbourne: Melbourne University Press.

—— (1977) *Ruling Class, Ruling Culture.* Melbourne: Cambridge University Press.

—— (1991) "Live fast and die young: The construction of masculinity among young working class men on the margin of the labour market," *Australian and New Zealand Journal of Sociology* 27: 141–71.

Connell, R. W., Ashenden, D. J., Kessler, S. and Dowsett, G. W. (1982) *Making the Difference: Schools, Families and Social Division.* Sydney: George Allen & Unwin.

Connell, R. W., Davis, M. D. and Dowsett, G. (1993) "A bastard of a life: Homosexual desire and practice among men in working class milieux," *Australian and New Zealand Journal of Sociology* 29: 112–35.

Connell, R. W. and Irving, T. (1992) *Class Structure in Australian History: Poverty and Progress,* 2nd edition. Melbourne: Longman Cheshire.

Connell, R. W. and Wood, J. (2002) "Globalization and scientific labour: Patterns in the life-history of intellectual workers in the periphery," *Journal of Sociology* 38: 167–90.

Cunneen, C. and Lynch, R. (1988) "The socio-historical roots of conflict in riots at the Bathurst 'bike races'," *Australian and New Zealand Journal of Sociology* 24: 5–31.

Davies, A. F. (1967) *Images of Class.* Sydney: Sydney University Press.

Dempsey, K. (1990) *Smalltown: A Study of Social Inequality, Cohesion and Belonging.* Melbourne: Oxford University Press.

Devine, F. (1998) "Class analysis and the stability of class relations," *Sociology* 32: 23–43.

Elkin, A. P. (1945) "Introduction," in Walker, A., *Coaltown: A Social Survey of Cessnock.* Melbourne: Melbourne University Press.

Emmison, M. (1985) "Class images of 'the economy': Opposition and ideological incorporation with working class consciousness," *Sociology* 19: 19–38.

Emmison, M. and Western, M. (1991) "The structure of social identities," in Baxter, J. et al., *Class Analysis and Contemporary Australia*. South Melbourne: Macmillan.

Encel, S. (1970) *Equality and Authority: A Study of Class, Status and Power in Australia*. Melbourne: F. W. Cheshire.

Erikson, R. and Goldthorpe, J. H. (1992) *The Constant Flux*. Oxford: Clarendon Press.

Gilding, M. (1999) "Superwealth in Australia: Entrepreneurs, accumulation and the capitalist class," *Journal of Sociology* 35: 169–82.

Glaser, B. G. and Strauss, A. L. (1967) *The Discovery of Grounded Theory: Strategies for Qualitative Research*. Chicago: Aldine.

Gleeson, P. (1996) "'No yobbos here': Education as a vehicle for social class transition," *Australian Journal of Social Issues* 31: 95–112.

Graetz, B. (1983) "Images of class in modern society: Structure, sentiment and social location," *Sociology* 17: 79–96.

—— (1986) "Social structure and class consciousness: Facts, fictions and fantasies," *Australian and New Zealand Journal of Sociology* 22: 46–64.

—— (1990) "Private schools and educational attainment: Cohort and generational effects," *Australian Journal of Education* 34: 174–91.

Hancock, K. (2002) "Work in an ungolden age," in Callus, R. and Lansbury, R. D., *Working Futures: The Changing Nature of Work and Employment Relations in Australia*. Sydney: Federation Press.

Hiller, P. (1975a) "The nature and social location of everyday conceptions of class," *Sociology* 9: 1–28.

—— (1975b) "Continuities and variations in everyday conceptual components of class," *Sociology* 9: 255–87.

Holton, J. R. and Martin, W. (1987) "The class structure of metropolitan Adelaide," *Australian and New Zealand Journal of Sociology* 23: 5–22.

Inglis, C. (1999) "Middle class migration: New considerations in research and policy," in Hage, G. and Couch, R. (eds.), *The Future of Australian Multiculturalism*. Sydney: Research Institute for Humanities and Social Sciences, University of Sydney.

Kelly, P. (1994) *The End of Certainty: Power, Politics and Business in Australia*, revised edition. St. Leonards, NSW: Allen & Unwin.

Kriegler, R. (1980) *Working for the Company: Work and Control in the Whyalla Shipyard*. Melbourne: Oxford University Press.

Lever-Tracy, C. (1983) "Immigrant workers and postwar capitalism: In reserve or core troops in the front line," *Politics and Society*, 12: 127–57.

Lever-Tracy, C., Ip, D. and Tracy, N. (1991) *Asian Entrepreneurs in Australia: Ethnic Small Business in the Chinese and Indian Communities of Brisbane and Sydney*. Canberra: AGPS.

—— (1996) *The Chinese Diaspora and Mainland China: An Emerging Economic Synergy*. New York: St. Martins Press.

Lever-Tracy, C. and Quinlan, M. (1988) *A Divided Working Class: Ethnic Segmentation and Industrial Conflict in Australia.* London: Routledge and Kegan Paul.

McDonald, K. (1999) *Struggle for Subjectivity: Identity, Action and Youth Experience.* Cambridge: Cambridge University Press.

Martin, B. (1998a) "The Australian middle class, 1986–1995: Stable, declining, or restructuring?" *Journal of Sociology* 34: 135–51.

—— (1998b) "Knowledge, identity and the middle class: From collective to individualised class formation?" *Sociological Review* 46: 653–86.

—— (2001) "The changing experience of the middle class," in Dow, G. and Parker, R. (eds.), *Business, Work, and Community: Into the New Millennium.* South Melbourne: Oxford University Press.

Martin, B., Riemens, W. and Wajcman, J. (2000) "Managerial and professional careers in an era of organisational restructuring," *Journal of Sociology* 36: 329–44.

Martin, J. I. (1967) "Extended kinship ties: An Adelaide study," *Australian and New Zealand Journal of Sociology,* 3: 44–63.

—— (1970) "Suburbia: Community and network," in Davies, A. F. and Encel, S. (eds.), *Australian Society: A Sociological Introduction,* 2nd edition. Melbourne: F. W. Cheshire.

Noble, T. (2000) "The mobility transition: Social mobility trends in the first half of the twenty-first century," *Sociology* 34: 35–51.

Oxley, H. G. (1978) *Mateship in Local Organization: A Study of Egalitarianism, Stratification, Leadership, and Amenities Projects in a Semi-industrial Community in Inland New South Wales,* 2nd edition. Brisbane: University of Queensland Press.

Pakulski, J. and Waters, M. (1996) *The Death of Class.* London: Sage.

Peel, M. and McCalman, J. (1988) *Who Went Where in Who's Who 1988: The Schooling of the Australian Elite.* Parkville, Victoria: History Department, University of Melbourne.

Pusey, M. (1997) "Inside the minds of middle Australia," *AQ: Journal of Contemporary Analysis* 69: 14–21.

—— (2003) *The Experience of Middle Australia: The Dark Side of Economic Reform.* New York: Cambridge University Press.

Richards, L. (1990) *Nobody's Home: Dreams and Realities in a New Suburb.* Melbourne: Oxford University Press.

Richardson, S. (1998) *Reshaping the Labour Market.* Cambridge: Cambridge University Press.

Savage, M., Barlow, J., Dickens, P. and Fielding, T. (1992) *Property, Bureaucracy and Culture: Middle-class Formation in Contemporary Britain.* London: Routledge.

Sennett, R. (1998) *The Corrosion of Character: The Personal Consequences of Work in the New Capitalism.* New York: W. W. Norton.

Skeggs, B. (1997) *Formations of Class and Gender: Becoming Respectable.* London: Sage.

Stratton, J. (1993) "Bodgies and widgies: Just working class kids doing working class things," in White, R. (ed.), *Youth Subcultures: Theory, History and the Australian Experience.* Hobart: National Clearinghouse for Youth Studies.

Strauss, A. L. (1987, 1990) *Qualitative Analysis for Social Scientists.* New York: Cambridge University Press.

Wajcman, J. and Martin, B. (2001) "My company or my career: Managerial achievement and loyalty," *British Journal of Sociology* 52: 559–78.

Walker, L. (1993) "Girls, schooling and subcultures of resistance," in White, R. (ed.), *Youth Subcultures: Theory, History and the Australian Experience.* Hobart: National Clearinghouse for Youth Studies.

—— (1998a) "Chivalrous masculinity among juvenile offenders in Western Sydney: A new perspective on young working class men and crime," *Current Issues in Criminal Justice* 9: 279–93.

—— (1998b) "Under the bonnet: Car culture, technological dominance and young men of the working class," *Journal of Interdisciplinary Gender Studies* 3: 23–43.

Ward, R. (1958) *The Australian Legend.* Melbourne: Oxford University Press.

Watson, I. (1993) "Life history meets economic theory: The experiences of three working-class women in a local labour market," *Work, Employment and Society* 7: 411–35.

Weakliem, D. and Western, M. (1999) "Class voting, social change, and the left in Australia, 1943–96," *British Journal of Sociology* 50: 609–30.

Western, M. (1999) "Class attainment among British men: A multivariate extension of the CASMIN model of intergenerational class mobility," *European Sociological Review* 15: 431–54.

—— (2000) "Class in Australia in the 1980s and 1990s," in Najman, J. M. and Western, J. S. (eds.), *A Sociology of Australian Society,* 3rd edition. South Yarra, Victoria: Macmillan.

Wild, R. A. (1974) *Bradstow: A Study of Status, Class and Power in a Small Australian Town.* Sydney: Angus and Robertson.

Williams, C. (1981) *Open Cut: The Working Class in an Australian Mining Town.* Sydney: George Allen & Unwin.

—— (1988) *Blue, White and Pink Collar Workers in Australia: Technicians, Bank Employees and Flight Attendants.* Sydney: Allen & Unwin.

Winter, I. and Bryson, L. (1998) "Economic restructuring and state intervention in Holdenist suburbia: Understanding urban poverty in Australia," *International Journal of Urban and Regional Research* 22: 60–75.

Wooden, M. (2002) "The changing labour market and its impact on work and employment relations," in Callus, R. and Lansbury, R. D., *Working Futures: The Changing Nature of Work and Employment Relations in Australia.* Sydney: Federation Press.

Zadoroznyj, M. (1999) "Social class, social selves and social control in childbirth," *Sociology of Health and Illness* 21: 267–89.

FURTHER READING

Connell, R. W., Ashenden, D. J., Kessler, S., and Dowsett, G. W. (1982) *Making the Difference: Schools, Families and Social Division.* Sydney: George Allen & Unwin.

Martin, B. (2001) "The changing experience of the middle class," in Dow, G. and Parker, R. (eds.), *Business, Work, and Community: Into the New Millennium.* South Melbourne: Oxford University Press.

Western, M. (2000) "Class in Australia in the 1980s and 1990s," in Najman, J. M. and Western, J. S. (eds.), *A Sociology of Australian Society,* 3rd edition. South Yarra, Victoria: Macmillan.

CHAPTER EIGHT

Talking about Class in Britain

FIONA DEVINE

British sociologists who were interested in the subjective dimensions of class in the past used to talk about class consciousness. Attention focused on the extent to which members of a class are aware of their collective interests and could be mobilized by class-based organizations in pursuit of those interests. They were not really interested in the collective capacities of all social classes, however. Rather, interest centered on the working class and its capacity to challenge class inequalities via the trade unions and the Labour Party. Within this remit, sociologists debated whether working-class consciousness was declining in the face of economic, social, and political change in the second half of the twentieth century. These "big" theoretical issues usually translated into empirical research on class identities. It included the study of popular perceptions of the class structure, people's willingness to place themselves in a class category and the extent to which these class categories shape people's social and political proclivities. The study of class identities, however, has been beset with a major problem: namely, whether people's ability to identify themselves as belonging to a certain class actually means that class is salient in their lives. Do they see the world primarily in class terms? Do they understand their own lives through the lens of class? The problem is not just a theoretical curiosity. It is a methodological issue as well. Are people happy to talk about class because sociologists ask them questions about class? Do they kindly oblige when asked to assign themselves to a particular social class?

Debate about class identities and the salience of class in people's lives in Britain has waxed and waned for many years. It has recently enjoyed a new momentum, however, in the context of debates about the demise of class analysis since the decline in class identities has been crucial to critics of the sub-discipline (see, for example, Beck 1992; Crook et al.

1992). The debate has also been rekindled with the growth of interest in social identities in sociology more generally (see, for example, Hetherington 1998; Jenkins 1996). This chapter addresses the controversy around class identities and the salience of class in people's lives. The next section summarizes the old and the new sociological debates on class identities. A renewed interest has seen sociologists argue that people actually prefer to distance themselves from class, that they have mixed feelings about class and they do not interpret their own lives in class terms even if they acknowledge class inequalities in wider society. The discussion about the pejorative feelings people express about class is to be welcomed. The third section discusses the methodological problems associated with the study of class identities. The major charge leveled against sociologists is the tendency to impose their own preoccupations about class on the general public. The ways in which sociologists have responded to this criticism and how they have sought to avoid this problem are discussed. The growing recognition of the difficulties of talking about class, of dis-identification, is refreshing. Some of the awkwardness about discussing the negative topic as class is considered in relation to my own comparative research on social mobility in Britain and America.

The fourth section discusses some spontaneous talk about class among British middle-class doctors and teachers from the comparative social mobility project. Unlike their American counterparts, it will be seen that the British rarely articulated a middle-class identity when they spoke of their family background. There was much talk, however, of class among people from working-class backgrounds and, furthermore, they often interpreted their life experiences through the lenses of class. It will be seen that talk about the middle class and the working class was not confined to a discussion of innocuous descriptive labels but to categories implicitly loaded with issues of status and hierarchy, feelings of superiority and inferiority and judgements of moral worth. The middle class, for example, was often spoken of in a derisory way as being too demanding, pushy, snobbish, and elitist. An undercurrent of class conflict, of struggles over moral worth, might explain why a middle-class identity was rarely claimed. The fifth section considers how the renewed interest in class identities and the salience of class in people's lives might be sustained. Obviously, research on class identification and dis-identification can be extended beyond the working class to the middle classes. More importantly, there is much exciting work to be done on the feelings and emotions that the topic of class evokes and the contexts in which it is articulated and where there is silence. The methodological implications for qualitative work of this kind are addressed. The study of class subjectivities, it will be argued, has much to contribute to a rejuvenated class analysis and the study of social identities in sociology.

CLASS IDENTITIES AND THE SALIENCE OF CLASS

In the 1950s, sociology was still a small and not very well-established discipline in Britain that was dominated by the study of local communities (Kent 1981; Eldridge 1990). These community studies (Dennis et al. 1956; Kerr 1958; Stacey 1960; Tunstall 1962) captured various dimensions of everyday experiences including the dominance of class in people's lives during this era. It was from these studies that sociologists described a "traditional" working class whose work and home lives were still dominated by economic constraint. They worked, for example, in harsh occupations like mining for relatively low pay and they lived in dense communities in poor houses and had little in the way of consumer durables. Most importantly, these conditions generated a fierce sense of occupational and community solidarity which was the bedrock of a strong working-class consciousness. Workers saw the world in terms of "them" and "us," two classes of employers and workers who occupied different worlds. In the late 1950s and early 1960s, however, there was much media-inspired debate about the demise of this "old" working class and the rise of a "new" working class. Commentators (Abrams et al. 1960; Zweig 1961) described how the age of affluence saw the emergence of a "new" working class with higher standards of living, greater consumer aspirations and, most significantly, a different view of class. A strong working-class consciousness was discarded by a working class who saw themselves as middle class and adopted a more middle-class outlook on life.

The embourgeoisement thesis, as it became known, was quickly refuted by sociologists and, most notably, by John Goldthorpe, David Lockwood and their colleagues (1968a, 1968b, 1969) in the *Affluent Worker* Series. Goldthorpe and Lockwood (1963) easily exposed the conceptual problems of the thesis that a more favorable economic climate had led to the assimilation of the working class into the middle class. In their subsequent research among factory workers in Luton, however, they developed their own, more modest, account of social change. Different working conditions generated an instrumental orientation to work while new housing conditions sustained more privatized lifestyles. Drawing heavily on Lockwood's (1966) paper on the social sources of working-class imagery, they also considered how workers' social perspectives had changed. Unlike the "traditional" working class, their workers viewed classes in terms of money, with differences in income, wealth, and standards of living being the most important determinant of class. Those who subscribed to a "money model" image of the class structure outlined a large central class, which included most workers, including themselves and which they either called middle class or working class. No significance was attached to the manual/non-manual divide and similarities rather than differences in lifestyles were emphasized. The new working class, in other words were not class-conscious radicals outside the system but people whose aspirations for material prosperity lay within the prevailing order (Goldthorpe et al. 1969: 147–54).

The *Affluent Worker* series became a landmark study in sociology since the three volumes appeared in the late 1960s as sociology grew and became more established in universities around the country. The Luton team's findings on class consciousness and class imagery were the source of much controversy. There was considerable interest in Lockwood's (1966) paper of working-class images of society although there was much critical comment about the way in which he described a quite deterministic relationship between workers' immediate milieux of work and community relations and their images of class and their place in the class structure. Numerous studies showed that workers, often in similar circumstances, had different world views and indeed, there was considerable doubt as to whether members of the working class held clear and consistent images of the class structure and their position within it (see, for example, the contributions to Bulmer 1975). More importantly, in the late 1960s and 1970s when Marxist thinking was more buoyant, the Luton team's characterization of the working class as essentially conservative consumers integrated into the capitalist system did not go down well. Subsequent debate led to a growing consensus that members of the working class did not simply endorse existing socio-political arrangements but were highly ambivalent about them. Rather, workers pragmatically accepted class inequalities and their position within the class structure not least because it was hard to imagine how a more equal society might be achieved (Parkin 1972; Mann 1973).

As many have already argued (Newby 1982; Marshall 1983), the consensus about working-class ambivalence led to an impasse in the study of working-class consciousness. Moreover, the depressed economic climate in the late 1970s and early 1980s fuelled a different debate about whether class fragmentation and sectionalism were undermining class identities. This debate was addressed in a major national study of class conducted by Marshall and his colleagues (1988) who sought to explore, among other things, the extent to which class is a salient social identity or whether other social identities are important in shaping socio-political perspectives. The Essex team asked respondents to place themselves in a class. Over half (60 percent) placed themselves into a particular social class rising to 90 percent when asked to do so (Marshall et al. 1988: 143–4). In contrast, less than a fifth (19 percent) identified with another social grouping, the most frequently mentioned groups being business and religious groups (27 percent and 21 percent respectively) (ibid.: 148–9). They argued, however, that a high level of class identification was not indicative of a radical class consciousness. As previous researchers had concluded, an "informed fatalism" prevailed. People's class background and class identities had a powerful influence on voting behavior but they are not the basis of a more substantial mobilization of class interests. Marshall and his colleagues did not "blame" individuals for their lack of class consciousness but challenged the political parties – specifically the Labour Party – for failing to mobilize (working-) class interests in the political arena.

The importance of class identities to political proclivities was subsequently confirmed in my own research (Devine 1992a). In the 1980s, I returned to Luton and to the car workers at Vauxhall to ascertain whether Goldthorpe et al.'s findings had stood the test of time. I also asked my interviewees about class and politics. The discussion on class evoked strong pejorative feelings on the topic although subsequent discussion revealed distaste for status distinctions more than anything. The interviewees also described the class structure in terms of money, income and wealth, and associated standards of living. They distinguished between two major classes not unlike the division between "them" and "us" of the old working class although they described them rather differently. The upper class consisted of rich people with vast amounts of money who enjoyed a leisured life. The other class was a mass central class of "ordinary people" or "ordinary working people," terms used interchangeably with reference to working class or even the middle class. Like Goldthorpe et al., this class was seen to embrace both the middle class and the working class and similarities in consumption and lifestyles were emphasized. If there were differences, the working-class interviewees certainly did not begrudge the middle class for they too had invariably worked hard to get where they were. It was in the sphere of politics, however, that a more precisely defined working class identity was voiced as part of an allegiance to the trade unions and the Labour Party although it was accompanied by a critical evaluation of them (Devine 1992b).

Once again, interest in class identities and the salience of class in people's lives waned in the mid-1990s as debate shifted to the alleged emergence of an underclass in Britain. This was an especially trenchant debate as sociologists sought to refute the view – among Conservative politicians and sections of the media – that the cultural predispositions of such groups as young single mothers were the cause of their poverty (Westergaard 1992). Out of this political debate, however, came an important study of young working-class women and class identification. Influenced by Bourdieu (1984), Skeggs (1997) found the young women rejected any identification with the working class and were anxious to distance themselves from a category that had such negative moral con-notations. They dis-identified and dissimulated from a working class that has been pathologized and stigmatized for women as dangerous, dirty and without value. The label, therefore, was a source of pain and shame. Distance from class, Skeggs (1997: 75) argued, was achieved by claims to respectability which influenced how the young women dressed, how they decorated their homes, how they brought up their children, and so on. While clearly influenced by perceptions of "others," they did not identify with the middle classes. The young women disliked what they saw as the knowledgeable pretentiousness of the middle class. Claiming respectability, therefore was a way of enjoy-ing independence from class labels – working class or middle class – although carving out such independence induced feelings of fear, anxiety, uncertainty, and unease so their escape attempts were not unequivocally successful. That they did not escape from its effects con-firmed the power of class to Skeggs (ibid.: 95).

Skeggs's work enjoyed acclaim for the novel way in which she spoke about class subjectivities drawing on Bourdieu's (1984) work on the generation of different "capitals." The major criticism leveled against Skeggs relates to her exaggerated account of the pathologization of the working class implying that working-class identification has all but dis-appeared (Savage 2000: 116). Bradley (1999), in her study of men and women in a range of middle-class, lower middle-class and working-class occupations, told a somewhat different story. The majority (80 percent) of her respondents believed class inequalities shaped British society and could identify a structure of different classes. However, they experi-enced considerable difficulties when asked to place themselves in a par-ticular class. Nearly half (47 percent) of her sample were unwilling to do so, seeing class in pejorative terms and anxious to distance them-selves from it. Interestingly, the majority (34 percent) of those willing to assign themselves to a class identified with the working class rather than the middle class (11 percent) even though most were in middle-

and lower middle-class jobs. There was "considerable ambiguity" about their class position. Her respondents also found it easier to talk about their family background in class terms. In these discussions, a strong loyalty to working-class origins and values was expressed (Bradley 1999: 154). It was a counter-discourse to the stigmatization of the working class that meant that a pride in the working class and a positive evaluation of its values remained. It was for this reason that her respondents were reluctant to describe themselves as middle class even when they worked in middle-class occupations.

Bradley's respondents, therefore, were aware of changes in the boundaries between the middle class and working class and their own experiences of social hybridity and class mobility caused confusion about where they might place themselves. It was in this sense that current class identities were weak (Bradley 1999: 158). Savage et al. (2001; see also Savage 2000) also explored the salience of class identities among a mixed class group and came to similar conclusions. A third of their sample (33 percent) were unwilling to identify themselves with a class although just under half of the sample (46 percent) saw themselves as middle class while a significant minority saw themselves as working class (21 percent). Nevertheless, the majority (71 percent) was ambivalent about their class identity. They could identity class inequalities in society at large but they expressed reluctance and often hesitated to define their own class position. A class identity, therefore, was not strong especially when it challenged their individuality and defined them by their social background. That said, Savage, Bagnall and Longhurst also found that a class identity was often strong in the telling of life histories especially if it involved a move away from their class background. Like Bradley (1999), they noted a pride in being working class, especially among men, indicating that the "moral force of working-class identities" endures. They were a minority, however, as were "reflexive class identifiers" who played with the different levels. The majority, however, distanced themselves from and were defensive about class. Like my own research (Devine 1992), their respondents were keen to be seen as "ordinary" whether they considered themselves middle class (in the middle) or working class (working people). Nobody wanted to be a "snob" or be seen to be culturally superior.

Savage and his colleagues concluded (2001: 888) that "class identities are generally weak." What is not entirely clear from their analysis, which is somewhat clearer in Bradley's work, is who is saying what? Are those who occupy middle-class positions more reluctant than their working-class counterparts to talk about class? Is a middle-class identity more problematic – more often denied and left unarticulated – as

Bradley suggests? How members of the middle class talk about class is an issue I consider in my most recent empirical work on social mobility in America and Britain. Before turning to this material, however, some of the methodological difficulties of studying class identities are considered further.

THE DIFFICULTIES OF STUDYING CLASS IDENTITIES

Sociological research on class consciousness and class identities has always been beset by methodological difficulties. In the early 1970s, for example, Jennifer Platt who was a member of the *Affluent Worker* team wrote a dissenting paper outlining some of the difficulties surrounding the interpretation of the evidence on class imagery. She expressed her unease about the way the respondents "did not make, or did not grasp" a distinction between the determinants and correlates of class. It led Platt (1971: 417) to wonder whether other interpretations of the data were equally plausible and, for example, whether "the references to money could mean only that it was a conveniently observable, and easily conceptualizable, correlate of class differences rather than being seen as their fundamental cause." Indeed, later studies (Beynon 1975) suggested that behind an apparently pecuniary orientation to work lay a more fundamental moral and political interpretation of power relations at work. Over 10 years later, Marshall and his colleagues (1988: 189) considered the difficulties of interpreting similar empirical material. They also found that income was the most widely used criteria for assigning people to different classes. Class conflict was seen in terms of distributional struggles over money. Following Platt's lead, however, they concluded that the data should not "be taken as unambiguous evidence of a widespread and simple pecuniary instrumentalism" for "it is entirely possible that statements about money are a shorthand form of offering wider assessment about social control, power or social justice more generally" (ibid.: 189).

In fact, the difficulties of interpretation did not trouble critics of the Essex study while more basic problems about the questionnaire did. Saunders (1989), for example, was highly critical of Marshall and his colleagues' conclusions about the salience of class in people's lives and the insignificance of other social identities. The high level of class identification, he argued, was an artifact of the numerous questions on class that preceded the class identification questions. Indeed, there were 12 questions (including supplementary questions) about class, including questions asking respondents to describe people belonging to the upper class, middle class and working class beforehand. It was no wonder, Saunders argued, that class seemed so salient in people's lives. Marshall and his colleagues had imposed their preoccupation with class on the general public! Nor was it surprising that other social identities were so insignificant when, following the battery of questions on class, respondents were asked "Apart from class, is there any other major group you identify with?" Given the quite different vagueness to the term "any other major social group," it was amazing that nearly a quarter of the sample could answer the question. Saunders was very doubtful, therefore, about their findings and the conclusions they reached from them. He argued instead that the salience of social identities is highly contextual so that people have a variety of social identities and their importance varies in different contexts (see also Emmison and Western 1990; Devine 1992b; Roberts 2001: 9).

Saunders was correct to point out the problems with the questionnaire and the conclusions that were undoubtedly strongly asserted. In their reply, Marshall and Rose (1989, 1990) effectively conceded to Saunders by qualifying their conclusions and emphasizing the salience of class in the sphere of politics. Nor could they deny that other social identities might be important to different aspects of people's lives. This debate aside, there are other interesting substantive findings and methodological issues arising out of the Essex study that were not discussed at the time. It is interesting to note, for example, that when asked if they thought they belonged to a social class, a majority (60 percent) answered in the affirmative. That is to say, a substantial minority (40 percent) did not think they belonged to a particular social class even after the battery of questions on class was put to them. In a footnote, Marshall and his colleagues noted that these percentages were rather different from Runciman's study (1966) where respondents were asked a similar question of a comparable study 20 years earlier. They quickly concluded that the differences between the findings were an artifact of the different questions asked. The lower response to the question inviting people to place themselves into a particular class resulted in their own "much less leading question" in comparison to Runciman's query. They discounted the idea that their findings might be evidence of a decline in class identities between the 1960s and the 1980s (Marshall et al. 1988: 166–7).

It is certainly true that there are considerable difficulties comparing the findings from slightly different questions in two cross-sectional surveys. It cannot be inferred that the lower percentages in the second survey are indicative of a longitudinal decline in class identities. Nevertheless, the current debate about class identities that has highlighted how people prefer to distance themselves from class leads one to suggest that Marshall et al.'s findings need to be considered in a fresh light. Is it the case that sociologists have long overlooked people's reluctance to assign themselves to a class and carried on regardless? When sociologists have ploughed on to ask people to place themselves into class, have they simply obliged when really the topic means very little to them? So far, the discussion has focused on these problems in relation to quantitative research. It would be naïve to think, however, that qualitative researchers do not also confront similar difficulties. In my previous research (1992a), for example, a discussion of class was far from easy. It provoked considerable unease because the interviewees had strong pejorative views about class and some of the older interviewees spoke with considerable bitterness about the effects of class on people's lives. Many did not know what to say about such a negative topic, often distancing themselves from it by referring to its importance in the past and its declining significance. At the same time, when asked, they were also prepared to acknowledge its continued effects, their place in the class structure and their class identity.

If the interviewees had not been probed further to elaborate their answers, however, it is open to question whether they would have pursued the conversation themselves. Mindful of the points raised by Saunders (1989), Bradley and Savage and his colleagues did not ask their respondents about class until the very end of the interview. They certainly cannot be accused of putting class in people's minds but, arguably, asking them at all leaves open the possibility that class would not have been mentioned or talked about in different ways when discussed spontaneously. In actual fact, Savage and his colleagues (2001: 880) found a third of their respondents spontaneously used the term class in the interview and especially when they were asked about the kind of people that lived around them. Unfortunately, they do not tell us how class was discussed in this context. That class was raised in the context of talking about people that lived around them suggests that class was important in some respect in this aspect of their lives. The way in which people talk about class spontaneously, therefore, might be another way of exploring the salience of class in different aspects of people's lives. Of course, this sort of empirical material is not without its limitations since what people might say about class might be extremely brief. Nevertheless, it is yet another way of exploring the context in which people talk about class that might provide further insight into the salience of class in people's lives.

The next section draws on a qualitative study of social mobility in America and Britain and the informants' spontaneous remarks about class. Before turning to the empirical material, however, how the research was done needs to be discussed. The research was a comparative qualitative study social mobility in the US and the UK focusing on how the middle class reproduces itself over generations (Devine 1998, 2004a). It involved in-depth interviews with doctors (physicians) and teachers (educators) in Boston, US, and Manchester, UK. Physicians were chosen as an example of a high-level middle-class occupation known, in the past at least, for its high level of occupational inheritance and domination by men. Educators were chosen as a typical low-level middle-class occupation known to be more open to men and women from working-class origins and still dominated by women. A total of 86 interviews were conducted with the informants and their partners (who, of course, were not necessarily doctors or teachers). The British sample (on which the next section concentrates) comprised 45 interviewees. They were aged between 32 and 63 and they had 27 children among them. Given the considerable growth of the middle class, especially in the second half of the twentieth century in Britain (Goldthorpe 1987), it came as no surprise that the final sample was very heterogeneous including those from middle-class backgrounds, those from lower middle-class origins who enjoyed (short-range) mobility into the professions and those from working-class backgrounds who enjoyed long-range mobility into medicine and teaching.

The intensive interviews for my research were conducted by way of life histories. The interviewees were asked to describe their early childhood, their experiences of education and their subsequent work histories. Attention then turned to their children and how they helped or were currently guiding them through the education system into good jobs. The final interview schedule, therefore, did not include any explicit discussions of class. In Britain, however, just under half of the sample made a spontaneous reference to class in the interview. In the majority of cases, an explicit reference to class was made as they described their family standard of living when they were growing up. Those from middle class or lower middle class backgrounds rarely used the category, however, in comparison to those who came from working-class backgrounds who explicitly described their background as working class. There were references to class in other points in the interview as the interviewees described their own education, work histories, and their children's education. When the interviews were conducted in the US, what was striking was the way in the majority of the American interviewees spontaneously described their standard of living in class terms and invariably to describe it as middle class or lower middle class (even when it did not seem to be the case). Those who were socially mobile rarely used the term working class and talked about being blue collar or poor (Devine 2004b). The comparative research, in other words, highlighted how middle-class identities were rarely articulated. The silence, in other words, was deafening and worthy of further investigation.

SOME SPONTANEOUS TALK ABOUT CLASS IN BRITAIN

Unlike their American counterparts, the majority of thee British interviews talked about their family standard of living without any reference to class. Most of those who did not talk about class were from middle-class or lower middle-class backgrounds, at least according to the limited information on their parents (usually their father's) occupation and employment status. In reply to the question, "How would you describe their family standard of living when you were growing up?" they did just that. The interviewees spoke of consumption goods, like a car or a television that their parents owned and whether they enjoyed holidays or not to convey a sense of their childhood circumstances. More often than not, however, the interviewees spoke in general terms about being "comfortable" – a frequently used word – and how they did not want for anything. At the same time, they emphasized that they were not wealthy and that they lived within a budget. They were neither wealthy nor poor but somewhere in the middle, at neither extreme but ordinary. This emphasis on "ordinariness" echoed the views of my working-class informants (Devine 1992a) and Savage and his colleagues' (2001) mixed-class sample. This emphasis was common among the interviewees even when some of them clearly had much more comfortable lifestyles than others.

Only a tiny minority of those from middle-class or lower middle-class backgrounds, therefore, actually described their family circumstances in class terms. The daughter of a self-employed pharmacist, Celia Watson, described herself as middle class although with a little uncertainty, as she said:

> I would describe it as middle class. My mother had help in the house. She didn't work. Looking back on it, it probably wasn't. My father had to work very hard. Maybe it was middle class . . . We had nice holidays but we always stayed in flats rather than hotels. But I and my sister never wanted for anything. We were quite comfortable.

The label "middle class" was used in an innocuous descriptive manner. It was a shorthand way of conveying her standard of living on the assumption, of course, that I knew what the label conveyed. Others used the term "lower middle class" to convey a less affluent lifestyle. David Hill's father, for example, was a bookkeeper and his mother did "school meals" later in life. He said:

> I suppose in some respects we were reasonably well off in that Dad did have a regular job, it was not a brilliantly paid job and we grew up in a typical semi-detached. We classed ourselves as lower middle class really. We never had a car. We had a TV when they'd been out quite a while. I am sure it was tough during the war when you couldn't get thing and that, but we were never without.

Most of the interviewees, however, were remarkably silent about their class background. It was not an identity they articulated (Kitzinger and Wilkinson 1993).

In contrast, most of the interviewees who came from working-class backgrounds explicitly described their family background as "working class." Their working-class background was not hidden but articulated, sometimes with pride (as in Bradley 1999). Some of the interviewees used the label "working class" in a shorthand way to describe their standard of living. Economic constraints were acknowledged although many emphasized that they were not poverty-stricken. Like their middle-class counterparts, they distanced themselves from the extreme and portrayed themselves as more in the middle of some sort of continuum. For others, the discussion of being working class led onto a discussion of respectability and status. Diane Willis, a teacher whose father and mother were weavers in the cotton industry, described her family background as

> very working class but very respectable working class. My father earned a very low wage all the time and when I was at grammar school I was always aware that my father was one of the poorly paid people of parents in the school but my parents were committed church goers and therefore had a certain amount of status in the community.

The claim to respectability was a defense against any moral judgements against her family and the reference to the high status they enjoyed contrasted, implicitly, with the lower status associated with the rough working class. The interviewee, therefore, was well aware of the moral judgements made against the working class described by Skeggs (1997) but there was a strong pride and challenge (Bradley 1999) to such negative representations of the working class in her comments too.

When these interviewees spoke about class, therefore, the discussion was not confined to harmless labels but touched on issues of status, questions of superiority and inferiority and, thus, judgments about worth. The moral undertones of class emerged out of other spontaneous references to class. Few of the middle-class respondents made any reference to class in accounts of their education but there were exceptions. One middle-class interviewee, the wife of a doctor, was highly class-conscious in that she told her life story almost entirely through the lens of class. Janet Jones was the daughter of a general practitioner and a teacher who described her childhood as "very middle class." Her parents decision to send her and her sister away to board at a prestigious ladies college was discussed in class terms. As she explained:

> I grew up in S. It was not a very middle-class area which was why we were schooled out of the area . . . Central S. was a very poor working-class area. It would have been difficult for us because they would have been patients. A lot of the children would know your father. Anyway, I don't think the academic aspirations of the local schools were the aspirations my parents had.

Her parents were anxious, it seems, to keep their daughters physically separate so that they would not be "polluted" by the working class (Walkerdine et al. 2001; Skeggs 1997). Moreover, the middle class was associated with academic aspirations while the working class was not. By implication, although not stated, the lack of academic aspirations among the working class explained why they occupied lowly working-class positions.

Such an explicit discussion of middle-class superiority was extremely rare. What is interesting to note, however, is that many of the interviewees of working-class origins were at pains to demonstrate their parents' high educational aspirations as if responding to Janet's remarks. Moreover, they stressed that their parents' aspirations had been shaped by the fact that economic circumstances had thwarted them when they were young. Thus, they may have lacked economic capital but they did not lack cultural capital (Bourdieu 1984). Barbara Coombes, who became a doctor, was the daughter of a factory worker and a weaver who described her childhood standard of living as "working class." Her family lived in a "two up two down and bog at the bottom of the yard." On her father's influence on her education, she said "My father had been quite clever but had not been able to go to a grammar school because in those days you had to pay so he was keen that I should have all the opportunities that he had missed." Similarly, John Willis, the son of a welder, described how his mother taught him to read at an early age although not, he stressed from his own experiences of teaching,

> so much the kind of middle class thing you get now where everything's laid on and the parent will sit next to the child and read to them and provide them with this, that and the other. It was always the presumption in the family that we were going to succeed and that we were going to do it.

It is interesting to note here how John's comments involved deriding the advantages of the middle class and thereby claiming a different kind of moral superiority.

Most of the working-class interviewees were, indeed, very successful at school but some had very negative experiences of the education system that they explicitly discussed in class terms. Paula Lewis felt she met, in her words, the "class system" on going to grammar school. The teachers judged her by the fact that her father was a miner. As she explained:

> I realized that people were making all sorts of assumptions about me but from nothing that I did, in fact, against the evidence of everything that I did. It didn't matter if I was an A student there and I'd passed the eleven plus. They still had me down for Woolworth's in the first week as far as I could see.

Her subsequent experiences meant that "I couldn't wait to leave. They'd done a good job you know. They'd convinced me that I would be lucky to get a job at all." Paula left school at 16 and worked for a number of years in low-level clerical work. After being made redundant, she went to night school initially to get A levels so that she would be better qualified than other candidates for clerical jobs. Academic success, however, propelled her on to university and she completed a degree in her late twenties. As a mature graduate, however, she found her career options were limited and she decided to pursue a teaching career albeit reluctantly. She was well aware of the effects of her working-class background on her education and subsequent work history and she expressed strong feelings of resentment about the way it which it had held her back. Unlike Savage et al.'s respondents (2001: 876), class was not "out there" but very close to home.

It was very "close to home," of course, when the interviewees discussed their own children's education. All now occupying middle-class professional jobs, the interviewees still sought to distance themselves from being seemingly "pushy" middle-class parents even if they originated from the middle classes. Mary Bull was the daughter of a teacher and a nurse. She followed her father to university before going into teaching herself. Margaret only mentioned class once in the discussion of her sons' education. On her choice of secondary school for them, she said:

> We liked the atmosphere and the discipline. There were the usual resources. It was a well-resourced school and the intake actually mattered to us as well, the actually, um (pause) sounds very snobbish, doesn't it, but the actual intake, the pupils, yeah . . .

In some discomfort, she went on to say:

> Yes, I always felt that my younger one, sort of when he was about 10 or 11, he was one of those who could go either way. Put him with the wrong group and he'd follow the wrong way. So I didn't want him having that opportunity of doing it. Let's put him with the right ones (laughs) and take him that way. I mean I might be doing him a great disservice here (laughs).

Pressed on what she meant by the "right ones," Margaret conceded, "Yes, middle class, yeah, yeah (laughs), sounds snobbish but . . . (laughs)." Even though she wanted her son to be influenced by middle-class friends, distancing herself from a snobbish and elitist middle class was very important.

These sentiments were echoed by the interviewees originally from the working class although now in middle class-occupations. Like Mary, Sarah Proctor also described how a move to a new house was influenced by the quality of the local state schools, making reference to such middle-class preoccupations in an apologetic and embarrassed way. As she explained, "I started looking around for an area where I liked the state schools which is why I moved to C. Isn't that awful? Terribly middle class and teacherish." Here, engaging in middle-class practices was seen in a pejorative fashion. Linda Underwood was concerned about the elitism of the middle class and her own experiences influenced decisions about her daughters' schooling. The daughter of a welder and a housewife, she discussed the elitism she met at medical school. She talked about how

> it was quite a shock to my system. There isn't the same class system in Wales actually. It's a smaller community so everyone mixes really. I found

people at medical school all seemed to come from exactly a very narrow strata. I think there were only a few of us whose parents were professional. Yeah, I thought it was very elitist.

Now a general practitioner and married to a doctor from a well-established middle-class background, Linda and her husband could afford to send their children to private school but chose not to because "it's partly the elitist element which I don't like. I think sometimes it fosters the kind of we're better than anyone else 'cos we got more money attitude which I don't like."

FUTURE DIRECTIONS IN RESEARCH ON CLASS IDENTITIES

Although talk about class was not the central focus on my research on social mobility, the interviewees' spontaneous remarks were very revealing about the place of class in their lives as well as their feelings towards and moral evaluations of other classes. A middle-class identity was rarely articulated either among those who were from well-established middle-class families or those from lower middle-class positions. This silence is somewhat surprising of the former but not of the latter group. Arguably, the lower middle-class respondents were a hybrid group, as Bradley (1999) has described, who might have been able to distance themselves from the working class but who did not necessarily see themselves as middle class or as well-established middle class. Where such an identity was articulated, it was usually spoken of in an innocuous descriptive manner. In sharp contrast, an identification with the working class was often articulated by the socially mobile. Discussion of working-class origins was not, however, confined to a simple description of particular working and living conditions. A defensiveness and pride – which appeared to be two sides of the same coin – were often expressed with considerable feeling. That is to say, there was a clear awareness of the moral judgments made of the working class and attempts to resist any judgments of inferiority were made either through defense or by offense. In this respect, therefore, Skeggs's (1997) account of dis-identification with the working class and Bradley's (1999) description of working-class pride are not as far apart as they might first seem.

Similarly, implicit and explicit references to class that arose elsewhere in the interviewees' narratives revealed the way in which class was associated with status, hierarchy, feelings of superiority and inferiority, and judgments about moral worth. That said, explicit expressions of middle-class superiority were rarely expressed with ease and often couched in euphemisms of class (Reay 1998a). Most of the interviews, in fact, made derisory comments about the middle class. Being middle class, it seems, was associated with being too demanding, pushy, snobbish and elitist and the interviewees were eager to distance themselves, not surprisingly, from such a label even where they engaged in such practices themselves. The apparent superiority of the middle class was rejected. So too was the inferiority of the working class. The socially mobile interviewees rejected any characterization of the working class as lacking in cultural capital as well as (or because) they did not have economic capital. On the contrary, they asserted their high aspirations that were fuelled, in part, by past constraints on their life-styles. Resentment and anger were expressed about the effects of class on their lives including their educational and occupational histories. Class was not just "out there" but "close to home." Moral judgements and claims to superiority were also made against the middle class, including the ease of their achievements in comparison to their own accomplishments. Arguably, an undercurrent of class conflict, of struggles over moral worth, became apparent. This underlying tension might explain why the British middle class do not articulate and, indeed, go to some length, to distance themselves from the class label.

The discussion of some empirical findings from my research has been extremely brief. Nevertheless, it shows there are a number of exciting areas of research still to be pursued. The study of class identities has, more often than not, concentrated on the working class although there is no reason why it should be confined to one class. This is not to say that research on the working class should cease. On the contrary, there is still much work that could be done for past research invariably concentrated on working-class families, couples with children, although it was usually husbands who were interviewed. Skeggs's work was so innovative, in part, because she talked to a group of young working-class women whose experiences of and views about class had never been heard. Charlesworth's (2000) powerful ethnography of the experiences of unemployed young men – their economic powerlessness and political dispossession – should also be noted here. While research has been done on young men and women from ethnic minorities (see Back 1996), the intersection between racial and class identities has yet to be fully explored. A focus on young people, of course, often highlights how things are changing for their everyday experiences are located in a different economic, social, cultural and political climate from their parents. This is not to say that the middle aged or the old should be neglected for their classed life experiences should be voiced too. They, too, will have experienced change in their lifetime, such as the decline of the trade unions, of working men's clubs, changes in family and community life, and so on, which will have shaped and maybe changed their identities. The study of working-class identification and dis-identification is far from exhausted.

Then there is the middle class or, more accurately, the middle classes. Despite the huge growth of the middle classes in the twentieth century (Goldthorpe 1987; Savage et al. 1992), there has been surprising little in the way of research into middle-class identities. Arguably, the middle class have been ignored because they are seen as an essentially conventional and conservative class unlikely to challenge the system so to speak. Yet, the lived experiences, practices, class, and other social identities are crucial for understanding middle-class formation (Wacquant 1991). Again, it is easy to identify different groupings within the still heterogeneous middle classes who could be researched. The experiences of the socially mobile are interesting for it seems that an identification with the working class often remains strong (see also Reid 1998). As Bradley (1999) rightly suggests, this identification with the working class prevails as part of a loyalty to family and friends and the social world of which they were once members. Indeed, it might be that identification with the working class is stronger for the socially mobile than for those who remain in the working class, who know of the changing experiences of working-class life and whose identification with the working class also changes over time. The well-established middle class, however, should not be forgotten either for they are not a static entity, immune from change, even if they are good at reproducing their privileges and power across generations (Devine 2004a).

Discussion of the socially mobile, however, highlights the fact that so many people cannot be categorized as unequivocally working class or middle class. Arguably, sociologists have been too quick to categorize people into such distinct groups (see Reay's discussion of middle-class and working-class women and their children (1998b)). There is considerable hybridity that has implications for class identification or dis-identification. Acknowledging this hybridity suggests, as Savage and his colleagues (2001) have argued, that the common features of class ambiguities should be explored. This is undoubtedly true although research on commonalities should not necessarily preclude the study of differences for few would dispute that people's everyday experiences at work and at home are different because they are classed experiences that are "lived" in distinct social spaces. Be that as it may, an important issue is how this research is undertaken. Previous research which has asked people to place themselves into particular social classes now seems very mechanical and unimaginative. This research may have tapped into people's cognitive understanding of class but it neglected the affective dimensions of class. Again, the most recent work on class and other social identities by Skeggs, Bradley and Savage and his associates tap people's feelings about class in particular and inequalities more generally. The evidence suggests that class evokes often powerful emotions and such strong feelings that people do not always want to express them or find it difficult to do so.

If further research into class and other social identities is to tap the feelings and emotions evoked by class, there are important methodological issues to address. There has been an increasing tendency to do qualitative research by way of interviews in various guises and to present them as almost emotionless conversations. The remit of qualitative research, in other words, has narrowed over recent years. If we are to acknowledge that class cannot always be articulated, as Skeggs (1997) following Bourdieu (see, most recently, Bourdieu et al. 1999) has argued, and that much is left unstated, then we have to take a much more careful look at all the "noise" that has been previously unacknowledged in interviews: namely, how people react to questions, their body language, hesitations, nervous laughter, and so on. In other words, a lot more observation of interviewees' minds and bodies (see Crossley 2001; Walkerdine et al. 2001) needs to go on in the interview situation and be discussed more explicitly in the writing of qualitative research. It should be more ethnographic in form. It is easy to imagine the objection that would be leveled against this research agenda, however. Sociologists of class could stand accused of imposing their preoccupation with class on the general public, and worse, continue to do so when people have long stopped talking about class. This objection cannot be ignored but, arguably, it can be addressed. The study of (class) subjectivities can listen to how people draw on their experiences of and talk about inequalities without ever using the language of class. Indeed, thinking about the contexts in which class is articulated and the contexts in which it is not voiced may be the direction in which future research on class subjectivities should go.

Conclusion

This chapter has addressed the current debates about class identities and the salience of class in people's lives. There is a growing consensus in Britain that class identities are now weaker than they once were and my discussion on the way in which middle-class identities are rarely articulated confirms this conclusion. That said, it is difficult to argue that class identities are weak for everyone for working-class identities remain strong for certain groups of people. Thus, whether class identification is weak across the board is open to debate. Be that as it may, the study of class subjectivities is far from dead. The growing interest in social identities in sociology has highlighted the importance of the construction and process of identity formation, both internally within ourselves as we construct our uniqueness and externally via out interaction with other individuals and institutions. Further research on class identification or dis-identification could embrace these concerns. Moreover, the study of social identities has highlighted both the individual and collective dimensions of social identities. Interest in the subjective dimensions of class was confined to the collective properties of class identities in the past. There is room, as Savage and his colleagues (2001: 888) have also argued, for an exploration of the individual dimensions of class identity and how people actively and reflexively draw on classed experiences in the formation of social identities. To be sure, the links between individual and collective class identities are also worthy of further exploration.

REFERENCES

Abrams, M., Rose, R., and Hinden, M. (1960) *Must Labour Lose?* Harmondsworth: Penguin.

Back, L. (1996) *New Identities and Urban Culture.* London: UCL Press.

Beck, U. (1992) *Risk Society.* London: Sage.

Beynon, H. (1975) *Working for Ford.* Harmondsworth: Penguin.

Bourdieu, P. (1984) *Distinction.* London: Routledge.

Bourdicu, P. et al. (1999) *The Weight of the World.* Cambridge: Polity Press.

Bradley, H. (1996) *Fractured Identities.* Cambridge: Polity Press.

—— (1999) *Gender and Power in the Workplace.* London: Palgrave.

Bulmer, M. (ed.) (1975) *Working-Class Images of Society.* London: Routledge and Kegan Paul.

Charlesworth, S. J. (2000) *A Phenomenology of Working Class Experience.* Cambridge: Cambridge University Press.

Crook, S. et al. (1992) *Postmodernisation.* London: Sage.

Crossley, N. (2001) *The Social Body.* London: Sage.

Dennis, N., Henriques, F., and Slaughter, C. (1956) *Coal is Our Life.* London: Eyre and Spottiswoode.

Devine, F. (1992a) *Affluent Workers Revisited.* Edinburgh: Edinburgh University Press.

—— (1992b) "Social identities, class identities and political perspectives," *Sociological Review* 40: 229–52.

—— (1997) *Social Class in America and Britain.* Edinburgh: Edinburgh University Press.

—— (1998) "Class analysis and the stability of class relations," *Sociology* 32: 23–42.

—— (2004a) *Class Practices: How Parents Help their Children Get Good Jobs.* Cambridge: Cambridge University Press.

—— (2004b) "Middle-class identities in America," in Devine, F. et al. (eds.), *Investigating Social Stratification.* London: Palgrave.

Eldridge, J. (1990) "Sociology in Britain: A going concern," in Bryant, C. G. A. and Becker, H. A. (eds.), *What Has Sociology Achieved?* London: Macmillan.

Emmison, M. and Western, M. (1990) "Social class and social identity: A comment on Marshall et al.," *Sociology* 24: 241–53.

Goldthorpe, J. H. (1987) *Social Mobility and Class Structure in Modern Britain,* Oxford: Clarendon Press.

Goldthorpe, J. H. and Lockwood, D. (1963) "Affluence and the British class structure," *Sociological Review* 11: 133–63.

Goldthorpe, J. H., Lockwood, D., Bechhofer, F., and Platt, J. (1968a) *The Affluent Worker: Industrial Attitudes and Behaviour.* Cambridge: Cambridge University Press.

—— (1968b) *The Affluent Worker: Political Attitudes and Behaviour.* Cambridge: Cambridge University Press.

—— (1969) *The Affluent Worker in the Class Structure.* Cambridge: Cambridge University Press.

Hetherington, K. (1998) *Expressions of Identity.* London: Sage.

Jenkins, R. (1996) *Social Identity.* London: Routledge.

Kent, R. A. (1981) *A History of British Empirical Research.* Aldershot: Gower.

Kerr, M. (1958) *The People of Ship Street.* London: Routledge and Kegan Paul.

Kitzinger, C. and Wilkinson, S. (1993) "The precariousness of heterosexual feminist identities," in Kennedy, M. et al. (eds.), *Making Connections.* London: Taylor and Francis.

Lockwood, D. (1966) "Sources of variation in working-class images of society," *Sociological Review* 14: 249–67.

Mann, M. (1973) *Consciousness and Action among the Western Working Class.* London: Macmillan.

Marshall, G. (1983) "Some remarks on the study of working-class consciousness," *Politics and Society* 12: 263–301.

Marshall, G. and Rose, D. (1989) "Reply to Saunders," *Network* 44: 4–5.

—— (1990) "Out-classed by our critics," *Sociology* 24: 225–67.

Marshall, G., Rose, D., Newby, H., and Vogler, C. (1988) *Social Class in Modern Britain.* London: Hutchinson Education.

Newby, H. (1982) *The State of Research into Social Stratification in Britain.* London: Social Science Research Council.

Parkin, F. (1972) *Class Inequality and Political Order.* London: Paladin.

Platt, J. (1971) "Variations in answers to different questions on perceptions of class," *Sociological Review* 19: 409–19.

Reay, D. (1998a) "Rethinking social class: Qualitative perspectives on class and gender," *Sociology* 32: 259–75.

—— (1998b) *Class Work*. London: UCL Press.

Reid, I. (1998) *Class in Britain*. Cambridge: Polity Press.

Roberts, K. (2001) *Class in Modern Britain*. Basingstoke: Palgrave.

Runciman, W. G. (1966) *Relative Deprivation and Social Justice*. London: Routledge and Kegan Paul.

Saunders, P. (1989) "Left write in sociology," *Network* 44: 3–4.

Savage, M. (2000) *Class Analysis and Social Transformation*. Buckingham: Open University Press.

Savage, M., Barlow, J., Dickens, P., and Fielding, T. (1992) *Property, Bureaucracy and Culture*. London: Routledge.

Savage, M., Bagnall, G., and Longhurst, B. (2001) "Ordinary, ambivalent and defensive: Class identities in the northwest of England," *Sociology* 35: 875–92.

Skeggs, B. (1997) *Formation of Class and Gender*. London: Sage.

Stacey, M. (1960) *Tradition and Change*. Oxford: Oxford University Press.

Tunstall, J. (1962) *The Fisherman*. London: MacGibbon and Kee.

Wacquant, L. J. D. (1991) "Making class: The middle class(es) in social theory and social structure," in McNall, S. G. et al. (eds.), *Bringing Class Back In*. Oxford: Westview Press.

Walkerdine, V., Lucey, H., and Melody, J. (2001) *Growing up Girl*. Basingstoke: Palgrave.

Westergaard, J. (1992) "About and beyond the 'underclass': Some notes on influences of social climate on British sociology today," *Sociology* 26: 575–87.

Zwieg, F. (1961) *The Worker in an Affluent Society*. London: Heinemann.

FURTHER READING

Devine, F. (2004) *Class Practices: How Parents Help their Children Get Good Jobs*. Cambridge: Cambridge University Press.

Savage, M. (2000) *Class Analysis and Social Transformation*. Buckingham: Open University Press.

CHAPTER NINE

Research on Gender Stratification in the US

Christine L. Williams, Patti A. Giuffre, and Kirsten A. Dellinger

The sociology of gender has experienced tremendous growth and development in the United States. Although stratification researchers have long considered gender to be a major locus of social inequality, sociologists have only begun to understand the dynamic processes involved in the reproduction of sexism, thanks in large part to the efforts of qualitative researchers. In this chapter we will begin by identifying the key theoretical and empirical questions that have organized the field of gender studies in the US over the past 50 years. Next, we will discuss how qualitative researchers have contributed to the growth of the field. Finally, we will discuss our own research as an example of qualitative work that expands the understanding of gender. We conclude with some ideas about the future directions the field is likely to pursue.

Key Theoretical Preoccupations

Prior to the second wave of feminism in the United States, gender stratification was understood entirely in terms of roles, known as "sex roles." This was a reflection of the dominance of structural functionalism in the 1950s and 1960s. This theory argued that men were socialized to fit an instrumental role, and women to fit an expressive one. Talcott Parsons and Robert Bales, who were the leading proponents of the theory, wrote:

> It seems quite safe in general to say that the adult feminine role has not ceased to be anchored primarily in the internal affairs of the family, as wife, mother and manager of the household, while the role of the adult

male is primarily anchored in the occupational world, in his job and through it by his status-giving and income-earning functions for the family. (Parsons and Bales 1955: 14–15)

When women did enter the work world, they noted that it was typically in support occupations that drew on their expressive personalities: teacher, nurse, and secretary. All social institutions, including the legal system, religious institutions, schools, and the family, promoted this differentiation of roles, they argued, because it resulted in a cohesive and stable social order.

Although structural functionalists stressed the importance of socialization, and recognized some historical and cultural variation, they maintained that sex roles ultimately derived from men's and women's complementary reproductive functions. Women were socially destined to provide the unconditional love of a mother to a child, so if they did enter paid work, they tended to serve in dead-end pink-collar jobs that would not place them in competition with men or interfere with their childrearing responsibilities. Men's role in the family was to impose impersonal rules and discipline the children, traits that were reinforced by their primary attachment to the sphere of paid work. Although some individuals might escape this standard socialization, society typically dealt with them harshly, condemning them to outsider status by labeling them deviant or even mentally ill.

Feminists were early antagonists of structural functionalism because it was often interpreted as a justification for the status quo. If sex roles are functional and promote stability in the social system, it is easy to assume that the social system is as it "should" be and should not be changed. In *The Feminine Mystique*, Betty Friedan (1963) interpreted structural functionalism in this light and labeled the 1950s "a functional freeze in social science" (Johnson 1993: 103). And as Judith Stacey and Barrie Thorne pointed out much later, by translating gender into expressive and instrumental roles, Parsons assumed that men and women are simply different kinds of people rather than considering gender as an expression of power of one group over another (Stacey and Thorne 1985). Even feminists today, who have attempted to resurrect the potential of structural functionalist analysis in a radical direction, agree that Parsons, in particular, failed to "problematize power" (Johnson 1993: 102).

In this vein, feminists pointed out that sociologists never referred to "race roles" or "class roles." Instead of being benign and beneficial to society, feminists saw sex roles as sexist and the product of male dominance. Marxist feminists in Britain seized on the analogy of class antagonism to explain men's power over women: men's rule over women in the family, they argued, was tied to their control over economic resources brought about by capitalist industrialization (Engels 1972; Barrett 1980). Early Marxist feminists argued that women's roles as housewives placed them in a unique relationship to the means of production. The work they did in the home aided in the reproduction of the workforce and produced surplus value for capitalism (Glazer 1984). This branch of Marxist feminists known as "housework feminists" argued that women's work in the home should be industrialized (Benston 1970) or remunerated (James and Dalla Costa 1973). Later Marxist feminists explored the complex interface of capitalism and patriarchy as dual sources of women's oppression (Hartmann 1976; Eisenstein 1979) and emphasized the importance of examining the historically situated nature of the sex/gender system (Rubin 1975).

Marxist feminists saw virtually all forms of masculine and feminine difference as something imposed from the outside, the consequence of economic inequality. In the late 1970s and 1980s, some psychoanalytically-influenced theorists sought to moderate this view by investigating how gender was internalized. Nancy Chodorow (1978) asked a simple yet profound question about the division of labor in the home: Why do women mother? In so doing she demonstrated that gender identity and gender inequality are not simply imposed by social training or by the economic domination of men over women. Women's primary responsibility for child care both shapes and is shaped by the unique psychic structure of men's and women's personalities. In the pre-Oedipal stage of development both girls and boys form a primary attachment with a woman, usually their mother. At the age of three, boys are often forced to break this attachment and shift their identification to the more distant male figures in their life, usually their fathers. Girls are not required to make such a profound shift and consequently maintain a closer psychological attachment to and identification with their mothers. This asymmetrical treatment in childhood often results in adult women with unconscious cravings for nurturing, holding, and intimacy, and adult men who define their masculinity as a rejection of these very qualities. Women will then turn to mothering to satisfy their unmet emotional needs which adult men are seemingly incapable of providing.

Chodorow's explanation for why women mother was applied to other matters, such as the cultural devaluation of women (Benjamin 1988), men's domination of science (Keller 1985), unhappiness in heterosexual marriage (Rubin 1983), and the persistence of occupational gender segregation (Williams 1989). Men's power throughout society is sustained by a largely unconscious definition of masculinity that rejects as inferior and foreign anything associated with femininity. Hester Eisenstein wrote that Chodorow allowed us to see that "the sexual division of labor and women's responsibility for child care are linked to and generate male dominance" (1983: 214).

This line of psychoanalytic theorizing understood gender inequality as a reflection of both socially structured inequality and individuals' internalized needs and dispositions. But, in general, feminist sociologists resisted the view that anything other than power or force could account for gender stratification. Cynthia Epstein, for example, categorized the psychoanalytic feminists as "maximalists" because in her view the argument that gender difference is deeply ingrained through early influences assumes that the differences between men and women are overwhelming and intractable. She called herself a gender "minimalist" instead because she believes that men and women are inherently similar and that gender differences are social constructions and subject to change depending on the social situation (Epstein 1988).

In the 1990s, interest in social constructionism was at a high tide in the US. The most influential gender theorists emphasized "doing gender" and "performativity" (West and Zimmerman 1987; Butler 1990; West and Fenstermaker 1995). Gender was conceptualized as malleable and contextual, a product of everyday interactions that, when repeated often enough, gave the impression of being natural and inevitable when in fact they were artificial and contingent. Every interaction is a performance in which individuals are assessed on their ability to conform to normative conceptions of gender. This "doing gender" perspective was adopted by many feminist researchers who examined how interactions on the job perpetuated traditional notions of appropriately feminine and masculine work and resulted in the gender segregation of jobs (Leidner 1993; Pierce 1995).

Judith Butler (1990) took social constructionism a step further when she suggested that gender *and sex* are both fictions that are performed through the body in order to regulate sexuality in the context of mandatory reproductive heterosexuality. Butler and other postmodernist feminists drew on the works of Foucault and Derrida to argue that how we study the world is a form of domination itself (Nicholson 1990). From this view, all categories and definitions of social life, especially those crafted by experts, should be subjected to skepticism and intentionally subverted to reveal their connection to power, hierarchy, and domination (Bordo 1993). In the field of gender studies, subversion was understood as any challenge to stereotypical expectations about how men and women ought to behave in daily interactions. Butler uses the example of dressing in drag: A man who dresses as a woman, she argues, mocks the notion of a true, original gender identity and has the potential to subvert the gender order and cause people to rethink their essentialist views of what is natural for men and women. In this way, postmodernist feminists forced us to question the very nature of "structure" and opened the door for a discussion of resistance and change in everyday social practices.

This focus on gender subversion through individual acts of resistance resonated with third-wave feminism. The third wave was made up of mostly young college women in the 1990s who, like the second wavers of the 1970s, were politically active on issues of abortion rights, homophobia, and sexual violence, but who perceived their forebears as "male bashers" (Findlen 1995; Heywood and Drake 1997; Baumgardner and Richards 2000). They were uncomfortable with what they saw as the bland androgyny of the earlier generation of feminists, and sought instead to cultivate a unique feminine style that was at once subversive and highly sexualized (Green and Taormino 1997). The shift to interaction as the site for the reproduction of gender was empowering to this younger generation of feminists because it implied that anyone could undermine the status quo by making "gender trouble" (Butler 1990).

Because of its focus on resistance and subversion, the social constructionist perspective led many scholars to study diversity in men's and women's experiences, thus opening up research on race and class differences in the experience of gender. However, with its focus on individual resistance, the perspective tended to underplay the constraining power of structured inequality (racism, capitalism, sexism). Some scholars argued vehemently about the limitations of social constructionism, most notably Patricia Hill Collins. Arguing from a black feminist perspective, she maintained that there is a complex matrix of domination which grants privilege to individuals depending on their race, gender, and social class. Individual acts of resistance cannot by themselves overcome this power structure (Collins 2000; Collins et al. 1995).

Australian R. W. Connell (1987) introduced the notion of hegemonic masculinity and emphasized femininity to discuss gender diversity in a framework of power. These have become enormously influential concepts in US gender studies. Connell suggests that there is a definite hegemonic ordering of versions of femininity and masculinity at the societal level ranging from legitimate and protected to illegitimate and subordinated. These versions do not represent the actual femininities and masculinities that individuals experience in their daily lives: "the public face of hegemonic masculinity is not necessarily what powerful men are, but what sustains their power and what large numbers of men are motivated to support" (1987: 185). Connell argues that the structured fact of men's dominance over women provides the basis for the construction of "hegemonic masculinity" which is defined in opposition to other competing masculinities and to women (Connell 1987, 1995). This perspective made room for a discussion of multiple versions of masculinity and femininity without abandoning recognition that specific versions are most powerful at any given historical moment.

And so in a strange way, we have come full circle. This shift brings us back to the project that Parsons originally saw himself undertaking, integrating all levels of analysis in his theory of social action. In the 1950s he wrote, "neither personalities nor social systems can be adequately understood without reference to culture, to each other and to the relations of these three to each other" (Parsons and Bales 1955: 33). Over the past 50 years, the major currents in the field of gender studies have at times privileged a focus on identity and at others on culture or structure as the source of gender differentiation and inequality. Now there is a recognition that all three levels are important. The current challenge for the study of gender is to examine how gender inequality is perpetuated – and resisted – at structural, cultural, and individual levels and to examine the *processes* through which these levels are linked (Acker 1990; Britton 1997).

The Importance of Qualitative Research

In the United States, there are two strands of empirical studies of gender stratification: qualitative and quantitative. Feminists are at the forefront of both types, but few scholars combine the two methods. Quantitative researchers have documented the wage gap, degrees of occupational segregation, the unequal allocation of housework and child care in the home, and the prevalence of sexual harassment and discrimination. Qualitative researchers often refer to this literature to frame their investigations, but many are wary of an over-reliance on these studies. Some of the problems are generic to all quantitative studies having to do with measurement issues, and some are specific to the study of gender stratification. Here we review three of the problems of quantitative methods identified by qualitative feminist researchers: (1) the problem of counting; (2) using sex as a variable; and (3) treating gender as a property of individuals and not institutions and organizations.

Problem of counting

Counting social phenomena is a problem for all social scientists, but may be especially pronounced for gender scholars because many of the topics of interest defy quantification. How do you quantify child care, housework, or sexual behavior? These activities merge seamlessly into daily life, making them difficult to categorize and count. This is in contrast to paid work, for example, where surveys can ascertain the proportions of men and women employed in various jobs, the number of hours they worked, the amounts they were paid, the benefits they received, and so on. But even in this area, some gender scholars are skeptical about the ability of quantitative studies to grasp the full picture of gender inequality. Men and women may do the exact same job, for example, but they may be called by different titles: the woman may be called a "secretary" while the man is called an "administrative assistant." Even pay is tricky to quantify since it seems to be the case that men exaggerate their earnings and women under-report theirs.

Many of the problems with counting were exacerbated when the field of sociology was controlled almost exclusively by men. During that time, quantitative sociologists used categories for analysis that were derived almost exclusively from men's experiences. A classic example is the study of social status: In the 1950s and 1960s it was assumed that a woman's socio-economic status was identical to that of her father or her husband, so no independent studies were undertaken of women's position in the stratification system (Acker 1973). Similarly, sociologists treated time away from paid work as "leisure" time, which is a far more fitting assumption about men's experience than women's, given women's responsibility for most of the family work.

Women sociologists were the first to argue that new categories were needed to reflect women's experiences. In the 1970s and 1980s, debates on feminist methodology arose about whether quantitative methods could ever fully comprehend gender inequality. Some researchers privileged qualitative methods as being more in line with the goals of feminism (e.g. Smith 1979; Devault 1990). Dorothy Smith argued that a "sociology for women" must be truthful to women's understandings of their intimate daily lives. She maintained that everyday life inherently defies categorization – and hence quantification – because of its contingency and paradoxical nature. Marjorie Devault (1991) demon-

strated this in her study of women's family work. Using in-depth interviewing she showed that a plethora of tasks were involved in preparing
family meals, but for the most part, women did not consider this activity "work" but an expression of love. She argued that qualitative
methods are necessary because they allow respondents to discuss their
experiences at length on their own terms without forcing them into
pre-given categories that are derived from (or at least sanctioned by)
men's understandings of social life.

Other feminist sociologists argued that qualitative methods are not
inherently more valid or feminist than quantitative methods. Shulamit
Reinharz (1992), for example, argued that any method could be feminist. Further, Joey Sprague and Mary Zimmerman (1989) noted that
the criticisms of quantitative methods made by some feminist
researchers (including the critique of objectivity and of the power relations embedded in research) can be made against qualitative research
as well. Today US gender researchers have reached a sort of détente.
Both quantitative and qualitative methods are used by feminists, and
the limitations of both approaches are generally acknowledged by both
sides.

Treating sex as a variable

Quantitative studies frequently use sex as an independent variable.
Some feminists argue that treating sex as a variable essentializes what
researchers are wanting to explain by collapsing the conceptual distinction between sex and gender. Most sociologists agree that sex is
defined as the different biological and reproductive characteristics that
men and women are born with or develop (e.g. genitalia, chromo-
somes). Gender, on the other hand, refers to the social and cultural
constructions of masculinity and femininity. Using sex as an independent variable presumes that biological differences are causing changes
in behaviors or attitudes. Interestingly, some quantitative sociologists
have begun to use the terms "sex" and "gender" interchangeably on
surveys when they probably mean "sex." This elides the problem but
does not eliminate it because "gender" in this case is defined entirely
by biology.

Advocates of the "doing gender" perspective are among the most
ardent critics of using sex or gender as an independent variable. Since
they understand gender as an emergent property of interaction, it is
more like an "effect" than a "cause" of social behavior. Biological sex
becomes irrelevant to this understanding of gender inequality. If you

are biologically female, but you dress and act and "pass" as a man, then you *are* a man as far as society is concerned. The rise of postmodernism in sociological studies of gender has complicated the matter even further by challenging the assumption that "sex" is a biological category. The notion that there are two – and only two – sexes is culturally constructed, they argue, and they point to societies that recognize more than two sexes and speculate about the possibilities of even more (Fausto-Sterling 1993).

Similar concerns have arisen about the use of "race" as a variable. Since most theorists now recognize that "race" is a social, and not a biological, category, it is a mistake to assume that differences in social behavior are caused by racial differences. Using "race" as an independent variable is criticized by some as a form of racial essentialism that promotes racism. Likewise, using "sex" or "gender" as a variable is gender essentialism that promotes sexism.

Gender and organizations

Quantitative studies tend to treat gender as a property of individuals. *Individuals* are considered masculine or feminine, while *organizations* are considered gender-neutral. This approach tends to ignore the ways that gender is institutionalized in society. Joan Acker (1990) introduced the notion of "gendered organizations," arguing that assumptions about men's and women's abilities become embedded in jobs and organizations. Some of these assumptions are built into what she refers to as "organizational logic." For example, men and women must be able and willing to have little or no family life if they are to be successful doctors or attorneys. These types of deeply embedded – and unquestioned – job requirements favor men and discriminate against women. They are forms of institutionalized sexism that are virtually impossible to ascertain using quantitative methods.

Several qualitative studies have demonstrated the usefulness of Acker's gendered organizations framework. Dana Britton's (1997) in-depth interview study with men and women correctional officers is perhaps the best example. Britton found that prison policies often appear gender-neutral on the surface but actually benefit men officers more than women officers. Many officers noted that they were unprepared for working in the women's prisons because their training focused exclusively on men's prisons. When asked if she was prepared for her work in the woman's prison, an officer said, "I would have to say no, because at the training academy, they teach you on the man's aspect, not the women's prison. Everything they teach you in preservice had to do with the men's unit" (1997: 807). Officer training also stressed the importance of acquiring highly touted masculine qualities like aggressiveness and physical strength, while ignoring the equally important skills of diplomacy and empathy, which are more typically associated with women. Male officers benefit from this type of training; women feel unprepared and at a disadvantage. A quantitative survey could ask respondents whether their training prepared them for the job and how much their training prepared them for the job, but such inquiries would be unable to discern the organizational processes that result in these outcomes. Often, respondents do not recognize the taken-for-granted gendered assumptions of their jobs. Only by discussing their personal experiences at length and observing their workplaces do the patterns emerge.

Critiques of qualitative methods

Perhaps the two most common criticisms of qualitative research are problems with reliability and inability to generalize. Some researchers argue that qualitative studies are more difficult than quantitative ones to replicate (Sprague and Zimmerman 1989; Williams 1991). One reason for this shortcoming is that qualitative researchers are more likely to engage in face-to-face observations and interactions with their respondents. The qualities and appearance of the researcher – including their age, race, ethnicity and gender – can influence the findings. Quantitative researchers who rely on mail-in forms or telephone surveys are perceived as less vulnerable to this problem. However, this problem of "interviewer effects" is a concern to all researchers. The conventional solution is to study only people who are "like" ourselves, possessing similar race and gender characteristics.

Those who violate this normal practice and interview people who are unlike themselves can nevertheless provide important insights into their subjects' experiences, but they must be alert to how respondents will frame their views according to the gender- and race-context of the interviews. Qualitative researchers may in fact be better able than quantitative researchers to assess their impact on their respondents. Because they use the flexible method of in-depth interviewing, they can monitor rapport in an ongoing way, and thus detect and respond to their respondents' feelings about them. Examples include Christine Williams' study of male nurses (1995), Mary Waters' study of African-American immigrants (1999), and Nancy Foner's study of nursing home attendants

(1994). These researchers did not share the same gender, race, or class backgrounds as their respondents, but by creatively negotiating their "differences," they were able to discern important insights from their investigations.

Along with charges that qualitative studies are difficult to replicate, qualitative research is criticized for its inability to generalize findings to the population. These criticisms are inaccurate because qualitative research does not attempt to generalize findings to the population based on small, nonrandom samples. It would be grossly inappropriate to state, even tentatively, that a study of 20 women surgeons represents the population of all women surgeons. The goal of qualitative research is to describe as truthfully as possible individuals' definitions of their situations, and the meanings they attribute to their behaviors. Because the goal is one of interpretation – not generalization – qualitative researchers often attempt to choose their sample theoretically and not on the basis of representativeness and probability.

Interestingly, even though they are based on nonrandom samples, qualitative studies can help researchers attain diverse samples or examine experiences of groups about which we know very little. Qualitative sociologists typically rely on case studies and snowball sampling, when respondents volunteer the names of other people who might agree to be interviewed. In contrast, quantitative researchers have to rely on random samples, where each member of the population has an equal chance of being included in the study. Random samples are very costly to generate; usually this type of study has to rely on funding from government agencies or private foundations. Moreover, quantitative researchers typically do not get to choose which questions are asked; questions are decided upon by government officials and consultants. This limits the kinds of research questions that can be addressed. And although random samples are excellent for statistical purposes, they are notoriously bad at identifying hard-to-reach populations, such as the homeless, prostitutes, drug users, and illegal immigrants. They also fail to reach the opposite end of the stratification hierarchy: corporate executives, celebrities, and politicians, for example, almost never volunteer to answer survey questions in person or over the phone. They are reluctant to identify themselves, they have little time to spare for a research study, or they tend to be suspicious of the motives of researchers.

Qualitative researchers can overcome some of this reluctance by joining groups and establishing a reassuring rapport with respondents. Recent in-depth interview studies of hard-to-reach populations include Lauraine LeBlanc's study of punk girls (1999) and Pierrette Hondagneu-Sotelo's study of Mexican immigrant domestic workers (2001). Both of these studies relied on snowball sampling techniques. Ethnographic methods are also useful for infiltrating inaccessible settings and getting an up-close view of behavior that people may be embarrassed to admit to researchers. One the best examples is Judith Rollins' (1985) study of black domestics. Rollins worked as a domestic for white women employers and recorded their treatment of her. She also interviewed other African-American domestic workers. Her research demonstrated the importance of exploring perspectives of both the powerful and powerless and the contradictions inherent in relationships between them. This information would be virtually impossible to find using quantitative methods.

In short, qualitative methods are able to overcome some of the research problems inherent in quantitative studies. But the goals of the two types of study are quite different. Quantitative researchers aim to discover general patterns of behavior that apply to the population as a whole. In gender studies, this translates into a concern with differences in men's and women's incomes, political affiliations, living arrangements, health behaviors, and so on. Qualitative researchers, on the other hand, seek to understand the motives for people's behaviors from their own points of view, and they seek out respondents whom they believe will be especially knowledgeable and familiar with the processes that interest them. Their findings do not apply to the population as a whole, but they help to refine theories about how and why gender differences are reproduced. These different goals result in a more or less bifurcated field of gender stratification in the US.

QUALITATIVE STUDIES OF SEXUAL HARASSMENT

To illustrate the strengths of qualitative research to understand gender stratification, we will now turn to a discussion of our studies of sexual harassment. Sexual harassment is considered one of the major barriers to women's economic success. It is legally defined in the US as any unwanted sexual acts or words that are an explicit or implicit condition of employment and that result in gender discrimination. Research has shown that women often leave jobs because of sexual harassment, or their work performance suffers because they are under constant stress of being treated as a sexual object.

Sexual harassment law does not specify what specific behaviors constitute sexual harassment. It only states that the acts must be "unwelcome," "unreasonable," or cause "an intimidating, hostile, or offensive working environment." Although these are subjective conditions, many quantitative sociologists and organizational researchers have devised objective lists of behaviors that they think constitute sexual harassment in order to measure its prevalence. (Susan Bordo (1993) calls this the "grabs and gropes" approach to identifying harassment.) These lists vary a great deal, and cover an enormous range of behaviors, every-thing from leering to sexual assault. Workers are asked to indicate on a survey form whether they have ever experienced such behaviors in the workplace. By using such lists, researchers estimate that 40 to 50 percent of women workers have experienced sexual harassment (Welsh 1999).

This figure does not represent how many people actually label their experiences as sexual harassment, however. Even those respondents who indicate that they have experienced offensive or unwanted sexual behaviors rarely answer "yes" to the survey question, "Have you ever been sexually harassed?" So why don't people label their experiences as sexual harassment?

At least part of the answer lies in the fact that sexual harassment is a feature of many jobs, especially in the predominately female service sector. Many women are employed in jobs where they are routinely sub-jected to deliberate or repeated sexual behavior that is unwelcome, as well as other sex-related behaviors that they consider hostile, offensive, or degrading. They rarely label their experiences sexual harassment, however, because they are institutionalized as part their jobs; as Acker would say, they are in "gendered organizations" where the taken-for-granted rules and assumptions discriminate against women. In some highly sexualized occupations, workers are required to sign consent forms indicating that they acknowledge the highly sexual nature of their employment and that they promise not to bring suit against the company for these sexual elements. Those who refuse to put up with such requirements end up quitting or being fired, or never taking the job in the first place.

In one study of the restaurant industry (Giuffre and Williams 1994), we found that waiters and waitresses gradually learn to accept sexual harassment as part of their jobs. For example, one waitress claimed that customers often "talk dirty" to her:

> I remember one day, about four or five years ago when I was working as a cocktail waitress, this guy asked me for a Slow Comfortable Screw [the name of a drink]. I didn't know what it was. I didn't know if he was making a move or something. I just looked at him. He said, "You know what it is, right?" I said, "I bet the bartender knows!" (laughs) . . . There's

another one, "Sex on the Beach." And there's another one called a "Screaming Orgasm." Do you believe that? (Giuffre and Williams 1994: 387)

This waitress works for an organization that subjects all employees to sexual comments as a condition of employment. In fact, we picked this occupation to study precisely because the environment was sexualized, so workers would be likely very knowledgeable and reflective about how to draw the line between sexual behavior that was and was not sexual harassment. This waitress personally finds sexy drink names offensive, but she neither complains about it nor labels it sexual harassment: Once it becomes clear that a "Slow Comfortable Screw" is a "legitimate" and recognized restaurant demand, she accepts it (albeit reluctantly) as part of her job description. The fact that the offensive behavior is institutionalized makes it beyond reproach in her eyes.

Another example comes from case studies by Kirsten Dellinger (2002) and Dellinger and Williams (2002) of two organizations in the magazine publishing industry, one that publishes a pornographic heterosexual men's magazine, and the other, a feminist magazine. These case studies were also selected because they are highly sexualized, but in vastly different ways. At the porn magazine, given the pseudonym *Gentleman's Sophisticate*, one of the workers talked about how she learned to tolerate the offensive behavior at her workplace. Tina, who is an editor, was responsible for writing the captions beneath the sexually explicit pictorials. She said:

It used to be so hard . . . It used to be like, torture. And now . . . you get used to what it's supposed to sound like . . . So it's easier to write . . . I mean they're funny – you really have to have a sense of humor, that's the one requirement to work here. You gotta be able to have anything go off your back. Because there's just so much, you know. You gotta have a really open mind.

When Tina started working at *Gentleman's Sophisticate*, she described the sexual aspect of her job as "torture." She was subjected to an offensive working environment that made her feel uncomfortable. In this sense, her experience could be interpreted as sexual harassment. But instead of labeling it sexual harassment, she eventually learned to define it as "funny" – something not to be taken seriously.

These examples highlight the experiences of individuals who are uncomfortable with the sexual elements of their jobs. There are, of course, many people who seek out and enjoy jobs that are highly sexualized. Meika Loe, who studied the "Bazooms" restaurant chain (where she was employed for some time as a waitress), reported that 800 women applied for the job when she did (Loe 1996). In our studies, we've also found that some people are drawn to work environments where sexuality is a major part of the job. In Patti Giuffre's study of doctors and nurses in a teaching hospital, she found that some high-ranking professional women enjoy the sexual elements of their jobs. A woman surgeon admitted that in the operating room, "[There's] teasing and joking and pinching and elbowing. It's fun. That's one reason people like being in that arena. That's part of the camaraderie" (Williams et al. 1999: 86). But even in these cases, workers still draw boundary lines between sexual behaviors that they consider pleasurable, tolerable, and harassing.

Based on our qualitative studies of sexual harassment, we have identified four criteria used in labeling behaviors as sexual harassment. That is, when asked if they have ever been sexually harassed, the workers we have interviewed answered "yes" only if one of the following conditions were met. These criteria are not necessarily consistent with the legal definition of sexual harassment, but our goal is not to determine whether these individuals would stand a chance of prevailing in a court of law. Nor are we interested in what proportion of men and women experience sexual harassment on the job. Rather, we seek to understand how workers actually apply the label "sexual harassment" to their experiences in the workplace. As qualitative sociologists, our goal is to understand the meaning of sexual harassment from the perspectives of working people, in particular, how they draw boundaries lines between sexual behavior they consider harassing, and behaviors they consider tolerable or even enjoyable. What follows is a description of what "sexual harassment" means to those we interviewed.

1   *Violence or physical force.* Some workers label their experiences as sexual harassment only when violence or physical force was involved. For example, when asked if she had ever been sexually harassed, a waitress described being thrown into a walk-in refrigerator by a co-worker who had earlier made a pass at her. In the hospital study, doctors and nurses reported that patients frequently behave in sexually inappropriate ways, but some only labeled these experiences as sexual harassment if physical force was used (granted that the patient was in full command of his or her mental faculties). For instance, a nurse described a patient who tried to pull her into the bed with him; she reached down to take his pulse and he yanked her hand onto his erect penis. In response, she hit him and threat-

ened to tie his hands with restraints to the bed (Giuffre and Williams 2000).

2   *Organizational power and authority.* Sexual harassment researchers have found that in general, people think of sexual harassment as something that mainly occurs between bosses or managers and their employees. A great deal of psychological research based on vignettes asks mainly college students whether certain behaviors constitute sexual harassment, and in most instances, agreement is strongest when the behaviors occur between supervisors and subordinates. We found support for this in our study of restaurant workers. Some respondents who enjoyed flirty and raucous behavior with their co-workers drew the line at management. Cathy, for example, said that she and the other waitpeople talk and joke about sex constantly. "Everybody stands around and talks about sex a lot . . . isn't that weird? It's something about working in restaurants . . . we all sit around and talk about sex." She said that talking with her co-workers about sex does not constitute sexual harassment because it is only "joking." Not so with her manager:

My employer is very sexist. I would call that sexual harassment. He kind of started saying stuff like, "You can't wear those shorts because they're not flattering to your figure . . . But I like the way you wear those jeans. They look real good. They're tight." It's like, I want to say to him, "You're the owner, you're in power. That's evident. You need to find a better way to tell me these things." We've gotten to a point now where we'll joke around but it's never ever sexual, ever, I won't allow that with him.

Cathy acknowledges that her manager has the right to tell her what to wear, but he crosses the line when he personalizes his directive, by saying to Cathy "I like the way you wear those jeans." This is offensive to Cathy because it is framed as the manager's personal preference, not the institutional requirement of the job. Note that the rule itself is not problematic in her view; the manager is simply asked "to find a better way to tell me these things."

3   *Race/ethnicity and sexual orientation.* Nothing in sexual harassment law specifies the characteristics of the assailant and victim, but our restaurant study suggests that race/ethnicity and sexual orientation are keys to understanding workers' definitions of their experiences as sexual harassment. The white women waitresses who tolerated and even enjoyed sexual bantering and touching from the white waiters drew the line when the same behavior came from the mostly

Latino kitchen staff. For example, Ann said that she and the other waitstaff joke about sex and touch each other "on the butt" all the time, and when asked if she had ever experienced sexual harassment, she said:

I had some problems at a previous restaurant but it was a communication problem. A lot of the guys in the kitchen did not speak English. They would see the waiters hugging on us, kissing us and pinching our rears and stuff. They would try to do it and I couldn't tell them, "No. You don't understand this. It's like we do it because we have a mutual understanding but I'm not comfortable with you doing it." So that was really hard and a lot of times what I'd have to do is just sucker punch them in the chest and just use a lot of cuss words and they knew that I was serious. And there again, I felt real weird about that because they're just doing what they see go on every day.

In addition to double standards based on race/ethnicity, there were also double standards that seemed to apply in interactions between straights and gays, especially between straight men and gay men. Jake, who is straight, said that he talks and jokes about sex all the time in the restaurant: "When men get together, they talk sex," he said, regardless of whether there are women around. He admitted that "people find me offensive, as a matter of fact," because he gets "pretty raunchy" talking and joking about sex. When asked if he had ever been sexually harassed, he said,

Someone has come on to me that I didn't want to come on to me . . . He was another waiter. It was laughs and jokes the whole way until things got a little too much and it was like, "Hey, this is how it is. Back off. Keep your hands off my ass." Once it reached the point where I felt kind of threatened and bothered by it.

Only when the talk and bantering were initiated by a gay man did Jake call it sexual harassment. Such fears of sexual harassment of straight men by gay men are sometimes institutionalized. This is the case with the military's "don't ask, don't tell, don't pursue" policy, and other anti-gay hiring practices throughout the labor force.

4   *Workplace norms.* Dellinger's study, which compares the editorial departments of a porn magazine and a feminist magazine, highlights the importance of workplace norms in understanding how workers define sexual harassment.

At *Gentleman's Sophisticate,* a "locker room" culture prevails. The editorial department, evenly composed of men and women workers, is a place filled with bawdy joking and bantering. Sexual put-downs and braggadocio are common, but this joking is almost never about personal matters. Tina says joking is "just business and never personal." When Bill is asked if he ever talks and jokes about sex at work, he says, "No. Not at all. I just don't want to talk about sex . . . especially with women, because everything could be misconstrued especially in these times when people are so sensitive." But when asked if he jokes about sex in regards to the magazine, he says that happens "all the time":

> Oh yeah, we laugh at a lot of stuff. Some of it is so ridiculous, you know, how many positions can you come up with and have it artful? We laugh at the pictorials. We laugh at the color. We laugh at the choice of girls. Yeah, we do that a lot. Sure. But to me that's in the abstract.

Talking and joking about sex are fine if it is about the magazine, or if it is "abstract." If it is concrete talk about an individual's sexual behavior or desires, then it is "sensitive" and likely to be "misconstrued," possibly as sexual harassment.

In contrast to the "locker room" culture at *Gentleman's Sophisticate,* a "dorm room" culture prevails in the all-woman editorial department at *Womyn,* a feminist magazine. Editors at *Womyn* frequently reflect on and share their opinions about topics ranging from date rape to sexual harassment to the nature of sexual pleasure and desire. The workplace climate is intensely personal: People talk and joke about their own sex lives and what they do and don't like to do in bed, as well as have serious conversations about their sexual identities and their relationships. This sharing creates very close bonds among the workers. Stacey explains:

> It's just like all of us hanging around all the time. We're so touchy. And we're always having parties just together without our partners. And so we're always dancing together and having sleepovers and stuff.

While talk of "the personal" is taboo and possibly constitutes harassment in the locker room, it is normative and expected in the dorm room. But this doesn't mean that sexual harassment doesn't exist at *Womyn;* rather, workers there define it differently than workers at *Gentleman's Sophisticate.* From the perspective of the editors at *Womyn,* sexual harassment is defined as behavior that involves the exploitation of someone in a less powerful position by someone who has organizational power over them.

This study suggests that workers define sexual harassment as behavior that deviates from the cultural norms governing sexual behavior in their workplaces. Clearly, there is no single set of behaviors that editors in the two organizations would agree constitute sexual harassment. Editors at *Womyn* would surely object to normative behaviors at *Gentleman's Sophisticate*, and vice versa. Workplace norms have local validity; behavior that is normative in one organization or department can inspire outrage in another.

CONCLUSION: FUTURE AREAS FOR RESEARCH

Our studies suggest that workers' definitions of sexual harassment vary depending on the social and cultural context. We believe that it would be impossible for quantitative surveys to tap into the vast array of meanings associated with sexual behavior at work; only through qualitative case studies can we begin to understand how workers confront different norms at different workplaces. Our studies also point to the ambiguity that many individuals experience when confronted with offensive sexual behavior. Sexual behavior at work is rarely "all good" or "all bad"; the meaning of any specific act is a product of negotiated meanings in interaction, involving institutionalized job requirements, complex double standards and varying expectations that people bring with them to their jobs. Quantitative surveys tend to ignore such ambiguity or average it away.

Research on sexual harassment addresses just one aspect of gender stratification, but it serves as a good illustration of how differences between men and women are the product of individual, cultural, and structural forces. As we noted in our discussion of theory, all three levels are important for understanding sexual harassment. Our studies also demonstrate that a full understanding of gender cannot be achieved without considering race and social class in our analysis. But we are just beginning to understand how these different forms of inequality overlap and reinforce each other. One of the challenges in the future will be to systematically explore how different groups of women, and different groups of men, already segregated into different jobs on the basis of race and social class, experience gender discrimination and sexual harassment.

Another challenge for gender scholars is to address the positive aspects of gender and sexuality in organizations. Sociologists have used qualitative methods to understand inequality, oppression, and discrimination in a number of settings. What we have de-emphasized are pleasures and empowerment in organizations. As we have noted in this chapter, workers often feel ambivalent about their experiences of sexual harassment and exploitation. Workers can and do experience sexual behaviors as both unwanted and simultaneously pleasurable, but researchers almost never examine the pleasurable aspects. Future research should also explore the types of organizations that are empowering and for whom, with special attention paid to men and women of different racial and ethnic backgrounds, cultures, sexual orientation, social classes, and organizational statuses. As examples, some types of organizations are empowering for heterosexual women but not for lesbians. Likewise, professional workplaces might be empowering for women managers, but not for the service workers employed in these organizations or for the domestic workers employed by successful women in their homes. Understanding how stratification enhances the pleasures of some while imperiling others is necessary to achieve a complete picture of the reproduction of inequality.

A third challenge facing gender researchers in the United States is to incorporate international perspectives into our understanding of gender stratification. There is growing recognition in US sociology that we are extremely parochial; we rarely cite or even recognize the contributions of gender researchers around the world (Bose 2002). In the study of sexual harassment, for example, US scholars typically ignore the different legal and cultural understandings of the phenomenon in other countries (for an exception, see Saguy 2000). This not only limits our conclusions, it causes us to miss out on understanding the global processes that link together forms of gender inequality around the world. We hope that volumes such as this one will be an important step in promoting greater international awareness and collaboration.

REFERENCES

Acker, J. (1973) "Women and social stratification: a case of intellectual sexism," *American Journal of Sociology* 78 (4): 936–45.

—— (1990) "Hierarchies, jobs, bodies: A theory of gendered organizations," *Gender and Society* 4: 139–58.

Barrett, M. (1980) *Women's Oppression Today: Problems in Marxist-Feminist Analysis.* London: NLB Press.

Baumgardner, J. and Richards, A. (2000) *Manifesta: Young Women, Feminism, and the Future*. New York: Farrar, Strauss, and Giroux.

Benjamin, J. (1988) *The Bonds of Love: Psychoanalysis, Feminism, and the Problem of Domination*. New York: Pantheon Books.

Benston, M. (1970) "The political economy of women's liberation," in Tanner, L. N. (ed.), *Voices from Women's Liberation*. New York: Signet.

Bordo, S. (1993) *Unbearable Weight: Feminism, Western Culture, and the Body*. Berkeley, CA: University of California Press.

Bose, C. (2002) "From the Editor," *Gender and Society* 16: 5–7.

Britton, D. M. (1997) "Gendered organizational logic: Policy and practice in men's and women's prisons," *Gender and Society* 11: 796–818.

Butler, J. (1990) *Gender Trouble: Feminism and the Subversion of Identity*. New York: Routledge.

Chodorow, N. (1978) *The Reproduction of Mothering: Psychoanalysis and the Sociology of Gender*. Berkeley, CA: University of California Press.

Collins, P. H. (1995) "Symposium on West and Fenstermaker's 'doing difference'," *Gender and Society* 9: 491–4.

—— (2000) *Black Feminist Thought: Knowledge, Consciousness, and the Politics of Empowerment*, 2nd edn. New York: Routledge.

Connell, R. W. (1987) *Gender and Power: Society, the Person and Sexual Politics*. Cambridge: Polity Press.

—— (1995) *Masculinities*. Berkeley, CA: University of California Press.

Dellinger, K. A. (2002) "Wearing gender and sexuality 'on your sleeve': Dress norms and the importance of occupational and organizational culture," *Gender Issues* 20: 3–25.

Dellinger, K. A. and Williams, C. L. (2002) "The locker room and the dorm room: Workplace norms and the boundaries of sexual harassment in magazine editing," *Social Problems* 49: 242–57.

Devault, M. L. (1990) "Talking and listening from women's standpoint," *Social Problems* 37: 96–116.

—— (1991) *Feeding the Family: The Social Organization of Caring as Gendered Work*. Chicago: University of Chicago Press.

Eisenstein, H. (1983) *Contemporary Feminist Thought*. Boston: G. K. Hall & Co.

Eisenstein, Z. (ed.) (1979) *Capitalist Patriarchy and the Case of Socialist Feminism*. New York: Monthly Review Press.

Engels, F. (1972) *The Origin of the Family, Private Property, and the State*. New York: Penguin.

Epstein, C. F. (1988) *Deceptive Distinctions: Sex, Gender, and the Social Order*. New Haven, CT: Yale University Press.

Fausto-Sterling, A. (1993) "The five sexes: Why male and female are not enough," *The Sciences* 33: 20–5.

Findlen, B. (ed.) (1995) *Listen Up: Voices from the Next Feminist Generation*. Seattle: Seal Press.

Foner, N. (1994) *The Caregiving Dilemma: Work in an American Nursing Home*. Berkeley, CA: University of California Press.

Friedan, B. (1963) *The Feminine Mystique*. New York: W. W. Norton.

Giuffre, P. A. and Williams, C. L. (1994) "Boundary lines: Sexual harassment in restaurants," *Gender and Society* 8: 378–401.

—— (2000) "'Not just bodies': Strategies for desexualizing the physical examination of patients," *Gender and Society* 14: 457–82.

Glazer, N. Y. (1984) "Servants to capital: Unpaid domestic labor and paid work," *Review of Radical Political Economics* 16: 61–87.

Green, K. and Taormino, T. (eds.) (1997) *A Girl's Guide to Taking Over the World.* New York: St. Martin's Griffin.

Hartmann, H. (1976) "Capitalism, patriarchy, and job segregation by sex," *Signs* 1: 137–69.

Heywood, L. and Drake, J. (eds.) (1997) *Third Wave Agenda.* Minneapolis: University of Minnesota Press.

Hondagneu-Sotelo, P. (2001) *Domestica: Immigrant Workers Cleaning and Caring in the Shadows of Affluence.* Berkeley, CA: University of California Press.

James, S. and Dalla Costa, M. (1973) *The Power of Women and the Subversion of the Community.* Bristol: Falling Wall Press.

Johnson, M. (1993) "Functionalism and feminism: Is estrangement necessary?", in England, P. (ed.), *Theory on Gender; Feminism on Theory.* New York: Aldine de Gruyter.

Keller, E. F. (1985) *Reflections on Gender and Science.* New Haven, CT: Yale University Press.

LeBlanc, L. (1999) *Pretty in Punk: Girls' Gender Resistance in a Boys' Subculture.* New Brunswick, NJ: Rutgers University Press.

Leidner, R. (1993) *Fast Food, Fast Talk: Service Work and the Routinization of Everyday Life.* Berkeley, CA: University of California Press.

Loe, M. (1996) "Working for men – at the intersection of power, gender, and sexuality," *Sociological Inquiry* 66: 399–421.

Nicholson, L. (ed.) (1990) *Feminism/Postmodernism.* New York: Routledge.

Parsons, T. and Bales, R. E. (1955) *Family, Socialization, and Interaction Process.* Glencoe, IL: Free Press.

Pierce, J. (1995) *Gender Trials: Emotional Lives in Contemporary Law Firms.* Berkeley, CA: University of California Press.

Reinharz, S. (1992) *Feminist Methods in Social Research.* New York: Oxford University Press.

Rollins, J. (1985) *Between Women: Domestics and their Employers.* Philadelphia, PA: Temple University Press.

Rubin, G. (1975) "The traffic in women: Notes on the political economy of sex," in Reiter, R. R. (ed.), *Toward an Anthropology for Women.* New York: Monthly Review Press.

Rubin, L. (1983) *Intimate Strangers: Men and Women Together.* New York: Harper & Row.

Saguy, A. C. (2000) "Employment discrimination or sexual violence? Defining sexual harassment in American and French Law," *Law and Society Review* 34: 1091–128.

Sargent, L. (ed.) (1981) *Women and Revolution: A Discussion of the Unhappy Marriage between Marxism and Feminism.* Boston: South End Press.

Smith, D. E. (1979) "A sociology for women," in Sherman, J. A. and Torton, E. (eds.), *The Prism of Sex: Essays in the Sociology of Knowledge*. Madison, WI: University of Wisconsin Press.

Sprague, J. and Zimmerman, M. K. (1989) "Quality and quantity: Reconstructing feminist methodology," *The American Sociologist* 20: 71–86.

Stacey, J. and Thorne, B. (1985) "The missing feminist revolution in sociology," *Social Problems* 32: 301–16.

Waters, M. (1999) *Black Identities: West Indian Immigrant Dreams and American Realities*. Cambridge, MA: Harvard University Press.

Welsh, S. (1999) "Gender and sexual harassment," *Annual Review of Sociology* 25: 169–90.

West, C. and Fenstermaker, S. (1995) "Doing difference," *Gender and Society* 9: 8–37.

West, C. and Zimmerman, D. (1987) "Doing gender," *Gender and Society* 1: 125–51.

Williams, C. L. (1989) *Gender at Work: Men and Women in Non-Traditional Occupations*. Berkeley, CA: University of California Press.

—— (1991) "Case studies and the sociology of gender," in Feagin, J. R., Orum, A. M. and Sjoberg, G. (eds.), *A Case for the Case Study*. Chapel Hill, NC: University of North Carolina Press.

—— (1995) *Still a Man's World: Men Who Do Women's Work*. Berkeley, CA: University of California Press.

Williams C. L., Giuffre, P. A. and Dellinger, K. A. (1999) "Sexuality in the workplace: Organizational control, sexual harassment, and the pursuit of pleasure," *Annual Review of Sociology* 25: 73–93.

FURTHER READING

Britton, D. (2003) *At Work in the Iron Cage: The Prison as Gendered Organization*. New York: New York University Press.

Hondagneu-Sotelo, P. (2001) *Domestica: Immigrant Workers Cleaning and Caring in the Shadows of Affluence*. Berkeley, CA: University of California Press.

Naples, N. (2003) *Feminism and Method: Ethnography, Discourse Analysis, and Activist Research*. New York: Routledge.

CHAPTER TEN

The Japanese Paradox
Women's Voices of Fulfillment in the Face of Inequalities

Yuko Ogasawara

Studies of Gender Stratification in Japan

In this chapter, I will consider the issue of gender inequalities with specific reference to Japanese women and employment. I will begin by an overview of studies of gender stratification in Japan, and discuss how works utilizing quantitative research methods have made a valuable contribution to outlining patterns of women's economic activities and highlighting their disadvantages compared to men. Next, I examine qualitative studies of Japanese women, which have usually asked different sets of questions of their subjects, given their different concerns about people's life experiences. These studies have generally focused on understanding women's hopes and dreams, fears and concerns as they lived their ordinary lives and produced a picture of women who are neither pitiful nor powerless.

I then extend the insights provided by the existing studies of Japanese women with a discussion of my own qualitative research on female clerical workers. I argue that while a quantitative analysis is useful in clarifying how the distribution of economic resources favors men, qualitative work is necessary to understand what the unequal distribution of resources *means* to the lives of women and men placed in a particular institutional context. I conclude the chapter by proposing three new directions for future qualitative research on gender inequalities in Japan.

Gender is fast becoming one of the key theoretical preoccupations of researchers of contemporary Japan, as there is an increasing awareness that women and men are not the all-embracing and de-sexualized human beings as once studied. Japanese society has long been viewed as a homogeneous and seamless whole. Because no major conflicts of

interests are assumed in a harmonious society, it was difficult to enter-
tain the idea that women's interests and world-views would be different
from those of men. Even though women's social experience was seldom
reflected in what was considered universal to Japanese, the gender bias
was rarely taken note of, or worse yet, was concealed.

Spectacular post-war economic growth attracted many students to
the study of political economy of Japan, and above all, to the study of
organizational behavior and labor relations. The so-called "lifetime"
employment, seniority pay, quality control circles, and enterprise union,
among others, quickly became the most controversial and thoroughly
studied aspects of Japan's political economy (Johnson 1989). In discussing labor and employment, however, workers were treated as disembodied, abstract individuals whose gender and sexuality need not be
commented upon. In reality, it was men's work experience and not
women's that was studied, but this male-centered view was taken for
granted. Research on male employees, particularly in large companies,
that said nothing about the issues of women's working lives and consciousness, was regarded as the study of Japanese labor and management (Cole 1979; Roberson 1998).

Gender studies have brought to light that knowledge hitherto implicitly considered universal was in fact that regarding men. More and more
studies of contemporary Japan have focused on women, successfully
delineating their life course and experiences that are different from
those of both men and Western women (Lebra 1984; Iwao 1993;
Fujimura-Fanselow and Kameda 1995; Rosenberger 2001). Most studies
pointed out the existence of a sharp division of labor for Japanese men
and women and the emphasis on the nurturing role in the family on
the latter (Imamura 1987; Smith 1987; Allison 1991). Japanese women's
participation in the public sphere of gainful employment, the state and
municipal politics, and cultural institutions was found to be sporadic
and intermittent. Among these, the most studied area that has produced many substantial arguments is women's participation in the labor
market (Takenaka 1983; Saso 1990; Kumazawa 2000). The use of quantitative research methods mainly by labor economists and sociologists
has shown unambiguously that Japanese women have limited access to
various economic resources such as good pay, high positions, and stable
employment (Brinton 1993; Machiko Osawa 1993; Mari Osawa 1993;
Seiyama and Imada 1998).

More than anything else, the limited nature of women's presence in
the world of paid work is considered to manifest itself in the M-shaped
distribution of female labor force participation rate by age. The percentage of women working peaks twice in the age groups of twenties

and late forties with a dip in between caused by family demand. Partly due to the prevalence of late marriage in recent years, the drop has shifted somewhat towards older age groups, but the overall pattern remains remarkably consistent. Since such a dip can no longer be observed in labor force participation rates of women in most other industrial nations, Japanese women's working patterns are not only dissimilar to those of Japanese men, but are an anomaly among those of women in other industrial nations.

The distinct life-cycle pattern of Japanese women's employment has caused much controversy among scholars both in the West and in Japan. Numerous studies sought to separate factors contributing to or discouraging women's continued employment, including, among others, the effects of discriminatory employment policies, education, cohort, occupation, and husbands' social status (Tanaka 1987; Brinton 1993; Imada 1996; Akachi 1998; Hirata 1998; Seiyama 1999). One of the important findings is that the association between women's higher-education attainment and labor market participation after marriage, which can be observed in most Western industrial societies, is weak in Japan (Hirao 1997; Seiyama 1998; Tanaka 1998).

Despite women accounting for about 40 percent of the total number of employees in Japan, the frequency of women taking part-time, temporary, or other non-standard jobs is another major departure from men's work patterns that exacerbates the impression of women being less of a worker than men. The proportion of women with non-standard work arrangements is rapidly increasing, reaching almost half of total female employees in 2001 in comparison with men's ratio of just over 10 percent. The tendency is particularly strong among women returning to the labor market in their forties and fifties.

Mari Osawa (1993) was one of the first to point out the problematic nature of part-time work in Japan, which often demanded as long working hours as standard work. Osawa found that it was impossible to define part-time work in any other way than that it was a job of low-status. The majority of part-time employees work for significantly less pay than the full-time. The former are also far less likely to enjoy various fringe benefits and employment rights, including the right to complain about unfair dismissal and the right to take maternity, child- or parent-care leave granted as standard workers by law. In addition, many do not have pension and health insurance coverage.

Women are not only over-represented in part-time work but are segregated into a few selected occupational categories (Aiba 1997; Brinton 1998; Komagawa 1998). However, horizontal sex segregation measured either by industry or by occupation was not found to be greater in Japan

than in other Western countries (Mari Osawa 1993). It has been argued
that the more serious problem in Japan is the vertical segregation. In
her recently published study of female managers in Japan, Renshaw
(1999) described how she was told repeatedly that there were no female
managers in Japan. Even if we agree with her argument that women
managers are made invisible in Japan, the fact remains that there are
very few of them. Only 2.2 percent of *bucho* (department heads) and
4.0 percent of *kacho* (section heads) in all firms employing 100 or more
workers were women in 2000 (Ministry of Health, Labour and Welfare
2001).

Perhaps nowhere else is Japanese women's inferior status in the
economy better reflected than in their low levels of wage. The wage difference between the sexes has been found to be substantial with
women's average monthly scheduled cash earnings accounting for only
65.5 percent of men's in 2000 (ibid.). This is a minor improvement
from 60.2 percent ten years ago, making Japan unlike many Western
countries where similar gaps have decreased considerably over the years
(Kawashima 1983; Machiko Osawa 1993). Some studies detect a steady
tendency for the difference between the sexes to decrease in recent
years in Japan among the so-called standard workers (Hori 1998;
Mitani 1996), but when half the women working have non-standard
employment arrangements, the rapidly rising difference in the wage
between part-time and full-time workers is an alarming trend. The ratio
of average hourly earnings of female part-time to female full-time
workers dropped 11.5 points in the past 22 years and reached the low
of 66.9 in 2000 (Ministry of Health, Labour and Welfare 2001).

It is not that the Japanese government has done nothing to improve
women's working conditions. There have been some post-war legal
reforms, the most important of which is the implementation of the
Equal Employment Opportunity Law in 1986 and its amendments in
1999. However, the reforms have been undermined by various enterprise practices so that the total effect turned out to be disappointingly
limited (Upham 1987; Lam 1992). For example, the introduction of a
supposedly gender-neutral tracking system permitted a small number
of elite women into the managerial track; 3.5 percent of all such
workers were found to be women in 2000 (*Nihon Keizai Shinbun*, June
8, 2000). However, for the vast majority of women, segregation became
even more rigid under the new system, which now officially delegated
them to the clerical track.

Statistics summarizing Japanese women's status in the labor market
are depressingly low, and give much credence to the view that Japan is
a quintessential case of a society with large gender inequality. However,

qualitative studies of women in Japan offer some surprising insights into their lives. By asking questions about how individual women think, feel, and behave in their everyday lives, these studies negate the picture of women who are only to be pitied.

QUALITATIVE STUDIES OF JAPANESE WOMEN

The quantitative research focus on numbers related to women's economic activities such as workforce participation rates, employment status, and wage gap has enabled it to clarify the extent to which the distribution of economic resources was skewed in favor of men. While these studies are valuable in outlining aggregate patterns of women's activities in paid work, they do not clarify distinct motivations or behaviors. In contrast, anthropologists and sociologists conducting qualitative studies of the lives of Japanese women are generally more concerned about individual women in their relations to a particular institutional context. These researchers seek to understand women's aspirations and dreams as well as their struggles and their pains as they live their ordinary lives. Some of the questions asked include: What are Japanese women's notions of selfhood? How do women balance their commitment to self and society? What is their passion for life and how do they pursue it? What are their concerns and desires, challenges and triumphs? How do they express their joys, hopes, and dilemmas of everyday life? What is the nature of their relationships with people around them and what are their feelings towards them? What responsibilities and influences do they have for?

One of the earliest attempts to answer such questions was made by American sociologists who carried out fieldwork among urban middle-class housewives (Lebra et al. 1976; Vogel 1978; Imamura 1987). These researchers found that industrialization in Japan did not result in the weakening, much less the breakdown, of traditional sex roles that assigned women to the domestic sphere and men to the public sphere. Rather, a housewife continued to be a socially valued female career, as suggested by the famous title of Vogel's article "Professional housewife." Even though the domestic work did not produce cash earnings, it was nevertheless considered comparable to men's paid work. Many women seemed to enjoy total autonomy in the family, which they expressed as being their *ikigai* (sources of self-fulfillment). These studies were so successful in depicting women as autonomous and powerful figures in the domestic realm that they created a new stereotype of Japanese women.

Many subsequent studies rich in ethnographic material on women's daily lives similarly eschewed the view that Japanese women were dependent, deferential, and powerless. For example, Lebra (1984), who collected life histories from women in a small city in central Japan, found typical Japanese husbands to be totally dependent on their wives for housework. According to Lebra, husbands' childlike dependence gives wives leverage to exercise power by making their services absolutely necessary.

One of the most optimistic views of women's status in Japan is offered by Iwao (1993). She agrees with most students of Japan that women are excluded from public arenas such as policymaking and business. But because of this, they are freer than men, who must spend long, grueling hours on the job to support their families. Pointing out that concerts and museums in Japan are almost always packed with women but seldom men, Iwao maintains that many women can and do engage in culturally enriching activities, for which men seem to find no time. Women can also decide to work on their own terms, part-time, without the worry of making a living. Iwao concludes:

> Today it is, in a sense, the husbands who are being controlled and the ones to be pitied. The typical Japanese man depends heavily on his wife to look after his daily needs and nurture his psychological well-being. The Confucian ethic of the three obediences formerly binding women could be rewritten today as the three obediences for men: obedience to mothers when young, companies when adult, and wives when retired. (1993: 7)

The fearful fate of retired men is also noted by Allison (1994). A husband's power over his wife is sometimes quickly lost when he ceases to bring home a check.

Although most studies describe how women enjoy autonomy in the household, there are some that examine women in the workplace. Studies utilizing qualitative research methods illuminate aspects of Japanese women's working life that have not been addressed by quantitative analyses. Condon (1985), for example, argues that because most single women are relieved of serious work and family responsibilities, their shorter working hours and large disposable income allow them to enjoy extensive shopping, various hobbies, gourmet dinners, and overseas travel. It is not an exaggeration to say that young female office workers are among the biggest consumers and trendsetters of contemporary Japanese society. Similarly, Kelsky (1994) details how young clerical women use their financial resources to support a vibrant subculture of their own through which they find opportunities to defy as well as to escape traditional gender hierarchies.

Nor is it only young single women that emerge as powerful figures. Hamabata's (1990) concern is with *okusama*, the wives of presidents of family-owned businesses, who are adept at cultivating, maintaining, and using a network of kin across industry and finance to protect and promote their interests. Middle-aged part-time women in Kondo's (1990) study of a small confectionery factory in Tokyo claim a central space for themselves within the informal structures of the workplace. The women play the role of surrogate mother for younger male full-time artisans, and invite them home for a hot meal, lend them money, and run bank errands. Kondo maintains that because superordinates, such as parents and bosses, assume the position of caregiver in Japan from whom subordinates are encouraged to seek indulgence, women workers gain power over the younger men by casting themselves as mothers.

In sum, the views of Japanese women presented in qualitative research are often radically different from what is expected from studies relying only on quantitative methods. In the former work, women are not pitiful or powerless. Instead most women portrayed maintain surprisingly positive attitudes towards life and seem content with the roles they play in the society. Certainly, their choices are limited, but within these constraints, they exercise the freedom to plan, organize, and carry out their lives in a way not possible for men whose life is confined and regimented to an extreme degree by corporate demands. Few women seem eager to change their place with men who are expected to dedicate their entire lives to the company. Because paid work is optional for many women, they have the latitude to seek meaning and self-fulfillment in work (Rosenberger 2001). The parallel attitude in men may be condemned.

There are pitfalls in the argument, however, that women play a different but equally vital role in the society as men. It is not only that this line of reasoning has often been used to justify unfair treatment of women. By emphasizing women's difference *from* men, the claim serves to mask the diversity *among* women. When women's views and experiences are opposed against those of men, there is a tendency to regard women as a monolithic group holding same or similar interests. In reality, it is often only the interests of a certain group of women, for example, the urban middle-class housewives, that are taken into account. It is clear that the autonomy and freedom alluded to by Vogel, Iwao, and others are premised on the lifestyles of women who do not have to work to sustain a living. Such an assumption, however, clearly do not apply to working-class women. The room to enjoy leisure or the search for meaning and fulfillment in optional work is more severely circumscribed for less fortunate women (Roberts 1994; Rosenberger 2001).

As living standards continue to rise and education costs for children mount, more and more housewives are forced into becoming wage earners. Most critics agree with Higuchi (1985) who maintains that the "new division of labor" has replaced the old, with women assuming the dual role of paid and unpaid work while men continue to engage only in the former. Women's increasing participation in the labor market brought about the new configuration of sex roles and not the dismantling of them. Moreover, the dual role that women now assume seems dangerously synonymous to dual burden (Hochschild with Machung 1989).

The second pitfall, therefore, related to the first is the slipperiness of the distinction between autonomy and burden and the ease with which the former can turn into the latter. For example, the fact that many Japanese women hold the family purse strings has often been pointed to as the symbol of women's domestic autonomy. However, instead of considering budgeting as a source of power, some women feel this responsibility is a burden. The exclusiveness of women's roles in the domestic sphere can quickly become oppressive. In a number of well-known writings by journalists, the loneliness and misery of a wife whose husband is constantly working and absent are documented (Saito 1982; Hayashi 1985). The meanings of unpaid work have been at the center of much-heated debate in Japan among scholars, critics, and housewives called *shufu ronso* (domestic labor dispute), which began in the 1950s and lasted for over 20 years.

The focus by qualitative research on individual women's thoughts, feelings, and experiences thus highlights one of the most puzzling paradoxes of gender inequalities in Japan that quantitative research alone would not have discovered: why are there frequent reports of satisfaction and fulfillment by women even as they face extreme limitations and inequalities? Do we find in Japanese women an alternative mode of women's empowerment, which the Western feminist movement has been looking for? Was it wrong to assume that the experience of gender inequality was the same everywhere? Or, conversely, can we safely discount women's professions of satisfaction with their roles? Is this just that women have learned to adjust and accommodate their images and aspirations to restricted rewards offered by the society? Or, is this due to the pervasiveness of ideology that valorizes the nurturing role and virtues of perseverance for women?

In my own research on women office workers, I have found neither reasons for discounting women's proclamation of contentment to be adequate. However constrained, women's exercise of power is *real*.

RESEARCH ON WOMEN OFFICE WORKERS

In spite of their visibility, female clerical workers, often called office ladies or OLs for short, have not been studied as individuals. The prevalent depiction has been that they are the victims of severe sex discrimination practiced by Japanese firms (Cook and Hayashi 1980; McLendon 1983; Lo 1990; Saso 1990). It is assumed that they quit shortly and move on to become wives and mothers, and their polite language and gentle demeanor are often taken at face value. In my study, I sought to find out whether they were really as powerless and as subservient to men as they seemed. In order to observe daily interactions among OLs and salaried men and relate them to structural conditions of employment, I conducted participant observation at a large bank in Tokyo, where I was employed as a temporary worker. I also interviewed 30 office ladies and 30 salaried men working in various large Japanese firms so that I could assess the universality of what I observed in a particular workplace.

Structurally, female clerical workers are discriminated against in the bank. Clerical women are called "girls" while the men are never referred to as "boys." They perform many routine jobs such as filing, copying, and typing, and more menial chores including wiping desks, cleaning ash trays, and pouring tea for their bosses, male colleagues, or visitors. They are frequently spoken of as being "office wives," who look after the needs of dependent men. Furthermore, while men are evaluated individually for their work performance, most women in the bank are automatically given grade "C" on a scale of A to D. This is because the purposes of evaluations are different for male and female employees. For men, evaluations are made primarily to help the management decide whom to promote. Since the company does not intend to promote clerical women, serious evaluations of their work are considered to do more harm than good by disrupting harmonious relationships among them. Some women are therefore not even aware that they are evaluated.

It is precisely because female office workers occupy such subordinate positions in Japanese firms, however, that they can enjoy a certain degree of freedom. Freed of the responsibility of making a living, many women have time and money to enjoy a variety of self-expressive activities as consumers of goods, culture, or travel (Kelsky 1994). In addition, they are freer than men to express their feelings at work. They can often decide according to their likes and dislikes the order in which they do their work and the extent to which they will go beyond the minimum to help out a busy man or cover his mistakes. They can also ignore or refuse a man's request to work. They can publicly humiliate him by *sosukan* (denying him news of what is going on) or by highly elaborate gift-giving practices. Women are relatively safe to demonstrate their non-compliance to men, because they have little to lose in the way of promotion. They do not have permanent positions and career opportunities in the first place. If something goes terribly wrong, they can always quit the company, unlike men who must continue working.

One of the ways in which women resist male authority is scrutinizing the behavior of men in the office and constantly sharing information about their observations. They review, judge, and comment on men's every move day by day, hour by hour. In so doing, they are particularly alert to men's disagreeable behavior, which they report to each other during their lunch break. Although women rarely discuss discrimination directly, many seem to be keenly aware of the situation in which they work and have a clear sense of their rights and responsibilities as well as those of men. The two sexes have unequal rights in the organization, and most women think that responsibilities should reflect this discrepancy. For example, they often believe that it is men's responsibility – not theirs – to make sure that work gets done, because it is men who ultimately enjoy the fruits of the labor in the form of higher earnings or promotion. Men must, in this way, pay their dues for treating women unequally. Those who do not pay are criticized as "free riders." Such men include those who are arrogant, those who remain indifferent to women's needs and complaints, those who do not provide generous treats, and those who demonstrate little aptitude for business. Women's talk sometimes escalates to the level of seriously damaging a man's prospect for promotion. This is possible because it is customary for a company to take into account a man's ability to supervise female subordinates in evaluating his potential as a manager.

Although many women energetically review and comment on male behavior, it is obvious that this criticism is possible only because they do not compete with men for promotion. Women can laugh at men making desperate efforts to please their superiors because they usually do not have to do the same to support themselves and their family. Nevertheless, in spite of constraints, many women continue to scrutinize and criticize men. Indeed, women's persistent gaze calls into question conventional understandings and customs in the male business world.

When women laugh at men who try to accommodate whatever their bosses demand, they highlight how funny and pathetic – truly how abnormal – "company people" are. By exposing the hitherto taken-for-granted work attitudes of many men, women throw doubt on the basic values of salaried men.

Women's critique of values and lifestyles of "company people" seems to have found audience among men. Most men I interviewed admitted that they missed their family. For example, a banker told me:

> Women in the company are perhaps to be pitied. But women have the home. My daughter, for instance, is very close to her mother. I make efforts to join the family by helping with household matters, but it's difficult when I have to spend so much time away from home . . . The company is a place where lonely men are compelled to throng because they have been shut out from the home and have nowhere else to go.

Another man working for a manufacturer of heavy electrical equipment similarly related his desire to spend more time with his family. Because his work keeps him in the office until late at night, his small daughter, who sees her father only infrequently, begs him to "call again," thinking that he lives somewhere else. Many men are aware that company and work are depriving them of their time with their family.

Decades ago, a man could expect promotion or pay rise in return for hard work. However, as the Japanese economy continues to suffer from prolonged recession and newspapers report incidents of bankruptcy, lay-offs, and pay cuts as everyday matters, a man can no longer count on a company to reward him for his dedicated services. It is no wonder that more men are beginning to question whether putting such a high priority on work really makes sense. Increasingly there is talk that work is not worth the sacrifice of one's family life and personal interests.

Gerson (1993) has found that a significant proportion of American men would actually prefer to work less and parent more. She therefore argues that economic and occupational structures are more firmly divided by gender than by the preferences of individual men and women. Gerson's argument applies even more to Japan where men suffer from exceptionally long hours of work. Their rights to care for their children are minimal, as evidenced not only by long working hours but also by the prevalence of *tanshin funin* (transfer without the family). A typical Japanese firm does not take family matters into consideration when relocating its employees. Because a man must be prepared to receive a heavy penalty should he refuse the company request to transfer, he is obliged to leave for a new post, leaving behind his family who cannot or will not join the father. Concerns for children's education are said to be the predominant reasons for families to stay behind, but often the wives, some of whom have full-time jobs, are reluctant to move as well. Even *tanshin funin* overseas is not uncommon.

Several workers have taken *tanshin funin* to court, suing the company for the infringement of the fathers' rights to care for their children. However, Japanese courts have thus far found the company requests for relocation to be within "reasonable" bounds, and have yet to grant workers such rights. The wish to renounce long-established male privileges and claim new rights to care for their children has also given rise to a number of men's liberation movements, including "*Otoko mo Onna mo Ikuji Jikan o! Renrakukai*" (Child Care Hours for Men and Women Network) (Ikujiren 1989; Toyoda 1997).

Japanese men on average enjoy higher status and higher pay than women, but it is difficult to say with confidence that they have more freedom than women. Sexual division of labor assigns men roles more advantageous than women, but the fact remains that set roles are imposed upon them. Moreover, the enforcement of social roles seems stronger for men than women. Whereas women can nowadays choose family, work, or both, albeit with considerable constraints, men are not free to choose family; they *must* work. Those who do not will face more discrimination than women who do not choose marriage and motherhood. Unless retired, homemaking husbands are regarded with great suspicion. Currently few men in Japan can escape from male roles that demand long working hours and the sacrifice of time to spend with family or just relax. That the danger of *karoshi* or *karojisatsu* (death or suicide due to overwork) is present and is not limited to a select number of workers has been documented forcefully by Kawato (1998) and Kamata (1999).

Witnessing men's life painted as nothing but hard work, many Japanese women say they do not wish to change places with men. Judging their voices as attitudinal adjustments to low expectations or false consciousness is a misplaced attempt to transfer Western feminist assumptions to non-Western culture. Such a view only encourages the continuation of representing the Asian women as "Other" in European and North-American-centered discourses.

Micro-level analyses of power initiated by Homans (1961) and Blau (1964) have often been criticized for not being able to account for the rise of an unequal distribution of resources. The resources with which individual actors in the model enter an interaction are predetermined and outside the theory. A parallel criticism, however, can be made of macro-level studies of social stratification using quantitative data. These works explain well how resources are distributed unequally among socially stratified groups. However, they do not elucidate what individual members of a group *do* with their resources, what these resources *mean* to their lives, and how they *feel* about them. Moreover, without first understanding what an unequal distribution of resources means to people concerned, we cannot begin to examine how changes can be made, who will most likely initiate them, and how.

Although men as a group have considerable advantage over women as a group in developing lucrative professional careers in Japan, some men may not want to succeed in work. For a man whose preference or priority is taking care of his children, Japanese society may be equally, or even more, oppressive. While their problems were different, the lives of single fathers in Japan examined by Kasuga (1989) were no less easy than those of single mothers. Although most fathers could find jobs that paid reasonably, they could not *keep* them because the hours they demanded were not compatible with child care.

It is sometimes assumed that members of a dominant group can always exercise power against members of a subordinate group. For example, in her remarkable study of how the work environment affects human feelings, Hochschild (1983) argues that women's subordinate position requires them to control their own feelings more than men must. She writes, "High-status people tend to enjoy the privilege of having their feelings noticed and considered important. The lower one's status, the more one's feelings are not noticed or treated as inconsequential" (ibid.: 172). However, I have found that under certain conditions, Japanese men in positions of authority care more about the feelings of subordinate women than subordinate women do about the feelings of men in authority. Moreover, men do not necessarily feel powerful in their roles as breadwinners. Whether or not particular members of the dominant group can enjoy their resources and the extent possible should be analyzed, not taken for granted.

NEW DIRECTIONS FOR RESEARCH

The above discussion suggests three promising directions for the future research to move forward. First, it is clear that studies must take note of the diversity among Japanese women and that qualitative research on social inequalities has the advantage in this respect. However enticing it may be to document women's subordination with statistical figures and paint in one large stroke the prototypical life of Japanese women, it is important to remember that "only particular women exist, situated in particular contexts" (Tamanoi 1990: 21). Individual members of a society differ not only by gender but also by class, ethnicity, sexuality, region, and disability, among other things. In stressing women's subordination to men, we must not forget that there are minorities among women, too. Women can and often do take part in oppressing others.

It should be remembered at the same time, however, that there is a danger for qualitative studies to over-emphasize the diversity among women. A focus on society as being made up of individuals with infinite differences may lead to an erroneous impression that all such differences are of similar nature. Then, even if members of a society do not enjoy equal access to resources and opportunities, such a difference may easily be dismissed as *personal* in nature – something that is based on individual preference, ability or chance. Emphasizing diversity, in other words, is dangerously close to losing sight of the structural problems that lie beneath the surface variability. For example, a time-stretched elite woman who is struggling to combine motherhood and career and a part-time housewife suffering from poor working conditions may seem to share little. However, a closer look reveals an important commonality between them in that both women's problems are related to a society that prescribes a domestic role for women. The difference among the sex and that between the sexes must clearly be distinguished. Qualitative studies will enable sensitive researchers to take note of diversity among women and at the same time stay attuned to structural inequalities.

Second, it is necessary to include men in qualitative research on gender. To be sure, men as a group loomed large as oppressors of women in existing studies of gender. In treating men as members of a dominant group, it has been taken for granted that their interests, preferences, and expectations converge and that they are enjoying their advantageous position in the society. Such an assumption may have contributed to making men's lives seem deceptively less problematic than women's. Surprisingly little has been examined about Japanese men besides their roles in the political economy. We know little about their lives apart from work, what they enjoy doing, and what their feelings are about their lives. In these respects, it is not an exaggeration to say that Japanese men have been studied less than Japanese women.

If urban middle-class housewives are considered the prototypical Japanese women, then white-collar employees of large corporations are their male counterparts. The image of salaried men with lifelong commitment to a firm continues to be hegemonic as a symbol of masculinity in Japan. Although there is greater amount of individual and class-related diversity in men's work experience than the standardized description of Japanese men suggests, there remains a serious bias in the existing research. Qualitative work on Japanese women has countered the unidimensional description of submissive women, but except for few studies (Roberson 1998), there have not been enough attempts to dismantle the ready stereotypes of men's experiences and identities.

That there exist diverse forms of masculinity and that there are hierarchical relationships among them have been pointed out most notably by Connell (1987). In his study of changing gender identities among Japanese men, Taga (2001) examines the oppression experienced by homosexual men and men who consider themselves not "manly" enough. Sexual division of labor and the prescriptions of masculinity and femininity constrain not only women but also men, although the effects of such limitations are usually more detrimental to women. Qualitative studies of gender must treat both women and men as gendered and sexualized human beings.

Finally, there is a need to bring women and men together analytically. Despite gender being a relational concept, Japanese women and Japanese men have long been studied separately as though each lived in the detached world of their own. This is a legacy of the development of gender studies in Japan. Years after the publication of classic works on male white-collar workers by Vogel (1963), Rohlen (1974), and Clark (1979), among others, Japanese women were suddenly "discovered" as worthy of a serious study. Research on women was added on to the existing literature, but comprised a separate area. It was regarded as studies on a special subject undertaken by specialists, typically female researchers, and was not to be incorporated into the mainstream studies of organizational behavior and labor relations in Japan.

The relegation of Japanese women's studies to a separate and special area was not confined to English-language literature, but was prevalent also among Japanese scholars and researchers (Kimoto 2000). One of the most telling cases of such treatment can be found in various surveys on female workers carried out by the government agencies. For example, the former Ministry of Labour conducted a survey of women employed in the managerial track several years after the implementation of the Equal Employment Opportunity Law. According to the results reported in national newspapers in 1994, 60 percent of the managerial-track women considered they had disadvantage in promotion (*Nihon Keizai Shinbun*, March 30, 1994). The National Personnel Authority conducted a similar survey of female government officials and found that 49 percent were dissatisfied with their performance evaluation (*Nihon Keizai Shinbun*, May 8, 1995). What can we tell from these government agency surveys? In fact, very little.

That more than half the women in managerial track think they are disadvantaged in terms of promotion or that almost half the female government officials are not happy with their evaluation does not in itself reveal much, because there are no clues as to how to interpret these figures. We cannot judge the ratios to be either high or low unless the same questions are asked, for example, of male employees and officials and comparisons are made between the answers provided by the two sexes. It is difficult to understand why large-scale surveys sponsored by the government agencies were carried out with such a glaring shortcoming in the design. However, when we remember that studies of female workers were treated as something completely different from the mainstream studies of male workers, we begin to understand why. The defective survey design was indeed the common sense of the time.

The single focus on women may have served to call attention to the voices that tended to be ignored in the mainstream studies. With the proliferation of research on Japanese women, we can be assured that their voices will never again be muted. However, there continue to be few studies that analyze women and men together and examine their relations and interactions. It is high time to incorporate research of Japanese women into the mainstream work, for surely the former have much to contribute to the development of the latter.

Future studies of gender in Japan will merit greatly from the use of qualitative research methods that bring both women and men into the analysis of inequality as gendered and sexualized beings with their variability and structural commonality. Consideration of women's and men's thoughts, feelings, and experiences and concerns about their hopes, dreams, and fears are no less important than aggregate statistics on patterns of behavior to understanding the nature of gender inequalities in Japanese society.

REFERENCES

Aiba, K. (1997) "Unrecognized inequality in the Japanese workplace: Structure of organizational sex segregation," PhD dissertation, Washington State University, Washington, DC.

Akachi, M. (1998) "Kikon josei no chii tassei katei ni okeru sedaiteki hennka" [Intergenerational change in the process of married women's status attainment], in Seiyama, K. and Imada, S. (eds.), *1995 SMM chosa shirizu: Josei no kyaria kozo to sono henka* [1995 SSM survey series: Changing career structures of women]. Tokyo: SSM Chosa Kenkyukai.

Allison, A. (1991) "Japanese mothers and obentos: The lunch-box as ideological state apparatus," *Anthropological Quarterly* 64: 195–208.

—— (1994) *Nightwork: Sexuality, Pleasure, and Corporate Masculinity in a Tokyo Hostess Club.* Chicago: University of Chicago Press.

Blau, P. M. (1964) *Exchange and Power in Social Life.* New York: Wiley.

Brinton, M. C. (1993) *Women and the Economic Miracle: Gender and Work in Postwar Japan.* Berkeley, CA: University of California Press.

—— (1998) "Jimushoku no kakudai: Josei no shugyo patan ni kansuru beikoku to higashiajia no hikaku rekishiteki kenkyu" [The evolution of the clerical sector: A comparative-historical view of women's work patterns in the US and East Asia], *Nihon Rodo Kenkyu Zasshi* 453: 36–49.

Clark, R. (1979) *The Japanese Company.* New Haven, CT: Yale University Press.

Cole, R. E. (1979) *Work, Mobility, and Participation: A Comparative Study of American and Japanese Industry.* Berkeley, CA: University of California Press.

Condon, J. (1985) *A Half Step Behind: Japanese Women Today.* Rutland, VT: Tuttle.

Connell, R. W. (1987) *Gender and Power: Society, the Person and Sexual Politics.* Stanford, CA: Stanford University Press.

Cook, A. H. and Hayashi, H. (1980) *Working Women in Japan: Discrimination, Resistance, and Reform.* Ithaca, NY: Cornell University Press.

Fujimura-Fanselow, K. and Kameda, A. (eds.) (1995) *Japanese Women: New Feminist Perspectives on the Past, Present, and Future.* New York: Feminist Press.

Gerson, K. (1993) *No Man's Land: Men's Changing Commitments to Family and Work.* New York: Basic Books.

Hamabata, M. M. (1990) *Crested Kimono: Power and Love in the Japanese Business Family.* Ithaca, NY: Cornell University Press.

Hayashi, I. (1985) *Kateinai rikon* [Divorce within the family]. Tokyo: Chikuma Shobo.

Higuchi, K. (1985) "Shufu to iu na no 'zaken'" [The "seat right" called housewife], *Sekai* 478: 24–7.

Hirao, K. (1997) "Work histories and home investment of married Japanese women," PhD dissertation, University of Notre Dame, Indiana.

Hirata, S. (1998) "Joseiteki shokugyo to shokugyo keireki" [Female occupations and occupational career], in Seiyama, K. and Imada, S. (eds.), *1995 SMM chosa shirizu: Josei no kyaria kozo to sono henka* [1995 SSM survey series: Changing career structures of women]. Tokyo: SSM Chosa Kenkyukai.

Hochschild, A. (1983) *The Managed Heart: Commercialization of Human Feeling.* Berkeley, CA: University of California Press.

Hochschild, A. with Machung, A. (1989) *The Second Shift.* New York: Avon Books.

Homans, G. C. (1961) *Social Behavior: Its Elementary Forms.* New York: Harcourt, Brace, and World.

Hori, H. (1998) "Danjokan chingin kakusa no shukusho keiko to sono yoin" [The decrease in the wage gap between men and women and its causes], *Nihon Rodo Kenkyu Zasshi* 456: 41–51.

Ikujiren (ed.) (1989) *Otoko to onna de "hanbunko" ism* ["Sharing half"-ism by men and women]. Tokyo: Gakuyo Shobo.

Imada, S. (1996) "Joshi rodo to shugyo keizoku" [Female labor and employment continuity], *Nihon Rodo Kenkyu Zasshi* 433: 37–48.

Imamura, A. E. (1987) *Urban Japanese Housewives: At Home and in the Community.* Honolulu: University of Hawaii Press.

Iwao, S. (1993) *The Japanese Woman: Traditional Image and Changing Reality.* Cambridge, MA: Harvard University Press.

Johnson, C. (1989) "Studies of Japanese political economy: A crisis in theory," in The Japan Foundation (eds.), *Japanese Studies in the United States, Part I: History and Present Condition.* Ann Arbor, MI: Association for Asian Studies.

Kamata, S. (1999) *Kazoku ga jisatsu ni oikomareru toki* [When a family member is driven to commit suicide]. Tokyo: Kodansha.

Kasuga, K. (1989) *Fushi katei o ikiru* [Living the family of father and child]. Tokyo: Keiso Shobo.

Kawashima, Y. (1983) "Wage differentials between men and women in Japan," PhD dissertation, Stanford University, Stanford, CA.

Kawato, H. (1998) *Karo jisatsu* [Overwork suicide]. Tokyo: Iwanami Shoten.

Kelsky, K. (1994) "Postcards from the edge: The office ladies subculture of Tokyo," *US-Japan Women's Journal* (English Supplement) 6: 3–26.

Kimoto, K. (2000) "Rodo to jenda" [Labor and gender], *Ohara Shakai Mondai Kenkyusho Zasshi* 500: 2–16.

Komagawa, T. (1998) "Ginko ni okeru jimushoku no seibetsu shokumu bunri" [Occupational segregation by gender in banks], *Nihon Rodo Shakaigakkai Nenpo* 9: 151–75.

Kondo, D. K. (1990) *Crafting Selves: Power, Gender, and Discourses of Identity in a Japanese Workplace.* Chicago: University of Chicago Press.

Kumazawa, M. (2000) *Josei rodo to kigyo shakai* [Female labor and corporate society]. Tokyo: Iwanami Shoten.

Lam, A. (1992) *Women and Japanese Management: Discrimination and Reform.* London and New York: Routledge.

Lebra, J., Paulson, J. and Powers, E. (eds.) (1976) *Women in Changing Japan.* Boulder, CO: Westview.

Lebra, T. S. (1984) *Japanese Women: Constraint and Fulfillment.* Honolulu: University of Hawaii Press.

Lo, J. (1990) *Office Ladies, Factory Women: Life and Work at a Japanese Company.* New York: M. E. Sharpe.

McLendon, J. (1983) "The office: Way station or blind alley?", in Plath, D. W. (ed.), *Work and Lifecourse in Japan.* Albany, NY: State University of New York Press.

Ministry of Health, Labour and Welfare (2001) *Chingin kozo kihon tokei chosa* [Basic survey on wage structure]. Tokyo: Ministry of Health, Labour and Welfare.

Mitani, N. (1996) "Kintoho shikogo no josei koyo" [Women's employment after the implementation of the Equal Employment Opportunity Law], *Nihon Rodo Kenkyu Zasshi* 433: 24–36.

Nihon Keizai Shinbun (1994) "Sogoshoku josei 6 wari 'shoshin nado ni furi,' 8 wari 'noryoku hakki' 'shigoto tsuzuketai' 7 wari"[60 percent of women in managerial track profess "disadvantage in promotion," 80 percent report "demonstration of their capabilities" and 70 percent "wish to continue work"], March 30.

—— (1995) "'Noryoku hyoka ni fuman' 49%, kanrishoku no josei komuin" ['Dissatisfied with performance evaluation' 49 percent, female managers of public officials], May 8.

—— (2000) "Josei sogoshoku zentai no 3.5%" [Women accounting for 3.5% of the total employees in the managerial track], June 8.

Osawa, Machiko (1993) *Keizai henka to joshi rodo: Nichibei no hikaku kenkyu* [Economic change and female labor: A comparative study of Japan and the United States]. Tokyo: Nihon Keizai Hyoronsha.

Osawa, Mari (1993) *Kigyo chushin shakai o koete* [Overcoming corporate-centered society]. Tokyo: Jiji Tsushinsha.

Renshaw, J. R. (1999) *Kimono in the Boardroom: The Invisible Evolution of Japanese Women Managers.* Oxford: Oxford University Press.

Roberson, J. E. (1998) *Japanese Working Class Lives: An Ethnographic Study of Factory Workers.* London and New York: Routledge.

Roberts, G. S. (1994) *Staying on the Line: Blue-Collar Women in Contemporary Japan.* Honolulu: University of Hawaii Press.

Rohlen, T. P. (1974) *For Harmony and Strength: Japanese White-Collar Organization in Anthropological Perspective.* Berkeley, CA: University of California Press.

Rosenberger, N. (2001) *Gambling with Virtue: Japanese Women and the Search for Self in a Changing Nation.* Honolulu: University of Hawaii Press.

Saito, S. (1982) *Tsuma tachi no shishuki* [The wives' gloomy middle ages]. Tokyo: Kyodo Tsushinsha.

Saso, M. (1990) *Women in the Japanese Workplace.* London: Hilary Shipman.

Seiyama, K. (1998) "Trends of educational attainment and labor force participation among Japanese women," in Seiyama, K. and Imada, S. (eds.), *1995 SMM chosa shirizu: Josei no kyaria kozo to sono henka* [1995 SSM survey series: Changing career structures of women]. Tokyo: SSM Chosa Kenkyukai.

—— (1999) "Josei no kyaria kozo no tokusei to doko" [The characteristics of women's career structure and its trends], *Nihon Rodo Kenkyu Zasshi* 472: 36–45.

Seiyama, K. and Imada, S. (eds.) (1998) *1995 SMM chosa shirizu: Josei no kyaria kozo to sono henka* [1995 SSM survey series: Changing career structures of women]. Tokyo: SSM Chosa Kenkyukai.

Smith, R. J. (1987) "Gender inequality in contemporary Japan," *Journal of Japanese Studies* 13: 1 25.

Taga, F. (2001) *Dansei no jenda keisei* [Men's gender formation]. Tokyo: Toyokan Shuppan.

Takenaka, E. (1983) *Josei rodo ron* [A treatise on female labor]. Tokyo: Yuhikaku.

Tamanoi, M. A. (1990) "Women's voices: Their critique of the anthropology of Japan," *Annual Review of Anthropology* 19: 17–37.

Tanaka, K. (1987) "Women, work and family in Japan: A life cycle perspective," PhD dissertation, University of Iowa.

Tanaka, S. (1998) "Kogakurekika to seibetsu bungyo" [Higher education and the sexual division of labor], in Seiyama, K. and Imada, S. (eds.), *1995 SMM chosa shirizu: Josei no kyaria kozo to sono henka* [1995 SSM survey series: Changing career structures of women]. Tokyo: SSM Chosa Kenkyukai.

Toyoda, M. (1997) *Otoko rashisa to iu jubaku* [A spell called masculinity]. Tokyo: Asuka Shinsha.

Upham, F. K. (1987) *Law and Social Change in Postwar Japan.* Cambridge, MA: Harvard University Press.

Vogel, E. F. (1963) *Japan's New Middle Class: The Salary Man and His Family in a Tokyo Suburb.* Berkeley, CA: University of California Press.

Vogel, S. H. (1978) "Professional housewife: The career of urban middle class Japanese women," *Japan Interpreter* 12: 16–43.

FURTHER READING

Brinton, M. C. (ed.) (2001) *Women's Working Lives in East Asia.* Stanford, CA: Stanford University Press.

Imamura, A. E. (ed.) (1996) *Re-Imaging Japanese Women.* Berkeley, CA: University of California Press.

Ogasawara, Y. (1998) *Office Ladies and Salaried Men: Power, Gender and Work in Japanese Companies.* Berkeley, CA: University of California Press.

CHAPTER ELEVEN

Catching Up?
Changing Inequalities of Gender at Work and in the Family in the UK

Harriet Bradley

Leyla is a married woman in her late forties with two children who works as an English teacher for the New Deal,[1] the British Labour Government's program for getting the long-term unemployed into jobs. Leyla was born in India, to very highly educated and successful parents; she herself won a scholarship and was started on a promising career as a scientist, completing a Master's and commencing her PhD in biology. She is a competent statistician, with considerable research experience.

However, once she got married everything changed. She left India to follow her husband, a medical scientist around the globe, including some Middle East countries where it would be hard for a woman to pursue her career. Finally, they ended up in England, where her husband did further training. During this period she managed to get some hours of part-time lecturing in biology, but found it impossible to obtain secure employment or to find any work as a researcher, so she moved into English language teaching. Meanwhile, her children were growing up and her eldest is at university. She describes her current priorities as "looking for a house to buy" and "being set towards my children because I want to see them through whatever they are going, their future."

Leyla, who was interviewed for a project about minority women in trade unions,[2] is happy with her life and her domestic role. She enjoys her New Deal teaching work and although she retains interest in recommencing a PhD she sees it as quite unlikely: "I have left that for such a long time, it's such a complex field and you have to be so much up front that I really don't know whether I would be able to go back and start." While she has no regrets about the course her life has taken she muses on the differences in gender equality she perceives between India and Britain, challenging some western stereotypes that portray women of the developed societies as oppressed victims of "backwardness":

> In India you don't really struggle so much to be equal, you have a lot more equal opportunities, like, you don't, if you have a female boss it is nothing new. It is so taken for granted . . . My aunts they are scientists, my uncles are scientists and they all work in premiere research institutions . . . nobody had ever raised issues about being a woman and being side-tracked. But since I came here I found that was a lot more prevalent. And I thought, how can such a developed country have such an issue? When I look at it, I can see here that women are paid less than men . . . For example, my daughter has taken up electronics and it was like, oh God, a girl in engineering, but that's not the case in India.

Despite these national differences, Leyla's history is fairly typical of the life experiences of women of previous generations, my mother's generation and to some extent my own. Such women, as Sylvia Walby (1997) has noted, were brought up in a gender regime in which women were oriented towards domesticity. Giving up work to prioritize the care of home, husband and children was seen as normal; and most women accepted without much complaint the differences in gender roles, and the inequalities of power, pay, and status that accompanied them. It was only when crises disrupted the smooth running of their family lives – divorce, a husband being made redundant or falling ill, children leaving home (the "empty nest" syndrome) – that some women started to question the status quo. Some became involved in the "second-wave" feminist movement which erupted in the 1970s and had their views changed for ever; others merely suffered from the sense of malaise and lack of fulfillment that American feminist Betty Friedan so tellingly described as "the disease without a name" (Friedan 1965). But many women remained perfectly content with their lot, especially those like Leyla who were reasonably comfortably off with husbands in well-paid, secure jobs.

However, it is argued that all this has changed as a result of upheavals in economic and family life over the past three decades. Long-term male unemployment has occurred, causing particular problems for older men who find it hard to secure new jobs. There has been a "feminization" of the labor force (Bradley et al. 2000) linked to the decline of manufacturing and increase in service employment. Divorce rates have soared and 10 percent of households are lone-parent families. Where there are two partners, dual-earning has become the norm. Sociologists have interpreted these changes as resulting in a major upheaval to existing gender norms and a challenge to gender inequalities. In

Gender Transformations (1997) Walby speaks of a new gender regime in which women as well as men expect to work for most of their lives and are oriented to the workplace. Hochschild (1997), commenting on these events in America, believes that both men and women are fleeing from the family and childcare into work because they find themselves more valued there and their self-esteem is heightened. Crompton and Sanderson (1990) have documented the use made by women of the "qualifications lever" to compete more equally with men in the labor market thus beginning to overthrow the long-standing patterns of gender segregation in the workplace. Bradley (1999) has described how there has developed a "climate of equality" whereby women are no longer prepared automatically to accept that they should be subordinate to men or confined to inferior jobs. It has even been argued that men are now "losing out" to women as young women have become equally or more successful in school and university examinations (Steinberg et al. 1998). In Britain in 2002 girls once again achieved higher grades than boys in the GCSE school exams, causing another wave of panic as to what is going wrong with "our boys." In 2001, 56 percent of girls as compared to only 45 percent boys gained five of more grades A–C at GCSE (or grades 1–3 in the Scottish equivalent SCE). At the important A-level stage, which determines university entrance, 34 percent of girls compared to 27 percent of boys aged 17–19 gained two or more passes (or three or more in Scottish Highers) (EOC 2002)

But how profound have the effects of these changes really been? Do we live in a "post-feminist" age with gender inequalities a thing of the past? Is gender segregation at work, the channeling of the sexes into "men's work" and "women's work" (see Bradley 1989), breaking down? Are men holding the babies? Is the gender pay gap diminishing? This chapter seeks to explore these questions by looking at data on women's experiences from three qualitative research studies carried out over the past decade. The first of these studied gender segregation in the North East of England in the early 1990s; the second is currently exploring the life trajectories of young women and men in Bristol; and the third investigates the situation of British-Asian, British-African and British-Caribbean women within trade unions in London and the South West. These studies are used to trace out changes in the attitudes and behavior of women and men in the face of undeniable socio-economic change. But before starting to discuss these studies, I want to offer a brief overview of previous social science approaches to the analysis of gender inequalities; and I shall then consider the type of methods that have been used in such analysis, focusing in particular on the contribution of qualitative research techniques.

THE STUDY OF GENDER AND INEQUALITY

The study of gender is a relatively recent phenomenon in social science. This is primarily because relations between men and women have traditionally been seen as *natural* rather than *social*, a view that is far from extinct today. This view is often apparent when talking to managers and employers about women and men as employees; and it is also characteristically held by many of my first-year undergraduates, before exposure to social science thinking has sensitized them to the fact that no social phenomena can be viewed as purely natural. At the time when the social science disciplines were being formalized and institutionalized in the nineteenth century, such biological thinking on women and reproduction was at its strongest; as Sydie (1987) shows, this view of men as cultural products and of women (or "woman" as Victorian thinking had it) as natural is demonstrated in the work of the "founders" of sociology, Marx, Weber, and Durkheim.

The neglect of gender continued into the early part of the century, despite the achievements of the first wave of feminists and the production of a few pioneering studies by women academics, e.g. Clark (1919), Schreiner (1911), Pinchbeck (1930), Klein (1965). Where the study of the relationships between women and men did enter social research was in relation to the family, which in contrast was firmly seen as a social institution. However, continuing naturalist assumptions about gender (the maternal instinct, "man the hunter" and "woman the homemaker") meant that family relationships were not habitually viewed in terms of inequality; rather, as in the work of Talcott Parsons, the gender allocation to men of economic and instrumental functions and to women of nurturing and expressive activities was seen as linked to biological programming and a logical way to organize society. The family and relationships between men and women were also important topics within social and cultural anthropology; but here, too, the study of difference in what women and men did was seen as an aspect of culture and not related to inequality.

All this changed dramatically in the 1970s with the advent of second-wave feminism. Suddenly gender emerged as a key sociological concept and one that was framed in terms of oppression and inequality (Oakley 1981). A new generation of female social scientists, more or less directly influenced by feminist politics, produced an outpouring of studies, both historical and contemporary, both theoretical and empirical, which posited gender as a major axis of social inequality. Influenced by the political agenda of the Women's Liberation Movement, as formulated at the famous Ruskin Conferences in 1970 and 1971, the empirical scope of this research was wide: Oakley (1974) produced her pioneering studies of housework, Sharpe (1976) and Hunt (1980) studied gender socialization, Spender (1989), David (1980) and Stanworth (1981) looked at education and inequalities in schooling, Beechey (1977), Pollert (1981) and Westwood (1984) investigated gender relations in the workplace, the Dobashes (1979) and Hanmer (1983) opened up the topic of domestic violence, Wilson (1977) and Land (1978) studied the gendered nature of the welfare state and British social policy, Doyal (1985) and Graham (1984) looked at women's health and medical oppression, Oakley (1980) and Lewis (1980) explored maternity and motherhood, while Randall (1982) and Lovenduski (1986) documented women's under-representation in political institutions. Meanwhile more theoretically inclined sociologists such as Barrett (1980) or Mitchell (1975) tried to marry (in Hartmann's (1981) well-known metaphor) the study of gender inequalities with the analysis of capitalism. An interest in sexuality and sexual orientation as aspects of gender inequality also developed, strongly influenced by the work of American feminists, Millett (1971), Firestone (1979), and Rich (1981). This multifaceted nature of the study of gendered inequalities is exemplified by a key text of British feminist sociology, Sylvia Walby's *Patriarchy at Work* (1986), which offered an integration of liberal, Marxist and radical feminist theorizing. Famously, Walby posited six interrelated sets of social structures as constituting the basis of a system of patriarchy: "The key sets of patriarchal relations are to be found in domestic work, paid work, the state, male violence and sexuality: while other practices in civil society have a limited significance" (1986: 51).

In a later, equally influential text, *Theorizing Patriarchy* (1990), she reiterated this list but reconceptualized the last item as "patriarchal relations in cultural institutions" (ibid.: 20). A chapter in the book is devoted to each of these aspects of male domination and gender inequality.

While the study of gender and inequality proceeded on this broad base, the tendency of 1970s' and 1980s' British feminism to lean towards Marxism meant that work lay firmly at the heart of the emerging sociology of gender. Waged labor and women's employment, domestic labor and housework were acknowledged by all schools and tendencies as being at the core of gender inequality. It is significant that Walby's definition of patriarchy starts with domestic work and paid work and the first two chapters of Theorizing Patriarchy are entitled "Paid Employment" and "Household Production;" while another key early contribution, *Women in Britain Today*, an Open University text edited by

Beechey and Whitelegg (1986), looks at four areas: the family, employment, education and health (in that order).

The above list of contributions to the study of gender relations, it should be said, is by no means exhaustive. This was an incredibly productive period when social scientists influenced by the feminist movement began the process of mapping out the dimensions of gender difference and inequality across every area of social life. Yet, despite the insights it offered, this body of work was soon to come under quite savage attack, both in Britain and America.

A typical text, *Destabilizing Theory* by Michele Barrett and Ann Phillips (1992), announced a "paradigm shift" away from the feminist theory of the 1970s and 1980s. Approaches which had formerly been distinguished under the labels of liberal, Marxist or materialist, and radical feminism now were lumped together under the label of "modernist" feminism. This, it was claimed, had now been superseded by a new perspective, that of post-structuralist or postmodern feminism. Another adherent of this change, Ann Brooks, described the coming of "post" forms of feminism in these glowing terms:

> Postfeminism represents . . . feminism's coming of age, its maturity into a confident body of theory and politics representing pluralism and difference and reflecting on its position in relation to other philosophical and political movements similarly demanding change. (Brooks 1997: 1)

As the name implies, the new theorists were skeptical of the structural analysis offered by their predecessors: the idea of societies as holistic systems displaying regular patterns of social activity was attacked by a new generation of social theorists who saw the social world as disorderly, incoherent and fragmented. Postmodernists were particularly hostile to the Marxist attempt to explain the workings of society in terms of a capitalist mode of production, although, as Pollert (1996) has argued, they were more chary of denouncing the key feminist concept of patriarchy, despite its connotations of a society regularly ordered on the basis of gender distinction.

While this attack on systemic and structuralist theories was one launched on all brands of sociological thinking, there were more specific criticisms of "modernist" feminism. The old analyses of gender inequality were seen to be insensitive to differences between women, especially those related to ethnicity and culture. Moreover, the prevailing approach to gender as a form of oppression was seen to construct women as victims of an all-encompassing male power. Rather, declared the new postmodernist theorists, women should be seen as active constituents of their own social world and as empowered rather than oppressed. There was a change of focus: the mood of the new analysis was to celebrate and document gender as a form of cultural difference, rather than expose it as a dimension of material inequality. The political thrust shifted, in the terminology of Nancy Fraser (1995) and Charles Taylor (1992), from redistribution (of economic resources) to recognition (of distinct cultural identities). Thus the old topic of gender and class was virtually abandoned, giving way before studies of issues such as sexuality, the body, representation, media, identity, and nationality. In short, feminism had taken a sharp "cultural turn" and the study of gender inequalities in the family and workplace was seen as rather "old hat." This shift has been strongly marked in Britain, the USA and Australia; some European societies, such as the Scandinavian countries, are less receptive to postmodernism and post-structuralism and continue to research in the older mode.

This was not to say that the exploration of gender inequalities in Britain was abandoned, because, ironically, this had now become accepted as an important topic within the sociological mainstream. Recent introductory textbooks, such those by Giddens (1997) or Fulcher and Scott (1999), now contain substantial sections on gender and inequality. Thus, for example, research into the gendered division of labor carried on within the sub-specialisms of the sociology of work; projects dealing with gender segregation, part-time work, motherhood and childcare, homeworking, domestic labor, ethnic minority women in the labor market and within trade unions are contained within the major program on The Future of Work funded by the Economic and Social Research Council (ESRC). The ESRC is also currently funding a major national survey on domestic violence.[3]

Findings from projects of this kind continue to highlight gender inequalities at home and at work. Studies of domestic labor persistently demonstrate that around 70 percent of housework is done by women, although men are likely to participate more where both couples work part-time. Childcare remains identified as the responsibility of women, so that it is the mother who in the main gives up work when children are born or takes time off when children are ill. This is what Hochschild (1989) has called the "second shift" and her work established that there are similar patterns in America.

While highly-paid professional and managerial women are able to "buy out" of the constraints of childcare and housework by employing nannies, au pairs, child-minders and cleaners, such work is mainly carried out by women reinforcing the idea that childcare is "women's work." The 1991 census showed that 90 percent of those employed in

domestic caring occupations were women (Crompton 1997). Habitually, as the research of Gregson and Lowe (1994) and of Anderson
(2000) shows, domestic work is carried out by low-paid working-class
women or, especially in London, by equally low-paid and often abused
and mistreated migrant women, from the Philippines, Eastern Europe,
Africa or Latin America. In the worst cases, Anderson describes how
migrant women may be beaten and threatened, made to sleep in cup-
boards and on floors, work incredibly long hours and suffer sexual
harassment from their "madam's" husband. *Doing the Dirty Work* indeed!
These studies are important, because while they affirm that all women
have in common an identification as responsible for domestic labor, it
also can constitute a major axis of exploitation among women. Middle-
class women seem prepared to treat their servants as virtual slaves:

> I'm looking for a domestic help . . . I have three children and expect her
> to begin work at 6.30–7.00 and work as long is as needed.

> I want someone to live-in . . . she'll work twenty-four hours of course . . .
> a friend of mine told me Filipinos are willing to work twenty-four hours
> a day. (Healy 1993: 31, quoted in Anderson 2000)

Such expectations by middle-class women are no doubt fostered in
some cases by the "long hours" culture which has become typical of the
advanced capitalist economies. This is one major obstacle for women
in attaining equality with men in the workplace as Judy Wajcman's work
on managerial women shows (1998). Like many other recent studies,
this highlights the increasing demands made by employers and organizations on their employees' time and commitment. To get to the top,
employees often have to be prepared to get in at breakfast time, work
late several evenings, give up their weekends for conferences and training sessions. Such demands are simply incompatible with the responsibilities of child-rearing, but, as Wajcman points out, even childless
women suffer in contrast to men, because they don't have wives to look
after them! The career success of top managers and professionals is
often built upon the unpaid labor of the wives whose work in the home
frees men up to put in the hours that mark them out as deserving of
promotion.

The work of management, as Wajcman describes it, is built on pre-
sumptions which reflect the experience of masculinity. In order to
flourish in this environment women have to learn to "manage like a
man." It is not surprising, as Judi Marshall's work on women managers
has shown (1995), that many give up the struggle, returning to full-time

motherhood, setting up businesses or seeking out less competitive orga-nizational contexts. Another study of high-flying women, Linda McDowell's *Capital Culture* (1997) highlights the way women are seen as outsiders and intruders in the male-dominated world of the City of London because of the bodily visibility of their gender and their sexu-ality. Her respondents struggled to find acceptable clothing for work which was not seen either as dowdy and unfeminine or as overly provocative and sexual. McDowell argues that female bodies are viewed as inappropriate in workplaces where the normal form of embodiment is male and desexualized. Although this might seem a relatively trivial issue, it is in fact crucial in highlighting the way that rules and values in workplaces are decided by men on male terms. As a result, women often feel excluded and marginalized in a way that affects their self-esteem and confidence in developing a career. Male monopoly of what I have elsewhere labeled "symbolic power" (Bradley 1999) is a major factor in maintaining patterns of gender segregation.

Thus, despite the advances of feminization, research has shown that established patterns of gender segregation are remarkably robust, as will be discussed later. Moreover while middle-class highly-educated women have made some inroads into male occupational strongholds in management and the professions, even if not managing to mount to the top jobs, in the lower tiers of the occupational hierarchy gender segregation remains very strong. There are few women lorry or train drivers, garage mechanics or building laborers; and few men typists, cleaners or beauty consultants. The continued existence of gender seg-regation underpins the pay gap between men and women which will be discussed in a later section. But perhaps even more important than pay is the concentration of women in part-time work which brings with it lower rewards, benefits and career advancement opportunities. While 66 percent of women and 79 percent of men aged 16–64 are in employ-ment, 44 percent of women employees are part-time, as compared to 8 percent of men. In 2002, the British Equal Opportunities Commission reported a continued 18 percent gap between the hourly wage rates of full-time men and women. Between full-time men and part-time women the gap is a worrying 41 percent (EOC 2002).

The persistence of gender inequalities at home and at work and indeed in most other areas of social life is marked enough in the soci-eties of advanced western capitalism, but is dramatically greater in other parts of the world. It has often been pointed out that across the globe women do most of the work and men control most of the wealth. Female poverty is stark in many parts of Africa and Asia, and in almost all countries poverty, like work, has been feminized. This then, must be a strong justification for a return to the analysis of material aspects of gender relations. It may be too extreme to claim, as Bryan Turner has done, that "the cultural turn has been a disaster for sociology" (2002), but I would certainly argue that feminism in its preoccupation with post-thinking has taken a wrong turn.

However a re-turn to material factors, and in particular to the study of class and its interrelation with gender, needs to be handled shrewdly and delicately. We should not countenance a return to the monolithic and masculinist frameworks of stratification and class analysis which prevailed in the 1960s and 1970s, with their neglect of gender and ethnicity. Postmodern and post-structural feminism does have valuable lessons to teach us and we can learn from its insights. We need to be sensitive to the way inequalities are framed by context, to the variations within and across categories and to the fluidity of social life. As I have argued in previous work, the way ahead should involve attempts to explore the interaction of different dynamics of inequality in specific settings and work through these towards sociological generalizations. Thus we can develop an account of inequality which takes on board complexity and contradiction and avoids unilinearity. I shall try to illustrate this in my discussion of three qualitative projects studying gender inequalities. But first I need to say something about methodologies used in research into gender.

VOICING WOMEN: QUALITATIVE RESEARCH ON GENDER

In contrast to the study of class and racial inequalities, the study of gender inequality, at least within British social science, was initially marked by an advocacy of qualitative methods. This can, I believe, be in part attributed to the close links between the "academic wing" of feminism and its activist political counterpart. A key principle which informed the work of early feminist sociologists was that their writing must be accessible to non-academic women and thus kept free of excessive jargon or scientism. Thus Ann Oakley produced two books from each of her first big empirical investigations: *Housewife* (1976) and *From Here to Maternity* (1981) were targeted at the general public of women, while *The Sociology of Housework* (1974) and *Women Confined* (1980) were more explicitly academic. Second, a major concern of those interested in empirical research into gender was to excavate the buried experiences of "invisible women" and to free their voices from the silence imposed on them by male cultural dominance and especially by the male bias which had shaped the curriculum within the academic disciplines (Spender 1980, 1989). Case studies and interviews seemed the best way to achieve these objectives, along with exploration of women's texts and writings. A related distrust of mainstream (or "malestream") science was a third factor in the inclination to use of qualitative techniques; male-dominated social science was seen as overly rationalist and technocratic, privileging the use of "hard" statistical and experimental techniques over the "softer" approaches of ethnography and observation and tending to problematize notions of "experience" as too subjective. By contrast, feminist methodology emphasized that experience was the building material of all knowledge and that the experience and the "standpoint" of the researcher were integral to the formulation of knowledge (Harding 1987). While feminist researchers did not reject entirely the more orthodox techniques of "positivist" science, they saw them as far from immune to criticism, and they strongly confirmed the value of qualitative studies.

Thus, some of the first and important studies of women's work were case studies (for example, Pollert 1981; Westwood 1984) based on extensive participant observation. Miriam Glucksmann even gave up her academic post for a while and went to work in a factory to prepare for a book *Women on the Line* (1984), which she published under the name of Ruth Cavendish. These books sought to redress the balance within industrial and occupational sociology which was centered on the study of male workers (miners, car workers, lorry drivers, and chemical operatives). They also exposed the inequalities of the sexual division of labor and started to explore the link between these and women's domestic role.

Good ethnographic work, though, is time-consuming and difficult to arrange and therefore expensive, and there has been a drift away from this to interviews and surveys of various types. This also reflects the return to the mainstream of many feminist sociologists who are interested in the study of gendered work. There is now less suspicion of quantitative techniques; for example, Oriel Sullivan (1996) has carried out complex statistical research on housework, a subject notoriously difficult to measure. A difficulty here is that large-scale surveys, too, are expensive. Thus, much large-scale research into gender inequality has been based on the analysis of statistics already collected by government, such as the work of Hakim (1991), of Arber and Ginn (1991) or Blackburn and his associates (1993). On a few occasions major surveys which deal with gender issues have been sponsored by government or research organizations, examples of which are the Women and Employment survey or the ESRC's Social Change and Economic Life initiative (1994).

By and large, researchers into gender inequality have tended to affirm the value of both types of research and a current trend has been to combine both methodologies. Here one can cite Angela Dale's ongoing research into Bangladeshi women in Oldham which combines analysis of national and local labor market statistics with interview work among local women's organizations. Another current example is Irene Bruegel's research into gender segregation at work, which links data from national surveys on employment like the Labour Force Survey to a number of case studies of organizations in different occupational sectors.[3]

Researchers into women's employment and into domestic labor, however, have still continued to look favorably on smaller-scale and intensive methods, particularly in order to uncover the complexity of gender relations and the subtleties of power. Quantitative studies, such as those referred to above, are excellent in revealing patterns of gender difference; longitudinal and comparative techniques can expose national variations in such patterns and how they alter over time. But though they are absolutely necessary to show us *what* has been happening they are less good at answering the question *why* and inadequate to answer the question *how*, that is, they can inform us on correlations, on structures and on outcomes, but they do not help us much with understanding actions, agency, and process. Moreover, large-scale national or regional surveys inevitably cover up, in the process of statistical averaging, variations and complexities that may underlie general patterns. Unless they are very large, indeed, they cannot, for example, tell us very much about some of variations of experience among Britain's smaller minority groups, especially if these are further broken down by age and social class. Nor are they well designed for uncovering the subtleties of identity and culture that are particularly of interest to current researchers into gender.

Seeking to tease out these aspects of gender relations (variations, identities, agency, and change) researchers have employed a wide range of qualitative techniques. These include participant observation; semi-structured and unstructured interviews; life history analysis of various types; narrative study; textual and discourse analysis; and diaries and logging of daily activities (especially useful for studying household tasks). While many of these studies are inevitably small and localized, taken together they can start to show the complexities and contradictions that lie behind the often apparent stability of gender divisions. At the same time, qualitative work allows research influenced by feminism to stay true to one of its first principles: allowing women to give voice to their own views and experiences that often are not heard in the public domain.

An important recent trend is to try to get a rounded picture of gender divisions and inequalities in different sites and contexts by using a mix of qualitative and quantitative techniques. This was the strategy employed by Dale and Bruegel in the studies mentioned above. Similarly, one of the three pieces of research drawn upon in the next part of this chapter, the Bristol Young Adults Study, employed a mix of investigative tools. A loosely ethnographic initial phase of fieldwork involved observation of workplaces, informal interviews with employers and agencies handling employment and training issues, visits to schemes run by agencies and in-depth semi-structured interviews with young adults identified by employers, agencies and through personal contacts of the research team. This was followed by a systematic exploration of young adult's employment trajectories, by means of a household-based survey interview with a sample of 1,100 young adults carried out by NOP. Sampling was based upon a quota of addresses in selected census enumeration districts in four zones of Bristol chosen for their contrasting socio-demographic statistics. Finally, a set of follow-up in-depth interviews were carried out with a sub-sample of 80 survey respondents. In this way we sought to acquire a feel for the specifics of the context (the Bristol labor market), a broad statistical picture of the position of young adults within it in terms of labor market gains and losses, and insight into the resources provided to young adults by their life experiences and the processes by which they negotiated their paths through the structure of labor market opportunities. This methodological mix allowed us to study the way that inequalities of gender, class, and ethnicity interact and to explore this within a given context. In this way researchers can explore the important insights offered by the postmodern and post-structuralist critics of modernist feminism, that gendered experience is *differentiated* and *tied to context*.

Studying Gender Inequality and Segregation of Work

Breaking through: employees in Tyne and Wear

Before discussing the Bristol study I want to say a little about an earlier study which was carried out in five organizations in the North East of England. This involved semi-structured interviews with 200 women and men, 40 in each organization. The interviews were carried out in 1992–3, around a decade ago. The context of this research was the feminization of the labor market in Tyne and Wear; women were about to become a majority of the workforce and male unemployment was very high. Long-term unemployment following the collapse of local traditional industries such as shipbuilding, mining, and steel might be handed from father to son, while new jobs tended to be "women's work" in the service or public sector; 82 percent of women worked in services and 49 percent in the public sector (Bradley 1999).

But despite these processes of feminization, gender segregation remained strong, even in the five case-study organizations which had been selected as key areas of female employment and all of which professed commitment to equal opportunities. In the five organizations 44 percent of the interviewees said they worked mainly with their own sex, and only 27 percent reported working equally with both sexes. Many women in these organizations felt very strongly that women were still discriminated against:

> Men get favored more . . . Men get the prime jobs.

> The men have a better prospect. The men get more pay than women. The men get away with a lot more.

> It's a male-dominated firm. The main man's job is management and naturally the fitters . . . Women can't go no further.

Some of the segregation could be put down to custom and practice and the entrenched attitudes of men, especially those in control of staffing decisions. However, the women believed that women's responsibility for childcare and household work was still the main barrier to gender equality:

> To me that's the only thing that holds women back, it's looking after the children.

> If you're a married woman, the opportunities are there but carrying it out that's a different thing. If you want to get on, like, the girls, there are one or two of them trying to be managers, they have to be in at all times. But if you're a married woman you couldn't do it. It always ends up being the woman's responsibility, no matter how good your husband is, and even if it doesn't, you feel guilty. Especially as everyone thinks you should be looking after the children, they make you feel guilty.

Nevertheless, this did not mean that nothing had changed. Some of the managers I spoke to were keen to promote women and the trade unions, too, were to varying degrees committed to gender equalization. Thus I described what I called a "climate of equality" developing. Central to this were women's own attitudes. The women I spoke to were not prepared to accept automatically that they would occupy positions subordinate to men. Many of the younger women spoke of their determination to have careers and to "make something of themselves." Some of them professed a desire to become managers. They were taking much less time out of the labor force to bring up their children, often returning to their jobs soon after maternity leave. While women over 50 had taken an average of over 10 years out of employment, for the women under 30 it was only one year. They believed that it was necessary for both partners to work if a household was to maintain a decent standard of living, especially as they knew that their menfolk were vulnerable to unemployment. All this contrasted with earlier studies such as those of Cavendish and Pollert who found that women accepted the idea of male breadwinners and saw their own work as secondary.

Perhaps the most striking finding was that older women whose children were grown up were particularly committed to their jobs; many regretted their lack of qualifications which cut them off from promotion and advancement while they saw inexperienced graduates take positions they felt they deserved. Here was an untapped source of energy and enthusiasm which we will encounter again when we discuss the case of the minority ethnic trade unionists. This seemed to me the most interesting example of the raised expectations and ambitions of women: yet their history of being "secondary earners" and homemakers had contributed to their sense of frustration as they confronted the still unbroken "glass ceiling" and pondered how to "break through." While some expressed anger and bitterness about the situation, there was also a spirit of gritty determination among many of these older women: "Men are still given preferential treatment . . . but it was my generation who took them on. We're breaking through!"

Back to the future? Young adults in Bristol

Ten years on, one might assume that women had made further progress to equality, especially given their continual gains in educational achievement, along with commitment of the New Labour government to equal opportunities. However, research currently being carried out in Bristol by a team of researchers among young adults revealed a much more complicated and contradictory picture. The age-group covered in this study is 20–34. We should therefore expect that if, indeed, there have been significant recent changes in gender roles and in gender attitudes they would be displayed among this generational group. We anticipated them to be more "progressive" and egalitarian in their attitudes to gender roles than the older North East sample.

Certainly we did find that some of our young women were very work-oriented and ambitious, in line with the North East study. They thought seriously about their lives, made career plans, underwent training subsequent to their undergraduate degrees and had managerial ambitions:

> I would love to be my own boss, have my own company, doing something.

> I'd quite like to run my own company when I'm a bit older. So I guess what I thought was this – in my thirties I'd get as much experience as I could together working with other people and then in my forties I'd think about setting up my own business. I think the teaching has made me realize I can't work for other people, long term, I'm too bolshy . . . So I think if I ran my own company, although it would be hard work and all sorts of risks involved, then I'd have that control . . . So I guess that's my life plan.

> At the moment it's my degree and then following that it's my, erm, job or career if you like it . . . I don't know definitely what I am going to try and do but I'm aiming for some kind of management role, probably in training or education – along the lines of that. But something that's challenging and not repetitive and comes with a lot of responsibility and new things to deal with.

Compared to the older women of the North East study, these younger women seemed to have less sense of being trapped by school failure or a disadvantaged background. For example, Katrina came from what is seen as one of Bristol's problem estates, got married and had three children early in life and worked in a mix of low-paid caring jobs. But now she is on the first steps of a career which she has carefully planned out:

> This isn't where it ends. This is just where it begins . . . I've decided to go for the degree because the social work qualification is changing and in a couple of years everyone will need a degree. Plus you've got more scope for employment. And eventually after I've been in social work for a number of years, and I hope I do well, and my children are older, I hope to do a degree in child psychology Eventually I'm hoping . . . that later in life that will be the career that I turn to.

Both men and women seemed prepared to take advantage of openings offered by labor market flexibility and by opportunities for "life-long learning." They were ready to embrace both academic and vocational

Table 11.1   *Has having children caused you to do any of the following?*

	Women (N = 297)	Men (N = 100)
Stop work altogether	150	9
Work fewer hours	94	17
Change your type of job	35	6
Choose particular type of job	24	4
Earn less money	37	3
Only work at certain times of day	74	17
Miss out on promotion	22	1
None of these	27	56

Some 20 women with children for some reason did not answer this question.

types of training as part of their career development and to make major switches in career as part of their self-development. For example, Anita was a high-flier with a BA and a PhD who was pursuing a successful career as a management consultant, but when we interviewed her, she was pondering on making a major change in her life and perhaps returning to education.

However, this picture of heightened female aspiration is only part of the picture. Not all the young adult women we interviewed were like Katrina and Anita. For many of them, domestic responsibilities and pre-occupations loomed large and remained an impediment to gender equality in the labor market. This finding was even more marked in the responses to the household survey.

Table 11.1 illustrates this. We asked our survey respondents how having children had affected their working lives. As Table 11.1 shows, over half of the women had given up work altogether and many reported other constraints on their employment. Only 27 of the 297 women with children had been unaffected in this way, compared to over half of the men with children.

Not only are women still the ones who bear the practical responsibility for children, but there is strong evidence that children continue to have a much more important place in their priorities than men. We asked all our respondents to choose out of a list of items up to three which were currently most important in their lives. Table 11.2 summarizes their responses.

Table 11.2 indicates a clear difference in priority between men and women, with men putting career and breadwinning at the top, while women are more likely to prioritize children and family. Indeed, when

Table 11.2 *Percentage of respondents mentioning each priority (up to 3 mentions per respondent)*

		Women	Men
1	Sorting out my life	36	38
2	Earning a living	36	48
3	Developing career/job	41	57
4	Studying/gaining qualifications	31	30
5	Bringing up children	53	20
6	Spending time with partner/family	52	44
7	Spending time with friends	34	38
8	Sports or other leisure activities	9	19

we asked the young adults what they would ideally like to be doing in the future, 10 percent of women opted for full-time motherhood. There were not a large number of prospective "househusbands": only 1 percent went for this option. Given that the vast majority (89 percent) of those women who did not yet have children hoped to do so in the future, we have a picture that is not very different from previous generations. In fact, our young adults' attitudes to family and gender roles were much more traditional than we had expected. Some 25 per of women and 29 percent of men chose father working full-time and mother not working as the best arrangement for families with young children. Only 8 percent of both sexes favored both parents working full-time and the most popular arrangement was father full-time/mother part-time, which was chosen by 38 percent of both sexes.

Given these attitudes and constraints, it is not surprising that women's labor market position continued to be worse than that of men. As this was not a workplace study, we cannot produce much evidence about gender segregation; but we do have figures on income. Altogether, our young adults were a low-paid workforce, but women were doing considerably worse than men as Table 11.3 shows. The majority of them earned less than £12,000 per annum, and twice as many men were in the top-earning bracket.

Although clearly income differences are linked to occupational class, the gender difference persisted across classes. Roughly the same proportion of men and women were in professional and managerial jobs but, of these, 33 percent of men, as opposed to 17 percent of women, were in the top income band, while among the unskilled and semi-skilled grouping 85 percent of women, as opposed to 59 percent of men, earned less than £12,000.

Table 11.3 *Young adults' incomes by gender (excluding students)*

	Women (%) N = 452	Men (%) N = 315	Total (%) N = 767
Low Under £12000	70	48	61
Medium £12000– £19999	23	37	29
High £20000+	7	15	10

The idea that women are "catching up" with men, let alone over-taking them, thus becomes doubtful. But this finding also throws doubt on Walby's contention that the impact of the domestic sphere on women's employment has reduced and that the "traditional impact of life cycle events on women's employment rates has ceased" (Walby 1997: 55). It looks as if she may have overestimated what she refers to as "immense differentiation between the lives of younger and older" women, especially among the lower socio-economic groupings, where we found traditional patterns and attitudes to be the most strongly manifested.

Keeping up the struggle: ethnic minority women in unions

This brings us to the important issue of differences among women and here I will refer briefly to another current study, the Double Disadvantage project which explores the position of minority ethnic women in trade unions. Interviews were carried out with 60 women drawn from four case-study unions. The majority of women were African Caribbean and many were in their forties and fifties. Most of the women were in London, with others being located in the South West, the West Midlands and the North West.

We had noticed in the Bristol Young Adults' Study that some of the most determined and success-oriented young women were Asian and African Caribbean. This strong sense of energy and commitment to career, self-development, and education emerged again in the union study. Women described having made a change of occupation late in life after experiencing blocks to advancement because of their ethnicity, or having started out on a career after rearing children on their own. Often this involved getting a new qualification or some other kind of retraining: "Blair talks about education, education, education. I talk about training, training, training. Anything I can do that will empower you with knowledge, I will do that."

We also found that for women who had experienced the frustrations of lack of recognition or promotion in their workplaces, becoming a union activist, with the chance of becoming a paid official, was an alternative type of career move.

But despite their dynamism and enthusiasm, women had almost universally experienced racial stereotyping and discrimination. When they described the division of labor in their workplaces it was strongly reminiscent of the accounts offered in the North East study, but with the element of ethnic hierarchy added in. Management positions remain the province of white males:

> The cleaners here are all black, black or Filipino, the people in the canteen, black, Filipino, er, clinic clerks, black, Asian, you know. African or black nurses get talked down to a lot. Um, in the hospital the sisters are all white, we haven't got one black sister in the department.

> It's dominated by men, the council on the whole. We've got quite a few senior solicitors, but there are no black ones.

> As in most retail stores the race composition is mainly black, it's predominantly black, on the lower levels, but, like, in terms of management it's pure whites . . . The store manager is white and the deputy manager is white, the assistant manager is white, the whole of the personnel team which comprises 12 people are white.

Like the women in the North East, the union women felt disadvantaged and angry that their merits were not recognized. They reported, in just the same way, having trained newcomers who then got promoted above them. But in their case they linked the discrimination to racism:

> The jobs that are for black people who work here are either, um, in manual grades or on very low clinical grades . . . Nobody else started at grade 1, it took me years to actually move up to the academic scale, whereas people in my own department have been given lesser grade, lesser responsibility, get moved up above me.

It's always been deemed that if you are black, you cannot manage, it's a bit like saying you cannot supervise. It's just the assumption that we are not able to do it. I have heard many reasons, people say it is because of our temperament, it's that. You know, you people are all very highly strung.

For these women, established patterns of the gender division of labour along with race discrimination had combined to block their progress and confine them to lower-paid positions. If they did not always agree with the term "double disadvantage" to describe the combining of the dynamics of gender and ethnicity, it was because they were aware of the other kinds of disadvantage suffered by their menfolk. For example, many African-Caribbean boys fail to achieve at school, and unemployment is especially high among Asian and African-Caribbean men. This illustrates the need to unpick the complexities of gender difference and the dimensions of inequality. In the UK, minority and working-class men are more prone than women to unemployment; minority and working-class women are more likely to experience low pay and dead-end jobs; women of all classes and ethnic groups are affected by vertical segregation and constraints imposed by domestic responsibilities especially childcare, although typically they handle family relations in rather different ways.

CONCLUSION: FUTURE ISSUES IN THE STUDY OF GENDERED INEQUALITIES

Leyla's story told at the beginning of his chapter offered an example of a typical woman's life among an older generation of women. Recently Walby and others have suggested that gender inequality may be diminishing among a younger generation brought up not to expect a life of domesticity and "secondary" status as a breadwinner. However, my discussion based on three fieldwork-based studies has suggested a less optimistic and more complex scenario, with marked continuities as well as change. While some young women appear more work-oriented and well equipped to compete in the labor market, pay equality has not been achieved, gender segregation persists and motherhood still means that women fall behind in the labor market. Moreover, especially in their thirties, women voluntarily tend to become more focused on parenting than on work, refusing the more economic orientations of men. Men still expect their partners to look after children and do more of the housework. That these attitudes still persist so strongly among young adults suggests that unless time out of work for mothering is not penalized, women are unlikely to catch up with men, despite their higher qualification levels.

In discussing the findings I have tried to point to some of the complexities and contradictions of gender divisions. Processes of social change are not experienced in a simple way with single consequences. Different groups of women find themselves differently positioned as a consequence of the feminization of the labor force, the growth of the knowledge economy and the spread of service work. Leyla's comments about the greater sexism in England than India illustrate how gender is nationally and culturally variable. Moreover, different women respond differently to the web of constraints and opportunities in which they find themselves positioned. This illustrates the *differentiated* nature of gender inequalities.

Gender inequalities are also *context-tied*. Part of the reason why the young adult women did not seem so uniformly career-oriented as we had expected is that the Bristol labor market is more buoyant and less depressed than that of Tyne and Wear. Though there is some long-term male unemployment, it tends currently to be confined to the multiply disadvantaged, rather than affecting former skilled manual workers as it has done in the North East. The need for dual earners in a household, or to be able to assume the breadwinning role if necessary, is not so pronounced in Bristol. Thus, many of the young adults have a greater degree of choice in the decisions they make about their working and home lives. Again, in the North East, there is a very small minority ethnic population and the workplaces in my study were almost entirely white. The retail organizations and hospitals of London, however, display a division of labor that is not just gendered, but highly ethnicized.

In such circumstances, it is important not to look at gender inequalities alone. The two later studies in particular demonstrate the importance of exploring the *multiple positionings* of class, gender, and ethnicity in which we are all located: labor market experience is different for women and men of different classes and ethnic groups.

This chapter, then, has advocated the use of qualitative research to reveal the complexities and contradictions of gender and to explore these in a way that is sensitive to variability, context, and multiple positioning. Nevertheless, it is still possible to draw some sociological generalizations across the three studies. First, it is clear that labor market segmentation on the base of gender and ethnicity persists despite the decades of change. Second, women's domestic roles continue to shape their employment histories and there is little sign of the much vaunted "new man" sharing parenthood and housework equally with his partner.

Taking these two factors together, we can state one thing with some certainty. In this period of change, the winners continue to be white, middle-class men: to be a woman, black or working-class is to be at a disadvantage, especially in terms of income. And if you are a woman *and* black *and* working-class – you are likely to have a struggle on your hands!

NOTES

1   The New Deal is the most recent of many British Government policies designed to get people (back) into employment. It consists of a set of programs targeted at special groups (young people, lone parents, older unemployed, etc.). A key aspect of the programs is that they are targeted at particular needs and involve the development of an individualized plan for each client, along with a mentoring system.
2   *Handling Double Disadvantage: Ethnic Minority Women in Trade Unions.* ESRC grant L212 25 2061, Future of Work Programme Phase 2. Research Team: Harriet Bradley, Geraldine Healy, Nupur Mukherjee. The other current project referred to in this chapter is *Winners and Losers: Young Adults' Employment in a Changing Labour Market*, ESRC grant R000 23 8215. Research Team: Steve Fenton, Jackie West, Will Guy, Ranji Devadason. As well as team members, the following graduate students conducted interviews for this project: Matthew Cole, Lucy Collins Teresa Dibble, Glyn Everett, Emma Head, Lorna Henry, Judi Kidger, Mojgan Rhabani, Hugh Ortega Breton. Details of the earlier project, *Gender Differentiation within Trade Unions*, ESRC grant R000234124, can be found in *Gender and Power in the Workplace* (Bradley 1999).
3   Both these programs of research, which have been completed and are currently being written up, formed part of the ESRC's *Future of Work* initiative.

REFERENCES

Anderson, B. (2000) *Doing the Dirty Work*. London: Zed Books.
Arber, S. and Ginn, J. (1991) *Gender and Later Life*. London: Sage.
Barrett, M. (1980) *Women's Oppression Today: Problems in Marxist Feminist Analysis*. London: Verso.
Barrett, M. and Phillips, A. (1992) *Destabilizing Theory*. Cambridge: Polity Press.
Beechey, V. (1977) "Some notes on female wage labour in capitalist production," *Capital and Class* 3: 45–66.
Beechey, V. and Whitelegg, L. (1986) *Women in Britain Today*. Milton Keynes: Open University Press.

Blackburn, R., Jarman, J. et al. (1993) "The analysis of occupational gender segregation over time and place: Considerations of measurement and some new evidence," *Work, Employment and Society* 7 (3): 335–62.

Bradley, H. (1989) *Men's Work, Women's Work.* Cambridge: Polity Press.

—— (1999) *Gender and Power in the Workplace.* London: Macmillan.

Bradley, H., Erickson, M., Stephenson, C. and Williams, S. (2000) *Myths at Work.* Cambridge: Polity Press.

Brooks, A. (1997) *Postfeminisms: Feminism, Cultural Theory and Cultural Forms.* London: Routledge.

Cavendish, R. (1982) *Women on the Line.* London: Routledge.

Clark, A. (1982, 1st edn 1919) *Working Lives of Women in the Seventeenth Century.* London: Routledge.

Crompton, R. (1997) *Women's Work in Modern Britain.* Oxford: Oxford University Press.

Crompton, R. and Sanderson, K. (1990) *Gendered Jobs and Social Change.* London: Unwin Hyman.

David, M. (1980) *The State, the Family and Education.* London: Routledge and Kegan Paul.

Dobash, R. and Dobash, R. (1979) *Violence against Wives.* New York: Free Press.

Doyal, L. (1985) "Women, health and the sexual division of labour," *Critical Social Policy* 7: 21–32.

Equal Opportunities Commission (2002) *Facts about Women and Men in Great Britain.* Manchester: EOC.

Firestone, S. (1979) *The Dialectic of Sex.* London: Women's Press.

Fraser, N. (1995) "From redistribution to recognition? Dilemmas of justice in a post-socialist age," *New Left Review* 212: 68–93.

Friedan, B. (1965) *The Feminine Mystique.* Harmondsworth: Penguin.

Fulcher, J. and Scott, J. (1999) *Sociology.* Oxford: Oxford University Press.

Giddens, A. (1997) *Sociology,* 3rd edn. Cambridge: Polity Press.

Graham, H. (1984) *Women, Health and the Family.* London: Harvester.

Gregson, N. and Lowe, M. (1994) *Servicing the Middle Classes.* London: Routledge.

Hakim, C. (1991) "Grateful slaves and self-made women: Fact and fantasy in women's work orientations," *European Sociological Review* 7 (2): 101–21.

Hanmer, J. (1983) *Violence against Women* (Unit 15 of U221). Milton Keynes: Open University Press.

Harding, S. (ed.) (1987) *Feminism and Methodology.* Milton Keynes: Open University Press.

Hartmann, H. (1981) "The unhappy marriage of Marxism and feminism: Towards a more progressive union," in Sargent, L. (ed.), *Women in Revolution: The Unhappy Marriage of Feminism and Marxism.* London: Pluto.

Hochschild, A. (1989) *The Second Shift.* New York: Viking.

—— (1997) *The Time Bind.* New York: Metropolitan Books.

Hunt, P. (1980) *Gender and Class Consciousness.* London: Macmillan.

Klein, V. (1965) *Britain's Married Women Workers*. London: Routledge and Kegan Paul.

Land, H. (1978) "Who cares for the family?", *Journal of Social Policy* 7 (3): 257–84.

Lewis, J. (1980) *The Politics of Motherhood*. London: Croom Helm.

Lovenduski, J. (1986) *Women and European Politics*. Brighton: Harvester.

Marshall, J. (1995) *Women Managers Moving On*. London: Routledge.

McDowell, L. (1997) *Capital Culture*. Oxford: Blackwell.

Millett, K. (1971) *Sexual Politics*. London: Sphere.

Mitchell, J. (1975) *Psychoanalysis and Feminism*. Harmondsworth: Penguin.

Oakley, A. (1974) *The Sociology of Housework*. London: Martin Robertson.

—— (1976) *Housewife*. Harmondsworth: Penguin.

—— (1980) *Women Confined*. Oxford: Martin Robertson.

—— (1981) *From Here to Maternity*. Harmondsworth: Penguin.

Pinchbeck, I. (1930, reprinted 1981) *Women Workers and the Industrial Revolution*. London: Virago.

Pollert, A. (1981) *Girls, Wives, Factory Lives*. London: Macmillan.

—— (1996) "Gender and class revisited; or the poverty of patriarchy," *Sociology* 30 (4): 639–59.

Randall, V. (1982) *Women and Politics*. London: Macmillan.

Rich, A. (1980) "Compulsory heterosexuality and lesbian existence," *Signs* 5 (4): 631–90.

Schreiner, O. (1911, reprinted 1978) *Women and Labour*. London: Virago.

Sharpe, S. (1976) *Just Like a Girl*. Harmondsworth: Penguin.

Spender, D. (1980) *Man-made Language*. London: Routledge.

—— (1989) *Invisible Women*. London: Women's Press.

Stanworth, M. (1981) *Gender and Schooling*. London: Hutchinson.

Steinberg, D., Elwood, J., Hey, V. and Maw, J. (1998) *Failing Boys*. Milton Keynes: Open University Press.

Sullivan, O. (1996) "Time co-ordination, the domestic division of labour and affective relations: Time use and the enjoyment of activities within couples," *Sociology* 30 (1): 79–100.

Sydie, R. (1987) *Natural Women, Cultured Men*. Milton Keynes: Open University Press.

Taylor, C. (1992) *Multiculturalism*. Princeton, NJ: Princeton University Press.

Turner, B. (2002) "Thinking right(s) sociologically," paper presented at the BSA Annual Conference, Leicester University, April.

Wajcman, J. (1998) *Managing Like a Man*. Cambridge: Polity Press.

Walby, S. (1986) *Patriarchy at Work*. Cambridge: Polity Press.

—— (1990) *Theorizing Patriarchy*. Oxford: Blackwell.

—— (1997) *Gender Transformations*. London: Routledge.

Westwood, S. (1984) *All Day, Every Day*. London: Pluto.

Wilson, E. (1977) *Women and the Welfare State*. London: Tavistock.

FURTHER READING

Bradley, H. (1996) *Fractured Identities*. Cambridge: Polity Press.

Delmont, S. (2001) *Changing Women, Unchanged Men?* Buckingham: Open University Press.

Pilcher, J. (1999) *Women in Contemporary Britain*. London: Routledge.

Walkerdine, V., Lucey, H., and Melody, J. (2001) *Growing Up Girl*. Basingstoke: Palgrave.

CHAPTER TWELVE

Gender and Work-Related Inequalities in Finland

PÄIVI KORVAJÄRVI

This chapter focuses on gender divisions in Finland. Moreover, it addresses gender inequalities in relation to paid employment. This might sound slightly narrow. However, work and employment are the areas of life that affect nearly every woman in Finland. In this sense, the perspective of gender inequalities in paid employment is rather far-reaching.

The analysis here emphasizes paid work, leaving out the attempt to reconcile work and family. Historically, womanhood was defined in the context of work rather than in the context of motherhood in Finland in the 1800s (Anttonen 2001). In addition, the women's movement strongly advocated women's right to paid work outside the home (Julkunen 1999). The housewife role, as a permanent life condition for women, hardly exists today. Nor has it ever been a dominant career solution for women in Finland. Most parents, mainly mothers, who have children under three years of age use the system of child care allowance that supports them to stay at home until the child is three years old without losing their jobs (Anttonen 2001). However, it has been stressed that women take care of the children at home only temporarily and the use of the allowance is related to the level of the unemployment rate among women (Salmi 2000). In today's Finland it is a self-evident fact that women do full-time work outside the home, partly because the country has a strong cultural orientation to work and partly because the public sector in which women usually work is large. In addition, living in a country where housing costs in particular are very high, both spouses have to earn a salary (Rantalaiho 1997).

Consequently, the majority of women in Finland belong to the active workforce. In 2001 over 65 percent of women aged 15 to 74 years old, and 70 percent of men of the same age, belonged to the workforce (Sta-

tistics Finland 2002). Women have made up nearly half of the workforce since the mid-1980s. In addition, the majority of employed women
work full-time. By international comparison part-time work is rather
scarce in Finland. Overall, part-time workers make up 12 percent of all
employees, whereas in the European Union part-time workers amount
to 17 percent of the workforce on average (ibid., Savola 2000: 18, 68–9).
Women more often work part-time than men; however, only 17 percent
of employed women do part-time work in Finland (Statistics Finland
2002). Younger women under 29 years old work part-time more often
than women in the older age groups. The reasons for this are not necessarily connected to the family situation. The main reasons for doing
part-time work are studies, or the fact that no other kind of jobs are
available (Savola 2000: 69). Furthermore, the general educational level
of employed women and men is high. In the 25–69 age group, women
are better educated than men (Lehto 1999a: 19).

The unionization rates of woman and men are exceptionally high in
Finland. In 1997 the proportion of unionized women was even larger
(83 percent) than that of unionized men (75 percent) (ibid.: 34). Today
the unionization rate of female-dominated bank clerks is over 90
percent. However, it is much lower among young employees; only half
of the employees under 25 years are unionized (Ylöstalo 2002: 183).
Company-based collective agreements are becoming common.
However, nationwide collective agreements guarantee that the wage differentials in the same occupations and jobs in the different regions of
the country are very rare.

The dominance of work-related issues concerning inequalities
between women and men has been clear. Thus, in the public debate,
the issues of gender (in)equalities concern women's situation in
employment. The aim of the Act on Equality Between Women and Men
(2002) is "to prevent discrimination on the basis of sex and to promote
equality between women and men." According to the Act, it is possible
to achieve this aim by improving the status of women, "particularly in
working life."

Despite this, there are still enduring workplace inequalities between
women and men that need to be explained. There is a clear wage gap
between women and men in favor of men. Women's average earnings
amount to 80 percent of men's average earnings. Educational level or
the length of the work history do not explain the wage differential
(Lehto 1999b). The aim of reducing and removing the gender wage
gap is recognized in the political agenda and in the mass media.
However, hardly anything seriously has been done to solve the problem.
The Act on Equality, because of its weak sanctions, does not work well

in this situation. In addition, occupational segregation and the gendered hierarchical segregation of positions in organizations are clear, although at the same time mobile (Kolehmainen 1999). Moreover, more women are unemployed than men (Statistics Finland 2002). A rather new phenomenon is that the number of fixed-term job contracts has increased. Interestingly, fixed-term job contracts are most common among highly educated women (Sutela 1999). The gender inequalities concerned have mainly been facts that can be shown statistically, although the ways of interpreting wage statistics, for example, are not unambiguous. This is why it is necessary to explore everyday gendering practices through qualitative research.

Thus, Finland provides an interesting case of gender inequalities in paid work because of the contradictory features of the situation of women in this country. The chapter begins with an overview of the research that has been done on gender inequalities in work-related contexts. Qualitative research has revealed the form of everyday activities and practices that are often ignored. In particular, qualitative data and qualitative methods of analysis have demonstrated the cultural and non-textualized practices that may result in inequalities and discrimination. After the overview, the qualitative methods of analysis are examined. Typically, the starting point has been the research questions, not a particular qualitative method of analysis as such. In addition, the research relationships have been a crucial point in many studies. Then, an investigation on women and men in two call centers is presented as an example of gender inequalities in a technology-based setting. It draws on a cultural perspective focusing on practices and models of thought used at work by different actors. Technology appears to represent both a bright future for all employees and a division of expertise along gender lines. Finally, an attempt to identify new areas of research on gender inequalities is suggested from the perspective of a rather homogenous society, such as Finland.

STUDIES ON GENDER INEQUALITIES IN WORK

Raija Julkunen (1984) provides an excellent overview of research on relationships between women and men in paid work in Finland. She analyzed how women and women's work were included in the Finnish sociology of work in the period from the Second World War until the early 1980s. Julkunen found that it was only female researchers who had been sensitive to women and inequalities between women and men at work. Researchers in the field of paid work and employment were mostly men who were interested in male (manufacturing) work. There was no place for women in the research. Thus workers in the textile or shoe factories, mostly female workers, were ignored. In some studies, women were a part of the research subject but subsequently excluded from the data because the "research setting had become complicated."

Julkunen (ibid.) summarizes women's position within the sociology of work from 1945 to 1983 as follows: (1) the focus of the research field was on men and it was called general sociology of work; (2) there was no research that would have conceptualized male wage earners from the viewpoint of gender; (3) gender could be either a background variable in the tables or there was no information according to gender available in research reports; (4) quantitative research had produced information on women's lower positions and gendered divisions of labor; (5) there was some research on women as a particular work force with particular problems, such as day-care arrangements; and (6) there were some signs of women's studies that took into account women's life totality, women's socialization, and women's qualifications. In short, until the beginning of the 1980s, women's position or gender relations in work were hardly examined using qualitative methods. Julkunen had to stop her analysis on the threshold of new emerging ideas of women's own cultures at work which inspired female researchers to use qualitative methods in studying gender inequalities in paid work.

It is fair to say, however, that a paradigm shift took place in the sociology of work with regard to gender during the 1980s and at the beginning of the 1990s. Female researchers from different disciplines doing research on work launched a network "Women and work," which was financed by state sources (the Academy of Finland). The relationships between "women" and "work" were considered to be ambiguous in two respects. They concerned the relationships between social structures and human agency.

On the one hand, at that time, it was thought that a job or an occupation included social structures that determined a "woman's" place in employment and in work organizations. Consequently, society, work, and employment were seen as given and women were studied as targets of social and structural impacts. In this view, women were found to be a homogenous social category in society. On the other hand, however, researchers stressed the ways in which women and women's activities shaped and changed social life and work. In this view, the aim was to shift the focus onto women as active subjects of their own lives in the context of work. Consequently, the idea was to study women's reality as multifaceted processes (Rantalaiho 1984: 199–201).

One way to examine the variety was to analyze gender contracts of working women. These contracts among female lawyers included the work contract, the care contract and the professional contract, which all were differently weighted and combined in a variety of ways in different phases of life. (Silius 1992). In practice, the paradigm shift from structural conditions to women's own activities and women's ways of acting at work concerned the relationships between female clerical workers and technological change (Korvajärvi 1990; Rantalaiho 1990). More and more female researchers became interested in women's experiences and goals in work and the tensions between work and family, from the viewpoint of both individual life histories and reconciliation of the two spheres in different phases of life (Strandell 1984). This also meant that women's activities and the relationships between women and men were not only conceived of as issues of (in)equalities in terms of social divisions, but also in terms of social practices and social processes. Even in research on women workers in the clothing industry (Lavikka 1997), the context of analysis was women's experiences and women's cultural codes in coping with organizational change.

Marja-Liisa Honkasalo (1984) studied forms of resistance that women workers used in the everyday factory work. The focus of the study was on mechanisms of power in female-dominated assembly plants. The aim was to reveal sophisticated micro-processes of power and resistance. The study was based on participant observation and the researcher took a job as an ordinary worker for five months in a factory. Everybody knew that she was a researcher. She discovered complex technological, social, and cultural ways in which the women workers' activities were controlled. It appeared that even the union representatives and the health care personnel reproduced women's subordination. However, Honkasalo found that women workers' resistance followed very different, and surprising, lines. This resistance did not directly affect the ways in which the women were controlled. When talking about control or controlling men, women laughed at, parodied and joked about the dominance of men. Women also used fantasies as a tool of their resistance. Furthermore, the researcher states that they also used even their bodily symptoms (e.g. headaches) as a form of resistance, i.e., chatting about bodily symptoms at work made the women's social community strong and united. Thus the female workers responded to the subordination. However, at the same time, the trade union activists did not take the female workers' resistance seriously. Honkasalo concluded that this kind of resistance would have been ignored in the working-class movement (e.g. trade union activities). Instead, active participation in the movement would have bound them tighter to the organizations that functioned without considering female workers' conditions and problems.

In the early 1990s, a number of feminist researchers launched a research project "Gendered practices in working life" (Heiskanen et al. 1990; Kinnunen and Korvajärvi 1996; Rantalaiho and Heiskanen 1997). The basic idea of the project lay in the tensions and contradictions of women's position in employment in Finland. On the one hand, at the time women were in a good position in comparison with many other countries: women worked full-time; women were better educated than men; women were more highly unionized than men; child care arrangements, including school meals, were provided by the welfare state; women's unemployment rate was lower than that of men; and women's place in employment was culturally accepted. On the other hand, however, the wage gap between women and men was clear; the hierarchical gendered segregation in organizations and the horizontal occupational segregation appeared to be permanent (Heiskanen et al. 1990). As described in the Introduction, the current picture is not dramatically different from that of the 1990s.

The project consisted of a number of studies and thus did not engage in one unambiguous theory only. Rather, different sources were used to illuminate the following key questions: What kind of gendered structures and practices frame the activities of women and men at work? How do structures and practices produce different positions for women and men? What kinds of silent contracts operate in the background? And in what ways do women and men contribute to the maintenance and change of those practices? (Heiskanen et al. 1990: 9–10). The core of the project lay in the problem of the relationships between social structures and people's everyday activities from the gender point of view. Therefore, the theoretical ideas were derived from both Anthony Giddens (1979) and Dorothy Smith (1987). All the background results and knowledge that shaped the joint effort were based on analyses which were extensively built on statistics or quantitative surveys. Moreover, the idea was to go beyond variables and numbers to the concrete everyday lives of women and men. The aim was to carefully look for and examine gendered practices embedded in the activities of people and in the structural and physical conditions of work organizations.

Joan Acker's (1990, 1992, 1997) conceptualization on gendered processes in organizations provided a fruitful starting point for studying gendered practices. She also participated in a one-week research seminar arranged by the project. According to Acker, gendered processes are a multifaceted angle on social systems. Therefore, social systems should be studied through daily practices, through the ordinary things that people do as they go about their daily activities. Acker (1992) distinguishes between the four sets of gendered processes in organizations: (1) the production of gender divisions; (2) the creation of symbols, images and forms of consciousness which explain, justify and oppose gender divisions; (3) interaction between women and men; and (4) internal mental work which means conscious construction of one's gender and sexuality and in which individuals at the same time reproduce the gendered structures and adapt themselves to the implicit and explicit gender demands of organizations.

Acker's conceptualization includes a broad range of opportunities for examining gendered processes not only in the actualities of the everyday work, but also in the institutional documents which frame people's activities at work, such as official occupational classifications or documents including collective agreements. Accordingly, although not strictly following Acker, the project "Gendered practices in working life" empirically covered different topics: statistical classifications, collective agreements, changing work organizations, reconciling work and family, information technology at work, sexual harassment, and experiments in changing gendered segregation. Some examples of the results within the approach are presented next.

The analysis on how gender is embedded in the statistical occupational classifications used by Statistics Finland showed that the ways in which terms such as "productive labor force," "occupations," "households" as well as "social and economic positions" are defined statistically are part of the legitimation of women's and men's wage differentials in society. Down the centuries, the model of males as breadwinners has been embedded in statistical classifications, and the descriptions of occupations have created a hierarchy between male technical and manufacturing occupations and female people-centered welfare occupations (Kinnunen 2001). The case of collective agreements is important in the Finnish context because the wages, working time arrangements and other working conditions are regulated through the collective agreements. They are negotiated and agreed on the national level between the labor market partners. Thus there are only small wage differentials between the same jobs in the different regions of the country. However, the concrete practices of interpreting the work requirements in the agreement texts can produce wage differentials between women and men. For example, the agreement text concerning salespeople in retail trade stated that entry "into the better paid category requires special knowledge of the products on sale and the ability to guide and instruct the customer on their principles of operation." This statement was interpreted in the negotiations between the partners in such a way that the selling of various machines and equipment required of salespeople an ability to understand how these operate, but the selling of household appliances, groceries, fabrics or clothes did not. The former products usually came under the sphere of influence of male salespeople, whereas the non-operating products mostly came under the sphere of influence of of female salespeople. The example shows that a document without explicit gender expressions includes statements that result in wage differentials between women and men in retail (Martikainen 1997).

The study on gendering practices in changing work organizations showed that in clerical work organizations from 1986 to 1996 the ways in which clerical employees, mostly female, conceived of gender issues shifted towards informality and individualization (Korvajärvi 1998a). This means that gender issues in everyday work became obscured and they were mainly linked with individuals and individual bodies and intentions rather than groups or social categories of people. Thus, the move towards individualization of gender matters in paid work reflects the arguments that have been made in the broader contexts on institutional individualization (Beck and Beck-Gernsheim (2002: xxi–xxii). In addition, the result of the obscuring and individualizing of gender is a paradox, because it was precisely then that the inequalities between women and men were formalized through the enactment of the Act on Equality in 1987 and its renewal later. The topics concerning gender in clerical work organizations were related to the distance of gender, the distinction between the spheres of life, sexuality, and skills. Both women and men in different positions recognized that in society at large inequalities between women and men prevailed. However, they seldom discussed injustice or sexual harassment in their own workplace. Men in leading positions tended to see women as mothers and wives, whereas women stressed their role as wage earners. Sexuality was almost a non-existent topic in the work organizations, whereas skills and qualifications seemed to become more crucial when gender was defined in terms of appreciation at work. The change from service to marketing meant that the proper knowledge of how equipment works, for example, was not enough for an employee. Instead, expressive and bodily performances in order to convince the customer became crucial. The market-oriented performances tended to favor men in recruitment (Korvajärvi 1998a, 1998b).

One of the research areas among Finnish female researchers has been the academic sphere. Liisa Husu (2001: 325–6) has shown the discriminatory aspects in the academic community. Female interviewees seldom reported overt and harsh discrimination in academia. However, informal practices that remained hidden and unspoken had a discriminatory impact on women's career development and support, allocation of resources, and formal and informal divisions of labor. The picture remained rather stable from the early 1980s until the end of 1990s. At that time, sexual harassment appeared to become more serious than earlier. It is worth noting that the women interviewed did not find reconciling work and family as such to be a reason for discrimination in academia. In her participatory action research in her own academic community, Susan Meriläinen (2001) showed the existence of deep and unconscious models of thought that result in women's discrimination, although she herself avoids the term discrimination in her study.

To sum up, what seems to be permanent along gender lines is the division of researchers into female researchers who study women's work and male researchers who study men's work, with only very few exceptions. After the Second World War, until the early 1980s, women in paid work were mostly ignored and considered in a limited way. At its best, the category "woman" was used systematically as a background variable. In the mid-1980s different ideas began to emerge, and women's paid work received serious attention in the field of research in which a crucial paradigm shift occurred at the same time. First, the focus of research shifted from structural conditions to women's own activities and experiences at work. Second, the emphasis of research activities changed to reconsidering the dichotomy between social structures and human agency at work from the gender perspective. Consequently, the focus of research on women in paid work moved on to the gendered processes and gendering practices in work. Thus, it was more about how gender is done (West and Zimmerman 1987) and how gender is produced in the everyday activities of women and men in paid work and in its organizations.

QUALITATIVE APPROACHES TO INEQUALITIES IN WORK

The starting point in doing qualitative research on gendered practices has been to collect qualitative material. Personal interviews of individual employees have been the most popular way of gathering qualitative material on gender-related matters at work. Usually interviews have been semi-structured in regard to the topics of an interview, and usually one person has been interviewed only once. Interviews are also used as well as statistical and other quantitative research material in several studies to illustrate and to make the person behind the numbers more concrete (e.g. Kovalainen 1995). In addition, mostly non-participant observation, documents and texts, written accounts, and the emotions of the researcher herself have been used as research material. Thus, the idea behind fieldwork has been for researchers to familiarize themselves with the everyday life of their research subjects from different angles.

However, understanding qualitative research only as gathering rich data is too narrow a stance. Qualitative research is not "qualitative" without qualitative methods of analysis (Gubrium and Holstein 1997: 114–22; Denzin and Lincoln 2000). In my view, the interpretation practices of the researcher lie at the core of the analytical methods. Thus researchers are always an integral part of qualitative data, its analysis, and consequently, its results. Indeed, it seems to be typical of qualitative studies on gender and work to produce a sophisticated analysis of the research process in relation to the gathering of the research material. There are rich ethnographic descriptions concerning access to the organizations (Eräsaari 1995) and detailed narratives on the ways of data gathering in the different phases of the research (Korvajärvi 1998a; Husu 2001). The interaction between the researcher and those researched during the study process has been analyzed in several studies. The researchers have been sensitive to whether and in what sense the research relationships were equal or hierarchical, and whether the researcher felt the atmosphere of the interviews to be confidential. In addition, relationships between the language and reality and experiences have been evaluated. Moreover, the role of the audience in the interpretation process has been taken into account (Silius 1992, 122–8). In short, a detailed description of the research process has been part of the research text. However, two issues have not been reflected upon. First, it has often been ignored how integral the research relationships as such are to the research material and to its quality. Second, and consequently, studies have usually not been able to answer the question how the research relationships participate in shaping the research results. Thus, the rich reflection of the research processes has remained separate in relation to the substantive results, both in terms of conceptual and empirical generalizations.

In the area of gender and work, scholars have avoided strong engagements in the established ways of analyzing qualitative data, such as discourse analysis and conversation analysis which have gained a strong footing in the social sciences in Finland. Perhaps this is why qualitative studies on gender and work do not have an image of qualitative research as such, or an image of cultural research, which is also currently a strong approach in sociology in Finland (Allardt 2001). Instead, the studies on gender and work are known for their substantial topics.

Juxtaposion of results produced on gender inequalities within the same study both through quantitative and qualitative analyses has hardly occurred.

The starting point in the analysis of research data has been the research questions, not the method of analysis. Finding answers has meant endless efforts and crafts(wo)manship: reading the material of different research questions, first, forming broader categories and then concentrating on certain topics in the material (Husu 2001). It is a process of sifting through relevant material with regard to the research questions. In this type of context, qualitative material, usually interviews, is used as factual information. It is also used to illustrate and to enliven theoretically informed topics and research questions. The empirical material then confirms, opposes, and brings fresh insights into the theoretical configurations of the study (Silius 1992). In some studies, one label for the methods could be deconstruction; in a loose sense, this means that the subtexts between the lines and silences of the transcribed interview texts are taken seriously (Lavikka 1997; Korvajärvi 1998a).

The research questions and theoretical interests have directed researchers on what to look for. However, cultural analyses are not primarily about facts but also concern interpretations in relation to the conceptual configurations of the study. Thus also what is mentioned and what is silent in the interviews or in the documents provide fruitful information. An example of this type of research is the above-mentioned study on the documents of the collective agreements. The written documents did not mention "women" or "men" but the consequences of the definition of the "principles of operation" clearly meant different wages for women and men (Martikainen 1997). The other example is the study on the formation of the occupational classifications in the official statistics. More specifically, the focus is on the written arguments that concern the ways in which women and men are placed in the different classifications of occupations. The analysis revealed that the ways in which women and men were culturally both separated in the texts and connected to each other produced a hierarchical difference between women and men (Kinnunen 2001). This method has also called for crafts(wo)manship and effort in relating the research material to the relevant conceptual work. It also includes the idea that interpretations are contextual in terms of the place and time of the study and the research process, including the production of the research material. Drawing on reflexive interpretations means that the research process necessarily involves contingency and unexpected phases.

In a study (Kurvinen 1999) that focused on the changes and new solutions in the lives of those women who lost their jobs in banking, the same women were interviewed several times during the rationalization process of their bank. The central concept of the study was identity. The basic idea of the study was that, simultaneously with the changes in the bank, the women were working on changes in their identities. Kurvinen used several methods in the study: discourse analysis, narrative approaches, conversation analysis, and language analysis. However, she did not use one or two methods of analysis strictly, but created her own method. This included the analysis of the research relationships in different phases of the research process. The interaction episodes in the face-to-face interviews were analyzed. In addition, when reading and re-reading the interviews later, the researcher analyzed her cognitive interaction with the written interviews aiming to clarify for the reader her process of analysis and interpretation. During the research process, it appeared that the interviews did not necessarily contain coherent stories about how the women coped with the situation. Instead, these stories were fragmented and precarious. The stories were fragmented in different ways and all the stories had a continuity of their own, even though the starting point, losing their job in the bank, was the same in a rather homogenous region. Again, it is worth noting that in the case of bank clerks and their job loss, no interpretations could be done, perhaps because there was no material concerning what the process meant in terms of social inequality or class position. Rather, the results concern individual explanations, which were framed by different, even unequal life conditions, but which were not linked to the social divisions in society. Consequently, the job in the bank had meant something different for different bank clerks. For some, the job represented a success story, some had only drifted into the bank and, for some, it meant deep exhaustion. Accordingly, the change and losing their job had different meanings for the women. Thus, the women worked on their identities during the rationalization process following their individual work orientations.

In another study (Meriläinen 2001) that was targeted on changing gendered practices in the same academic community where the author herself was based, personal experiences, discussions in formal and informal situations, documents, interviews, and organized activities for the community were used as research material. Discourse analysis, (de)constructing stories and participatory action were used as methodical tools for analysis. The results showed that organizations are arenas in which sexual violence is produced and practiced both in reality and in the imagination. This is a rather exceptional result because extensive research on white-collar workplaces, for example, show that sexuality hardly exists in the everyday workplace according to interviews or observations (Korvajärvi 1998a). The results on gendered practices in the academic community demonstrate that gendering practices that resulted in women's devaluation were not necessarily based on conscious discrimination. Rather, they were based on a strong faith in the neutrality and objectivity of academic processes, in the neutrality of people's ways of thinking and in the equal opportunities that resulted in women's devaluation in many respects. What was crucial in producing the research results were the emotions of the researcher. The study began from an emotional involvement with the academic community. During the study it appeared that emotions gave important information. Moreover, in the process of achieving change, the emotions of the researchers and other participants were a powerful resource (Meriläinen 2001).

In addition to qualitative studies, Lehto (2002) and Järnefelt (2002) have made an interesting comparison between qualitative and quantitative methods in studying working conditions. More specifically, they investigated how the integration of qualitative and quantitative data could facilitate understanding everyday life at work. Their focus is on time pressure and gender equality at work. After conducting a structured survey, Järnefelt interviewed employees who, according to the survey, were greatly affected by time pressure at work. Women in particular suffered from workload pressures more often than men. Interviews started with general questions concerning time pressure at work. In addition to this, the employees were asked to think aloud why they had chosen to answer the survey the way they had done. The researchers conclude that through interviews they discovered experiences and impressions that were not available on the basis of the survey (Lehto 2002). For example, the difference between the concrete practices of women and men with regard to time pressure at work became clear. Time pressure among women was connected to the lack of personnel, whereas time pressure among men was mostly connected to the increasing demands of effectiveness and competition (Järnefelt 2002).

Gender equality at work was studied in a slightly different way. The employees interviewed were women and a couple of men who had reported in the survey on gender discrimination at work personally or in general. The interview consisted of certain themes that related to the survey questions. The interviewed employees linked gender equality at work with the pay, equal chances to develop oneself, appreciation and promotion opportunities. Gender and the appreciation of skills and qualifications were connected with challenging tasks, career promotion and pay, which formed a vicious circle. Consequently, the reasons for gender discrimination at work were difficult to explain. It is worth mentioning that, according to this study, as also in the study on women in the academic community, the employees interviewed seldom mentioned reconciling work and family as an element of gender equality. The employees tended to defend the equality of their own workplace. In addition, there was a tendency not to perceive the work situation from the perspective of gender discrimination and gender inequality (Pulkkinen 2001).

Qualitative research on gender in Finland has focused on the micro-processes present in everyday working life and on the cultural contents of the lines of argumentation in different textual documents. The studies have revealed subtexts that produce the wage gap, for example, between women and men. Moreover, they have opened perspectives on the cultural models of thinking, practices, and emotions that maintain and produce hierarchical differences between women and men at work. In addition, the use of qualitative methods in studies where quantitative methods has dominated have revealed micro-processes which result in women's and men's different situation in work organizations with regard to time pressure and gender discrimination at work. The results of qualitative research on gender and work provide a sophisticated picture on the continual formation of gender inequalities.

TECHNOLOGY AS A DIVIDING EDGE

Finland is said to be among the leading countries in the information society development measured by the number of Internet connections, wireless connections, and users of the Internet (Blom et al. 2002). In addition, it has been stated that Finnish society has managed, in a positive way, to combine the welfare state and technological innovations without reducing the power of the competitive market economy (Castells and Himanen 2001). However, there are also opposing accounts. Income differentials, as a whole in society, have started to increase remarkably (Uusitalo 1999). Moreover, it has been shown that (Blom et al. 2001) there is a risk among knowledge workers, who already constitute about 40 percent of the labor force, that inequalities among them will increase. Even though women and men are equally represented in numbers in knowledge work, the wage gap and the unequal distribution of power resources have put women in a disadvantageous position in knowledge work. Indeed, one conclusion of the study by Blom et al. (2001) is that it is crucial to examine the social and cultural practices and meanings on which the use and applications of technology are work based. Technology continuously sets new demands for employees and there is a risk that those who are not skilled in information and communication technology will drop out of the labor market (ibid.).

Customer service has been women's work in Finland. One rather recent aspect of the change in service work is the growing number of call centers, where customer service is done totally via the connections that information and communication technology offers. Studies of call centers have produced a growing body of research results demonstrating the strictly controlled position of women at work. Only a few studies have discussed the positive side of call center work (Frenkel et al. 1999). Having undertaken interviews and observations in four different call centers in Finland, I concentrate here on the relationships of technology and customer service representatives in two call centers by asking whether and how information and communication technology and the ways of using it work for or against inequalities between women and men at work. One of the call centers was an in-house call center within an insurance company, and another a firm to which other firms outsourced their services. In the call centers, the majority of customer service representatives were women who had permanent job contracts, who worked full-time as usual in Finland, and who were unionized. More broadly, the study linked with a larger project on the mobile boundaries of work in the information society. The aim was to examine how and in what sense it is possible for workers to be active agents in the workplaces of the information society. As mentioned above, hardly any studies on call center work have reported that customer service representatives had any opportunity to be active agents at work.

In all the call centers, the job content first appeared to be similar to me, as an outsider. Customer service representatives mainly took inbound calls, and seldom made outbound calls in order to sell something or to do an overview of the "needs" of potential customers. Customer service representatives mainly worked in an open-plan office; managers' offices were separated from the open-plan office by glass walls. Customer service representatives usually formed groups in the office; between three to six desks were placed in a circle divided by partitions. Every customer service representative had a screen and a keyboard on their desks; ergonomically, the settings gave an impression of a comfortable work situation. Everyone wore, as parts of their bodies, headphones which were plugged into the computer. Even when customer service representatives disconnected themselves from the computer, they wore their headphones when walking around in the offices.

Thus the physical aspects of the call center gave out the message of a clean and elegant technology which simultaneously represented bodily dependency for customer service representatives. Here I understand the ways of using technology at work in a broad sense. I consider technology not only as material equipment, but also as a symbolic device that contributes to the job content and to the image of the company. The call centers differed from each other with regard to what kind of significance technology and its applications had in the organization.

In the call center within the insurance company, information and communication technology intertwined with a change in the job content of customer service representatives who had the qualifications of insurance clerks. Insurance clerks were mostly middle-aged women and they were also officially entitled customer service representatives in the call center. In this call center, I conducted ethnographic fieldwork, consisting of observations, interviews, discussions and collecting any kind of available material, at three different times: in 1986, 1989 and 1996. During this ten-year period, the most striking changes took place in technology, in working space and in work content. In the mid- and the late 1980s, customer service representatives had computers and telephones that functioned separately. In 1996, the telephone and computer technologies were integrated into a joint system that recorded all the activities of customer service representatives. In 1996, the call center was located in an open-plan office with brand new furniture, indoor plants, pictures on the walls and a comfortable lounge, whereas during the earlier fieldwork rounds customer service representatives had common offices that they shared with several colleagues.

The content of work had clearly changed. In short, a shift from service to selling took place. To put it simply: earlier, customer service representatives answered customer inquiries, whereas later they had to take the leading role in the interaction in order to sell new insurance policies to the customer (even in situations when the customer was angry and complained about the insurance company). The job content had changed from customer-oriented service to company-oriented selling. The skills required of customer service representatives also changed. Previously, the customer service representatives spoke about the insurance policies with customers. Now, they had to "sell themselves to the customers" as a supervisor said. They had to create a personal and emotional relationship with the customer who then found it difficult to say "no" to the insurance policy as it also meant saying "no" to the friendly and convincing person at the end of the phone.

Interestingly, the gender composition in the call center changed. Until the end of the 1980s, there was only one man working in the call center (or in telephone support and sales, which was the proper name of the unit at that time). However, after information-and-communication-supported selling had been firmly introduced, men also entered the scene by being recruited to the call center. The supervisor in the unit was a woman. However, when the unit started to operate as an independent profit center, a man was nominated the head of the unit. Thus, extensive selling together with even more intensive use of information and communication technology brought men into the arena that earlier had belonged to women. The female supervisor in her recruitment practices stressed that she was looking for someone with the "soul of a salesperson," not specifically a woman or a man. The end result, however, meant men moving in and recruiting into a women's sphere of work. This is very exceptional. The general trend in Finland is that women have culturally more space to move within the segregated labor market. They move more often into men's occupational arenas than men move into women's occupational arenas (Kolehmainen 1999). Nobody explicitly said in the interviews that information and communication technology and the shift in the job content had transformed the job into a more attractive or more suitable job for men. Nor was the shift a sign of increasing inequality between women and men in the call center. However, as has been shown (Leidner 1993: 202–3), success in selling insurance policies that includes competition between the customer service representatives and the "battle of wills implicit in their interactions with customers," can be activities which let people interpret that the jobs are suitable to men. At the same time, this contains an implicit change in how customer service skills are appreciated along gender lines.

In the independent call center, women were also users of technology and men were experts in it. The middle-aged women usually had a commercial college education and their job title was "telephone operator." In this call center, I conducted ethnographic fieldwork consisting of observation, discussions, giving feedback on the fieldwork results and mainly of individual interviews between the spring 1998 and the summer 2001. During that time the call center company greatly expanded its activities both in terms of the number of workers and suppliers. However, in terms of profit, the company was not successful. Similar to the call center of the insurance company, the employees moved from small and crowded offices to an elegant open-plan office, the furniture, the colors and the ergonomics of which were designed by an architect. The jobs which entailed developing technology or providing support in technological matters either within the firm or for the customers were occupied by men. The personnel manager said, "Candidates are mainly women. However, last time all the guys who applied were recruited [a job in the IT HelpDesk]." The division between those who appeared as experts and those who appeared as users of information and communication technology followed gender lines. Expert tasks were appreciated by everyone but occupied by men. Expertise also meant that men were in the decision-making positions and women got supervisory or middle managerial positions. Women's tasks in those positions were to organize other people in everyday work, whereas men's tasks in leading positions were to make final decisions concerning the budget, technology, and co-operation with suppliers.

In addition, information and communication technology had important symbolic meanings. According to the interviews, this advanced technology served both women and men by providing a bright vision for the future. Information and communication technology was present as a subtext in all activities in the company. Call centers were a "hot topic" and "trendy workplaces." Information and communication technology created an optimistic atmosphere in the company, and the idea was that information and communication technology would make the constant growth of the company possible. Both female and male employees felt that they were part of something new at the top due to the advanced information and communication technology. On the one hand, technology was something to be admired. On the other, technology gave them a chance to keep their future in their own hands. Thus this technology-driven workplace provided them with an opportunity to control their own lives in terms of earning the necessary living.

This example does not mean that women are excluded as users of technology. The call center cases show that women master the use of the technology in their jobs, although it is not a skill that is appreciated in work organizations, as also reported in Britain (Callaghan and Thompson 2002). Using technology is, according to both women in lower positions and men in higher positions, as natural as the skill of reading and writing. In the advanced information society that Finland is said to be, the abilities to use technology appear to be self-evident, and only the development of technology or selling or supporting technology-related products or services makes a person an expert, who nearly without exception, are men. At the same time, women and men unambiguously supported their work situation. What was also interesting was the silence concerning control of work. The interviewees did not perceive the control that was available through the computer systems as a repressive power, and again the same result is reported in Britain (ibid.). However, the fact was that control was applied to customer service representatives. This meant that women more than men were the subjects of the control.

The case studies show that technology is multifaceted from the viewpoint of gender inequalities. In the first case study organization, the advanced use of technology was connected to the changing ways of interaction with customers. Technology-supported selling tended to get a male label in the call center. In the second case study call center, the division of employees into male experts and female users excluded women from decision-making processes and, consequently, prevented them from reaching higher positions, higher wages and higher status. In this sense, technology became "male." Despite the fact that the women had access to a new sphere of work, the processes of gender segregation continued to exist. At the same time, paradoxically, women felt that technology, either as concrete equipment or as a symbolic vision, had not been disadvantageous toward them. Quite the contrary, technology seemed to empower them by providing them with a bright future and enabling them to have a chance to earn their living. In spite of all this, the technology differentiated between women's and men's activities in the call centers. In short, the use of technology linked with the assumed male expertise in particular contributed to the maintaining of wage differentials and the hierarchical positions between women and men.

In Search of New Perspectives

There are a couple of obvious silences and gaps in the above descriptions. Studies on gender inequalities in work, the ways of using qualitative material and analysis and the description of the role of technology for customer service representatives in call centers did not include a single hint of sexuality or body at work. Indeed, it has been suggested that workplaces in Finland seem to lack sexual meanings, if we trust the interviews or observations conducted at workplaces. Clerical workers, for example, said that sexual harassment did not exist in their own workplace. However, nearly in the same breath, the same clerical workers said that they knew somebody at another workplace who had told them about harsh and overt sexual harassment occurring there. Thus the uncomfortable aspects of sexuality were located somewhere at a distance, not close at hand (Korvajärvi 1998a).

Nor have ethnicity nor race found an explicit space in studies that can be categorized as qualitative research. The race and ethnicity aspects were totally absent on the discursive level of the workplaces. It is clear in the sense that there were only white people at the workplaces. In fact, one characteristic of employment in Finland is that the labor force is very homogenous in terms of race, ethnicity, and nationality. Migrants and immigrants form a small minority group in the whole population and they are visible solely only in the capital. In addition, the unemployment rate of people of foreign nationalities is considerably higher than that of the citizens of Finland. However, in spite of this, I think that researchers should also study "whiteness" in terms of race or ethnicity in the societal conditions where an explicit everyday comparison is not possible. It makes sense to ask what kind of symbolic resource the white skin represents to us in the European context, for example, in which race differences are much more visible than they are in Finland. Furthermore, class inequalities among women is a topic which needs to be incorporated into the research agenda so that the heterogeneity of women's work experiences are better understood.

Qualitative research on gender in work in Finland shows that everyday practices contribute to the formation and maintenance of unequal divisions between women and men. These practices are not necessarily consciously shaped discrimination. Rather, they are taken for granted and remain implicit. It has been suggested that discursive practices have become crucial in shaping work organizations (Julkunen 2001). Accordingly, occupation, class or gender do not provide sources for the self and solidarity. Instead, new elements for shared organizational cultures are emerging (Casey 1995). An example of that kind of element is the increasing importance of information and communication technology. However, new elements include divisions that result in inequalities between women and men at work. These unequal divisions are embedded in the models of thought or in the lines of argumentation that can be revealed only in reflective qualitative research. As Meriläinen (2001: 49) has brilliantly put it: "What counts as 'equality' or 'discrimination' does not lie within the activity of phenomenon itself but within the social relations and interpretive processes that sustain it."

Qualitative research is based on the accounts, stories, and episodes which the interviewees explicitly produce or which the researcher explicitly observes. It has been my experience that clerical workers, for example, are not eager to talk about inequalities between women and men, except in society at large. Instead, the interviewees tend to keep silent on the inequalities at the workplace level, even though these inequalities appear as self-evident to the researcher. It is not that the employees do not recognize the inequalities. The point is that the employees like to maintain harmony in their closest social environment. Furthermore, there are also other silences that the employees hardly mention in Finland. These silences revolve around sexuality and the body, or the symbols of sexuality and the body. It has to be asked, for example, how sexuality and bodies are embedded in the expertise and visionary aspects of information and communication technology. This task, among other tasks, needs qualitative research material. In order to overcome the limitations of the explicit information in the interviews and observations, carefully planned settings of participatory action research would be useful when aiming to break the obvious silences in the practices of producing inequalities between women and men at work. This qualitative work needs to be combined with theoretical work and, in keeping with this volume, I would argue, with comparative work in different research settings.

ACKNOWLEDGMENTS

I am grateful to Bente Rasmussen and to the editors of the book for their constructive suggestions on this chapter. I am grateful to the projects 37201 and 49213 of the Academy of Finland for supporting the writing of the chapter. My warm thanks go to Marjukka Virkajärvi as well as to Fiona Devine for improving my English.

REFERENCES

Acker, J. (1990) "Hierarchies, jobs, bodies: A theory of gendered organization," *Gender and Society* 4: 139–58.
—— (1992) "Gendering organizational theory," in Mills, A. J. and Tancred, P. (eds.), *Gendering Organizational Analysis*. Newbury Park, CA: Sage.
—— (1997) "Foreword," in Rantalaiho, L. and Heiskanen, T. (eds.), *Gendered Practices in Working Life*. London and New York: Macmillan.
Act on Equality between Women and Men (2002) http://www.tasa-arvo.fi/www-eng/legislation/legis2.html (accessed 19 July).
Allardt, E. (2001) "Perspektiv och perspektivförskjutningar inom Nordisk sociologi" [Perspective and perspective movements in Nordic sociology], *Sosiologia* 38: 4–13.
Anttonen, A. (2001) "The female working citizen: Social rights, work and motherhood in Finland," *Kvinder, Køn and Forskning* 2: 33–44.
Beck, U. and Beck-Gernsheim, E. (2002) *Individualization*. London: Sage.
Blom, R., Melin, H. and Pyöriä, P. (2001) *Tietotyö ja työelämän muutos* [Knowledge Work and Transformations in Work]. Helsinki: Gaudeamus.
—— (2002) "Social contradictions in informational capitalism: the case of Finnish wage earners and their labor market situation," *The Information Society* 18: 333–43.

Callaghan, G. and Thompson, P. (2002) "'We recruit attitude': The selection and shaping of routine call centre labour," *Journal of Management Studies* 39: 233–54.

Casey, C. (1995) *Work, Self and Society after Industrialism.* London and New York: Routledge.

Castells, M. and Himanen, P. (2001) *Suomen tietoyhteiskuntamalli* [The Finnish Model of Information Society]. Helsinki: WSOY and Sitra.

Denzin, N. K. and Lincoln, Y. S. (2000) "The discipline and practice of qualitative research," in Denzin, N. K. and Lincoln, Y. S. (eds.), *Handbook of Qualitative Research.* Thousands Oaks, CA: Sage.

Eräsaari, L. (1995) *Kohtaamisia byrokraattisilla näyttämöillä* [Encounters on Bureaucratic Stages]. Helsinki: Gaudeamus.

Frenkel, S. J., Korczynski, M., Shire, K. A. and Tam, M. (1999) *On the Front-Line: Organization of Work in the Information Economy.* Ithaca, NY and London: Cornell University Press.

Giddens, A. (1979) *Central Problems in Social Theory.* London: Macmillan.

Gubrium, J. F. and Holstein, J. A. (1997) *The New Language of Qualitative Method.* New York and Oxford: Oxford University Press.

Heiskanen, T., Hyväri, S., Kinnunen, M. *et al.* (1990) *Gendered Practices in Working Life.* Tampere: University of Tampere, Research Institute for Social Sciences, Work Research Centre.

Honkasalo, M.-L. (1984) "Valta, valvonta ja naisten työ" [Power, control and women's work], in Husu, L. and Honkasalo, M.-L. (eds.), *Työ, nainen ja tutkimus* [Work, Women and Research]. Helsinki: Valtioneuvoston kanslia.

Husu, L. (2001) *Sexism, Support and Survival in Academia: Academic Women and Hidden Discrimination in Finland.* Helsinki: University of Helsinki, Department of Social Psychology.

Järnefelt, N. (2002) "Kiireen hallinta työn muutoksessa" [Managing time-pressure in changing work], in Järnefelt, N. and Lehto, A.-M., *Työhulluja vai hulluja töitä?* [Workaholics or Crazy Jobs?], Helsinki: Statistics Finland.

Julkunen, R. (1984) "Nainen suomalaisessa työnsosiologiassa" [Women in the Finnish sociology of work], *Sosiologia* 21: 146–62.

—— (1999) "Gender, work, welfare state," in *Women in Finland.* Helsinki: Otava, pp.79-100.

—— (2001) "Ammatti jälkiammatillisessa työelämässä" [Occupation in post-occupational work], *Ammattikasvatuksen aikakauskirja* 3: 16–23.

Kinnunen, M. (2001) *Luokiteltu sukupuoli* [The Classified Gender]. Tampere: Vastapaino.

Kinnunen, M. and Korvajärvi, P. (1996) *Työelämän sukupuolistavat käytännöt* [Gendering Practices in Work]. Tampere: Vastapaino.

Kolehmainen, S. (1999) *Naisten ja miesten työt: Työmarkkinoiden segregoituminen Suomessa 1970–1990* [Women's and Men's Work: Labor Market Segregation in Finland]. Helsinki: Statistics Finland.

Korvajärvi, P. (1990) *Toimistotyöntekijäin yhteisöt ja muutoksen hallinta* [Women's Social Collectives of Work and Coping with Change]. Tampere: University of Tampere, Work Research Centre.

—— (1998a) *Gendering Dynamics in White-Collar Work Organizations*. Tampere: University of Tampere.

—— (1998b) "Reproducing gendered hierarchies in everyday work: Contradictions in an employment office," *Gender, Work and Organization* 5: 19–30.

Kovalainen, A. (1995) *At the Margins of the Economy: Women's Self-Employment in Finland 1960–1990*. Aldershot: Avebury.

Kurvinen, A. (1999) *Tilinteon aika* [Time to Settle a Score]. Joensuu: University of Joensuu, Publications in Social Sciences.

Lavikka, R. (1997) *Big Sisters: Spacing Women Workers in the Clothing Industry*. Tampere: University of Tampere, Work Research Centre.

Lehto, A.-M. (1999a) "Towards equality in working life?", in Lehto, A.-M. and Sutela, H., *Gender Equality in Working Life*. Helsinki: Statistics Finland.

—— (1999b) "Gender pay differential," in Lehto, A.-M. and Sutela, H. (eds.), *Gender Equality in Working Life*. Helsinki: Statistics Finland.

—— (2002) "Laadulliset menetelmät kiireen tutkimisen apuna" [Qualitative methods in studying time-pressure], in Järnefelt, N. and Lehto, A.-M., *Työhulluja vai hulluja töitä?* [Workaholics or Crazy Jobs?], Helsinki: Statistics Finland.

Leidner, R. (1993) *Fast Food, Fast Talk: Service Work and the Routinization of Everyday Life*. Berkeley, CA: University of California Press.

Martikainen. R. (1997) "Gender matters in collective bargaining," in Rantalaiho, L. and Heiskanen, T. (eds.), *Gendered Practices in Working Life*. London and New York: Macmillan.

Meriläinen, S. (2001) *Changing Gendered Practices: A PAR Project within an Academic Work Community*. Helsinki: Helsinki School of Economics and Business Administration.

Pulkkinen, P. (2001) "'*Vähän enemmän arvoinen,*' tutkimus tasa-arvokokemuksista työpaikoilla," ["Slightly More Appreciated": A Study on Equality Experiences in the Workplace]. Helsinki: Statistics Finland.

Rantalaiho, L. (1984) "Naiset toimistotyössä" [Women in office work], in Husu, L. and Honkasalo, M.-L. (eds.), *Työ, nainen ja tutkimus* [Work, Women and Research]. Helsinki: Valtioneuvoston kanslia.

—— (1990) "Office work as women's work," *Polish Sociological Bulletin* 2: 63–74.

—— (1997) "Contextualizing gender," in Rantalaiho, L. and Heiskanen, T. (eds.), *Gendered Practices in Working Life*. London and New York: Macmillan.

Rantalaiho, L. and Heiskanen, T. (eds.) (1997) *Gendered Practices in Working Life*. London and New York: Macmillan.

Salmi, M. (2000) "Analyzing the Finnish homecare allowance system: Challenges to research and problems of interpretation," in Kalliomaa-Puha, L. (ed.), *Perspectives of Equality: Work, Women and Family in the Nordic Countries and EU*. Copenhagen: Nordic Council of Ministers.

Savola, L. (2000) *Naiset Suomen työmarkkinoilla* [Women in Finnish Employment]. Helsinki: Statistics Finland.

Silius, H. (1992) *Den kringgärdade kvinnligheten: Att vara kvinnlig jurist i Finland* [Contracted Femininity: The Case of Women Lawyers in Finland]. Åbo: Åbo Academy Press.

Smith, D. (1987) *The Everyday World as Problematic: A Feminist Sociology*. Boston: Northeastern University Press.

Statistics Finland (2002) *Labour Force Statistics 2001: Annual Review, Preliminary Data*. Helsinki: Statistics Finland.

Strandell, H. (1984) "Kolmen naissukupolven kokemuksia työstä ja perheestä" [Experiences in work and family by three female generations], in Haavio-Mannila, E., Jallinoja, R. and Strandell, H. (eds.), *Perhe, työ ja tunteet* [Family, Work and Emotions]. Helsinki: WSOY.

Sutela, H. (1999) "Fixed-term employment relationships and gender equality," in Lehto, A.-M. and Sutela, H., *Gender Equality in Working Life*. Helsinki: Statistics Finland.

Uusitalo, H. (1999) "Tuloerot kasvaneet jo kolmena peräkkäisenä vuonna" [The income differentials have increased during the last three years], *Yhteiskuntapolitiikka* 64: 465–79.

West, C. and Zimmerman, D. (1987) "Doing gender," *Gender and Society* 1: 125–51.

Ylöstalo, P. (2002) *Työolobarometri* [The Barometer of Working Conditions]. Helsinki: Ministry of Labour.

FURTHER READING

Czarniawska, B. and Höpfl, H. (eds.) (2002) *Casting the Other: The Production and Maintenance of Inequalities in Work Organizations*. London: Routledge.

Mills, A. J. and Tancred, P. (eds.) (1992) *Gendering Organizational Analysis*. Newbury Park, CA: Sage.

Index